HENRY DARGER, THROWAWAY BOY

Henry Darger,
Throwaway Boy

The Tragic Life of an Outsider Artist

Jim Elledge

Overlook Duckworth
New York · London

This edition first published in hardcover in the United States and the United Kingdom in 2013 by Overlook Duckworth, Peter Mayer Publishers, Inc.

NEW YORK
141 Wooster Street
New York, NY 10012
www.overlookpress.com
For bulk and special sales, please contact sales@overlookny.com,
or write us at the above address

LONDON
30 Calvin Street
London E1 6NW
info@duckworth-publishers.co.uk
www.ducknet.co.uk

For permission to use the following copyrighted material, grateful acknowledgment is made to the copyright holders of the following texts: Newberry Library for song lyrics ("O meet me at Riverview Park, sweetheart") and a note ("There was a priest out here the other night"); Special Collections and Archives, John T. Richardson Library, DePaul University, Chicago, Illinois (St. Vincent's Church Papers) for photographs of St. Vincent de Paul Church and of St. Augustine's Home for the Aged; Special Collections, Regenstein Library, University of Chicago (Burgess Papers) for excerpts from written texts—Nels Anderson's "Chronic Drinker, Stockyards Worker, Seldom Migrates, Many Arrests, Away from Wife Twelve Years: 'Shorty'" and "Young Man, Twenty-Two, Well Dressed, Homosexual Prostitute, Loafs in Grant Park"; "Case of Herman [One of Herman's early childhood . . .]"; "Case of James"; "Case of Mr. R."; "Charles, Age Twenty-Three"; Paul G. Cressey's "Report on Summer's Work with the Juvenile Protective Association of Chicago"; "David—Age Twenty-One"; "Degeneracy"; "Glossary of Homosexual Terms"; "Harold, Age Twenty One"; "Lester, Negro. Age 16. Only Child"; Paul Oien's "West Madison Street"; "[Passengers will please refrain]"; "Three children. (1) Brother who is now 19 (2) Sister 17. Mr. D 2"; and Myles Vollmer's "Boy Hustler—Chicago"; Special Collection, University of Illinois at Chicago Library, for photographs of tenement houses from the 1910 annual report of the Hull House, page 52, HHYB_1910_0052_5556; and Chicago History Museum (Gregory A. Sprague Papers) for excerpts from unpublished essays written by Gregory A. Sprague.

Cataloging-in-Publication Data is available from the Library of Congress

Book design and typeformatting by Bernard Schleifer
Manufactured in the United States of America
ISBN US: 978-1-59020-855-7
ISBN UK: 978-0-7156-4632-8

For David
&
For Howard Dean
(1930–2013)

Every picture seems to look at you straight in the face as if you had some secret to tell them, or as if you suspected them of knowing your thoughts.

—HENRY DARGER, *The Realms*

CONTENTS

Acknowledgments

I T'S TAKEN ME MORE THAN A DECADE TO COMPLETE THIS BOOK, AND because so much time has passed from when I first decided to write something about Darger (in April 2002) to when I handed the manuscript over to my editor (July 2012), I have a lengthy list of those who have been supportive.

As they have for so many other writers, the universities where I've taught have financially supported my work on this volume, and had it not been for that, the book wouldn't have been written. At Kennesaw State University, I'd like to thank Tommy and Beth Holder, who kindly selected my project for funding through their Tommy and Beth Holder Faculty Award; the Center for Excellence in Teaching and Learning for its Incentive Fund for Scholarship; and Rich Vengroff, dean of the College of Humanities and Social Sciences, for stipends. At Pratt Institute, I want to thank the Provost's Faculty Development Grant and Toni Oliviero, dean of the School of Liberal Arts and Sciences, for stipends.

The financial support I was given allowed me to conduct research at a number of institutions, to whose staff—many nameless to me—I owe a great deal of thanks. To that end, I'd like to thank the many individuals at the following institutions for their help: the Special Collections of the Regenstein Library, University of Chicago; the Newberry Library; the Chicago Public Library; the Chicago History Museum; the Special Collections and University Archives of the Daley Library, the University of Illinois at Chicago; the Special Collections and Archives of the John T. Richardson Library, DePaul University; the Henry Darger Room and the Robert A. Roth Study Center of Intuit: The Center for Intuitive and Outsider Art; and the Henry Darger Archives, Henry Darger Study Center of the American Folk Art Museum.

Three writers who published books about Darger before me have also been very helpful in understanding Darger's life, and to each of them, I owe a great deal of thanks: Michael Bonesteel for *Henry Darger: Art and Selected Writings*; John MacGregor for *Henry Darger: In the Realms of the Unreal*; and Michael Moon for *Darger's Resources*. Their books are extremely important to anyone researching Darger, as I discovered.

A number of individuals have also gone out of their way to be helpful in a variety of ways, and to them, I also owe my gratitude: Cleo Wilson, Heather Holbus, and Kevin Muchay of Intuit: The Center for Intuitive and Outsider Art; Lisa Stone of the Roger Brown Study Collection, the School of the Art Institute of Chicago; Michael Boruch; Betsy Fuchs; Judith and Clifford Berglund; and Kevin Miller, Anne-Marie Reilly, and Courtney Wager of the American Folk Art Museum. Brooke Davis Anderson, former director and curator of the Contemporary Center, the American Folk Art Museum, has been especially helpful, opening doors and pointing me in the right direction, and to her I owe many, many thanks.

Many colleagues have also been very supportive over the years, and to them, too, I owe my gratitude. These include Beth Daniell, Keith Bothelo, Anne Richards, Bill Rice, and Christian Hawkey. It was Christian who got me interested in Darger in the first place. While I was away on various research trips, my assistant, Terri Brennen, held down the fort with grace and savvy, and because of her, I was able to focus on this project without a second thought.

Others have had an important role in the production of this book, and they, too, deserve my acknowledgment, especially my wonderful agent, Adriann Ranta, and my editor, Dan Crissman, whose sensitivity to my manuscript has been gratifying and whose work in getting reprint permissions, herculean. My copyeditor, Mary Beth Constant, has sharp eyes and caught an embarrassing amount of mistakes—all mine—and my thanks go out to her. My graduate research assistant for 2011–12, Andrew Duvall, read my manuscript not once but twice and made many valuable suggestions on how to improve it, and to him, too, I owe a great deal.

I wrote the first draft of the manuscript on Condado Beach in San Juan, Puerto Rico, between the Atlantic Beach Hotel and the Atlantic Ocean. Each day, Manny, an employee of the hotel, would take a few minutes to say hello and ask how the book was going. Although a small act, it was very generous and became important to me, and I thank him for his interest in the book.

To my friends, all of whom are more family than "friends" implies, I send many thanks: Betty and Howard Dean; Alison Umminger, Mike Mattison, and Maggie Mattison; as well as Romayne Rubinas Dorsey and Damon Dorsey. In fact, David Groff, not only a dear friend but a comrade-at-arms, gratiously read and commented on early drafts and helped me find an agent. Without his help, this book would not exist.

And finally, I apologize to my partner of twenty-three years, Aelred (David) Dean, for making him listen to the most mundane as well as the most extravagant discoveries I made about Darger during the past decade, and I thank him for listening to me blather on and on about them. Such is love and the greatest support of all.

HENRY DARGER, THROWAWAY BOY

PREFACE

I BEGAN WORK ON *HENRY DARGER, THROWAWAY BOY* IN 2002 because I was tired of reading in articles, blogs, websites, and books that Darger was a pedophile, a sadist, or a serial killer—or some combination of them—without any sort of evidence. Their authors somehow believed that, by pointing to the torture of children that appears prominently on his canvases, they were offering evidence for their claims. It was also difficult to accept their assertions that he lived a completely hermit-like life, friendless and loveless for the eighty-one years and one day that he was alive. I didn't buy any of it.

I had attended an exhibit of Darger's paintings at the American Folk Art Museum that April, and while, like others, I was taken aback by the slaughter—there's really no other word for it—of children in many of his paintings, I wasn't willing to accept the commonly held belief that the figures represented Darger's desire, that by painting a child being eviscerated, strangled, or crucified he revealed that he wanted to harm children. That seemed to me to be the laziest sort of response, a quick and simplistic emotional reaction to figures that needed to be considered objectively. I didn't know then if I would be able to offer a solid alternative response to Darger's work, but I knew it was needed and I was willing to try.

Darger incorporated another group of figures, the little girls with penises, in as many of his paintings as he had the eviscerated, strangled, crucified, and otherwise tortured children. In fact, many of the children he depicted belonged to both groups. It was this second group that I understood—or thought I did—and that gave me at least some confidence that I might be able to add solid information to the little-known and mostly misunderstood life of Henry Darger.

During research for two of my earlier books, *Gay, Lesbian, Bisexual, and Transgender Myths from the Arapaho to the Zuñi: An Anthology* (2002) and *Masquerade: Queer Poetry in America to the End of World War II* (2004), I had discovered that for centuries, gay men had used the figure of the hermaphrodite, usually a female body with male genitalia, to represent themselves. To explain why they were men who were sexually and romantically attracted to men, they theorized that, although their bodies were decidedly male, their souls were female. In the late 1880s, German sexologist Karl Ulrichs, who was also gay, codified the theory in his work. The question that faced me was: Could Darger have known this theory and, if so, what might that say about him?

Over the course of the next ten years, I read everything I could to find out about the culture in which Darger was born and into which he grew into a young man. This included not only the usual histories of Chicago from approximately 1880 to the 1930s but also dozens of medical and legal articles pertaining to sexuality; scores of articles and official reports about everyday life—employment, leisure activities, immigrant experiences, alcoholism and addiction, slumming, absent parents (especially fathers)—among Chicago's poor; nearly a hundred fifty first-person narratives by gay men in the 1920s and '30s about their lives; census reports, birth and death certificates, wedding announcements, and obituaries; sociological studies and dissertations about vice, jack-rolling, hoboes, and the sexual activities of newsboys and other children; and a thousand-plus-page report that summarized an investigation into allegations of child abuse at various institutions including the Illinois Asylum for Feeble-Minded Children, where Darger had been incarcerated as a child. I even hired a lawyer and successfully sued the State of Illinois for access to Darger's records from the Asylum.

I've drawn many of the accounts of events described in this book from Darger's own writings—especially his novels, autobiography, and journals, which are housed at the Henry Darger Study Center of the American Folk Art Museum—but it should be noted that certain scenes are, by necessity, a literary reconstruction. There exists very little first-person testimony other than Darger's own incomplete, embellished, and often contradictory remembrances. I have relied on historical documentation, contemporary sources, and the work of other historians and scholars to fill in the gaps. Beyond the known facts, I have intentionally dramatized certain details of the events depicted in order to bring them to life for the reader.

Darger was a very private man, and though he expressed himself through his art, there exists no single piece of indisputable evidence of the motivations behind his paintings and writings, certain events in his private life, or even his sexuality. Indeed, the executor of Darger's estate, Kiyoko Lerner—who has graciously agreed to allow the reproduction of Henry's works in this book—has expressed her own doubts to me about whether or not Henry was gay. But upon-viewing the whole of what he left behind, the portrait of Darger that emerged during my decade of studying these sources became much clearer to me, and I've done my best to represent that in these pages.

The portrait of Darger that developed during my decade of studying those sources is the exact opposite of previously held views. There is absolutely nothing in his background to support the idea that he was a pedophile, a sadist, or a serial killer, although it's obvious that he was the victim of predators when he was a child. There is absolutely no evidence that he was mentally ill in any form until he was stricken with senility during the last years of his life. Most important, perhaps, there is absolutely no evidence that he was friendless and unloved. He suffered a great deal of trauma during his childhood and everyone he knew betrayed him, making it difficult for him to form alliances, platonic or romantic. Nevertheless, he had friendships, very close ones, throughout his life and formed a relationship that lasted for nearly half a century.

Regardless of anything else I might say about *Henry Darger, Throwaway Boy*, discovering that Darger loved another and was loved in turn made the ten years I spent on the project a reward I never anticipated but to which I am extremely thankful.

INTRODUCTION

A T 1:50 IN THE AFTERNOON OF FRIDAY, APRIL 13, 1973, HENRY J. Darger died in a nursing home located on Chicago's Near North Side. No one who knew him—not the nurse who attended him, not the physician who signed the death certificate, not any of the nuns who ran the nursing home in which he lived out his last days, and not even his landlord Nathan Lerner, who was the person who knew him best at that time—were aware of his work. No one had a clue that Darger was a novelist who illustrated his texts with hundreds of vibrant watercolors. More important, none suspected that Henry Darger was destined to become one of the twentieth century's most important painters.

Shortly before Darger's death, Lerner hired David Berglund, one of his tenants and Darger's neighbor on the third floor of 851 Webster, to clean out the room in which Darger had lived for forty-two years. He wanted to combine the Berglunds' apartment and Henry's room into a single rental. Swarms of yuppies had begun moving into the neighborhood, gentrifying it, and causing property values and rents to climb. Lerner knew he stood to make more money per month after the renovation.

Darger had become what at least some of his neighbors thought of as a Dumpster-diver and had stuffed his room with all sorts of "junk." As Berglund excavated Darger's room—throwing out armfuls of newspapers and magazines, scores of empty Pepto-Bismol bottles, dozens of pairs of scratched or broken eyeglasses, and men's shoes, too many for him to bother to count and all scuffed up and holey beyond repair—he discovered three novel manuscripts (and a host of other texts) that Darger had written as well as more than three hundred paintings that he had created to illustrate them. As fate would have it, Lerner was a respected artist in Chicago and he immediately halted the renovation, at least for the time being. The paintings had caught his eye, and in fact, he was instrumental in getting Darger's first exhibit, at the Hyde Park Art Center, organized.

From the very first, Darger's paintings elicited questions that weren't specifically about the art at all but rather about Darger's motives behind the paintings. Many reviewers—among them Pulitzer Prize winner Holland Cotter, *Time* reporter Robert Hughes, and Richard Vine, managing editor for *Art in America*—saw in Darger's paintings the mind of a sadist, pedophile, or serial killer at work. Others unwilling to make their own conclusions have quoted John Mac-Gregor, author of the first book-length study of Darger's work, accusing Darger of the same activities. Unfortunately, these influential writers and others were quick to voice their accusations, or parrot those of others, without conducting any real research to see if the accusations were accurate. They've claimed that the depictions in and of themselves are evidence for their allegations, but none ever explains *how* the images might be considered evidence. Stunningly, none has ever looked for an explanation for them in Darger's paintings or writings. None has ever investigated American cultural histories to try to find an explanation for the figures in the period during which he created them. Instead, the critical community largely staked all assumptions on either visceral reactions to the work itself or cursory details of Darger's life. As the Internet grew and became an important part of everyday life, the accusations became gospel, the consensus portrait of Darger bearing little similarity to the one that I found in my research.

While many who have written about Darger's art have considered his paintings a wish-fulfillment fantasy of torturing and murdering children, few have considered that it may very well be a confession of what happened *to* him and to other children he knew, an idea central to my interpretation. Similarly, they have used his institutionalization as a young boy as more ammunition for condemning him. As it turns out, the twelve-year-old Darger was committed to an asylum because he'd been caught masturbating, which then was considered a symptom of insanity as well as homosexuality, and that—and only that—gave his father the power to have the adolescent branded feeble-minded and institutionalized and has given rise to the wrong assumption that he was mentally unbalanced.

Just as previous writers have made all sorts of accusations about Darger's psychological state, they have simultaneously created an abridged—and largely inaccurate—version of his life. According to most accounts, Darger's mother died giving birth to his sister when he was very young. He lived with his father in utter poverty until he began a string of commitments to various institutions, the last one an insane asylum for children in Lincoln, Illinois, a tiny town south of Chicago. His father died while he was confined there, and Darger eventually ran away, walking nearly two hundred miles back to the Windy City. With the help of his godmother, he found work as a janitor in St. Joseph's Hospital on Chicago's Near North Side, his career for the rest of his working life. He was employed for fifty-five years in that menial job, and he lived below the poverty line his entire adult life.

So far, this version of events is almost right on the mark.

Hermit-like, the establishment version continues, he never had any friends or family, had no interaction with the culture in which he lived, and was mistrusted and even feared by the few people who knew him. He was known among those who lived in his building and in nearby houses and apartments as the neighborhood oddball who would pass them on the streets without a glance, much less a hello. He compulsively attended Mass and confession—several times a day, each day of the week—at St. Vincent's Church a few blocks from where he lived and, just as compulsively, created a vast number of paintings in which he depicted naked little girls. Mysteriously, he drew penises on a large number of them, depicting many being tortured and murdered by adults who are often wearing military uniforms and academic mortarboards.

After a long life of extreme solitude and perverted desires, this telling goes, which he must have occasionally satisfied, Darger fell into ill health. He had to give up roaming the alleys of Chicago's Near North Side, collecting odd items that he would stuff into his one-room apartment, and move into an old folks' home where he would die a few months later.

While the details of this version may seem true on the surface, the facts I've found are much more complex and paint a portrait of a bruised and damaged soul struggling to deal with the traumas of childhood and the cruelty of life at the fringes of society. Darger's critics also conveniently ignore his unwavering dedication to his art, his aggressive creativity, and, most tellingly, his forty-eight-year loving relationship with a man named William Schloeder.

Henry Darger, Throwaway Boy is not founded on hearsay or subjective reactions to his art but on items in the Darger archives at the American Folk Art Museum and at Intuit: The Center for Intuitive and Outsider Art, and in a huge assortment of public and private documents. This book seeks to solve the various mysteries that have surrounded Darger and his art since his debut exhibit in 1977. Perhaps most important for a clear understanding of Darger's life, it thoroughly examines the diagnosis of insanity that allowed him to be put away in the children's asylum in the first place. It also discloses what the depictions of the tortured children in his paintings mean and, in particular, what the "little girls with penises" represent. In the process, this book argues that the labels libelously assigned to him—sadist, serial killer, pedophile—have nothing to do with the person that Darger was.

Darger's novels and paintings deal with the abuse he suffered as a child in his neighborhood (now called the Near West Side) and in the various institutions in which he'd been warehoused by his father. They are confessions of fact, not fantasies. Because counseling has been a luxury for the well-to-do until very recently, Darger never received any guidance to help him through his trauma. Instead, he wrote and painted about it obsessively, trying to find relief from the guilt he felt and healing from the trauma that the sexual abuse caused. In one way or another, all of his novels and paintings express that experience. It is, in essence, his only persistent theme.

Regardless of how much he wrote or painted, Darger never obtained the emotional redemption that he sought from his experiences, and eventually the guilt and trauma that were intensified by many physical ailments and the death of William Schloeder impacted his life in negative ways. Tortured by the past and left utterly alone in the world, he withdrew into himself, becoming the odd, cranky old man whom his neighbors remembered scouring through garbage cans in alleys across Chicago's Near North Side. Nevertheless, his paintings have achieved international recognition and earned him a place in the pantheon of the most important and most misunderstood artists of the twentieth century—an unknown no more.

PART I

ONE BOY'S LIFE

CHAPTER 1

THE THROWAWAY BOY

THROWING HENRY AWAY

ON WEDNESDAY, NOVEMBER 16, 1904, HENRY DARGER SR., THE sixty-four-year-old father of a twelve-year-old boy, and Otto Schmidt, a local physician, huddled together over an application in the dim afternoon light of the lobby of St. Augustine's Home for the Aged. It was too cold outside to open the windows and let in fresh air, and the scent of astringents stung Darger's nose and eyes. Dr. Schmidt, who was used to the odor, hardly noticed. Some of the inmates were sitting in wheelchairs parked in the waiting room and the halls. Others were sequestered in their rooms, occasionally tied to their beds. He was used to them, too.

Ill health, lameness, and the effects of alcohol had sent Darger into this nursing home, a long, five-story red brick building at the corner of Fullerton and Sheffield in the Lincoln Park neighborhood of Chicago's Near North Side. A block west of the Fullerton elevated station, it opened its front door onto Sheffield. Because he was penniless, Darger's two younger brothers had scraped together enough cash to pay his entrance. Once he was in, no one cared if he had the payment for his stay or not. The Little Sisters of the Poor, the order

of nuns who ran the Home, were bound to keep him until his circumstances changed or he died, whichever came first, and his circumstances weren't about to change.

Darger admitted that he was being "kept by charity," unable to
care for himself or his son, on the application that Dr. Schmidt helped
him to fill out. If his poverty and physical condition weren't embarrassment enough, his son's behavior was. Finally, he was being forced
to admit that the boy was out of control and bound for perdition. His
son, who was also named Henry, mortified him and had been in and
out of trouble for the past couple of years.

The old man and the doctor were deep in conversation. In a low-
ered, authoritative voice, Dr. Schmidt reminded Darger that he'd read
all the medical literature on the subject, that there was no other alternative, that Darger had done everything in his power to help his son.
The boy's antics weren't his fault. He wanted Darger to be confident
that his decision would be best for the boy in the long run and that
there was no cure, only a slow spiraling downward into a type of
lunacy that most regarded as hell on earth. The doctor had examined
Henry Jr. several times during the past few weeks. He knew what he
was talking about. He was a physician, after all, and he was convinced
that hoping to change the boy's behavior was futile this late in the
game.

It hadn't taken much for the physician to earn Darger's trust. A
German immigrant, Darger knew Dr. Schmidt's reputation, as all of
Chicago's substantial German-American and German-immigrant population did. He wasn't just one of the Windy City's most trustworthy
physicians; he was also engaged in scores of altruistic activities, from
being "president of the Illinois State and Chicago historical societies"
to giving "vital support to cultural and commemorative activities
among his fellow German-Americans." His consultation with Darger
was pro bono, another reason for the man to put his faith in the doctor. Undereducated, a tailor by trade, Darger would have been hard-
pressed not to trust Schmidt.

With the help of Dr. Schmidt, Darger now understood the cause behind at least one of his son's problems. The application asked for the attending physician to identify the cause of the patient's—the boy's—insanity, and Dr. Schmidt wrote "self abuse" in a clear hand in the blank. Now twelve, the boy had been masturbating since he was at least six years old and had even been caught in the act in public. In their eyes, the boy was not only morally bankrupt but also criminal and a pervert of the very worst sort. A man was supposed to assert self-control, especially over the basest of his urges, but a man (or boy, for that matter) who gave in to his lusts had abandoned his manhood and feminized himself in the process, something that both the father and the physician considered insane. Society as a whole couldn't have agreed more.

Darger was both embarrassed to be discussing his son's nasty secret and relieved that he was finally able to discuss it with a physician who had kept up with the medical literature on adolescents, someone who wouldn't blame him for the boy's perversion. His brothers, Augustine and Charles, hadn't been at all understanding or supportive.

Being a man of science, Dr. Schmidt understood Darger's anxiety and calmed the old man's fears of being blamed or ridiculed for his son's habit. Schmidt even told him in a whisper that the vice reared its ugly head in the very best of Chicago's families, that even the Brahmins of Astor Street and Prairie Avenue were plagued by such monstrosities of modern, urban life. The old man's only consolation was that he knew that *he* wasn't responsible for his son's vice. The boy had been taught to masturbate by an older boy or a man in the neighborhood. It was one of the many vices the boy had picked up on the streets, he stressed to Dr. Schmidt, *not* inherited from him or his family. So when the admission application for the Illinois Asylum for Feeble-Minded Children asked how the boy had become insane, Dr. Schmidt conscientiously wrote, "Acquired." It was important for the father to place the blame for his son's condition where blame was deserved.

Schmidt assured Darger that the staff at the Asylum had handled boys just like his son before—many of them. He patted the old man's forearm. "As difficult as it's been," he told Darger, "you're doing the right thing. Never think otherwise." The doctor kindly filled out the rest of the application, using the information Darger gave him, but Dr. Schmidt wrote "Dodger," not "Darger," as Henry's last name on the application. Darger also made a mistake. He confused the year of Henry's younger brother Arthur's birth (1893) with Henry's (1892), making Henry a year younger on the application than he actually was. Defeated by circumstance—by his bad health, his poverty, and even by the boy's shenanigans—and eager to put the whole episode behind him, Darger quickly signed the application that allowed him to send his son to a "children's nut house" without noticing the mistakes. Neither father nor doctor could bring himself to tell the child why he was being sent to yet another institution, his third in seven years. Sealing the boy's fate was as much as they could muster that afternoon.

VICE

Henry Joseph Darger was born April 12, 1892, the year his father turned fifty-two. Seventy-six years later and in what must have been the throes of denial, Henry described him as "a kind and easy going man" without a hint of irony or rancor. His father immigrated to the United States from Meldorf, Germany, in 1874 and settled in Chicago as his two brothers, Augustine and Charles, had done a few years before him. All three were married, self-employed tailors. Immigrants who were members of the same family usually did everything they could to live under the same roof once they arrived in the United States to save money and preserve family ties. The Darger brothers were no exception. Within a few years, they and their wives moved to a building at 2707 Portland that was large enough for all of them. 2707 Portland wasn't far from Chicago's stockyards, and in the summertime, the winds carried the animals' stench into their open windows.

No record of how or when Henry's mother and father met exists, but she moved to Chicago from Bell Center, Wisconsin, at least by early 1890, and must have met Henry Sr. soon thereafter. Rosa and Henry were married on August 18, 1890. When he and Rosa married, they moved into an apartment at 350 24th Street, where Henry Jr. was born about a year and a half later, the third of his mother's children, the first of his father's.

Oddly, two distinctly different birth certificates were issued for Henry. The first, dated May 6, 1892—the one usually held to be the original—gives his birth as April 12, 1892, the date he would use all of his life. It lists Rosa's family name as "Fullman" and reveals that Henry was born at home, which was typical at the time. His father's occupation is listed as "tailor." On the second birth certificate, dated May 31, 1894, his birth was changed to May 28, 1894, making him two years younger than he actually was, and the place of his birth was also changed, to the Cook County Infirmary. The infirmary, which was often called the Cook County Almshouse or the Cook County Poor Farm, was notorious at the time as the last resort for Chicago's indigent. It was "established to provide long-term refuge for the most extremely destitute people in the Chicago area." Complicating matters is the fact that his father's occupation is listed as "unknown."

The information reported on the second birth certificate suggests that Henry Sr. may have abandoned his family for a short time, which would account for no one knowing how Henry Sr. made his livelihood. It also suggests why Henry's age is shaved off by two years. The fraudulent date may indicate that Rosa was trying to get some sort of public aid available only to families with children below a certain age, but would she have been able to talk one of the house physicians, Joseph J. Crowe who signed the birth certificate, into falsifying the document? Somehow, she apparently did, and if Henry Sr. and Rosa had separated, they soon reconciled.

Henry Sr.'s drinking had been playing havoc with his ability to provide for his family and may have had something to do with his and Rosa's separation. Unlike his brothers, both of whom were actively engaged in developing their businesses by, for example, advertising in the Chicago city directories, Henry Sr. ignored his, and it had gone into a tailspin. His financial situation became so unstable that he needed to downsize his family's lodgings. The Dargers moved out of their respectable but decidedly lower-class neighborhood and into what was then called "West Madison Street," a district full of desperation—on every street corner, in every saloon or burlesque theater, behind every closed door.

The Dargers moved into a coach house apartment a block and a half from the intersection of Halsted and Madison, the threshold to West Madison Street. Taking its name from its chief thoroughfare, it was one of Chicago's most notorious vice zones and known throughout the Windy City as a poverty-stricken amusement park of sensualities, excesses, and debaucheries of all types. It was also the home of many poverty-stricken families. Alcoholism, drug addiction, gambling, missing parents (usually the father), and illnesses such as tuberculosis ravaged its families. Homeless men and boys crowded its streets and milled around purposelessly, prostitutes of both sexes displayed themselves on street corners and along the thoroughfares day and night, and affluent men and women from other neighborhoods slummed there nightly in search of thrills of every variety. No family in the district, including the Dargers, would be immune to what were then called "social pathologies."

The Chicago city government publicly and officially acknowledged the neighborhood's vile character. It described the West Madison Street district as extending from "Halsted street to Hoyne avenue" and added that it was lined with houses of prostitution on both sides of the thoroughfare for "fully a mile and a half" west. One early Chicago sociologist described the vice district, and its rank sister-centers of the taboo (North Clark Street's Rialto and the Levee of the Near South Side), as overflowing with "cheap burlesque shows, dime museums, shooting galleries and lady barbers."

These houses from the Madison Street vice district are similar to the one in which Henry
and his father lived, behind the "main" house at 165 West Adams.

(COURTESY OF THE UNIVERSITY OF ILLINOIS AT CHICAGO LIBRARY, SPECIAL COLLECTIONS)

"Vice" was a catchall for both public and private activities of
all sorts, including dancing, drinking, gambling, and especially illicit
sexual activities. Even desire, regardless of whether it was ever acted
upon, was considered vice. Vice included prostitution, of course, but
also being in the audience of burlesque shows (which often included
stripteases, risqué stand-up comedians, and skits full of sexual innuendo), engaging in or witnessing "sex circuses" (what we would call
live sex shows), taking part in "taxi dancing" (in which men paid
women by the song to dance with them, often with highly salacious
movements), and engaging in any homosexual activity, whether at
home behind closed doors or behind stacks of crates in alleys. In the
earliest decade of the 1900s, no laws barred children from the saloons,
burlesque theaters, or whorehouses of West Madison Street, so children, including Henry, ran wild there.

TRAGEDIES

The Dargers set up housekeeping in a two-room apartment in the coach house behind the much larger main house at 165 West Adams Street. "Coach house" was a euphemism for a stable that had been slightly renovated for human habitation. It was dirt-cheap, dingy, and hugged the alley. Except on the sunniest of days at the height of summer, sunlight rarely vaulted beyond the front house into the backyard where the coach house stood. The stench left by the horses that had once been stabled there rose from the floors and wafted from the walls. The former stable wouldn't have been insulated either, so in the summer, the Dargers sweltered, sleeping stripped to their underwear, and in the winter, they shivered, sleeping in their street clothes.

At the beginning, Henry's life differed little from the life of almost any other child during the days when the nineteenth century was turning into the twentieth. He was breast-fed: "Nursed by mother 5 months." He contracted the same childhood diseases—"typhoid, measles, and mumps"—that thousands of other children did, and like them, he was "whipped" when he was naughty. Neither Rosa nor Henry Sr. was a spare-the-rod parent.

Then several tragedies befell the Dargers.

Although Henry was too young to remember him, his brother Arthur was born on May 23, 1893, a little over a year after Henry. Henry and his parents temporarily moved back in with his uncles and their families at 2707 Portland so that Rosa's sisters-in-law (Augustine's wife, Margaret, and Charles's wife, Ellen) and her niece (Charles and Ellen's daughter, Annie) could help with the delivery and keep an eye on Henry. After Arthur's birth, his parents and brother returned to their apartment, but Arthur lived for only five months. Then, three years later, eleven days short of Henry's fourth birthday, Rosa died giving birth to her third child with Henry's father. Rosa had succumbed to what was most commonly called "childbed fever," an infection caused by a lack of sterile conditions.

The effect of Rosa's death on four-year-old Henry—who would have heard her screams, seen her writhing in pain, smelled the stench from her body, been overwhelmed by his father's grief and the anxiety of his aunts and cousin who powerlessly watched her die—was so devastating that he was rarely able to bear mentioning her. He once confessed, "I do not remember the day my mother died," an all-too-brief acknowledgment of her death but, revealingly, he ignored his feelings about the event. Henry learned during the earliest days of his childhood to ignore his feelings whenever possible, developing denial as a strategy to cope with the tragedies and other problems that he faced. He would resort to it over and over again throughout his life, virtually until the day he died.

The baby Rosa bore was a girl.

Henry's father, now fifty-six and already beginning to decline in health, was suddenly single and saddled with an infant, while also responsible for his toddler son. In his grief-stricken state complicated by alcohol, his situation overwhelmed him, and he took the only way out that he knew, which happened to be the easiest. He gave his daughter up for adoption.

Henry recorded his sister's birth as succinctly as he had his mother's death. "I lost my sister by adoption," he recalled, adding, "I never knew or seen her, or knew her name." As with his mother's death, he never addressed his feelings about it. Henry's few words are the only record of the little girl's existence. No one filled out a birth certificate for her. No one filed papers for her adoption. Without Henry's stunted recollection, we would never have known she'd been born. In fact, with Henry's brief remark, she completely disappeared from history.

Now a widower who had lost three members of his family in less than three years, Henry's father surrendered without a fight to his grief and his sense of failure as a provider for his family. Already a heavy drinker, he pulled out all the stops and sank into an abyss of self-absorption and alcoholic stupor, dragging his only child, and the last remaining member of his immediate family, down with him.

A VERY DANGEROUS KID

By the time he was four years old, Henry's home life was a far cry from idyllic, but the rest of America wasn't faring any better. The year Rosa died, the country had sunk into the worse economic depression it had yet to experience. The country wasn't at all prepared to deal with the thousands of jobless, homeless citizens that the economic catastrophe produced nor the effect it was to have on families already living on subsistence-level incomes. Children as young as six years old went to work on the streets in unsafe, menial jobs with long or nighttime hours (selling newspapers, acting as messengers for area businesses, and even working as bootblacks) to help their families. Men unable to cope with their inability to support their families vanished never to be heard from again or turned to alcohol to suppress their anger and fears, and women, left to support their families, turned to whatever occupations were available to them, including prostitution.

Adding to the economic misery of native-born Chicagoans was the large influx of immigrants from various European countries and the migration north of southern-born African-Americans. Both groups were after the same goal, to make their and their children's lives better, but the result was more than a million people squeezed into the inner city of Chicago, which quickly became a metropolis of tenements. Often a dozen people, sometimes several families, were forced to live together in tiny apartments. The streets and alleys were filled with garbage and the feces of horses—the chief mode of transportation because automobiles were still very much a rare luxury—making sanitation and control of the various diseases, especially cholera and typhoid, that vexed Chicago virtually impossible.

At the same time, those lucky enough to have jobs seemed to strike often, clamoring for raises in their less-than-subsistence-level wages, for shift hours shorter than the typical ten-to-twelve-hour days, and for on-the-job safety measures. Thousands of stories surfaced with examples of tragedies resulting from unprotected machinery in a variety of industries. A machinist got his arm caught in a rapidly moving belt. It was jerked from its socket, and he fell 50 feet to the floor. His fellow workers, aghast at the man's shrieks, ran in panic from the shop. A young boy working in a coffin plant was decapitated and had both arms and both legs torn off when he was caught on shafting rotating at 300 revolutions per minute. A worker in a brick-making factory was caught in a belt and had most of his skin torn off.

It's no wonder that skirmishes and even full-blown riots seem to have broken out almost daily between union organizers and police and between blacks and whites, who were competing for the few available jobs.

Despite living in the midst of such turmoil and the utter poverty that characterized his childhood, Henry described his and his father's time together in glowing terms. What he recalled is often touching and, typical of Henry, extremely brief. He mentioned that, "besides being a tailor," his father "was a very good cook." He also admitted "our meals were not scant, and I loved the pancakes the most." Their meals were very modest, filling but far from nutritious. Henry's typical Christmas was just as modest. He "mostly always got colored picture or story books" and "chicken for dinner." Henry's father had become lame, a condition that was worsening with each passing year. In fact, it had become so bad by 1899 that the boy began taking on a considerable amount of the household chores. Henry "bought the food coffee milk and other supplies and ran errands" for his father. He was only seven years old.

Henry's relatives fared just as well as his father in Henry's recollections. He remembered them briefly but generously, calling them "easy going people." He recalled only one of his five cousins, Harry, who was twenty-one years older than he, but he didn't remember that Harry was Charles's son. Because all of his other cousins were much older than he, Henry probably never saw them or, if he had, he was much too young to remember them.

Henry did, however, remember a great deal of other things about his early childhood and included it in his autobiography, *The History of My Life*, which is divided into two separate sections. The first, only two hundred six pages, covers Henry's life, although he was unable or unwilling to record it chronologically as is typical for most auto-biographies. Instead, he drifted off from one topic, veered sharply away to another (and often several topics after that), returning to his starting place paragraphs or, more often than not, pages later, if then. His somewhat stream-of-conscious style makes understanding what happened at any given point in his life very difficult, and yet the over-all view he offers is remarkably clear.

The two-room apartment in which Henry and his father now lived alone was on the top, second floor of the coach house. It slouched on the south side of the alley, called Marble Place, between Monroe and Adams Streets. A rickety wooden staircase on the outside of the south wall of the building led up to their front door. It opened into "a kitchen with a large stove, and behind it a bedroom." The stove was fueled by pieces of wood and scraps of lumber that Henry found on the streets, in alleys, on abandoned buildings, and at con-struction sites and brought home. The bedroom also served for what Henry called their "living quarters," their living room. Its windows faced north. He spent hours staring out of them, daydreaming, "watching it snow, especially if there was a great big blizzard raging" or watching "it rain with great interest, also short or long showers." Henry often escaped into his imagination when he was bored or felt threatened.

The only decoration in the apartment that Henry remembered was a tintype of his paternal grandfather. Henry never met his grandparents, who had died in Germany by the time he was born, but he recalled, "What he looked like, I would have been dreadfully scared of my Grandfather. Especially because of the awful mustache, and horseshoe in shape. That probably made him look more fierce and stern than he was." He also never met his mother's parents. As was common among the poor, Henry and his father shared their one bed. A stable stood across the alley, and the whinnying of horses and the rattle of wagons punctuated the day.

When he was five, Henry began attending St. Patrick's Elementary School, a squat building, administered by the clergy of St. Patrick's Church, less than a block away from their apartment. Henry first attended its so-called "girls' school," which every girl *and* boy attended through the third grade. When they reached fourth grade, boys enrolled in St. Patrick's Academy for Boys. Both the boys' and the girls' school buildings were red brick and four stories tall. The girls' school stood west of the church at 145-147 West Adams, and the boys' was to the north of it, at 135 Desplaines. The church stood between them, on the corner of Adams and Desplaines. Because Henry's father had taught him how to read before he ever went to school, he was allowed to skip second grade.

From the get-go, Henry had difficulties at school. He disliked his teacher, a nun, so much that he skipped school for a whole week. She was too "strict severe, and prime," meaning "prim," for his tastes. He was punished for minor infractions by being made to write one sentence repeatedly, often more than two hundred times, but making mistakes in the three R's or breaking classroom rules weren't his only, and not even his major, problem. Already small for his age, he was a year behind his classmates physically and emotionally when he enrolled in the Academy for Boys, making him an easy target for whatever the other, larger boys wanted to do to him.

Once, one struck him "on the nose with the palm of his hand," and in retaliation, Henry claimed that he put the boy "in a hospital for a long time." Another bully, who was a "much bigger boy" than he, taunted him. To get even, Henry slung "a half brick" at his knee and "nearly broke" it. One of Henry's most outrageous moments of bravado was when he claimed that, during his childhood, someone had tried to humble him and in retaliation, Henry not only put him "in a hospital for a year" but also "got away with it." Such bluster is quite likely the defense mechanism of someone who, as a defenseless child, had been hurt over and over again and needed to substitute a fantasy in which he wasn't hurt and was, instead, victorious to ease the pain of being repeatedly victimized by predators of various sorts.

As bullies targeted him, he in turn picked on smaller and even more defenseless children. Henry "hated baby kids, those though who were old enough to stand or walk." He often played on a "third floor porch of the building" near the coach house where he lived, and other, mostly younger, children played there, too. He "was a meany one day" when, for no reason but "spite," he "shoved a two year old child down and made it cry." Not a soul was around to catch him in the act, and the child didn't tattle on him, but his shame over hurting a defenseless child haunted him the rest of his life. At about the same time, he flung "ashes in the eyes of a little girl by the name of Francis Gillow." This time he was caught, and his father had to pay for her medical attention. To teach his son a lesson (and because the Dargers were so poor), the money his father would have spent on Henry's Christmas gifts went to pay Francis's medical bills. By his own admission, Henry could be "a very dangerous kid."

In one of his rare moments of self-analysis, Henry declared that the reason he physically abused other children was because he never had a brother or sister, but he never explains why that would compel him into violence. It was a rationalization he'd created to mask the real reason. Like many other children who have been bullied or physically abused, he turned his anger on those smaller and weaker than he.

Henry claimed that, when he was a little boy, he had a sudden moment of empathy that changed his life. For some reason that Henry never understood, he made a 180-degree turn in his actions toward younger, smaller children. Suddenly, he wanted to "love them," not harm them anymore. They became "more to me," he recalled, "than anything more than the world." Although barely more than a baby himself, Henry was somehow able to intuit that, just because boys larger than he were mistreating him, he didn't have the right to harm others smaller than he. His epiphany would guide him for years to come.

Henry's anger-induced violence made him an exceptionally difficult child, especially when it came to adults disciplining him. He "would take no scouldings or authority from anyone" but his father. Once, one of his teachers, a nun, punished him for "cutting up in class," and in retaliation, Henry "slashed her on face and arm" with a knife he carried. His father, who had earlier paid for the Gillow girl's medical expenses, now had to pay for the nun's, and Henry was expelled from school. His only comment about the episode was that he would retaliate for any punishment that was doled out to him, even if he deserved it. This wasn't hollow bragging.

After Henry's mother died, his father rarely took any interest in him. Henry recollected only two occasions when he did. Once was when he spent hours teaching Henry how to read, using the newspaper as a textbook. The only other time was when he and his father walked a few blocks from their coach house apartment to watch a huge fire:

> Once on a late summer afternoon my father took me to a big one close to home on the cornor of Washington street close to Halsted.
> We stood watching it across Washington street on the south side. He told me it was a tar factory.

When Henry recounted the story of the tar factory fire, he was always quick to admit "I was scared of burning buildings on fire for fear of falling walls or other debris," and often ended with "I did not go near the fire that day any more as I was afraid." He and his father stayed only a little while. The fire was so intense that it "raged all night," and he could see from their coach house apartment that it kept "the sky all lighted up" until the next morning.

Fires were common in those days, and Chicago had a special notoriety for them. Many smaller, yet devastating, ones broke out every week in residential neighborhoods all over Chicago because of someone's carelessness with the wood stoves on which everyone in those days cooked and heated their homes. Henry once "put lots of newspaper beside the stove near the wall" in their coach house apartment and "set it on fire." His father caught him at it just in time, put it out, and "boxed" his ears "good and proper" as punishment. His father did it again a few days later when he caught Henry ready to start another one. Slapping his son was one way Henry's father taught the boy not to play with fire, but taking him to see its destructive potential was another way. Regardless of which was the more effective, Henry recalled that "every 4 of July, I shot off all types of firecrackers and never was hurt or burned once, I was so overcareful." Henry also confessed that, as a child, he was "crazy about making bonfires," quickly adding that he was so careful that he was never "scorched, singed or burned." Despite his father's good intentions, Henry also learned how to use fire as a weapon, one as dangerous as the knife he'd used to slash his teacher.

One summer before Henry's eighth birthday, one of his neighbors, a fruit and vegetable peddler, accused him of stealing wooden crates from the stacks he kept in his yard. Incensed at the accusation, Henry snuck onto the man's property, moved a few crates away from the larger heap, and set them on fire. He promptly returned home and sat down with his father on the front steps of the coach house in the cool evening. Suddenly, "both noticed a light of brightness" at the peddler's. Pretending not to know what was going on, Henry left his father's side to investigate and discovered that "the shebang including the side of the house, was one high towering mass of singing flame."

He was sure, he claimed, that "the few crates" that he had "set afire" had not caused the inferno, but he was still relieved when the larger mass of "blazing crates crashed down, bouncing and covered the spot" where he had "made the little one." It obliterated any evidence that might have pointed to him as the arsonist. Luckily for the peddler, the fire only scorched the outside of his house. And luckily for Henry, he escaped punishment.

It's difficult to understand where Henry found the where-withal to commit a felony. To plan, then execute such a crime says volumes about the child and his environment, both in and out of the home. It also underscores the anger that was beginning to build in Henry because of the physical, and possibly sexual, abuse that he had been enduring and that would, when he was pushed too far, explode into violence. Try as Henry might to whitewash these neg-ative experiences of his early life, they were extraordinarily intense, and their effect on the boy leaches acid-like through his memories of his childhood.

Although Henry had many run-ins with children and adults in the neighborhood, the Andersons, a family who lived next door, saw Henry for what he was: a lonely, troubled little boy in need of help. Mrs. Anderson lived "in an old wooden three story house" with her "son and older daughter. His name was John and her name was Helen." The entire family took a liking to Henry. Helen sometimes checked in on Henry at his home when his father wasn't there, and when she did, she made sure that Henry's hands were clean. John sometimes took Henry to "a Salvation Army Sunday School" behind Henry's father's back. It was one of many secrets Henry kept from his father during his childhood. Mrs. Anderson, who was a widow and solely responsible for providing for her own children, generously invited Henry to have meals with them when his father wasn't around. Whether Henry's father knew about his son's relationship with the Andersons is unclear, but because of his poverty, it's extremely unlikely that he paid Mrs. Anderson to babysit Henry. More likely, she took care of Henry, feeding him and paying at least some attention to him, purely out of the goodness of her heart.

Henry thought that his father left him unattended so often because he was "very busy every day except Sundays and holidays." That sounds like another example of Henry's denial or, more probably, a lie his father told him to cover the tracks he made from one saloon to the next. Had his father been so busy at his job, the Dargers would've been living a better life. Henry's father's absence didn't just result in a breakdown in their relationship; it led to Henry putting himself into dangerous situations. The six- to eight-year-old Henry became an easy target for adults.

Child predators were common in West Madison Street, and Shorty, one of the dozens of hoboes that sociologist Nels Anderson interviewed during the first decades of the 1900s, was one. Shorty had lived on West Madison for years. Dressed as poorly as the rest of the district's denizens, he slept in the cheapest of the dozens of flophouses there when he had the change, but more often than not, he collapsed in one of the many free homeless shelters that dotted the vice district. Paunchy with drink, nearly bald, and donning a perpetual necklace of sweat and dirt, he was particularly attracted to the young boys who were lured to the district with its promise of easy money and excitement. Without much coaxing, he admitted to Anderson that "as long as there were any 'punks' on Madison Street," he would be sexually contented. In almost the same breath, he declared, "Give me a clean boy, every time."

In hobo argot, a "punk" was a boy (also called a "lamb" or a "kid") who had sex with an older man (called a "wolf") for money or protection or because he enjoyed sex with men. When Anderson told Shorty that he doubted that there were many men in West Madison Street who engaged in male-male sexual contact, Shorty told him there were "hundreds of them," and he added that "a lot of them big guys in the city are doing it too. There's more people doing it than you think—it's natural."

Although there's no direct evidence to indicate that he had been sexually victimized yet, Henry coolly recounted an experience that he had with an adult that shows the threat of sexual victimization with which he lived daily. When he was seven or eight years old, he often played on Adams Street a few blocks west of the coach house apartment. One day, one of West Madison Street's homeless, a wolf like Shorty, was out to kidnap a lamb like Henry. He spotted Henry and moved in. Henry saw the wolf stalking him, and afraid, the boy ran toward home to the intersection of Halsted and Adams, where he felt safe enough to stop and look back. The wolf was closing in, so Henry picked up half a brick, took aim, and threw it as hard as he could. At the same moment, a streetcar trundled by, shielding the would-be attacker from Henry's brick. It shattered the streetcar's "front side window" instead, and by the time the streetcar clattered past, the wolf had disappeared. Henry never told a soul about what had happened because he knew he would be "whipped" if his father found out. Henry kept this and other experiences secret from his father—or tried to.

BE GOOD, OR I'LL PACK YOU OFF TO DUNNING!

One evening in 1899 or 1900, when Henry was seven or eight, Henry's father answered the knocking on their apartment door to find the authorities standing outside. Over the previous months, they had caught Henry in various delinquencies, and they had finally decided to do something about it. The first step was to confront Henry Sr. with a list of the boy's illicit activities, which included being out late at night without parental supervision. They were polite but stern, recited Henry's myriad other infractions to the father, and then led the boy out the door and down the rickety stairs to the street. His father watched them until they disappeared in the darkness of the gangway between the main house and its closest neighbor. Henry later claimed that they eventually dropped him off at a "small boys home at Morton Grove."

Authorities never removed a boy from his home except in the most extreme situations, usually after he had a long history of run-ins with cops on the beat, so it's safe to assume that before he was eight years old Henry had a record and was well known to the police as a troublemaker. Henry never liked to discuss his experiences growing up in the West Madison Street district, except with very sparse and vague comments, because his experiences were too painful for him to admit to himself and too embarrassing for him to admit to others, including the readers of his autobiography. At worst, the comments obstruct the true nature of many unsavory incidents. At best, they are clues that, when examined closely and within the context of the culture in which he lived, give snapshots of Henry's life.

Several other men who also grew up in that neighborhood at about the same time as Henry gave clearer and more detailed accounts of their childhoods than Henry did. One in particular, who adopted the pseudonym "Stanley," wrote an amazing chronicle of his life that's the core narrative of what has become a classic of sociology, *The Jack-Roller: A Delinquent Boy's Own Story*. It offers a portrait of a typical boy's life in Chicago in the early 1900s, and the context it offers can be used to unveil the mystery of Henry's childhood, shining a very strong light on his accounts.

Like Henry, Stanley was the only child of a foreign-born father, and his mother also died when he was four. Both boys were small for their age; were intelligent but irrationally defensive; often reacted violently to any provocation, whether mild or harsh; and were sent to an institution at least once before being removed permanently from their fathers' homes. Stanley was born only a few years after Henry, and his portrait of West Madison Street—a "haven," he called it, "for bums, prostitutes, degenerates, and the rest of the scum of the earth" —confirms what can be assumed from Henry's clues.

Among the hoboes and the high rollers, the prostitutes and the gin runners, Stanley recalled other, even less desirable denizens of the vice district. "West Madison Street and vicinity," he wrote, "was a rather dark section of the city" and was the playground for "a lot of homosexuals." Chicago sociologist Clifford R. Shaw, who edited Stanley's autobiography and added his own commentary to it, noted that the boys who lived in the West Madison Street vice district "invariably come in contact with homosexuals" and that "among those who submit to their advances, a large proportion . . . become jack-rollers, exploiters of homosexuals and drunkards." Two varieties of jack-rolling were common among boys from the late 1880s through the mid-1930s or so: robbing drunks after they'd passed out on a park bench or on the sidewalk and mugging homosexuals whom they'd enticed into out-of-the-way places or accompanied home or to a hotel with the promise of sex for a price. Stanley and his friends, who worked together in the underworld as a gang, engaged in both types. Shaw summarized his findings by stating that "cases of 'jack-rolling' and homosexual practice are especially common" among the boys who rambled along West Madison Street, Henry's childhood playground.

Stanley admitted to being his gang's bait for luring homosexuals into construction sites, condemned buildings, the wooded areas of parks, alleys, hotel rooms, and other out-of-the-way places:

> As I'd walk along Madison Street there'd always be some men to stop me and coax me into having sex relations with him. My friend and I used this little scheme to entice men into a room to rob them. This very day a fellow stopped me and asked for a match. I accommodated him, and he started a conversation. He was about eight years my senior, and big and husky. He said he was a foreman in a machine shop, and when I said I was out of work, he promised to get a job for me at his shop. He invited me to have supper with him up in his room, which was built for light housekeeping. He was a kind guy, with a smile and

a winning way, so I went up to have supper on his invitation. We ate, and then he edged up close to me and put his arm around me and told me how much I appealed to his passions. He put his hand on my leg and caressed me gently, while he talked softly to me.

I had to wait a few minutes for my buddy to come to help put the strong arm on this man. I couldn't do it alone. My buddy had followed us all the time and was only waiting for a chance to come to my rescue. Finally he came and we sprang into the fellow with fury. He started to grab me and my buddy dealt him a heavy blow.

We found thirteen dollars in his pocket. Since he had tried to ensnare me I figured I was justified in relieving him of his thirteen bucks. Besides, was he not a low degenerate, and wouldn't he use the money only to harm himself further?

Stanley also recalled a jack-rolling episode that went sour. Again, he was the bait:

One day my partner didn't show up, and right then and there I lost all my nerve. I needed someone with me to steal. I was too cowardly to steal alone.

A companion made me brave and gave me a sense of security. I couldn't to save my soul steal a dime alone.

Because Stanley doesn't mention that he escaped, he must have submitted to the man's desire, and in fact, Stanley admitted that he sometimes engaged in sex with men that had nothing to do with jack-rolling at all but had everything to do with his own sexual urges. Some men, he confessed, asked him "to do immoral sex acts with them," and he sometimes "yielded to them." Nevertheless, it wasn't just anonymous men in West Madison Street with whom Stanley had sexual contact. Dr. Healy, Stanley's caseworker, reported that Stanley told him that some of the "older boys" in his gang with whom he jack-rolled did "bad things to him in the public baths."

Although Henry claimed that the authorities took him to a home for "small boys" in Morton Grove, then a village about ten miles northwest of Chicago's Loop, no such place existed until 1904, at least four years too late for Henry's story. However, officials had founded the Cook County Insane Asylum, popularly called Dunning (the original land owner's name), just after the close of the Civil War. An architectural monstrosity, it rose out of the prairie not too far from Morton Grove and is almost certainly where the authorities took Henry.

Dunning was a poorhouse, a hospital, a mental institution, and a hellhole. Stories of body snatching and grave robbing there circulated in the local newspapers throughout its first fifty years. In 1889, three male nurses—Charles Richardson, Charles J. Croghan, and Frank Pesha—were indicted for murdering inmate Robert Burns by beating and kicking him to death. Dunning's notoriety became so pervasive throughout the Chicago area that "Be good, or I'll pack you off to Dunning!" was a threat that more than one frustrated parent levied against an incorrigible child. Ashamed of having been locked up there, Henry camouflaged Dunning as the gentler-sounding "small boys home."

Although then on the outskirts of Chicago, Dunning wasn't as isolated as one might think. A decade before Henry was born, the Chicago, Milwaukee, and St. Paul Railroad, dubbed the "crazy train" by locals, connected Dunning to the Loop. Later, as Chicago's border began to inch farther and farther westward from the Loop, Dunning became accessible by streetcar, the cheapest mode of transportation available and an easy trip for the staff that lived in Chicago and commuted to and from work.

Days before Henry's father hopped onto the streetcar that took him to Dunning to retrieve his son, he had to meet with the authorities to discuss the case. He knew quite a bit about his son's activities even before they met. He knew that the boy carried weapons, a "long knife" and a "longstick." He knew Henry was violent—so violent, in fact, that the victims of the boy's anger had accumulated substantial medical expenses. The old man also knew that the boy was odd—so odd that he was a puzzle. Henry "cried once when snow" that he was watching from their bedroom window "stopped falling," and his father couldn't help but to stare at him with a "queer" expression on his face. He was astounded. He had never seen a boy cry over the weather before.

He didn't like the boy's antisocial behavior, but he could sweep it all under the rug without a second thought. He was just a boy, after all, and a small one at that. Older and bigger boys picked on him constantly, and for him to pick in turn on others younger and smaller than he was only natural. He was sure of it. Still, Henry Sr. admitted that if his wife was still alive, her touch would surely have set the boy on an entirely different path.

But the worst of the boy's behavior was the most persistent—and extraordinarily embarrassing to him. Since he was six years old, Henry had frequently engaged in what was then called self-abuse. To Henry's father, it was a mark of the deepest perversity, of a depravity so intense that no one wanted to acknowledge it, much less discuss it with the boy. *He* didn't. That was certain.

The authorities' record of Henry's shenanigans corroborated everything the old man knew and added a few things he didn't. They reminded him that for every good Samaritan—a social worker, a colleague of Jane Addams, a cop on the beat, and others like them—that one might come across on West Madison Street, there were hundreds of wolves like Shorty who cruised every nook and cranny looking to pick up lambs like Henry. Lambs were also called "kids" or "brats," and during a long rant in which Henry deplored how adults treated children during his own childhood and how they should be punished harshly for it, he added in a brief aside, "I was like a little devil if called 'kid.'" It suggests he had been some wolf's kid—perhaps for the thrill of the sexual pleasure of it, perhaps as a way of making a little money, just like Stanley—but perhaps he had also actively resisted, failed, and resented becoming a lamb, becoming angry whenever "kid" was applied to him.

While living with his father in utter poverty, Henry was somehow able to buy "paint boxes" and "other interesting articles," but he never explained where a child less than eight years old might have gotten the money for such luxuries. Whatever paltry salary his father was making at the time went for rent, food, and alcohol—not necessarily in that order—or for footing the medical bills of those whom Henry had attacked. Given Henry's penchant for bragging about his accomplishments, if he had had a legitimate job (as a shoe shine boy, newsboy, or messenger, all of which were occupations available to children as young as six), he would have mentioned it because it would have been another opportunity for him to brag. He didn't.

When he was an old man, Henry casually dropped a hint about how he might have earned money when he was a child. He said, "I used to go and see a night watchman in a six story building a short distance from where we lived." He began to visit the man around the same time that Mrs. Anderson was giving him dinner, a short time before he was led away to Dunning.

When his father was absent, which was much of the time, Henry was left to his own devices, and the neighborhood police caught him on the streets, going to or returning from his assignations with the "night watchman" (and perhaps, as Stanley's experiences suggest, with other men). Henry didn't visit the man in the factory only once. "I used to go" implies he did so often and suggests a relationship had developed between someone old enough to have a full-time job, which in those days was typically far younger than it is today, and a child no older than eight. Given Henry's father's absence, the man was likely a father substitute for the boy, but what Henry was for the man can only be surmised. Henry couldn't have carried on a mature conversation about anything that would have interested the man nor could the seven- or eight-year-old have been able to be one of the man's buddies and pal around with him. Had the night watchman been platonically and altruistically involved with the boy, giving him money because he wanted to help the needy child, Henry would have commented on it, as he had about Mrs. Anderson and her children, who gave him dinner and attention with no strings attached. Although the night watchman likely gave Henry money for sexual favors just as Stanley's "foreman" was prepared to do, the man also may have had very real affection for Henry. Henry certainly cared for him. As an odd man, Henry recalled the loss of the man's affection, which was extremely painful for him, and Henry called it a "sad remembrance," which shows that, regardless of the nature of the relationship, Henry enjoyed it enough to remember it fondly for the rest of his life. He mentioned their relationship only once and very briefly in his autobiography, and then he dropped the subject exactly as he had done when he mentioned his mother and sister.

Many dangers lurked on the dark avenues of West Madison Street, and it wouldn't have taken Henry long to learn about—and try to protect himself against—them. There was the potential for being caught by the authorities when out on a sexual escapade. Boys and men wanting to stay out of jail asked any man if he was a member of the police force before agreeing to engage in sexual activities with him. If the man was on the vice squad, for example, he had to acknowledge that he was, in which case the boy could back out without impunity.

The potential for being kidnapped into the "white slave trade" was also a danger. Although investigations into the white slave trade usually focused on white women and girls who were snatched, then sold into prostitution, a published report disclosed in 1914 that "young men"—and presumably boys—were also victims of the practice. In Chicago, the public's concern over the white slave trade grew so intense that it climaxed into a panic during the 1910s. Henry would have been aware of the panic and his own vulnerability. He would have been suspicious of any man approaching him for his sexual favors, making being in a gang of jack-rollers preferable to being on the streets alone. It also explains why being in a relationship with the night watchman became important to Henry. He wouldn't have been threatening to Henry after their initial contact.

Other chronicles besides Stanley's shed light on the environment in which poverty-stricken boys earned money by selling their bodies to whoever had the cash. One document after another mentions the down-and-outers who drifted to West Madison Street, the last stop on a journey that began with home, family, and financial stability and ended with homelessness, loneliness, and poverty. There were three stops, each a vice district, on their journey to rock bottom. "The usual procedure is North Clark [the Rialto], South State [the Levee], and then over to West Madison Street," the dead end for most of the men who drifted there. By the time they found themselves floundering in Henry's neighborhood, they were "utterly filthy and dilapidated run-down men"—each what Henry called a "skidrow bum."

Various "resorts" also sprang up in the area, and swarms of boys, and occasionally a girl or two, could be seen there, some playing, some working, but most simply loitering without any obvious purpose. "Resort" was a popular word at the time to identify a variety of entertainment establishments, from saloons, movie theaters, and burlesque houses to hotels that doubled as brothels. The most notorious resorts were within a block or two of Halsted and Madison, and the Haymarket, a burlesque theater, was one of the most popular. The performances on its stage were "as vulgar and sensuous as it is possible to find in any place save a house of prostitution. The vulgar jokes, the sensuous movements of young women and men performers have obviously only one purpose." Both women *and* men danced sensuously onstage to a loud and raucous ragtime band, taking their bows to the hoots and hollers of the mostly male audience titillated by the performances. Some of the young men performed in drag, a common occurrence in the early 1900s. Burlesque theaters became a marketplace where boys could offer their bodies in exchange for money. A social worker, who happened to be "taking in a burlesque show in a West Side theater," noticed "the almost unbelievable situation of little boys, as young even as ten years of age," in the audience "for the purpose of soliciting men for homosexual practices." Half a dollar was the going price.

Besides interviewing the hoboes of West Madison Street, Nels Anderson also spoke with a male prostitute whom he called "W.B.P." He noted that W.B.P. conducted "most of his soliciting along the lake front, in the parks, along Michigan Boulevard," and in the art galleries of Towertown, Chicago's bohemian neighborhood, that "stretched between the Water Tower and 'Bughouse Square,' the common nickname for Washington Square Park opposite the Newberry Library."

W.B.P. charged two dollars for his sexual favors, the "general price" for a male prostitute in the better parts of town. Then Anderson added, "W.B.P. seems to have contempt for the lads on West Madison street who do business for fifty cents," adding that a "good fag who keeps himself clean can get—good money—from six to twelve dollars a day."

The tall, slim eighteen-year-old Edward Stevens was already an expert hustler when he admitted to sociologist Myles Vollmer that, when he was fifteen, a stranger

> picked me up. It was on Madison Street. He said "Hello;" and I answered "Hello." He said "It's a nice night isn't it?" and I said "You bet." Then he said "What do you for excitement?" And I told him "O, most anything." Then he told me to come home with him, and I did. We took all our clothes off, and started to play around. He offered me $2.50 if I would go down on him, I did, and he shot in my mouth. It was the first time I ever did that. I didn't like it, but I wanted the money.

His openness embarrassed Vollmer, who wasn't much older than Stevens. Stevens was so jaded, he didn't blush, not even once, but stared eye-to-eye at Vollmer without blinking. Vollmer was the first to look away.

Had they been caught prostituting themselves by a cop on the beat instead of being spotted and interviewed by sociologists Anderson and Vollmer, W.B.P. and Stevens would have been arrested, convicted, and sent to jail. Henry was institutionalized in Dunning because a policeman in his neighborhood caught him going to or coming from the night watchman and likely engaging in other risky activities, many undoubtedly sexual in nature. To get Henry out of Dunning, his father had to guarantee, to the authorities' satisfaction, his eight-year-old son's future welfare. Given his poverty, his ill health, and his dependence on alcohol, he couldn't guarantee a thing. He was desperate. Something had to be done. He discussed the boy's antics with his brothers, hoping that one of them might take him in. They knew Henry was a handful, and neither wanted any part of being responsible for the welfare of such an incorrigible boy. So instead, he devised a plan to send the boy to live at the Mission of Our Lady of Mercy, where, the old man was sure, Henry would be kept safe from "grownups, and especially all types of strangers" who cruised the neighborhood ready to teach Henry even more perversions than he already knew.

Although the priest-run, Catholic-supported Mission of Our Lady of Mercy had been established as a haven for at-risk boys like Henry and had a wonderful reputation, its director, Father Dennis Mahoney, failed miserably to protect his wards from the dangers that lurked outside its doors and hid in the shadows behind its walls. Only a few days after he walked through the Mission's creaky front door, Henry was "tempted to run away." In fact, what happened to him there led him to declare, "If I knew where to go to be elsewhere taken care of I would have surely ran away."

CHAPTER 2

MERCY

ANNA DARGER

ANNA DARGER, HENRY'S UNCLE AUGUSTINE'S SECOND WIFE, was a parent and nobody's fool. She understood firsthand the many dangers Henry had faced daily in West Madison Street because she, her second husband, Joseph C. Sparr, and her two daughters from her first marriage had lived for a few years at the intersection of State and 26th Streets, at the threshold of Chicago's South Side vice district, the Levee. It was known internationally for its huge number of saloons, bordellos, and streetwalkers. Sparr and Anna were married on Christmas Eve 1879 before a justice of the peace in Chicago. She was thirty; he was forty-six. He owned the building at 2604 State, which had a saloon on the main floor and rooms above. They lived in most of the upstairs rooms and rented out those they didn't need. Many years earlier, he had been a butcher and owned a business with his brother, but he gave that up to be a saloon keeper when he discovered that alcohol was more profitable than meat. When her husband died in 1880, a few weeks before their son, Joseph A. Sparr, was born, she resolved to move her daughters and son into a safer neighborhood, one more suited to families.

Children who lived near the Levee were no better off than those, like Henry, who lived in West Madison Street. The boys and girls who lived in the vicinity not only encountered "prostitutes near their homes," but were also "in danger from vicious men and boys" who frequent such districts. "Court records show that vicious and degenerate men" sought out "young boys and girls and filled their minds with filthy and obscene suggestions and taught them lewd and unnatural practices." The sexual exploitation of children was virtually ubiquitous in the city's vice districts and unstoppable.

Anna had been a successful dressmaker when she met Sparr but gave it up to be a housewife when they married. She returned to her profession after he died, becoming so successful that, along with the profits from selling the building she and Sparr owned, Anna could afford to move into a better neighborhood. Within a year or two of his death, she and the children were living in an apartment at 2711 Portland, two doors south of Augustine and Charles Darger and their families. By 1894, both of her girls had married and moved into their own homes, and in 1896, Margaret, Augustine's wife, died of cerebral meningitis.

Anna was certainly aware of the Dargers and was friendly toward them, exchanging pleasantries when they met on the sidewalk or happened to leave or enter their houses at the same time. After Augustine mourned Margaret an appropriate amount of time, he began taking notice of Anna. She was a good mother and an industrious woman, making her own way in the world while attending to her boy. One thing led to another, and they tied the knot on February 13, the day before Valentine's Day, 1897. Anna moved with Joseph, who was then seventeen, into Augustine's home.

She had kept her eye on Joseph as he grew up, making sure he was safe and out of trouble. He had turned into a fine young man by anyone's standards, but Anna was aware that Henry, who was twelve years younger than Joseph, hadn't been as lucky. She never mentioned it to Augustine, but she considered her brother-in-law Henry little more than a penniless drunk who haunted the cheapest saloons in

West Madison Street while Henry ran wild and got into all sorts of trouble. As far as she was concerned, Henry's problems weren't the boy's fault but his father's.

When Henry Sr. realized he had to do something with his son, he came up with the obvious option first. He asked his brothers to take Henry into one of their homes.

It's possible that, initially, Augustine and Charles considered opening their doors, and their hearts, to the boy, and if so, Anna, who was Henry's most steadfast advocate, would have been for it. However, neither brother ended up taking on the responsibility of sheltering, feeding, raising, and—most daunting—controlling Henry. They knew he had slashed his teacher with a knife because she had punished him for an infraction of the class rules. Would he do that to one of them or to their wives if they scolded him? They knew he had thrown ashes in the eyes of a little girl, acting just like the bullies who had targeted him. Would he do that to one of the neighbors' children? They knew the police had caught him slipping out to visit a night watchman late at night, and they didn't want police knocking on their doors, Henry in tow. Even Anna had to admit the boy was too much to handle on a full-time basis.

On top of everything else, Henry's father must have also revealed his deepest shame to them when he asked them for their help. The boy had been habitually engaged in self-abuse.

At fifty-eight and fifty-five years old, Augustine and Charles were too old to deal with the trouble that they were sure Henry would bring into their lives. They couldn't take a chance on the boy. Too much was at stake. What if he actually murdered someone this time instead of just cutting her? What if the police caught him in the company of other perverts, all dolled up and prancing around the Loop? What if his monkeyshines got back to their customers or to their lodge brothers? Both were Masons and gossip like that could ruin them. They couldn't ignore the fact that his antics would throw their lives into an uproar.

Charles, the youngest of the Darger brothers, was already a grandfather and wasn't eager to take on the job of raising another youngster again. Ellen, his wife, was fifty-six and busy enjoying her grandchildren. Living with either Augustine or Charles would have been a boon for Henry, but it would be a no-win situation for them. They told their brother they couldn't take on the boy, family or not. He'd have to figure out what to do with the child without them, and that's exactly what Henry Sr. did.

Anna was forty-seven years old by the time she married Augustine and a little distraught that her youngest, Joseph, was growing up, rarely needed her now, and would be out on his own soon. She still had a nurturing streak a mile wide, and it didn't take much for her to surrender to her maternal instincts and take the boy under her wing whenever she had the chance. Henry Sr. was more than happy to let her.

In fact, Henry Sr. preferred to get others to do his dirty work for him whenever possible. Once he realized that he could give his son to the Mission of Our Lady of Mercy to be raised, he asked Anna to take the boy to be baptized a Roman Catholic. He had no intention of doing it himself. The Mission was free to any boy in need, regardless of his religious affiliation, but because the Roman Catholic Church ran it, Henry Sr. decided to help pave Henry's way into being accepted by the staff and children there by having Henry baptized a Roman Catholic. Henry was already attending school at St. Patrick's, so it made perfect sense.

Anna took Henry to St. Patrick's Church to be baptized on a snow-blanketed day at the end of winter in 1900, when he was nearly eight. Quite often, aunts and uncles become the godparents of the children being baptized, and following that practice, Anna probably became Henry's godmother that day. Too drunk, too ill, too lame, or too disinterested to walk the one block from his coach house apartment to the church, Henry's father didn't show up. As far as he was concerned, Henry was already out of his hair.

The following June, when it was time to drop the boy off at the Mission, Henry Sr. again asked Anna to do his dirty work, and again, she accepted. After all, she wanted the best for the boy, and even if no one else would admit it, she knew living with his father was far from nurturing. The old man was in his cups more often now.

At the same time, Henry was a unique child, as far as she was concerned. Creative and intelligent, a born storyteller, he spent hours coloring in the coloring books she or his father gave him as Christmas or birthday gifts. When he ran out of coloring books, he traced pictures he'd found in newspapers or magazines onto cheap paper and then colored them in. No one had taught him to do that. He figured it out on his own. Nothing seemed to stand in his way once he made up his mind to do something, and that somehow endeared him to her. Besides, he was smaller than most boys his age, and bigger ones easily bullied him. That pulled at her heartstrings.

When Henry Sr. first mentioned to her that he wanted to send the boy to live at the Mission, Anna had talked him into waiting until after St. Patrick's school year ended. If they moved him earlier, she explained, his schooling would be unnecessarily interrupted. Moving him after the end of the school year would give him all summer to become acclimated to his new home and surroundings before attending his new school. The transition would be easier on the boy. Henry Sr. gave in to Anna.

Henry Sr. had neglected to tell Anna that he'd come up with a way to ease his poverty a little. Once Henry was out of his apartment, he would rent space in his two-room, coach house apartment to a lodger, a common practice, to make a few extra bucks. The amount he could charge wouldn't be much, of course, but a little is better than nothing. Henry Sr.'s new boarder, a day laborer named John McKenzie, moved in by June 7, 1900. Anna had already dropped Henry off at the Mission.

THE MISSION OF OUR LADY OF MERCY

The Newsboys' Home, as it was initially called, was originally established in 1884 at 45-47 Jackson Boulevard in the Loop. Its goal was to help boys who hawked newspapers on the streets for a few cents a day: to get them off the streets, to give them shelter, and to herd them back to school if they were truant, as they most often were. The other boys on the streets, called "street arabs," and there were many, had to fend for themselves. In 1890, the Mission moved to 361-363 West Jackson, the epicenter of the West Madison Street vice district, and its director decided to open its door to any homeless boy, not just the newsboy. He changed its name to the Mission of Our Lady of Mercy, and it got a nickname that reflected its new inclusiveness, the Working Boys' Home.

The Mission of Our Lady of Mercy should have been a safe alternative to vice-ridden news alleys and flophouses where homeless boys usually congregated, but many of the boys at the Mission had already learned how to prostitute themselves for much-needed cash. At the same time, others were having sex with boys and men because they enjoyed it. As early as the very year in which the Newsboys' Home was founded, charges of homosexual conduct among the boys who lived under its roof surfaced in an article first published in Chicago's *Evening Journal* and then reprinted in the *Chicago Daily Tribune*. The reporter claimed that the boys "sleep in one dormitory," which was the attic room, "without any nightwatch after 10:30 o'clock, and they learn more evil in that dormitory in one night than they do on the street in a week."

Despite such accusations, the Mission gained a stellar reputation throughout all of Chicago due not only to the ease with which Church and civic authorities turned blind eyes to the article but also to the tireless efforts of Father Dennis S. H. Mahoney, its second director. The *Chicago Daily Tribune* began praising the priest and his efforts on behalf of boys almost as soon as he took over in 1899, the year before Henry went to live there. "He knows," the *Chicago Daily Tribune* trumpeted, "the waif as well as his theology, and immediately found his way to the hearts of the street arabs. No pastor ever knew or loved his flock better or more than Father Mahony," and "in all his advices and corrections," Father Mahoney was "always gentle, yet commanding," "a man of mild disposition," and "loved as well as revered" by the boys whose lives he changed. Praise of the priest's efforts continued for decades. One writer even claimed that, under Father Mahoney's direction, the Mission had "saved thousands of homeless boys" who had crowded the West Madison Street district "from perversion of faith and from temptations that had surrounded them." Henry's father and Anna may have missed the published exposé of sexual activities among the boys behind the Mission's walls, but they would certainly have been aware of the priest's glowing reputation.

Henry and his godmother, Anna, were perched in front of 361–363 West Jackson Boulevard, at the door to the Mission of Our Lady of Mercy. After she had arrived at the coach house apartment to pick him up, it had taken Henry all of a minute to gather his wardrobe together into a bundle. It was tucked under his arm. She was knocking on the door with one hand and holding his with the other. Her grip was so tight, he couldn't have broken away even if he had wanted to.

A three-story building, the Mission was capped off with an attic high enough to make the building a full four stories. It wasn't the tallest building Henry had ever seen, of course. Chicago was in the forefront of cities that were building what were beginning to be called skyscrapers, but the Mission was still imposing because of what it stood for, if not because of its size. It wasn't a prison, but it may as well have been as far as Henry was concerned. Although he still was living within an easy walk of his father's apartment and in a neighborhood that he knew like the back of his hand, Henry felt that he was about to find himself living a life so alien from the one he'd just

left that he'd never find his way back to his father's apartment again—
a metaphor that he would soon discover in *The Wonderful Wizard of
Oz,* which would become one of his favorite books.

It was the first week of June 1900. The summer sun beat down
on Anna and Henry as humidity hunkered over them. Henry shivered
and sweated at the same time. She noticed and knelt down, promising
him that she'd come to visit often, that she'd come right away if he
was ever in trouble.

At the threshold of the Mission, Anna hoped this would be the
beginning of a better life for her nephew. Within seconds, an elderly
woman opened the door, her salt-and-pepper hair pulled back into a
loose bun. Strands of her hair had slipped free and fallen forward
into her face. She was smiling at them both and, ushering them into
the foyer, introduced herself as Mrs. Brown, the Mission's matron.
The morning sun had entered through the seven-feet-tall windows
and brightly lit the first floor of the Mission, a sharp contrast to the
shaded coach house apartment he had shared with his father until
this morning.

Mrs. Brown may have reminded Henry of Mrs. Anderson. He
seems to have taken a shine to her immediately.

His godmother gave Mrs. Brown the bundle of his clothing. She
tucked it under her right arm and then offered her left hand to the
boy. The eight-year-old took it. His godmother watched them walk
toward the back of the foyer, listening to the matron point out what
was what in Henry's new home. She began chatting about the other
boys who lived at the Mission, telling him that most of them were
out, a few playing stickball or tag in the streets, some working at their
jobs as newsboys, shoe shiners, and similar occupations. What she
didn't add was that, right now, a large number would also have been
gallivanting throughout the neighborhood, darting in and out of the
burlesque houses and saloons that dotted the streets surrounding the
Mission, shoplifting, getting into fights, and otherwise attracting the
attention of cops on the beat.

They began climbing the stairs while Mrs. Brown explained that the Mission was such a wonderful place for boys his age to live. At the top of the first flight, they turned to begin the second. They not only disappeared from Anna's sight; she also couldn't hear them clearly anymore. Although she couldn't make out what the old woman was saying, she could hear Mrs. Brown's voice as she chatted away and her measured footsteps as they climbed all the way to the attic, where Henry would sleep for the next four years with all the other boys who lived at the Mission. Mrs. Brown decided to skip one other piece of information during their tour of the Mission. The Mission had bedbugs that, in a rare moment of humor bordering on comic relief, Henry once took delight in mentioning. "Our large sleeping room at times surely had the 'beautiful little creatures of a red color' known as bed bugs," Henry said, then joked, "Got the creeps?"

Henry's experience a few months earlier, when the authorities had taken him to Dunning, was much different than this. Everything about the situation felt different. Authorities hadn't dragged him to the Mission; his godmother had led him here by the hand. No one at the Mission was barking orders or glaring threateningly at him as they had at Dunning. Instead, Mrs. Brown hovered over him like a storybook grandmother. He was still in his old, familiar neighborhood, not out in the nondescript farmlands of northwest Chicago where Dunning blotted the landscape. He'd walked by the Mission plenty of times before coming to live in it. He'd played in the streets in front of it, too. He even already knew a couple of the newsboys who lived there by name and several others by sight.

None of that eased what must have been his overwhelming sense of abandonment. He had been tossed out like a scrap of spoiled meat, and street-savvy eight-year-old Henry knew it. Maybe not now, but soon he would have realized that not one soul he knew had offered to look after him. Only total strangers, like Mrs. Brown, wanted to take care of him, but that was only because she earned her livelihood by looking after boys like him. Because of Henry and the other boys who lived at the Mission, Mrs. Brown could buy food for her table and pay her rent.

Henry's move into the Mission marked the end of any substantial relationship he may have had with his father. The shift in Henry's perception of his father's actions, from liberating him from Dunning to jailing him in the Mission, happened so quickly that it confused the boy. Why the change? To punish him? He hadn't done anything recently that he hadn't done hundreds of times before without a peep from his father. It didn't make sense. Without answers to his questions, he ended up blaming himself for his father's drastic change toward him, adding to his already deep well of frustration, anger, and guilt.

CLASS CLOWN

When Henry moved into the Mission, he left the Catholic-run St. Patrick's School and began attending the Skinner School, a public school. Henry was a bright, engaged student who "excelled in spelling" but was "rather poor in figures and geography." He enjoyed reading, and his father had taught him to read before he ever went to school. Henry's favorite class was history, which he claimed he "almost knew by heart." He was especially fond of the Civil War, which had ended only thirty-five years earlier. Henry told Ella A. Dewey, his teacher, that he didn't believe the history books when they reported the number of soldiers who died in specific battles because he had read "three histories that told different losses." He deduced that, because the books' authors contradicted one another, no one could know exactly how many soldiers had been lost.

Being the new kid on the block is always difficult, even under the best of circumstances, and it demands that the new boy balance on the thin line between asserting himself and acknowledging the hierarchical power structure that already exists. In an attempt to fit in, Henry decided to play the class clown. He didn't tell jokes, and not understanding how delicate the balance that he had to negotiate was, he took it too far.

Henry "was a little too funny and made strange noises" with his "mouth, nose and throat" during class. He wanted his classmates to think he was a clever, fun-loving boy and hoped that they would laugh. His plan backfired. Instead of being invited into the fold as he'd hoped, the other boys and girls were so aggravated by Henry that they gave him "saucy and hateful looks." Some even told him that, if he didn't stop it, they'd put him in his place after school. His stored-up anger got the best of him, and instead of tempering his behavior, Henry did the opposite.

After a few weeks, Miss Dewey, who had given up trying to control Henry's behavior, complained to her principal, Ella R. Coles, about his disruptions in her classroom. Coles finally decided to expel him. This was the second time that his actions had gotten Henry kicked out of school, and one more example of the many times that, instead of dealing with Henry's problems and making an attempt to help him, adults simply tossed him out.

After a few days, Father Mahoney went to Mrs. Coles and asked her to reinstate the boy. At that meeting, Henry's frustration, anger, and guilt began welling up and threatened to explode, but Father Mahoney saw what was happening and gave Henry a look that calmed him down. After what seemed like hours to Henry, Mrs. Coles relented. She allowed Henry to return to Miss Dewey's class, but she told him "very sharply and angrily" that this was his last chance, that there would be no more nonsense out of him, and that, if he disturbed the class again, he would be expelled and would never, ever be allowed to return to Skinner School. Henry caught on. As soon as he returned to Miss Dewey's classroom, he changed his behavior drastically. He never made another peep and became "one of the best behaving boys in school."

Henry was repentant, accepting the fact that he'd done wrong and deserved punishment. However, in virtually all other situations in which he found himself accused of an infraction, Henry refused to acknowledge his guilt or accept the consequences of his own actions. In fact, he often claimed that he either didn't understand what was wrong about his behavior or that he couldn't remember having done anything wrong in the first place. Denial was Henry's main coping strategy, and it was becoming a strategy to preserve his self-respect. Throughout his childhood, teachers, neighbors, priests, and all sorts of other adults could accuse him of anything or dole out whatever punishments they wanted for all sorts of charges, but his mantra-like rejoinders—*I didn't know it was wrong* and *I don't remember doing it*—allowed him to think of himself as innocent when his own accounts later in life often reveal he was anything but.

Henry insisted that his father visited him at the Mission "often, in the winter and the summer" and "especially on the Fourth of July and Christmas," but he recalled details of only one visit that his father made. More likely, Henry was covering for his father's lack of interest in him, as he had often before. Quite lame by now, the old man might have found the four-and-a-half-block walk from the coach house apartment to the Mission too much to handle, but he could have taken public transportation. Two different streetcar lines ran within a block of the Mission, making visiting his son for at least a few hours every weekend extremely easy.

Luckily for Henry, Anna took her vow as a godparent seriously. Henry recalled that he had no sooner gotten settled into the Mission's routine than he'd had to call her to come to his rescue. One of the Mission boys saw two dimes that Anna had given Henry and accused Henry of stealing them from him. Believing the other boy, not Henry, Father Mahoney punished Henry by "wacking" his hands with a rubber shoe sole, a common form of punishment in Roman Catholic schools in the early days of the twentieth century. As soon as Henry contacted Anna, she hurried to the Mission to set the record straight.

Father Mahoney accepted her explanation and then punished the boy who'd accused Henry in the first place, but Henry had already been punished unjustly. His hand hurt for days, but his embarrassment lasted weeks longer. Father Mahoney never apologized to Henry, and Henry never forgot.

The laudatory phrases that newspapers had used to describe Father Mahoney contrast sharply with Henry's nickname for the man, "Father Meaney." Henry described him as "prime and very severe." He was an eagle-eyed, no-nonsense, hands-on authoritarian who was one step ahead of the boys in his charge. "Father Meaney" was, in fact, the opposite of Henry's father. Henry wasn't used to adult supervision, except for the perfunctory control that St. Patrick's School had meted out, and now, living at the Mission, he didn't like Father Meaney's iron fist one bit.

Henry was no angel. The boys at the Mission told on Henry often. As often as they told on him, the priests "whacked" him on his hands with the rubber sole of a shoe. But he, too, was a snitch. He recalled that one of the Mission's rules was that the boys weren't allowed to "climb to the top of their clothes lockers," but they often did. He claimed he was forced "to tell on them once when they did so," and it made the other boys angry. Some "of the bigger boys" even "told" him off.

One evening during dinner at the Mission, Henry "let out a big whopper of a poop." Some of the boys guffawed, while others yelled "phew" and fanned the air before their faces. Although Henry never admitted that he was the one who farted, the "oldest one there," probably James Tobin, who was eighteen, pointed at Henry, calling him by his nickname, "Crazy." Coming to his defense, Mrs. Brown slapped her hands together to get the boys' attention. When all were silent, she told Tobin, "If he is crazy he does not know any better." Another boy, John Manley, who sat facing Henry, whispered "It was you" to him. Although it's impossible to tell if Henry's fart was an accident or a sophomoric prank, an important fact emerges from the incident. Mrs. Brown exhibited an understanding of Henry that few others ever had, and she was unwilling to pigeonhole him. Because of her, Henry emerged from this incident virtually unscathed.

Mrs. Brown, who was likely Julia Brown, a widow who lived at 663 West Jackson, reacted to Henry as Mrs. Anderson and his aunt Anna had. All three women showed an unexpected and rare sensitivity to the boy and his plight, and their reactions to him reveal that there were things about Henry that brought out, in at least some women, a desire to help him and to focus on his more attractive and compelling attributes. Not only did Mrs. Brown recognize that Henry often did "not know any better" than to act as he did, suggesting with good reason there was something amiss with his family life before he came to the Mission, she also went so far as to offer to give him a home. One hot, June afternoon, as Henry walked past her house, she happened to notice him out of her window, went to her front door, and called him in to tell him that "she wanted to adopt" him. She had to get permission from his father, she told him, and she tried, but unfortunately for Henry, his father refused. He had someone else in mind, as Henry would later learn.

His father's rejection of Mrs. Brown's offer is tragic because she appears to have been a wonderful candidate for an adoptive parent. Having been the matron at the Mission for a number of years, she was used to boys who were headstrong and more than a little rough around the edges because of their experiences on the street. As important, she wasn't just a "good woman," as Henry himself realized, but was well-off financially. She could afford to retire from her job at the Mission, a rarity among adults at the dawn of the twentieth century.

Instead of giving Mrs. Brown permission to take his son under her wing and offer him all sorts of advantages that he couldn't even dream of, Henry's father brought another woman to the Mission as a prospective adoptive parent for Henry:

Once my father brought some woman relative to have me adopted by her, but Father Meaney was not there at the time, and Father Ohara could not do anything about it.

My father would have to see him.

He never did.

This is the only time that Henry gives any details about one of his father's visits to the Mission, and the fact that Henry's father considered the "woman relative"—perhaps a floozy with whom he drank or his lover, and probably not a "relative" at all—and not the sober, financially well-off Mrs. Brown as a fit parent for his son reveals his skewed perception of what a parent should be.

His father was probably jealous of Mrs. Brown, afraid she would replace him in his son's heart. He knew that Mrs. Brown would have been available physically *and* emotionally to Henry in ways that he never had been or would ever be. So instead of giving his son a foot up in the world by allowing Mrs. Brown to adopt the boy, he condemned Henry to a childhood without parental or familial love, surrounded by strangers who would never have Henry's best interests at heart. By rejecting Mrs. Brown's offer, Henry's father threw the boy to the wolves.

SOMETHING

During the four years in which he lived at the Mission, Henry had a sexual relationship with at least one other boy who lived there and probably with several others. He began describing the experience as if it were nothing out of the ordinary. "There was one boy," he recalled, "who was somewhat friendly and sometimes not. When he got angry at you, you knew it. He was not a bully though, nor tried to be," and then he announced the boy's name: "John Manley." John Manley arrived at the Mission shortly after Henry and took a strong, immediate liking to the smaller boy. "He wanted my company and friendship but was hot tempered and agresive," Henry admitted, "and I did my best to try and avoid him." "He wanted my company but was bossy," Henry complained. "He wanted my company always for sure I'll say again, but when I don't like anyone I wanted him to stay away," Henry said, adding with a hint of exasperation, "He would not do so." John Manley may or may not have been a bully, but he *was* insistent when it came to his interest in Henry. He never threatened Henry as the "skidrow bum" had, but he demanded Henry's "company." He didn't invite it. The phrase "keeping company" was popular in the 1800s and early 1900s as a synonym to "dating." At the same time, "friendship" was often used, depending on its context, to identify romantic liaisons between men, and this is especially so when the men called themselves "special friends" or "bosom friends."

Had Henry said only once that Manley wanted his company, it would be difficult to make anything of it. But mentioning it three times puts Henry's relationship with Manley into perspective—especially so with his emphatic "always for sure." It's clear that, at least initially, Henry wasn't particularly interested in the boy's advances. Still, Henry ends the confession suggesting that he gave in to Manley's desire. Manley would not leave Henry alone, so what could Henry do but give in? At eight years old and small for his age, Henry wasn't in a situation in which he could get by without being at least one boy's sexual property.

Historically, institutions that housed large numbers of boys often became the stage for sexual abuse. Boys too small or too weak to fend off the advances of other inmates or caregivers often simply surrendered to their advances, and this situation of predator and prey was not limited to the period of Henry's stay at the Mission. More than five decades after Henry gave in to John Manley, reports surfaced about another institutionalized boy, an eleven-year-old, who found himself the pet of one of the older boys, a fourteen- or fifteen-year-old. At his institution, an older, bigger boy would slip "into a younger or smaller boy's bed" after lights out, "threaten him into silence," and then force him into sexual activities. Often the bigger boy would form a relationship with the smaller one so that, during daylight hours, "the younger boy would receive favors" and even "protection" from the older boy, and at bedtime, the younger "would perform sexually" for the older. Eventually, the stronger boy might release the weaker one from their arrangement and move on to another boy who'd caught his eye, leaving the weaker boy fair game for the next strong boy who was interested in him.

When Henry moved into the Mission during the first week of June 1900, some twenty-eight boys were already inmates there. Four were Henry's age, two were younger than he, and twenty-two were older, some as old as eighteen. At the Mission, Henry no longer had the closed, locked door of his father's apartment for protection. At the Mission, he lived—and slept—among boys whose street smarts were sharper and more advanced than his and who were bigger and stronger than he. At the Mission, he had to be vigilant twenty-four hours a day, seven days a week, never letting his guard down. At the Mission, he was outnumbered.

Boys who were sexually abused in institutions often "retreated into a fog of dissociation and docile obedience," and they "viewed beatings, torture, and sexual assaults as if they were watching a film." Many of the boys were "so traumatized that they had trouble admitting what had happened to them," their denial causing emotional and physical problems later on in their lives. Henry was no exception.

John Manley's attraction to Henry eventually wore off, and helped by two other boys, the brothers Jim and John Scanlon, he accused Henry of something—what specifically that something was, Henry never fully divulged. But from clues he dropped, it appears that Henry was caught up in some sort of sexual escapade with Manley and the Scanlons. Either to deflect their role in it or to get even with Henry for something he did or wouldn't do, the others tattled on him before he could tattle on them, and Henry was blamed for whatever it was that had happened. Because each was just the sort of boy who was frequently eyed by the unsavory elements in the vice-ridden neighborhood, it would have been easy for the four of them to have formed a gang like Stanley's to jack-roll drunks and gay men who cruised West Madison Street. Likewise, it would have been easy for Manley and the Scanlons boys to do "bad things" to Henry, as the older boys in Stanley's gang had done to him, because they all slept in the same dormitory room, and no one—not even Father Mahoney or his assistant, Father Sylvester O'Hara, who lived together in a building next door—would have been there after ten thirty p.m. to police the boys.

Manley and the Scanlons took their complaint to Otto Zink, an "overseer" of some sort at the Mission, who in turn brought the boys' accusation to Mrs. Gannon, who had replaced Mrs. Brown when she retired, and to Father Mahoney. Years later, Henry recalled standing in front of Zink, Gannon, and Mahoney, but he claimed he didn't have a clue what he supposedly had done. However, he did remember that he hadn't bothered to deny the boys' charges—whatever they were. In his words, he "did not have the brains or courage to fiercely deny it." When Henry was innocent of some accusation, he was quick to remember, even many decades later, exactly what the accusation was and was vehement in his denials against it, but Henry's reaction in this situation is an obvious cover-up. He was again relying on denial to get through an unsavory experience. As so often before, Mahoney sided with Henry's accusers, and he "whacked" Henry's hands with the rubber sole of a shoe again. This time, Henry didn't contact his godmother, Anna, to ask her to set the record straight. Henry was obviously guilty, but of exactly what, he would never say.

Henry was also called on the carpet for moving his hands up and down and back and forth in the air, gestures that the adults around him probably identified as masturbatory, although he described them as "pretending it was snowing" or "raining." Whatever they were, the hand movements made Mrs. Gannon as well as "her son and Otto Zink and others" think Henry was "either feeble-minded, or actually Crazy," and they were quick to tell him, and Father Mahoney, so. Because of the movements of his hands and what Henry euphemistically called in his autobiography the "strange things" that he actually did, probably with Manley and the Scanlons, Father Mahoney felt compelled to contact Henry's father with an ultimatum.

All of the boys who lived at the Mission were exactly like Henry in one very important way. "The boys there all had parents," Henry realized, who "could not take care of them." They weren't orphans per se but had been institutionalized because their parents had been unable or unwilling to assume their responsibilities as parents. In essence, each of the boys had been abandoned and was simply a part of the flotsam and jetsam of West Madison Street. Henry was no stranger to street life and what went on there. Yet when his experiences on the street became too intense for him to handle, he had always had the door of his father's apartment to hide behind. It had been a refuge for him, even when his father was gone or too ill or drunk to respond to him.

Henry never revealed anywhere, not in his autobiography nor in any other document, what the "strange things" that he really did were, just as he never confessed what he, Manley, and the Scanlons had been up to, but as far as the priests and the staff were concerned, everything they knew about Henry pointed to one conclusion: "Crazy" didn't belong at the Mission, but somewhere else. The information they had compiled about Henry was all the ammunition they needed to demand that Henry's father do something else with his son, to find a different place for him to live, preferably miles and miles away from them. Henry Sr. had to devise another plan for taking care of his son and was quick to do so.

THE MASTURBATOR'S HEART

By the time the priests told Henry Sr. that he had to move his son out of the Mission, the old man had been a resident of the St. Augustine's Home for the Aged for more than a year. His health had declined so sharply that, by 1903, he couldn't take care of himself any longer. In early November of 1904, either Father Mahoney or, more likely, Father O'Hara took Henry to the office of Dr. Otto Schmidt at 109 Randolph in the Loop. Henry Sr. had contacted Schmidt, who was well known in Chicago for his work on behalf of Chicago's German-immigrant and German-American populations, to ask him for help with his son's perversion: his antics with the night watchman and the boys at the Mission as well as his history of habitual masturbation. When Schmidt agreed to examine the boy pro bono, Henry Sr. was in the physician's hip pocket.

Henry vividly remembered that, beginning in late October or early November 1904, "I was taken several times to be examined by a doctor who on the second time I came, said my heart was not in the right place." Twelve years old but no one's fool, the boy didn't believe the good doctor's diagnosis one bit. He didn't say so but thought, "Where was it supposed to be? In my belly?" He also realized that there was something strange going on. Neither the priest nor the doctor had said anything to Henry about why he was being examined in the first place. Henry didn't have a fever and wasn't throwing up. He hadn't broken any bones. Why were they taking him all the way to Dr. Schmidt's office in the Loop when he didn't need medical attention? Besides, the visits to Schmidt's office hadn't been like any others he'd had before because the doctor hadn't given him medicine or treatment of any kind. Something was going on, but he didn't know what.

Until the mid-1800s, people may have whispered about masturbation, what was then called "self-abuse," behind closed doors, but they rarely openly discussed it. Then, suddenly, the topic became a

St. Augustine's Home for the Aged, where Henry's father lived out his last years and died in 1909 and where Henry, too, lived for the last months of his life and died.

(Used by permission of Special Collections and Archives, John T. Richardson Library, DePaul University, Chicago, IL.)

virtual obsession among middle- and upper-class Americans, as well as among doctors and the growing number of men who devoted their lives to making America healthy through the self-help books they wrote. Considered a perversion and a sin, self-abuse sapped men's and boys' "vigor," a code word for their manliness or sexual potency—or so doctors and self-help writers believed. Each time a man or boy masturbated to orgasm, he significantly weakened his vigor and his body had to work overtime to replenish the store of sperm that he had just wasted. The more often he engaged in self-abuse, the more intensely his body was forced to work to replace it. Too much, too often, and his body would become extraordinarily debilitated, threatening his physical well-being and his mental capabilities. A man could even pass the perversion to his sons and from them to his grandsons, infecting his entire lineage and, ultimately, the whole of society.

The most celebrated of the self-help mavens at this time was John Harvey Kellogg of breakfast cereal fame. In his influential *Plain Facts About Sexual Life*, he echoed the sentiments of many others within and outside of the scientific community: "The seminal fluid is the most highly vitalized of all the fluids of the body," he claimed, and its "rapid production," which occurs after any discharge, whether through intercourse or masturbation, results in "manhood lost." To Kellogg and his contemporaries, only a man with no self-restraint would engage in as debilitating an activity as self-abuse, and a man whose "manhood" had been "lost" was a feminized man, a man on the same rung as a woman—sociopolitically, culturally, and psychologically. While a masturbator's body remained male, all other aspects of his being were female.

At the same time that Kellogg and a host of others were writing treatises against the loss of seminal fluid except in the hope of conceiving a child (and even then, orgasms had to be regulated so as not to overtax the body), other inventive minds were busy developing devices to stop boys and men from self-abuse. Some devices, like the masturbation belt, were constructed simply. Designed like a modern-day jock strap, encircling the waist as well as the thighs at the buttocks, the masturbation belt featured a pouch that offered support for the testicles, but it also had a sleeve into which the penis was inserted to protect it from stimulation. Another popular device to waylay self-abuse was a metal ring with spikes along its inside, fitted around the penis to prick it if it became aroused, the pain deflating the offending flesh. A third strategy had a similar outcome. Doctors sewed shut with wire the foreskins of some men and boys who didn't respond to other methods of ending self-abuse. If the penis became erect, it would strain against the wire, pulling the foreskin, causing pain and disrupting the erection. In more extreme cases, a number of authorities recommended cauterization of the penis. The sores that cauterization caused would deter the boy or man from manipulating his penis. If all else failed, physicians might resort to castration.

What is immediately evident when browsing such a catalog of tortures is the extremes to which some members of society, many of them leading voices in the health care field of their day, went to ensure that semen wasn't wasted but employed only for the perpetuation of the species. Like Kellogg, they believed that the individual who masturbated would succumb to a variety of illnesses—physical, mental, and spiritual—and that masturbators had lost their manhood, as defined by society, and thus were women. Some experts believed that this feminization was metaphoric, that although masturbators would become feminine in manner, dress, and attitude—even to the extent that they would adopt rouge and other makeup and take up women's jobs, becoming stenographers, clerks in department stores, dishwashers, etc.—their genitalia would remain in adequate working order. Others, however, were certain masturbation literally emasculated men. Kellogg believed "excessive masturbation . . . causes the penis to atrophy." Without a working penis, society in general would have agreed, a man is a woman. Nevertheless, neither Kellogg nor any of the others who supported him on this question ever suggested how many times a man might have a sexual climax before he was in danger of becoming a woman.

At the same time that Kellogg was trying to curb men's sexual activities, society was using the label "homosexual" to categorize a very specific group of men who had sex with other men—a label that did not include *all* men who had sex with other men. The medical and scientific professions, the police force, the Church, and even the typical citizen considered homosexual men female in every sense of the word except that they had male genitalia. For them, a homosexual wore makeup, sometimes wore his hair long, often even bleached it, dressed in women's clothing, and adopted a woman's name—

frequently, but not always, the name of a flower: Rose, Daisy, Violet. They were also feminine in their manner and called their kind "fairies," "belles," "pansies," "queens," or "queers."

Another class of men who had sex with other men was the opposite of the fairy. Because they were masculine as defined by the times, they weren't considered homosexual but *normal*. Society had no real term for the masculine men who either allowed the belles to perform oral sex on them or who took the penetrative role in anal sex. However, fairies called the normal men who exchanged sex for cash "trade." Some normal men had sex with fairies only to blackmail them, and fairies called those men "dirt." Normal men were often married; had children; held respectable, masculine jobs (as businessmen, police officers, soldiers, laborers, night watchmen, etc.); and kept their dalliances with fairies secret. It wouldn't be until the last decades of the twentieth century, after the Stonewall riots of June 1969, that "homosexual" would include anyone who desired same-sex sexual relationships regardless of whether that individual was effeminate or masculine, queer or normal, swish or butch.

Norms of the time held that the womanlike fairies willingly "inverted" their gender roles. Instead of acting like men and finding women to be their objects of desire, they flipped their gender identity upside down, "inverted" it, and acted as if they were women, desiring what women—i.e., heterosexual women—desire: men. Men who willingly inverted their gender identity weren't simply an utter mystery to most of society at the time; they were an outrage. In a culture in which women had few rights and privileges, most individuals believed that only an insane man would deny his male birthright and become an "invert"—another often-used term for a homosexual. Thus, according to the logic of the time, a man was an invert because he was insane. There could be no other explanation.

Physicians and heath gurus also linked masturbators to inverts. Summarizing a large majority of Americans' view, Dr. Henry Guernsey warned in his marriage manual, *Plain Talks on Avoided*

Subjects, that excessive self-abuse made men and boys "weak, pale, and feeble in mind, while all that was manly and vigorous has gone out of them." In short, medical professionals believed that A, habitual self-abuse made males effeminate; that B, inverts were effeminate; and that, therefore, C, men who masturbated were inverts—or would become inverts. In fact, by 1900, "masturbator" and "invert" had become interchangeable in many medicolegal texts as well as in the popular imagination. Like other boys who were known to engage in self-abuse, Henry was branded a homosexual—an invert—and so had to be crazy. It was logical. Sylvanus Stall, a Lutheran minister and self-proclaimed sexologist, summed up society's views in 1904, the year Dr. Schmidt examined Henry:

> A search in any insane asylum will show that a very large proportion of patients are made up from those who masturbate or who have syphilis. Stamp out these two evils, or rather curses, of the human race, and the supply that feeds our insane asylums, aye, and our penitentiaries, too, will become vastly lessened. Think of it! So many of the inhabitants of our prisons, asylums, and our poorhouses are composed of men and women who have offended against nature's laws by violating their own sexual nature.

Dr. Schmidt's very odd diagnosis of Henry's condition—his heart was in the wrong place—seems at best a mystery and at worse quackery at its most bizarre. What Henry didn't know was that, when Dr. Schmidt claimed that Henry's "heart was not in the right place," he was probably referring to an obscure article, "Ueber Herzerkrankungen bei Masturbanten" ("Concerning Heart Ailments in Masturbators"), published in 1895. Its author, Dr. G. Bachus, discussed a condition he diagnosed after treating a number of boys and men—the youngest nine, the oldest thirty-one—for habitual masturbation. Based on his examinations of his patients, Bachus postulated that, for individuals "who had masturbated a lot, enlargement of the heart sets in" and their hearts "usually stretch to the left and to the right, more seldom only to the left," resulting in the heart not being in its original "right place." He explained that "such an enlargement is generated by the increase and intensification of the heart's work that arises" to replenish the body's vigor after "frequent sexual acts."

Dr. Schmidt may never have read Bachus's article, but it's safe to assume that all physicians of Schmidt's professional standing would have been familiar with the most current texts in the basic medical specialties. He certainly would have been familiar with G. Stanley Hall's seminal two-volume study *Adolescence*. The single most important book of its day on the psychology of children, *Adolescence* not only mentions Bachus's concept of "the masturbator's heart," but in it, Hall also cited Bachus's article and linked it to what another physician, E. C. Spitzka, called "masturbatic insanity," a form of madness caused, he believed, by habitual masturbation. Hall also revealed that many authorities linked masturbation "in a more or less casual way with one or more of the morbid forms of sex perversion, or hold that it makes a psycho-physical soil which readily bears their dread fruit." The phrase "morbid forms of sex perversion" undoubtedly refers to homosexuality. In other words, Hall's *Adolescence* instructed thousands of physicians that masturbation leads to homosexuality, insanity, or quite often both.

When Dr. Schmidt told Henry that his "heart was not in the right place," he seems to have been offering the boy a diagnosis based on a medical misconception. What he meant was that Henry, now twelve years old, was homosexual—or becoming one.

Henry's father knew that Henry had been masturbating since he was six. They shared a single bed, as often happened in poverty-stricken families then, and Henry Sr. may have caught his son in the act or found evidence of it on their sheets or the boy's clothing. He knew the police had caught the boy sneaking off to visit the night watchman. What he didn't already know about his son's activities, the Mission staff was all too happy to tell him. Gannon, Zink, Mahoney, and O'Hara knew he had developed some sort of relationship with John Manley and the Scanlon brothers. He had even been caught masturbating in public while he was living at the Mission. They would have known, too, about the goings-on of the other boys throughout the West Madison Street vice district and how pervasive was contact with, and succumbing to, the sexual advances of men. After all, one of the Mission's goals was to protect them from such things. The staff would have realized that it was unlikely that Henry had somehow escaped being involved in male-male sexual liaisons on the streets, even if that activity comprised only jack-rolling episodes or sex for hire.

Everything that Henry's father had told the doctor about Henry's behavior was evidence that underscored Schmidt's diagnosis, and given Schmidt's diagnosis—based on a section of Hall's book, that was based on Bachus's article—it's no wonder that both doctor and father believed the twelve-year-old boy should be locked up. Henry, they believed, had to be crazy to act as he did.

As typically happened to Henry, no one bothered to explain to him what was going on or why, but they were eager to get rid of him. Years later, he came to believe that he'd been examined by Dr. Schmidt to see if he was "feeble-minded or crazy," and in a manner of speaking, he was absolutely right.

Unfortunately for Henry, neither Dr. Schmidt nor Henry's father had a hint about the goings-on at the Illinois Asylum for Feeble-Minded Children, the place where they were about to exile him. The activities behind its walls would elicit a government probe only a few years after the "cold windy threatening" day that Henry left Chicago for the Asylum in downstate Illinois. What he would face at the Asylum was devastating, and years later, he would admit, "Had I known what was going to be done with me I surely would have ran away"— virtually the same phrase he used to reveal his reaction to his life at the Mission of Our Lady of Mercy.

CHAPTER 3

THE HOUSE OF A THOUSAND TROUBLES

EXILE

ON NOVEMBER 16, 1904, THE DAY THAT HENRY SR. MET WITH Dr. Schmidt to fill out the application that would allow him to send his son away, twelve-year-old Henry was still living at the Mission of Our Lady of Mercy. Henry never revealed how he found out that he would be committed to the Illinois Asylum for Feeble-Minded Children, but he made it clear in his autobiography that no one, neither the priests nor Mrs. Gannon, ever told him why he was being sent there.

Given the Church's stance on homosexuality, and the reluctance of most people to discuss sexual matters in general, it was probably extremely difficult for either of the priests to explain to Henry what his relationship with John Manley and the Scanlon brothers—and his visits to Dr. Schmidt's office—had cost him and easier for them simply to ignore it. It's likely that Mrs. Gannon was just glad to be rid of him. Henry had been a problem for her from the moment she first stepped over the Mission's threshold, and even her predecessor, Mrs. Brown, who liked Henry, had also realized that he had difficulties fitting in, created trouble for himself and others, and was odd in habit and expression. Henry was a handful.

On the morning of Thursday, November 24, Tim Rooney arrived at the Mission and called for the boy. The Asylum was in a rural area downstate, near the state capital, and it would take many hours for Rooney to get to the Asylum and back by train. The town, Lincoln, was named after President Abraham Lincoln, emancipator of hundreds of thousands and hero to just as many schoolboys. His portrait, and that of George Washington, hung on the walls of most schoolrooms across the nation, as they did at Skinner School.

Henry was bitterly aware that others were keeping secrets from him, and that added to his frustration over not knowing why he was being sent away. Certainly, he hoped his father would suddenly sweep in and rescue him, as he had done when the police took him from his home to Dunning four years earlier. He hoped his godmother would arrive in the nick of time and make everything all right, as she had done when he was accused of stealing dimes at the Mission. Despite his hopes, no one rescued him.

Henry recalled years later that, once they were past Union Station's west entrance and through its cavernous waiting room, Rooney hurried him onto "the Chicago and Alton limited" with only a few minutes to spare. Rooney took the aisle seat and gave the boy the window. Henry heard a conductor yell, "All aboard," and then, a few seconds later, at precisely nine a.m., the whistle blew a loud and sharp warning. The train lurched forward, nearly throwing Henry against the back of the seat in front of him. He watched the city begin to pass by his window, slowly at first, then in a blur as the train zoomed faster than any streetcar he'd ever ridden.

After the train left the station at Joliet, just outside of Chicago, the conductor sauntered by, stopped, took their tickets, noted their destination, punched both tickets, and kept Henry's but returned

Rooney's. He exchanged pleasantries with Rooney. They knew one another slightly because Rooney had taken a number of other boys from Chicago to the Asylum in the past. The conductor would have easily guessed that Henry was, like the others, bound for the Asylum. While the men chatted, Henry glanced around the car, which was virtually empty, then turned his attention to the landscape outside his window.

By now, the urban buildings—only factories and warehouses, many now abandoned—were disappearing one after another as the skyscrapers had earlier. The train lumbered southwest, away from Chicago and toward St. Louis, and suddenly Illinois became a foreign land to the boy. Extraordinarily flat and empty, the landscape from the railroad tracks to the horizon was nothing but a long, continuous field, the view dotted every twenty or so miles with a farmhouse, a few outbuildings, and several trees bunched among them, an image that would haunt him until the day he died. This was the first time he'd been out of Chicago, and it was so alien to him that he thought he might as well have been on another planet a thousand miles in space.

Thick, bulbous thunderheads crowded the sky, and to pass the time, Henry imagined they formed the shapes of animals, ships, even the faces of people he already missed, especially his father and godmother. Clouds had fascinated Henry from the time he was a little boy. The clouds weren't simply harbingers of weather for him but toys. When he looked at them, his imagination was ignited. A cumulus might turn into a ship, a galleon like the *Nina*, *Pinta*, or *Santa Maria* that he'd learned about in Ella Dewey's class.

Long ago, he'd learned to escape into his imagination when things got too bad for him to handle, when he had no control. The places he could go in his imagination were safe, and he was always in control there. A stratus cloud that had spread itself out across the sky might look to him like the poppy fields in Frank Baum's *The Wonderful Wizard of Oz*, his favorite book. He understood Dorothy Gale's trials.

Like Dorothy, he'd been away from home for a long, long time, far longer, he figured, than she had. He wanted to go home, too. Unlike Dorothy, he didn't have a dog to love. He didn't have a trio of misfit friends to keep him company or help him in times of need. In fact, the trio that had attached itself to him, John Manley and the Scanlons, had gotten him into hot water. He didn't have a wizard promising help although the "night watchman" had done what he could. He recalled that, after a number of harrowing episodes with the Wicked Witch of the West (he pictured Mrs. Gannon), Dorothy returned home with Toto, safe and sound, and they lived happily ever after. He was certain her reunion wouldn't be his.

The trip was uneventful, and the train's rocking finally lulled Henry into a restless slumber. He slept off and on most of the way, and he woke with a start when Rooney patted his shoulder and said, "We're here, sport. Grab your things." It had taken Rooney several seconds to rouse Henry from his fitful sleep, a defense mechanism for the boy who felt kidnapped, snatched away from everything and everyone he knew.

The train depot at Lincoln, a patch of dirt with a tin roof but no walls, was nothing like Union Station. Henry hadn't eaten since breakfast, and he was weak from hunger. If Henry had looked into the twilit sky, he would have noticed that a spire pierced the sky. The three-story main building of the Asylum stood on a small rise of the grounds nearly three miles away, to the southwest, and that spire was the tip-top of the main building. In West Madison Street, buildings as tall as five stories surrounded him at all times, and in the Loop, they were much taller, but here in Lincoln, except for the Asylum's spire, the sky was empty of buildings, and such emptiness, something he'd never experienced before, would have made him feel vulnerable.

A buggy driver waved at them, and they boarded. He snapped the whip over the horse's head with a sharp "Giddyup," and Henry was on his way to the Asylum.

Rooney and the driver would've known each other, too, and

chatted on the three-mile trip to the Asylum, ignoring Henry. Before the train got too far way, Henry would have heard the conductor's "All aboard" followed by the train's shrill whistle piercing the evening's quiet.

The Chicago and Alton Limited lumbered off but then began to pick up steam as it moved away from the station and headed south to Springfield, Illinois, the next stop. After Springfield, it would chug southwest to St. Louis, and there, the passengers would transfer to another train that would trudge west to Kansas City and then swerve southwest, headed for Tucson. Puffs of its smoke billowed up higher and higher until they seemed to mingle with the thunderheads that blotted out the stars.

Henry was now "one hundred and sixty two miles away from Chicago," sitting on the bed of a buggy like a bag of flour or a load of firewood, and he was terrified. This wasn't the first time Henry had been taken from his home and institutionalized, but this time, it was meant to be forever.

THE ILLINOIS ASYLUM FOR FEEBLE-MINDED CHILDREN

Henry was exhausted and famished as he climbed down from the buggy with Rooney's help. The Asylum was the tallest building Henry had seen since leaving Chicago, and even in the near dark, he could see that it was enormous. The weather was just as cold in Lincoln as it had been in Chicago, but without the wind, the stillness made the cold seem more intense. As he and Rooney shuffled toward the Asylum's front door, Henry's breath swirled into wispy clouds in front of him.

The matron in charge assigned Henry "5007," the number on his application form, as his ID number and, without asking him his name, simply copied "Henry *Dodger*" onto the admission records.

She said "Follow me, boy" to Henry in a no-nonsense tone, turned on her heels, and led the way. Henry was lost immediately and wondered if he'd ever be able to maneuver the labyrinthine building. Overwhelmed by fatigue and hunger, as well as by the massive building, Henry was distracted and had a difficult time keeping up with her.

Suddenly, she stopped at a room in the northeast corner of the building, one of five on the second floor, turned as if to look at him (but looked over his head instead), and said, "This is it."

Here's where he would sleep. The room had plenty of large windows, and during the day, sunlight flooded the room. The beds were arranged as they'd been at the Mission: headboard to headboard, foot to foot, rows and rows of them. The aisles that separated one bed from the next were so narrow that there was barely enough room for boys to squeeze through. Henry scanned the room, trying to imagine what it'd be like sleeping there.

When twelve-year-old Henry arrived at the Asylum, a large percent of the individuals with whom he ate, worked, and slept were adults, not children. Beginning a few years before, the state had run out of space for convicts in penitentiaries. To solve the problem, authorities housed adult men on the second and third floors of the Asylum's north wing among the boys there. In fact, "just as many of the so-called boys and girls in public institutions" for feeble-minded children "were adults as were children." The Asylum's administration realized that "some of them" were "older than children," but it never arrived at the obvious conclusion: the strong inevitably victimized the weak physically and sexually.

Here and there, the walls, painted a bright white years ago, were bare except for streaks of dirt and smudges that the boys left on them when they roughhoused. The paint had begun to flake in places. Henry might have been a little surprised by the walls' bareness. The Mission had been full of Christian statuary, and a crucifix hung in every room so that, from the cross of his martyrdom, Jesus could keep a watchful eye on the boys who lived there, supervising their behavior *and* promising their safety. Henry was glad that here there were no crucifixes, no statues of the Blessed Virgin Mary, no framed prints of the Savior—blond and blue-eyed, handsome, and clean beyond all reckoning—knocking on the door of a home in a Middle Eastern village spread out under a starry sky. The Jesus who watched over the boys at the Mission from his crucifixes had never protected Henry, and he expected he wouldn't be of much help at the Asylum, either.

In the meantime, Rooney had left, his mission accomplished. He hadn't bothered to say good-bye to the boy, or even to the matron. Henry would never see him again, but he would never forget—or forgive—the man for stealing him from Chicago.

THE BEST LOOKING BOY
I HAVE EVER SEEN

Unlike the Mission, which was run by four people (the two priests, Mrs. Gannon, and Mr. Zink), the Asylum had a staff of nearly a hundred employees and operated on a strict pecking order. At the top was its director; at the bottom, inmates who held menial jobs with small amounts of responsibilities. All of the staff had specific duties that they were required to fulfill, and few, if any, were willing to do more than the minimum. The matron's duties wouldn't have included giving Henry a tour of the building, pointing out the lavatories, the play areas, or even the dining room. That would've been the job of one of the inmates.

The north wing was where the "bright boys" like Henry slept. They were those who had been sent to the Asylum for reasons other than mental debilitations. Some were habitual truants, others were constantly running away from home or creating insurmountable problems for their parents, others were children of the indigent and had nowhere else to go, and more than a few were, like Henry, self-abusers. Dr. Caudwell, who ran the north wing, had hired one of the "bright boys," William Thomas O'Neil, to be the head boy in the wing, and it would've been O'Neil's job, not the matron's, to show Henry the ropes. The same age as Henry, he was strikingly handsome, and years later, Henry would admit that he was "the best looking boy I have ever seen."

Thomas showed Henry the nearest toilet and shower rooms and then led him down the back stairs to the ground floor to show him the dining room. Henry heard noisy children and music emanating from somewhere. Thomas maneuvered Henry around the small groups of toughs who loitered in the halls and stared at the two as they quickly passed. Thomas mentioned that, behind the main building, there were cottages where the children who had real and often severe mental disabilities lived. They often didn't know how to use the toilet or dress themselves, and when the "bright boys" were accused of something especially bad, they were sent to one of the boys' cottages for a few days. They felt demeaned by the experience and were teased by the others.

At the dining room where the noise that Henry was hearing originated, Thomas opened the door to hordes of children presenting a pageant on a makeshift stage: some who wore chicken-feather headdresses were offering other children dressed in black crepe paper a few turkey drumsticks made of cardboard. The tables had been moved together. A few cornstalks from nearby fields were tied into bundles and leaned against a wall. A huge, blackened pot stood center stage. The children stood around it, trying to remember their lines. Few members of the audience were paying attention to the story unfolding before them. Most were caught up in their own dramas.

It was Thanksgiving Day.

Many of the children in the audience were making noises, speaking out loud (to one another or to children onstage), and fidgeting. Huddled here and there, the staff was torn between wanting to gossip with one another and having to keep an eye on their wards.

Thomas and Henry fell into silence, Henry walking behind
Thomas, who was leading him through the throngs of noisy children.
They circled around another group of children playing instruments
noticeably off-key for a much larger group that surrounded them.

When they reached the front door, which Henry had passed
through less than a half an hour earlier, Thomas opened it. They stood
outside in the quiet dark. It was freezing outside, but Henry didn't
mind. It was good being away from the loud commotion, verging on
chaos, inside. His and Thomas's breaths streamed out into the darkness; then a sudden burst of wind shredded them into nothingness.

From the front of the main building, Thomas pointed out the
playground and told Henry that the hospital, laundry, generator building, and others needed to keep the Asylum running were behind this
building. The next building to the south, only a faint silhouette now
in the darkness, was the school, and a tunnel connecting it to the main
building was used by the children when the snow was especially deep.
The Asylum owned a farm of several thousand acres a few miles
southwest. The "bright boys" worked there in the summers. During
the regular school year, the "bright boys" went to school and worked
part-time, pushing mops and brooms. Henry liked the idea of being
on a farm in the summer. He thought of all the barnyard animals pictured in the coloring books he once owned. He'd never seen a real
one in his whole life.

ROUTINE

Henry once declared that life at the Asylum "sometimes was
pleasant and sometimes not," but after a few months, he "got to like
the place and the meals were good and plenty." While he was living
with his father, Henry had run wild, and the Mission's routine, which
included atending school, curbed his activities a little, but only a little.
At the Asylum, routine filled the days of the inmates to brimming,

and it was strict and substantive there in ways it hadn't been at the Mission. The Mission was in the heart of a vice district; the Asylum was surrounded by fields. Boys at the Mission could slip off into the neighborhood's deepest recesses and emerge many hours later without their absence being noticed and sometimes with a little extra money in their pockets. The boys at the Asylum could also disappear for a time without being noticed, but there were too few places for them to go. They were obvious in the small town of Lincoln and were usually rounded up by Asylum staff or the police in short order—the boys, that is. The men were a different story. They would have been welcomed into Lincoln's saloons and whorehouses until they spent whatever money they might have had with them, and only then would the police have been called to round them up.

The children at the Illinois Asylum fell into one of two categories when it came to payment for their care: "bonded cases," which were those paid for by private individuals, usually their families, and "county charges," those too poor to pay and whose care was paid by their home counties. Half of the inmates at the Asylum were bonded cases, and the rest were county charges. Henry was supported by Cook County.

The Asylum was a huge complex of buildings, and for most of the time that Henry was there, Dr. Harry G. Hardt was its administrator. The main building had three floors with a basement and contained nearly one hundred twenty rooms connected by corridors and stairwells. The administrator's office and other public areas were spread across the first floor, and the second and third floors contained most of the dormitory rooms. These rooms had been built in clusters, three or four together, with an adjoining room for the attendant. Day attendants were "replaced by a watchman at night, who was not in any sense an attendant on the patients, but was more of a guard or fireman." The girls and women were housed on the south side of the building, and the boys and men on the north. The Asylum's property covered a total of eight hundred ninety acres, forty of which were its actual campus. Another four hundred were leased to area farmers, and the Asylum itself farmed the remaining four hundred fifty acres, using its harvest and its livestock to feed inmates.

Early in its history, the Asylum administration had decided that a typical curriculum of study wouldn't satisfy the children's needs because everyone associated with the Asylum assumed the children would never be released or, if they were, that they would only be able to take on menial occupations. Consequently, the administration adopted a practical curriculum "better suited to the feeble-minded." It included "arts, manual training, physical culture, phonetic drill and music" as well as "basketry, needlework, cardboard construction, reed, raffia, sloyd and Venetian iron work," training deemed more appropriate than the three R's for the children's usefulness to the Asylum as well as to society in general.

Henry's father had hoped that Henry would find training that was far grander than what the Asylum could ever provide. On the application for admission to the Asylum, question 48 asked, "Is the child capable of any useful occupation?" and Henry's father answered, "Yes." Then it asked, "If so, what?" and he replied, "Engineer." Instead, Henry was taught to sweep and mop floors in the main building of the Asylum.

Initially, Henry was among the children who went to school. (Because his father confused Henry's and his brother Arthur's birth dates, the Asylum records list his age as a year younger than he actually was.) He was "awakened at 5:00 a.m." and "after washing and dressing," then making his bed, he "did light chores"—sweeping and mopping floors, dusting furniture, emptying the trash in the main building—for a little over an hour, at which time "breakfast was served." Because Henry was one of the "'younger boys and girls,'" those under fourteen years and considered 'bright,'" he "began school around 7:30" with a lunch break around noon.

Meals were also strictly scheduled, with virtually the same menu each day. Henry's "breakfast consisted of fried or boiled beef, oatmeal, bread, and coffee," but on "special occasions," he and the other inmates would be served eggs. His lunch was basic but nutritious: "soup, in-season vegetables, occasionally meat, and always bread and coffee." At the end of the day, at around six, he had a dinner of leftovers from the two earlier meals, "plus an occasional sweet or seasonal fruit." He declared that "the meals were good and plenty," but in actuality, the children's food was far less in quality and quantity than what the staff who lived on the Asylum grounds ate. A report published while Henry lived at the Asylum disclosed that the children actually ate "wormy prunes, wormy oatmeal, and wormy cornmeal, together with tough and stringy beef, meat procured from ancient goats, loud-smelling fish and similar foods." Henry's assertion that the Asylum food was good suggests how poor his meals at the Mission must have been.

After supper, Henry and the other children were occupied with various activities: "On typical weekday evenings, especially in summer, they played baseball, threw horseshoes, or attended to personal needs. In winter, activities included skating, basketball, and playing musical instruments." On Saturdays and Sundays, Henry could take part in the dances that were held, although the children were separated by sex, with the boys dancing with older, female custodians. On the Fourth of July, children marveled at fireworks. On Christmas, there were pageants about Joseph and Mary's flight into Egypt or the baby Jesus's birth in a stable. On Easter, the children's choir sang the "Hallelujah" chorus, accompanied by the children's orchestra.

Henry had just gotten comfortable in his new life and its routines at the Asylum when it was rudely interrupted. At the beginning of the summer of 1906, he was "put with a company of boys" who were sent to work throughout the summer on the Asylum's farm some "three and a half miles" away. "American institutions" that housed the feeble-minded were most often built "in suburban or rural settings" with "extensive gardens, and most had fully operating farms."

"The rural setting"—respected physicians involved with caring for the mentally ill, such as Dr. Walter E. Fernald, supervisor of the Massachusetts School for Idiotic Children, and Dr. Charles Bernstein, director of New York's Willard Asylum for the Chronic Insane, theorized—would help cure the "feeble-minded," especially those like Henry whose mental illnesses the physicians associated with "urban society with its potential for vice, degeneracy, and abnormal behavior." The phrase "vice, degeneracy, and abnormal behavior" rings especially loud, given the reason why Henry was committed in the first place.

Fernald, Bernstein, and other authorities also considered the farms connected to the institutions "an outlet for restless boys who had reached their classroom potential." In fact, they believed that "hard work and fresh air" made the boys "well behaved and freed them from the sicknesses that disrupted institutional life. They were given a purpose suited to their abilities and temperament. Idleness and consequent bad behavior were unheard of."

The inmates sent to the farms were either too old to attend school, which was limited to those fourteen years or younger, or were troublemakers who created disturbances in and out of the classroom. All were among the "bright boys," were "often newly admitted to the institution as teenagers and young adults," and at the farms, were free "to be themselves." They were assigned specific chores, but in general, they "planted and tended the fields. Usually laid out for garden rather than cash crops, the farms became an important source of produce for the institution. As they purchased or rented more acreage, most institutions added cows and sometimes beef cattle to the farm." At the Illinois Asylum, "institutional authorities even experimented with a herd of sheep. The sheep, state officials boasted, provided work for 'boys of the school' and lamb" to eat "for institutions throughout Illinois at 'practically no expense for food or care.'" As far as authorities both inside and outside of the institution were concerned, the farms were, in a word, Edenic.

Henry spent his summers at what he and many others called the "State Farm," just south of Salt Creek. Beginning with his "earliest teens," he was sent there with fifty or more of the "bright boys," who ranged in age from fourteen or fifteen to much older. They lived "in a two storey building, containing simply a kitchen, dormitory, dining-room, and sanitary accommodations" under the supervision of a sole farm couple, the Ilmbergers, whose name Henry incorrectly remembered as "Allenburger." Alois and Annie Ilmberger were helped out by one or two male hired hands. After the summers were over, the boys returned to "the bughouse," Mr. Ilmberger's favorite name for the Asylum.

According to Henry, "the work" at the farm "was not hard" and the hours weren't horribly long. The boys began work "at eight in the morning" and "quit at four in the afternoon." They had "Saturday afternoons and Sundays" off and took their weekly bath on "Saturdays before dinner." Henry called the meals there "splendid" and swore that at breakfast he "was a glutton (if not a hog) for the oatmeal."

Henry "loved to work in the fields," and recalled one crop in particular that he tended: belladonna. Henry stated "that plant is used by chimest [chemist] for medicine and other needs," and he recalled that he "once used it for a sore knee." Its fruit is poisonous, and the boys assigned to picking it "had to wear protective gloves." Henry often grew rhapsodic and morbid in turn when describing it. "It is a strange but very beautiful tomato plant, called the 'Beautiful Lady' or in Spanish Belladonna," Henry said, then added:

It really was a most beautiful plant, with most beautiful little flow-ers before the tomatoes came.

There is where it got the name "beautiful Lady." But God help those who ever at[e] one of those tomatoes. We had very large easily seen, and easy to read signs (also electrilly lighted at night) warning tramps or hobos and visiting strangers about eating them, or anything of the plant.

Their original name well known by most is "The deadly night shade.

No hobo or anyone else went near them.

Henry liked the Ilmbergers, who probably seemed to him the epitome of the typical American family.

Ilmberger divided the boys from the Asylum into groups of three, each with an overseer. The overseers included two adults, Mr. West and John Fox, and the handsome William Thomas O'Neil.

SPECIAL FRIENDS

Whether he was at the Asylum or at its farm, Henry did his best to lose himself in the daily routine. He did the chores that were assigned to him and went to school, both of which helped to keep him busy, and like the other children, he took recess and other times set aside for play seriously, making the most of them. In warm weather, the boys played on the lawn between the main building and the school. He was entertained by the storms that passed through Lincoln year round. Some included thunder that grumbled louder than he'd ever heard. Others brought floods that seemed ready to sweep the Asylum away or snow that seemed endless and threatened to bury it. But as important as anything else, he was always on the alert for potential bullies on the prowl for blood or sex.

Not long after he arrived at the Asylum, Henry had run-ins with two troublemakers, George Hamilton and John Johnson. Except for identifying him as a problem, Henry never disclosed what twenty-year-old Hamilton did to him. His reticence suggests a possible sexual encounter, but he didn't feel the need to be secretive about Johnson. One day, Henry developed a severe toothache. Although slightly younger than Henry, Johnson was larger, and he began to tease Henry mercilessly. Johnson's horseplay threw Henry into a rage. As was typical with him when discussing an altercation with someone, Henry claimed that, after he was done with Johnson, the bigger boy never tried to bother him again.

Trouble at the Asylum wasn't limited to the boys, however. One day during class, Henry's teacher Miss Maud C. Duff was interrupted midsentence when a brawl between a janitor, whom Henry knew as George Hamford, and another, much taller man, whose name Henry didn't know, spilled from the hall into the classroom. Henry called their fisticuffs "a perfect storm or 'cyclone' of fist blows" and claimed it lasted nearly half an hour. Living in the heart of West Madison Street, Henry had seen many fights before this one, but none compared to the savagery with which the two men went at one another.

While they fought, Miss Duff was beside herself, unsuccessfully trying to calm the men down. The children were in the throes of pandemonium, some screaming and crying, others loudly rooting for one or the other of the men. One of Henry's classmates ran to get the principal, but she was terrified of the men, and instead of trying to break it up herself, she phoned Lincoln's police headquarters. Before the police could arrive, the janitor slugged his taller opponent with a perfect punch, and he slumped to the floor, knocked out. He lay there for a short time, then pulled himself together and left. Henry never knew what the fight was about, but he took a great deal of joy in retelling the tale. After all, a smaller man had triumphed over a larger one, and Hamford's victory made Henry, who was smaller than other boys his age, proud of the underdog.

The children took part in fire drills, too. The alarm would be sounded and the boys would rush to the east side of the building. A large chute was connected to one of the windows there, and they would jump into it and slide down to the ground and safety. One afternoon during a drill, one boy was afraid of the chute and refused to slide down it despite a few of the boys yelling at him, "What if the asylum had a fire?" The boy still refused to budge, so two of the larger boys grabbed him, dragged him to the fire escape, and pushed him down it. No one had to tell Henry twice. He remembered his own fear of buildings on fire. Besides, he thought that sliding down the chute was fun and jumped at the chance to do it any time he could.

Except for the time that Henry forgot to make his bed and had his ears boxed by Mr. Aurand, one of the men in charge of the "bright boys" in the north wing, he maintained that he was so well behaved that neither Aurand nor anyone else ever had an excuse for punishing him. In fact, Henry claimed that Aurand thought his behavior had become "marvelous" after getting slapped and that he considered Henry one of the best boys of the north wing. Unfortunately, Henry's bragging sounds incredibly fishy. More likely, after being slapped or otherwise punished any number of times, Henry wised up. He admitted as much. "I was not ever the talking back kind," he said, continuing, "I received that sort of training in the 'Bughouse' asylum as they called it." Then he added, "Who ever talked back to a superior there, got the real punishment and how," and "I never talked back. I did not dare."

Henry also claimed that he had no problem with any of the boys or men who lived with him in the north wing. He became close to several of the boys, whom he called his "special friends," and more than sixty years later could remember each of their names: "Jacob Marcus, Paul Marcus (no brother of the first mentioned), Daniel Jones, and Donald Aurand." In addition to them, Henry's relationship with William Thomas O'Neil grew, and O'Neil appears to have joined the coterie of Henry's special friends. Henry never described what constituted their friendship, keeping it a secret. Yet he dropped significant clues.

O'Neil "was no bully or exactly bossy," but he wielded a great deal of power because he was employed by the Asylum as Mr. Aurand's helper in the north wing and as an overseer for Ilmberger at the farm. Henry made it clear that, because of O'Neil's position and his need to keep on O'Neil's good side, he felt he "had to obey him and do his bidding," and then he added with a strong dose of sexual innuendo, "If you did you and he got along fine."

An Uncovering of Horrors

On December 23, 1907, an accident occurred in one of the boys' cottages, the small buildings behind the main one, which is where the boys who actually did have mental deficiencies of some sort lived. A sixteen-year-old epileptic had fallen on "an uncovered radiator, where he lay for several minutes," and was badly burned "on his left ear, neck, and face." When he was discovered, "the institution's matron sent the injured boy to the infirmary, where two physicians who treated him claimed the burns were minor." The boy, Frank Giroux, had entered the Asylum only nineteen days earlier and then only after long, heart-wrenching family discussions about whether to send him to the Asylum in the first place. As it turned out, the burns were hardly "minor."

The boy's father, Ben M. Giroux, coincidentally arrived at the Asylum the day after his son's accident, Christmas Eve, with gifts for Frank and other inmates. He hadn't received word about the accident before he left and didn't know about it until he stepped through the Asylum's front door. Giroux later testified that Dr. Hardt, who met him at the door, assured him that "it is nothing serious; it is a slight burn. Don't get worried over it." Hardt had been at his post for less than a year and was more concerned about the bad publicity the situation might generate and how that might affect his employment than about Frank's condition.

Almost immediately, Giroux took his son back to Chicago, where the family physician, Dr. Frank W. Lambden, examined him. Lambden discovered that the boy's injuries were "serious" and not at all "slight," as Hardt had claimed, and reported that he "was shocked at the extent of the injury." The burns were, he said, "very extensive," covering "the ear and back of the ear for about an inch and a half," extending "down towards the middle of the neck posteriorly, and along the cheek auteriorly." He also discovered that three burns "on the back part of the head had never been dressed at all." Lambden added, "The hair was matted in and crusted," and it took him "five days" of applying "moist dressings" to the wound before he could "separate the crusts and trim off the hair from the skull." The area behind the boy's ear had become "a seething mass of pus."

While examining the boy, Lambden discovered that the intense heat from the radiator had also "destroyed the middle ear," leaving Frank "absolutely deaf on that side." When asked to summarize his view of the asylum staff's caregiving, Lambden, who was not one to mince words when professionally outraged, said, "Anybody that would dress a wound in this way is either incompetent or criminally negligent."

As it turned out, Giroux was a man of some influence in Chicago, not only a successful theatrical agent who managed one of its best theaters, the Criterion at 1222 North Sedgwick Street on the Near North Side, but also, and more to the point, "a friend" of Chicago's mayor, Fred A. Busse. Giroux complained to another friend, State Representative John W. Hill. Hill finagled the creation of a committee composed of six other representatives from the Illinois General Assembly, with himself appointed its chair, to look into charges of abuse at the Asylum and other similar institutions throughout the state.

Beginning January 14 and ending May 7, 1908, the Special Investigating Committee met with forty-two different witnesses in sessions spread over seven days: on January 17, 23, 24, 30, and 31 and then on March 3 and 4. Newspapers also reported the testimonies, especially those that were bizarre or gruesome in nature, and they lodged in the public's imagination. Following the investigation, the General Assembly published the Committee's findings, which included hundreds of pages of testimony from past and current

Asylum employees, as well as from family members of some of its inmates. The Giroux case was only the tip of the iceberg.

In the morning of March 21, 1907, a Thursday, the custodian who had come to wake up Virgene Jessop noticed that rats had bitten and scratched the eight-year-old's arms, face, and abdomen. Caregiver Lucille Jordain testified before the Committee that Virgene's face "looked as if she had been—there was an impression on both sides where the skin was broken and the blood came to the surface—it looked as if it had been gnawed by something." Then she hastily added, "Her finger was just simply chewed up."

Two months later, in May, inmate Minnie Steritz "was severely burned while left unattended in a bathtub and died a week later." The severity of Steritz's condition had been hushed up. Minnie "had been badly scalded about the buttocks, the pubic regions, the posterior surface of the thighs, the flexor and extensor surfaces of both legs, and the dorsal surfaces of both feet. The hands had also been blistered. The skin was hanging in shreds and even in sheets, in places." She'd been forced to sit in boiling water as her flesh cooked.

When questioned by the Committee about Minnie Steritz, Dr. Hardt huffed, "The child was of such a kind, that the pain, I don't believe would affect her very much." However, he did know that "it would have been painful" to himself or to "any other normal being. She did not have the sense of pain developed to the extent of a normal individual." Dehumanizing the little girl may have helped Hardt to rationalize for himself the cruelty that befell her, but others in the courtroom were aghast by his hard-heartedness.

Then the Committee's investigations took a sharp turn in the public's mind, veering from the cruel to the ghoulish. Fifty-two-year-old inmate John K. Morthland, an epileptic, who had lived in neighboring Decatur and worked for the city until he was admitted into the Asylum, blamed his seizures on his "sexual indiscretion." While the report never clarifies what "sexual indiscretion" had plagued Morthland, the phrase probably referred in this case to either habitual masturbation or homosexual activity or both. To cure himself of the "sexual indiscretion," he decided to castrate himself. Self-castration was an extraordinarily desperate response to his situation, but as historian Ronald Hamowy as shown, "With such horror was masturbation looked upon by the psychiatric profession and so successful had the physicians been in communicating the monstrosity of these acts to an ignorant laity that . . . some" boys and men "surrendered themselves to mutilation rather than persist in the habit." In the 1800s, doctors in private practice and those assigned to institutions castrated boys or men to cure them of epilepsy, habitual masturbation, and homosexuality. In fact, the belief that castration cured all three was ubiquitous, even among the nonmedical public.

For "several years," two young men, eighteen and twenty years old, had "been much addicted to the habit of masturbation." Evidently, they had been engaged in mutual self-abuse and were, perhaps, romantically linked. In 1844, one of them "made efforts to overcome the habit, but not having moral courage sufficient," the twenty-year-old "made an agreement with his associate to perform the operation of castration upon themselves, and appointed a time for the purpose." They promised each other to keep their pact a secret. Unfortunately for the older one, who wanted to stop his sexual activities, his young friend had a change of heart at the last minute and backed out of their deal.

Not to be thwarted from his resolve, one night "before retiring," the twenty-year-old "applied a ligature (as is practiced upon some animals), tightly enclosing the testicles below it, and let it remain on the whole night. In the morning, finding the parts discolored, attended with considerable pain, and thinking the operation would be long and tedious," he went "to a secluded place, and removing the ligature, with a common jack-knife sharpened, he made an incision into the scrotum, drew down the spermatic cords," and then "severed them close to the abdomen." He hemorrhaged so badly from the wound that his self-mutilation was discovered, and he was taken to his family physician, who patched him up and reported that he was "doing very well."

Following that case, a "guilt-ridden" fifteen-year-old boy who, "being discouraged by his fruitless endeavors to free himself from the worst of all habits," or masturbation, "deliberately selected the privy as the theater of his operations, and holding the offending organ by the prepuce with one hand," he "took aim with a small pistol, and shot it, with the other." The .22-caliber bullet "entered the dorsal surface; running beneath the skin it entered the glans behind the corona, emerged on its dorsal surface, and again penetrated the prepuce before making its final exit." He, too, survived.

According to Asylum director Hardt, at about "9 o'clock on Saturday morning May 4," 1907, "Morthland borrowed a knife blade of another inmate, unknown to any one, and retired to a toilet room and severely cut his scrotum with the intentions of removing his testicles." He was treated in the Asylum's "hospital wards," and afterward, the physicians claimed that he was "doing nicely." Two days later, the "physician's Memo book," a record of the Asylum's house physicians' activities, reported that the patient was "doing fine" despite the "slight discharge from [the] wound," but by the next day, Morthland was "having convulsions and very restless." Then his condition took a sudden nosedive. On May 8, "John Morthland died at 12:30; death caused by Status."

It's impossible to know how many boys and men besides Henry were incarcerated in the Asylum because they masturbated or were homosexual or both, but Asylum records suggest that there were many. Unfortunately, the Committee was neither as straightforward in its conclusion as it needed to be nor as concerned about the welfare of the Asylum's inmates as its mandate required. In fact, it was unable, or unwilling, to distinguish between the sexual abuse of children and unappetizing baked goods: "When Harry Hardt's new baker at the Illinois Asylum began to bake doughy bread," the Committee's members "were as concerned that Hardt failed to dismiss the baker as they

6

were that inmates were being abused in other, usually more surreptitious, ways." Other than that hint of sexual misdoings, the Committee was utterly silent about sexual abuse behind the Asylum's walls. However, the Asylum's medical records aren't as guarded. They reveal that "some of the injuries" that boys suffered during this period, were "focused on the rectum and bleeding," which clearly implies "anal rape." It's no wonder that Henry would later call the main building of the Asylum "the house of a thousand troubles."

By now the Committee had become astounded by the Asylum caregivers' lack of compassion and professionalism. They hadn't expected a blissful picture, but they hadn't anticipated the torment that seemed to be everywhere, either. The newspaper-reading public was just as shocked and confounded by the goings-on behind the Asylum's walls, but the worst, in many peoples' minds, was yet to come.

Walter Kaak was considered "one of the brightest children in the institution," and he lived in the north wing with Henry and William Thomas O'Neil. In fact, Rooney had brought Walter to the Asylum, too. Although only fifteen years old, Kaak was assigned a job in the Asylum laundry operating a clothes dryer. This in itself was not unique. Most of the "bright" boys had jobs, but on August 28, 1907, he was left unsupervised.

At around three thirty that afternoon, Kaak "put his right hand in a partially empty extractor" that was "revolving at about 900 revolutions per minutes. This evidently was intricated by a few articles of clothing, causing a tremendous twist of the right arm, producing an amputation almost complete of the right arm close at the shoulder." Miraculously, Kaak kept his head. He reached over and turned the machine off before he was "ground to pieces." Instead of acknowledging the staff's—and, by extension, his—responsibility in the accident, Hardt asserted in a letter that "it was clearly" the result of the boy's "carelessness." Unlike Frank Giroux's family, Walter Kaak's was notified immediately.

During its investigation, the Committee caught wind of the incident and called Elizabeth Kaak, Walter's mother, to testify. "I never dreamed for one minute that the child was working in the laundry, at least, at a machine," she told them. When asked when she found out that her son had been put to work, she replied, "When I got down to St. Clair's hospital," where Walter had been taken for medical care, "the boy told me himself." After a few minutes on the stand, Mrs. Kaak added that Hardt had tried to rationalize leaving the boy unattended at the dangerous post by complimenting Walter's intelligence. Dr. Hardt, who was in the hospital room at the time, told Mrs. Kaak that "'Walter was one of their bright boys,' and he told me that he had him mop up the halls, and inside halls, and he said, 'We trusted him always.'"

Then Mrs. Kaak dropped a bombshell. According to her, Dr. Hardt admitted that Walter had written a letter to then-governor Charles S. Deneen to complain that "he was kicked and beaten." Instead of having Walter's complaint looked into, the governor forwarded the boy's letter to Hardt. Hardt was acutely aware of how damaging to his career the boy's comment could become, and Mrs. Kaak testified that he confessed to her that "I don't like to have any kind of trouble at all about this case, for I am too young a superintendent here to have trouble." Hardt again revealed that he was more concerned about his reputation and job than the truth or the well-being of the children in his care. With Hardt's unfeeling testimony about Minnie Steritz still fresh in their minds, the Committee members undoubtedly viewed Hardt's remarks, as recounted by Mrs. Kaak, unfavorably.

The Committee then called Walter Kaak to testify, and he related how he was kicked and beaten on his right side and back by a man named Stiegel. During dinner, Walter had wanted a cup of coffee. Stiegel wouldn't let him have it, so the boy got it for himself anyway. Stiegel beat Walter so badly for disobeying that his bruises lasted "two weeks."

After the beating and after Kaak wrote to Governor Deneen, "Dr. Hardt," Walter testified, "called me to the office and asked me why I sent that letter, and I said because I did not want to get kicked and beat around like that, and then he said if I did that again he was going to send me to the boys' cottage." When the Committee's chair asked Walter why he hadn't complained to Dr. Hardt about Stiegel's kicking and beating him in the first place, rather than writing to the governor, Walter replied, "I thought it wouldn't do no good" because "when Edgar Jones got hit it didn't do no good then, so I thought it wouldn't do no good when he kicked me, neither." T. H. Miller had beaten Edgar Jones with a board "all over the side and on the head and face" until his nose and mouth bled.

Then one of the asylum's staff physicians, Dr. William M. Young, took the stand. The Committee asked him, "Now, how are those boys sent to the laundry, at whose suggestion?"

Dr. Young replied, "That is done under Dr. Hardt's orders." He continued, "Mr. Miller, I understand, had taken the boy out there and told him that Dr. Hardt had sent him" to the laundry room.

"Is that laundry work," one of the Committee members asked, "considered safe work for inmates?"

Dr. Young dropped yet another bombshell when he replied, "No, sir."

"Why is it, then, doctor," he continued, "that they will put those inmates in charge of those dangerous machines?"

Dr. Young admitted, "I don't know."

The Committee deduced from the testimonies that Hardt had assigned Walter Kaak to the dangerous job to get even with the boy for complaining to the governor about his treatment at the Asylum, but the investigation also uncovered a fact about Walter that was ignored by the Committee and never reported in newspapers. He had been admitted to the Asylum on December 19, 1906, a little over two years after Henry. Like Henry, he wasn't at all mentally impaired but had been incarcerated by his parents because he was a habitual masturbator. Question 57 on the application for his admission asked, as it did on Henry's, "Is the child given to self-abuse or has it ever been?"

The answer that follows, filled in by his physician, is: "I fear he is. I think that is what is wrong."

It was well known and not at all concealed from the investigators that caregivers "were permitted to spank, box the ears of, and paddle inmates who were disobedient," but as the Committee discovered, they did much more. One staffer, Willard Ayers, testified that Eddie Kutz—an inmate, who, like Henry, was "one of the brighter boys" and had "a very bad temper"—had some trouble with attendant W. R. Beach. Beach "bruised" Kutz "considerably." Another caregiver, Q. E. Waller, testified that Kutz's "face was beaten up," that it was "badly bruised" and "bloody," as were his torso, arms, and legs. Beach beat Kutz so badly, in fact, that Kurtz's blood splattered the floor. He was "25 or 26 years old" and neither feeble-minded nor a child, but one of the "brighter boys" who slept in the north wing of the main building with Henry, William Thomas O'Neil, and Walter Kaak.

However, the Committee discovered that one of the most popular means of controlling disruptive older and younger inmates at the Asylum was not beating but choking them. William Wettle, an Asylum caregiver, testified in chilling detail about the practice:

Chairman Hill: Ever see one [of the inmates] choked with a towel?

Mr. Wettle: Yes, sir.

Chairman Hill: Who choked him?

Mr. Wettle: Mr. Robinson, the barber; he [the inmate] wouldn't sit still, you know, and he couldn't shave those boys. . . . Well, they wouldn't sit still and he couldn't shave him, so he says I will make him come to time and so he took a towel and he put it around his neck—

Chairman Hill: And choked him down?

Mr. Wettle: Choked him until he pretty near gave up.

Chairman Hill: Until he gave up and kept still?

Mr. Wettle: Yes, sir.

. . .

Rep. McLaughlin: The boy wasn't able to move?

Mr. Wettle: Oh, yes, he could move, but he got him under control.

Rep. McLaughlin: His face became blue?

Mr. Wettle: Yes, blue. He took a towel and laid it on the back of the chair and then just twisted it down.

Rep. McLaughlin: Twisted it so his tongue came out?

Mr. Wettle: Yes, and then he put it back in.

Near the end of Wettle's testimony, Chairman Hill decided to make a point about why the caregivers used towels instead of their hands. After all, a towel might not be available to the caregiver when he wanted to control an inmate. "When you choke anybody with a towel it doesn't leave any marks, does it?" Hill asked Wettle, and without missing a beat, Wettle replied, "No, sir."

After five months of inquiry into the events that transpired at the Asylum during 1907, the Committee ended its "uncovering of horrors." It printed all of the testimonies, various documents (such as letters to or from Hardt, excerpts from Asylum records that had some bearing on the investigation, etc.), and its conclusions in a tome of more than a thousand pages the following year. The Committee cited a number of the Asylum's attendants for "cruel or brutal conduct to the inmates." It also declared that "the record of the injuries kept during Dr. Hardt's" tenure as director "were of practically no value"; that meetings of the medical staff were too sparse and minutes of those meetings never kept; that there was "a want of co-ordination among the employees of the institution and a lack of discipline which has been greatly to its detriment"; that managerial procedures at the Asylum showed "a lamentable lack of efficiency"; and that the food served to the inmates "was seriously lacking" in "quality and oftimes in quantity."

It also addressed many of the individual cases brought to its attention. It noted "the careless and unprofessional treatment given" to Frank Giroux's "wound by the doctor in charge," calling the doctor's actions "not only reprehensible, but, in the opinion of the Committee, calls for severest criticism." "It is also the opinion of the Committee," the report continued, "that the supervision of institutions of this kind should be of such a nature that accidents" of the type that befell Minnie Steritz "would be absolutely impossible" and that "if through" an attendant's "neglect accidents of this kind occur, they are liable and most certainly will be prosecuted to the fullest extent of the law."

Among the more notable points that the Committee deemed necessary to articulate strongly was a comment about the incarceration of the mentally healthy with the feeble-minded and, similarly, of children with adults. "The Committee," the report reads, was "impressed with the fact" that the Asylum housed "inmates there who cannot properly be classed as feeble-minded, but may more properly be classed as incorrigible," and it recognized that "patients who had reached a certain age of maturity" should never be institutionalized with "children" and should instead "be promptly classified and placed in institutions more fitted for their reception." The "Asylum for Feeble-Minded Children should be what its name indicates, and, as far as possible, should be managed and conducted for the reception and proper treatment of children who are feeble-minded," suggesting that adults needed to be incarcerated in institutions created for adults and not warehoused among children. Focusing on the case of Minnie Steritz, it concluded with the most damning comment of all: "Apparently the screams of a child in pain do not attract much attention at this institution."

A STATE OF UGLINESS

Henry had tired to keep up a relationship with his father during the first few years of his life at the Asylum. He wrote him letters, and in return, his father sent him "once in a while catholic prayer books" and even a "musical harp." The harp didn't make Henry feel any less rejected. He didn't know how to play it, and there was no one at the Asylum to teach him.

Then, during the state-sponsored Committee's investigation of abuses at the Asylum, Henry was overcome by the worst personal tragedy he was to endure as a child. On March 1, 1908, a month before Henry's sixteenth birthday, his sixty-nine-year-old father died at St. Augustine's Home for the Aged, where he'd been living for the past five years. He had developed cirrhosis of the liver, which is often associated with alcoholism and a poor diet, and ascites complicated by chronic nephritis. Penniless, he was buried in a pauper's grave at the Catholic-run Mount Carmel Cemetery in Hillside, Illinois, a suburb west of Chicago.

Henry was so devastated by his father's death that, atypical for him, he recorded his emotional reaction to it:

> I did not cry or weep however.
>
> I had that kind of deep sorrow that bad as you feel I could not. I'd been better off if I could have. I was in that state for weeks, and because of it I was in a state of ugliness of such nature that everyone avoided me, they were so scared.
>
> . . .
>
> During the first of my grief I hardly ever ate anything, and was no friend to anyone.

He added, "I was even very dangerous if not left alone."

The elder Darger's death signaled to the boy that he was now irrevocably on his own. Henry knew his father had abandoned him over and over again, of course, even if he had become an expert at rationalizing it. His father had ignored Henry as he played in West Madison Street among predators of every sort, had sent him packing to the Mission of Our Lady of Mercy when the authorities began breathing down his neck, and finally had sentenced him to life in the

Illinois Asylum for Feeble-Minded Children because he'd grown embarrassed by the boy's sexual activities. Henry hoped his father might
rescue him from the Asylum as he had when Henry was locked up at
Dunning, but now, with the news of his father's death, he knew that
would never, ever happen. He also had to face the fact that the caregivers who had barked orders at him all of his life were no more concerned about him than the thrill seekers on West Madison Street had
been, and were just as predatory.

Henry began to complain about being sent to the Asylum's farm.
In fact, he seems to have made a fuss about it, but no one paid any
attention to him because, at the time, authorities believed so strongly
in the recuperative power of farm life. In later years, the painfulness
and the shame of the memories of his experiences on the farm made
Henry reticent about explaining his anxiety.

The director of another asylum in the Midwest during the early
years of the 1900s bragged that the "boys" sent to work at the farm
associated with his institution were "very glad to go to bed" after a
long day of milking cows, weeding vegetable patches, planting and
harvesting, sweeping out barns, stacking firewood, and other chores,
and that those who "have worked in the field all day require no night
watchman. They go to bed and sleep. An attendant sleeps in an adjoining room, but we have little anxiety about the boys during the
night. There are no locks on the doors, and the boys go and come as
they please."

The lodging of men and boys together, allowing them to "go and
come as they please," was a recipe for trouble. As Pulitzer Prize-
winning journalist Michael D'Antonio discovered at one institution
in the East, the older, larger boys (and sometimes attendants) who
came and went at night were called "night crawlers." Once the dormitory "lights were turned off," they

> would get into a younger or smaller boy's bed, threaten him into
> silence, and then teach him to engage in mutual masturbation and

oral sex. Often a relationship would evolve as an older boy claimed the younger one as a sort of pet. During the day, the younger boy would receive favors and protection. At night, he would perform sexually.

Even the Vice Commission of Chicago hinted at those very same comings and goings:

> Inquiries into the subnormal condition of boys and young men in certain [Illinois] State institutions, although not yet considered to be sufficiently scientific to be trustworthy, yet indicate that while feeble-mindedness decreased the strength of the sexual instinct with that of other capacities, the weakness of will and judgment lays these defectives open to temptation and exploitation.

The term "feeble-mindedness" reveals exactly to which institution the Commission referred, the Illinois Asylum for Feeble-Minded Children, the only institution in the history of Illinois with "feeble-minded" in its name.

With no one to stop the comings and goings of the night crawlers there, Henry and all the other smaller boys were probably easier targets at the farm than at the Asylum. The boys weren't watched at night at all. Days at the farm may have been Edenic for Henry, but his nights would have been a hell of exploitation. Now that his father was dead, he was forced to make a decision: stay at the Asylum and live with the sexual abuse there and at the farm or strike out on his own.

On June 8, almost exactly three months after his father's death, Henry couldn't bear another second of being at the farm and enduring his victimization there, and in a moment of self-determination, he took off alone on his first attempt to escape. He didn't get far. One of the hired hands, Mr. West—"that farms cowboy"—found him hiding in one of the cornfields. He bound Henry's hands together with a rope, and then, still on his horse, West led Henry back to the main farmhouse like an animal. The experience taught Henry an important lesson. He had to plan for the next time, not just leave on the spur of the moment, and he needed someone else to go with him. He waited nearly a full year before his next attempt.

On May 18, 1909, Henry took off again, this time with two of his Asylum friends, Paul Pettit and Theo Lindquist, in tow. The three were quickly rounded up and returned. Henry once claimed that the other two had talked him into taking off with them, but given his persistence in running away, it's likely that he was the instigator.

Thirty-five days later, on Wednesday, June 23, Henry ran away from the farm a third time. A friend accompanied him, although Henry kept his friend's identity a secret. They hopped a freight train that was headed north. Henry's friend got off at Joliet, just south of Chicago, where his family lived, and Henry continued to Chicago alone. Once inside the city limits, he jumped off. It began raining, and the rain turned into a thunderstorm. Suddenly, he was flummoxed by his situation. He was barely sixteen years old and hadn't bothered to plan what he would do after he arrived in Chicago. Where could he go, not just to get out of the storm but to live? How would he take care of himself? He had no answers, and all he could think to do was to turn himself over to the police.

The authorities didn't know what to do with him, either, and because he told them that he'd escaped from the Asylum, they sent Henry to the insane asylum at Dunning, his second stay in that hellhole. Nothing had changed. The inmates' screams day and night were as loud as they had been ten years earlier. The guards were just as brutal. Freezing in the winter and stifling in the summer, Dunning lacked hot water and had a lengthy record of attendants' abuse of inmates. Instead of being locked up there only a few days, as had happened to him when he was younger, he was incarcerated there for a month. Despite such a lengthy stay, he never once even hinted about what happened to him behind its walls, which may suggest how traumatic it had been for him. Authorities returned him to the Asylum around July 23.

On or around Sunday, July 25, Henry made his fourth escape from the farm. His friend Ernst Nordstrom and another boy whose identity he kept secret went along. Once the boys cleared the Asylum's property lines, they walked southeast through the countryside. Eventually, they met up with a farmer, a German immigrant like Henry's father and uncles, who lived a few miles away, near Decatur, and he offered the boys a job for a week. They drove "a wagon load of something the farmer sold" to the "nearest town" for him.

The boys' life with the farmer and his family was reassuringly ordinary:

> At meal times, breakfast dinner or supper, he said the Our Father, and sang some sort of a German hymn before we ate. He asked why we did not join him.
> We answered we do not know any German.
> His son and wife answered some parts.

All too soon, however, reality disrupted Henry's tranquility. Before the week ended, the farmer paid Henry and Ernst for their work and sent them on their way, but he "kept the other boy." Henry gave part of his pay to Ernst, and together they hitched a ride on "the Illinois Central to Decator Ill." Ernst couldn't keep out of sight, and authorities nabbed him in Decatur on the same day that they left the farmer, July 29. They returned him to the Asylum.

On the other hand, having learned to keep a low profile during his days in West Madison Street, Henry was free. With only a few cents left in his pocket after sharing his salary with Ernst, and with no one to ask for help, he "walked from Decator Ill to Chicago," one hundred sixty-five miles.

FOOL ENOUGH TO RUN AWAY
FROM HEAVEN

Henry's long, grueling two-week walk back to Chicago in early August 1909 gave him plenty of time to think, especially about his future. What was his life going to be like once he got home? Where was he going to find a job? Where would he live? He couldn't make up his mind if his decision to escape the Asylum had been a good one or not, and he ended up arguing with himself about it much of the way back, something he would do, off and on, the rest of his life. The argument was always the same. He "liked the work" on the farm "very much," but for some reason he couldn't (or wouldn't) articulate, he "did object to leaving" the Asylum when he and the others were sent to the farm to work. He "loved" the Asylum "much better than the farm, but yet" he "loved the work" on the farm. "Yet the asylum was home" to him. Around and around, back and forth he went.

Eventually, Henry came close to resolving the conflict:

> I can't say whether I was actually sorry I ran away from the State Farm or not but now I believe I was a sort of fool to have done so.
>
> My life was like a sort of heaven there. Do you think I might be fool enough to run away from heaven if I get there?

Henry felt that many aspects of his life before he was incarcerated at the Asylum were so difficult that, by comparison, being at the Asylum, and especially its farm, was a "sort of heaven." Now with no food and no place to sleep, he realized that at the Asylum he at least had three meals a day and a bed, even if others, invited or not, joined him. Over the years, his experiences with bigger boys and men had taught him how to cope with sexual situations so that when he arrived at the Asylum, he knew how to play lamb to the wolves who prowled the narrow aisles between the beds in the dormitory. His time there was occupied, too: first with school, then with work, and always with recreation of various types. He decided to run from the farm, rather than the Asylum proper, because the farm had only three or four adults who were too busy with their own responsibilities to oversee the inmates adequately. He could slip off without anyone noticing more easily at the farm than at the Asylum, but that didn't mean that he'd be any more successful at it there.

Henry's contradictions can be explained as another aspect of his defense strategy. His waffling over running away from the Asylum was similar to the time he was called on the carpet and "whacked" for something—he couldn't remember what, but he couldn't bring himself to deny it either—that involved John Manley and the Scanlon brothers. However this time, he claimed not to know why he preferred the Asylum to the farm, then flip-flopped to prefer the farm to the Asylum. "I liked the work" at the farm "very much," Henry said, "but still I don't know why, but I did object to leaving the home." Sex was at the core of both situations, although he was unable to admit his victimization even to himself.

At the same time, Henry showed all the signs of being in the throes of separation anxiety. He had spent nearly a decade of his life—much of his childhood, all of his adolescence, and most of his teen years—institutionalized. Running away forced him to come face-to-face with his terror over the unknown, what lay ahead for him in Chicago, and rightly so. His earlier experiences there were far from nurturing. Like a convict who's been imprisoned a long time, he wasn't sure that he could make it once he was beyond the walls of his captivity.

Years later, Henry would claim that his life at the Asylum had been "uneventful but busy," another phrase full of denial that he meant to camouflage what he really experienced there. Had it been as "uneventful" as he claimed, he wouldn't have been so determined to run away but would have settled in, accepting a life among the boys who meant something to him: William Thomas O'Neil, Paul Pettit, Daniel Jones, and Donald Aurand, as well as Ernst Nordstrom and Theo Lindquist, both of whom had tried to escape with him. They were so important to him that he remembered them in his books and on his canvases. He certainly would've remembered them during his two-week walk back to Chicago, wondering how they were faring at the Asylum and if they were still there.

As he drew closer to Chicago, skyscrapers began to appear, the tallest first, rising higher and higher along the horizon out of the farmland and small towns. Henry's mood began to change along with the landscape. Seeing the skyline of his hometown overwhelmed him. He took a deep breath, then another. The wind was blowing, carrying the stench of the stockyards with it. Henry hadn't realized until that moment how good the stink could be. He took yet another breath, one even deeper than those before, and held it as long as he could.

He thought of the cattle in the stockyards. The stench of their blood and manure in the slaughterhouse pens was the only way he knew they existed. He couldn't see or hear them, and he wondered if, by going back to Chicago where nothing would be guaranteed, where his future was a gamble, he was blindly penning himself up the way Armour and Company's employees corralled the cattle, letting them pace wide-eyed as they waited a fate they sensed but couldn't escape. A nullifying anxiety nearly stopped him dead in his tracks. He was seventeen now, a man, and not the child he was five years ago when Rooney knocked on the Mission's door and took him away. He was responsible for himself, but he wasn't sure how to be responsible.

For the past five years, when most adolescent boys had been figuring out their futures, getting jobs to help support themselves or their families, making friends with boys their own age or simply hanging out and enjoying life as only the young do, Henry had been in an asylum. He hadn't been apprenticed to a milkman, a stonemason, or a blacksmith—not even to a tailor, his father's occupation and one that, given the custom of the day, he probably would have followed had his life been more like other boys'.

Henry could imagine some of what he was to experience in Chicago now that he was back. He understood that he had been poverty-stricken as a child, which compelled him to do things he wasn't at all happy about now, but in a show of solidarity with his father, he thought—almost as if he were responding to someone's criticism of his father—that, no matter what their situations had been, at least their "meals" had not been "scant." If he couldn't find a job, he could return to jack-rolling or offer himself to older, financially-well-off men. He was certain that the queer community would welcome him— a blue-eyed, slim, boyish seventeen-year-old—with wide open arms, a street-wise lamb on his way to the wolves if there ever was one.

CHAPTER 4

TWENTY THOUSAND ACTIVE HOMOSEXUALS

REFUGE

ANNA HAD KEPT IN TOUCH WITH HENRY DURING HIS STAY AT THE Asylum. He mentioned getting letters from her occasionally, but she never visited him there. Because his decision to run away was on the spur of the moment, she wouldn't have gotten any word from him that he was returning to Chicago. He showed up on her doorstep unannounced and unexpected—and probably almost unrecognizable. The last time that she would have seen him was in 1904, when he was twelve. He was seventeen now, a little taller, perhaps a bit heavier.

He told her he'd hopped a ride on a westbound Illinois Central from somewhere near Decatur to just north of Lincoln, where he jumped off and began to follow the northbound railroad tracks back to Chicago on foot.

He kept away from the farms and villages between Lincoln and Chicago so the police couldn't spot him and return him to the Asylum, as had happened to his friend Ernst a few weeks earlier. At first, he tried walking during the day along the tracks and through the crops of soybeans and corn and sleeping at night. August is hot and muggy in central Illinois, often punctuated by showers, its rural areas full of mosquitoes and other bothersome insects after dark. The humidity, rain, and bugs bothered him so much that he was "hardly able to sleep" during much of the two weeks, and he decided to walk "many a night."

He hadn't eaten anything but what he could find in the fields along the railroad tracks, perhaps raw ears of corn, which would not yet have begun to ripen. When he arrived on her doorstep, he was sweaty and dirty from his two-week trek through the farmlands of central Illinois. He needed clean clothes, a bath, food, and sleep—and not necessarily in that order.

Always the person who helped Henry the most in his life, Anna invited him to live with her and Augustine—a "refuge," Henry later called their home—until he could get a job and his own place to live. He knew he couldn't stay for long, but he couldn't hide his happiness. It would feel good to be in a home, a real one, and to be safe.

It was the middle of August 1909. Henry was virtually unemployable in any meaningful occupation, but luckily Anna had connections on the Near North Side. She knew Sister Leno, one of the nuns who ran St. Joseph's Hospital at 740 Garfield, and she must have known Sister Leno quite a long time because she called the nun by her birth name, Nina. Sister Leno was one of the Daughters of Charity of St. Vincent de Paul, the group of nuns who founded St. Joseph's in 1868 and who were employed on all levels within the hospital, except as doctors.

A few days after Henry returned to Chicago, Anna spoke with Sister Leno. Anna mentioned all of Henry's good attributes—how he was a sweet, intelligent, creative child who would spend hours coloring in the coloring books that she and his father gave him, and how, after he'd filled in all of the pictures, he would trace people, buildings, animals, clouds, and all sorts of other things that he found in newspapers and magazines onto cheap paper and then color them. She explained his love of history, and how he once bragged to her how he'd argued with his teacher, Ella Dewey, about the number of soldiers killed in the Civil War.

She accentuated his troubled life: the loss of his brother, mother, and sister within just a few years of one another; his absent and alcoholic father; the utter poverty of his childhood; the vice-ridden neighborhood in which he grew up; the failure of the Mission to turn his life around, despite the good intentions and hard work of Fathers Mahoney and O'Hara, she added; and his institutionalization downstate in the Asylum. "But," she promised, "Henry's perfectly sane now" and ready—with God's and Sister Leno's help—to begin a new life. Anna laid it on thick, and Sister Leno was close to tears.

Anna left out all of the unsavory facts, of course: how he slashed his teacher with a knife so badly she needed medical attention, how he threw ashes into the eyes of a neighbor girl who also needed medical care, how he snuck out late at night to visit a man no one in the family had ever met, and how he engaged in "perversions." The last was so terrible that wild horses couldn't have dragged it out of her. She also left out the part about Henry escaping from the Asylum. As far as Sister Leno knew, Henry had been cured, then released.

Sister Cephas, who was the hospital's chief administrator and hired all the staff, offered Henry a job. The only opening at the hospital suitable for Henry was as a janitor, sweeping and mopping the floors, which happened to have been his job at the Asylum, but he would also dispose of all the trash from each floor of the hospital. St. Joseph's had a dormitory—a separate building on the premises for its single employees, both male and female—called the Workingmen's House. It stood behind the hospital and along Burling Street, and Henry would live there. In one fell swoop, the problems of where he would work and where he would live were solved, and Henry moved out of Anna and Augustine's home only a few weeks after his return to Chicago.

Despite its name, Henry didn't live among mostly men at the Workingmen's House, as he had at both the Asylum and the Mission. Most of the roomers were women, and they tended to be the hospital's nurses. Instead of sleeping in one large room with a substantial number of other boys and men as he was used to doing, Henry lived alone in his own private room, except for a short time when he had a roommate.

Unfortunately, Sister Leno couldn't keep a secret to save her soul. As soon as she learned that Sister Cephas had hired him, Sister Leno told Sister Rose, Henry's new supervisor, that he'd just been released from an asylum. Immediately, their imaginations turned Henry into their worst fear: a prowling lunatic who might, without warning, pounce on any of them.

Sister Rose was no better at keeping a secret than Sister Leno and was just as concerned about Henry. She warned a third nun about him, and she, in turn, passed the warning on to yet another sister until, as Henry quickly realized, word of his former life in the Asylum had spread throughout the sisters' quarters, then drifted throughout the lay staff. They began calling him "crazy," not just a nickname, as it'd been when he was at the Mission, but a label that, in the mouths of adults, carried more weight—and harm—than any nickname in the mouths of children.

As it turned out, Sister Rose wasn't just a blabbermouth. She had a vicious side, too. Some of her actions were as clichéd as they were cruel. Because of an "old injury" Henry received in a fight during his stay at the Mission, his right shoulder gave him pain when he used his right hand for any extended amount of time, so when sweeping or mopping, he used his left. Sister Rose constantly nagged him to use his right hand instead. Like many people of the time, she associated left-handedness with witches, Satan, and evil in general. He didn't tell her why he couldn't use his right arm. He didn't want her to know about his past behavior and give her another reason to nag, but he couldn't switch because of the pain it would have caused him. He ignored her orders, and she eventually gave up, never mentioning his left-handedness again. It was the only time he won an argument with another person while at the hospital, but there was no shortage of conflict.

Not long after he began working at St. Joseph's, Henry was searching through a poorly lit, closet-like room for cleaning items, and as he left the room, he almost ran into a young woman who, at that very moment, happened to be passing. His sudden appearance startled her. Compelled by the rumor that Henry was crazy as a loon, the woman complained to Sister Rose that he'd jumped out of the room to frighten her on purpose, and when Sister Rose called him into her office, she didn't give him a chance to explain that it was an accident. So sure that his lunacy was acting up, she gave him a dressing-down that shook the walls, informing him at the end of her rant and at the top of her lungs that she was sure he was still crazy. As bad as that was, it wasn't the end of her irrational dealings with him. She enjoyed using Henry as a whipping boy and did so as often as she could, something that didn't escape him. He complained that she railed at him for all sorts of things and liked to end her tirades with threats to ship him "back to the Lincoln Asylum."

Henry recalled that, when he was a child, "I was of the kind that only my father could tell me what to do, and would take no scouldings or authority from any one else." As an adult employed at a full-time job, he still bristled when anyone, supervisors or coworkers, ordered him about. Henry hated being under someone else's thumb, even when on the job, because it reminded him of being a lamb. The guilt that he had felt as a child after encounters with wolves in West Madison Street or at the Asylum would return, rising like bile from his gut to his mouth. An adult now, he couldn't stand being forced to feel helpless as he had as a child, and yet he knew he had to submit to his supervisors and others in positions of power. That caused him to brag about being victorious in fights, about refusing to allow others to boss him around, about standing up for himself. To boast about such actions, which were mostly fantasies, allowed him to appear assertive instead of docile, to feel empowered instead of ineffectual, and to be the hero of his own life instead of a victim.

From the beginning of Henry's employment with them, the Daughters of Charity showed Henry very little compassion or charity. He complained that he "dared not take off" from his job for any reason and then added, "You call that charity. Afraid I would be behind in my work and that would cost them (money)" He was never given vacation time or sick leave, even when he was very ill and "should have been in bed and under treatment!" But Henry wasn't the only employee who was treated poorly by his employer. The majority of U.S. workers labored long hours at mind-numbing, menial jobs like Henry's and received few, if any, days off for any reason, even for medical attention. Compared to many other workers, Henry had it good.

Newspapers and magazines at the time reported the hundreds of incidents of maimings and deaths among industrial workers, and *The Factory Inspector*, published from 1902 to 1907 by the International Association of Factory Inspectors, was in the forefront of reporting accidents "from unprotected machinery in a variety of industries." Among its many exposés was one about a "sawmill worker [who] fell onto a large, unguarded circular saw and was split in two." Elsewhere, at a navy yard, "a worker got caught in the large flywheel of the main steam power plant," and "his arms and legs were torn off and the lifeless trunk was hurled against a wall 50 feet away." Conditions for the laboring class would not change for decades, when labor unions were established and set standards for how employers had to deal with their employees.

Complicating matters for Henry was the fact that the nuns did everything possible to emasculate him. He was one of only a handful of men on the staff, excluding the doctors, and he was only a janitor, not anyone of any importance in the hospital hierarchy. Standing five feet one inch tall, he was shorter than the average adult male, and many of the nuns towered over him. On top of it all, they outnumbered him, just like the boys and the men at the Mission and the Asylum had, and because the nuns also ran the place, they could bully him without reprisal—and did.

FAMILY REUNION

During the brief time that he stayed with Anna and Augustine, Henry had the opportunity to reconnect, if only superficially, with his family. Conveniently, Charles and Ellen still lived at 2707 Portland with Augustine and Anna. After having nothing to do with Henry for almost a decade, not since he began living at the Mission, Augustine and Charles wouldn't have been exactly thrilled to become reacquainted with their nephew and hash over the past. He wasn't *really* family anymore. If anything, he was as close to being a stranger as a member of one's family could possibly be. Besides, their brother Henry's confession during a weak moment years earlier—that Henry had been engaging in perverted practices—would have made them nervous about being around the boy. Still, they felt they owed it to the memory of their brother, dead now for a little over a year, to offer Henry a place to live for a short time, but they made no bones about their reluctance to Anna.

She wasn't as concerned as Augustine and Charles were about Henry's history of acting up, although they brought it up around her as often as they could. She stood her ground against them. Maybe he'd grown out of it, she would've argued, always Henry's staunchest supporter. Maybe he'd changed.

During Henry's stay, Anna didn't bother to invite any of his four cousins, Charles and Ellen's children, over to become reacquainted with him. All were much older than he—Charles was now forty, Harry thirty-eight, Frederick thirty-six, and Annie thirty-three

—and were involved in their own families and occupations. Henry had rarely been around them when he was a child, far too long ago for him to remember them clearly. In fact, he recalled only Harry, who at best was a dim figure from his past.

Augustine and Charles, now sixty-six and sixty-five years old, minded their p's and q's when they were around Henry as Anna and Ellen had made them promise to do. They were old pros at small talk, something they'd learned while networking on behalf of their own small but successful businesses. (Of course, they steered clear of his life at the Mission and the Asylum, and while he may have mentioned some of his experiences there, telling them about his victimization would have been far too painful and embarrassing.) Once he was hired at St. Joseph's and knew where he'd be living, they asked him about his new neighborhood, known throughout Chicago for its hundreds of boardinghouses that offered rooms to let for reasonable prices and sometimes even offered meals along with the cost of rent. It had become headquarters for young men and women who had jobs and were, often for the first time, on their own as working adults. It was a very short distance north of Towertown, the epicenter of Chicago's artistic community, a bohemia as famous in Chicago for its painters, literary types, and sexual outlaws as Greenwich Village was in New York.

Towertown lay between the Chicago River and what's now called the Gold Coast, a quick ride by streetcar from the Workingman's House. By the time Henry returned to Chicago, many queer men lived there or just visited for entertainment. Home to bars, cafés, and restaurants, it welcomed queer men and women. Towertown had a seedy side, too: Bughouse Square, one of Towertown's most important queer hangouts, and several male-only bathhouses. Bughouse Square was the nickname of Washington Square Park, which is across the street from the front entrance to Newberry Library. During the day and early evening, local socialists and other politically minded men gave speeches on soapboxes there, but during the night, until the wee hours of the morning, queer men cruised the park, hoping to pick up other men for sex. Once they hooked up, they'd go to one or the other's place or, if that wasn't possible, to one of Towertown's Turkish baths, where for fifty cents they could have a room all night.

Augustine and Charles thought the glamour with which most people described Towertown was a bunch of horsefeathers and wondered if Henry thought so, too. Henry didn't let on that he knew anything at all about his new neighborhood yet—he'd been back in town for only a little while, he reminded them—much less Towertown. Anna hadn't had to warn him about minding *his* p's and q's. He'd learned the hard way at the Asylum when and how to do exactly that.

To keep their conversations away from any embarrassing lapses into silence, Augustine and Charles would have begun to reminisce about the past: their childhoods in Germany, their immigration to the United States, the Great Chicago Fire of 1871, even their older brother, Henry's father. Once Uncle Augustine mentioned how, as a teenager only a little younger than Henry was now, he had watched the battle at Meldorf between German and French forces during the Franco-Prussian War. He remembered it as if it were yesterday, and he took what seemed like hours to Henry to discuss in detail the devastation—of men, of the landscape—that he'd witnessed. Meldorf is where the Dargers originated, Charles reminded Henry, and where Henry's grandparents, now dead, had lived all of their lives. It was where the brothers had learned their occupation, but there was no opportunity there, so they moved to London. That's where Charles met Ellen and Augustine met his first wife, Margaret. The opportunities in London weren't much better than those in Meldorf, and the Darger brothers eventually set sail for the United States, where they'd be very successful—Augustine and Charles, that is.

The brothers slipped up once. Not bragging, just relating facts, Augustine mentioned that they'd been so successful and loved Henry's father so much that they had paid for him to enter the Little Sisters of the Poor, the nickname of St. Augustine's Home for the Aged. In the silence that followed what both brothers thought was a faux pas, Henry finally got a word in edgewise. He asked them what had happened to his little sister.

Augustine and Charles had likely expected Henry to ask them why they hadn't taken him in when he was set to the Asylum, and he caught them off guard. Charles told Henry the little bit they knew. They thought she'd been adopted, but they didn't know who had taken her. Years later, Henry would wonder if Charles was telling him the truth or not.

Then Henry asked them why his father hadn't brought the "woman relative" back to the Mission to adopt him as he had said he would. Henry had been thinking about how different his life would've been had he been given something resembling a normal life and not been exiled to the Asylum.

It would've taken Charles a little while to recall what Henry was talking about. That happened six or seven years earlier, and for him, it wouldn't have been important enough to remember. Henry's question triggered the memory, and he recalled his brother and that woman, whose name he couldn't recall. He told Henry to thank his lucky stars his father didn't go through with the adoption. She was a heavy drinker and would have turned him into one.

Henry probably had many other questions for his uncles, but these, and their answers, are the only ones that he bothered to record years later, revealing that they were likely the most important ones to him. Now seventeen years old, Henry would have been faced with an agonizing question: Why was his sister lucky enough to have been adopted when he was tossed out to strangers, to be victimized over and over again? The question not only intensified the guilt and anger that he'd felt since his childhood; it also remained unanswered for the rest of his life.

THOMAS M. PHELAN

In 1910, a few months after returning to Chicago, Henry met a man who would become an important figure to him during the first few years he lived at the Workingmen's House. Thomas M. Phelan arrived at St. Joseph's Hospital as a patient. He had developed "a sort of shaking sickness" that went undiagnosed, although doctors confirmed that "it was not palsy." Phelan was too poor to pay his medical bill, and to work off his debt, the Daughters of Charity put him in charge of the Workingmen's House. He had once studied for the priesthood but had been forced to stop his schooling because of an illness, and Sister Camilla, who had taken over from Sister Cephas when she retired, was certain that his experience as a seminarian would make him a good role model for the single men and women living there. Eager to pay his debt and to show the nun that she had put her trust in the right man, he quickly "took charge."

Phelan, already an "old man" of sixty-five, and eighteen-year-old Henry became roommates. The odd pairing of someone old and ill with someone young and, as far as the nuns were concerned, crazy had Sister Camilla's fingerprints all over it. She was likely hopeful that the almost-priest's influence would rub off on the boy, perhaps even cure him of his lunacy. In that, she was like Henry's father, who, years earlier, had sent him to the Mission, hoping that the priests there would be a positive influence.

For a few weeks, Henry and Phelan got along well enough. As soon as they began sharing a room, Phelan noticed that Henry scribbled in notebooks and even on loose sheets of paper as often as he could during his free time, often at night for hours at a stretch. He wondered what Henry was writing and dropped some hints that he was interested in it. Henry admitted it was the beginning of a novel that chronicled "the adventures of seven sisters—the Vivian girls—fighting for the Christian nation of Angelinia in an effort to stop the

country of Glandelinia from continuing its practice of child slavery."
Henry had enjoyed reading since early childhood, when he got "story
books" for Christmas, so it was almost second nature for creative
Henry to put pen to paper and write his own. Phelan's interest was
piqued. He offered to read what Henry had written so far and give
him an objective critique.

Henry was proud of how his novel was turning out, and he was
at the point that he wanted to show it to someone, not necessarily for
critical feedback but certainly for unqualified approval. Henry knew
neither of his uncles would be interested in tackling his manuscript.
Their favorite reading was the *Daily Tribune* or the *Chicago American*. Neither his aunt Anna nor the nuns would do, either. He didn't
know who among the nuns could read, but he was sure the story that
he was writing wouldn't be their, or his aunt's, cup of tea. He needed
someone used to reading, someone educated, and he finally decided
to open up to his roommate, who, having attended seminary, was
probably the most educated person he knew.

It had taken him several days to work up the courage to entrust
his manuscript with Phelan, but he finally did, secretly hoping Phelan
would fawn over it. Older than Henry by decades, Phelan had authority over Henry, lived with Henry in close quarters, and was ill—so he
would have been a natural surrogate for Henry's father. That, coupled
with the fact that Phelan had studied for the priesthood, may have
gotten the best of Henry, causing him to trust Phelan implicitly.

"Trash"—that's what Phelan called it when, after a few days, he
shoved the manuscript back at Henry. His reading material ran to the
sacred, not the secular. He subscribed to *The Victorian*, a Catholic
magazine focused on the family, and he believed that the only acceptable reading material for Christians were books and magazines aimed
at the pious, not a lot of rubbish about children in revolt against adults.

Unfortunately, Phelan's reaction wasn't at all what Henry
needed this early in the writing process. He was devastated but suffered his disappointment in silence. Then the manuscript abruptly dis-

appeared and, with it, a collection of pictures Henry had clipped from newspapers and magazines. Because he knew that children's adventure books like his were often illustrated, Henry had begun collecting pictures of children whose appearance matched what he imagined his characters, especially the Vivian girls, looked like. He planned on illustrating his novel by using the pictures the way an artist uses models.

Henry searched high and low for the manuscript—all over his and Phelan's room and every place in the Workingmen's House and the hospital where he'd been working on it to see if he'd put it down and forgotten to pick it up when he left.

Henry hated to admit it, but the manuscript and the pictures had disappeared without a trace. Still, he refused to be deterred. After a few days, he began rewriting the novel and clipping models for his characters from newspapers and magazines. Then, within days, he found the second manuscript, which was only a few pages long, in the trash.

It began to add up. Phelan called his novel "trash," and Henry found the second version in the trash. Phelan must have destroyed the first manuscript and the pictures and had tried to get rid of the second manuscript, too.

Henry accused Phelan of stealing and destroying his manuscript to his face, but Phelan denied everything. He even went so far as to call Henry names that were so terrible that Henry wouldn't ever repeat them. They were, he said, "slanders," and he admitted that he "resented" them. The slanders were worse than being called "crazy," and in a moment of self-determination, Henry decided to move out of the room he shared with Phelan.

WHILLIE

Henry had been living in his own room at the Workingmen's House for perhaps a year when another man, William P. Schloeder, entered his life. When Henry discussed the beginning of their relationship, he said that he "went seeing Whillie," as Henry referred to him, in 1911. The phrase echoes one that was used by heterosexual couples at the time: to "see" someone, to "begin seeing" someone, and other similar phrases most often referred to courtship.

Whillie lived with two of his three sisters (Elizabeth, who was called Lizzie, and Katherine) and his parents in the large building they owned at 634 Garfield Avenue. A block and a half east of the Workingmen's House, the Schloeders' home stood three stories tall and had enough space that they could rent out extra rooms on the upper floors to lodgers. It had a basement and a barn in the back against the alley. Its many windows allowed a great deal of sunlight into the family's life, and because it had been built a short distance back from the street, a small lawn in the front welcomed visitors and buffered the Schloeders from street noise. Whillie's sister Susan; her husband, Charles; and their two children lived in some of the rooms upstairs, but Whillie's younger brother had moved out of the house and was on his own. Whillie's father, Michael, who had bought the building years earlier, would die only a few months after Whillie and Henry met. Whillie's mother, Susanna, would continue to live there for decades.

Henry considered the Schloeders "well to do," and by the day's standards, they were. Employed for years as a tallyman, laborer, clerk, salesman, and other jobs in lumber mills, Whillie's father worked his way up in the industry until he became the owner and president of his own very successful lumber company, Schloeder and Schloeder, in 1891. Henry also described them as "very charitable, kind and good." At least, they were to him. Although his working life was full of stress caused by the nuns' mean-spiritedness and the boredom that was the nature of his job, his life away from St. Joseph's was much, much better. He'd found friendship and love.

Henry never revealed how he and Whillie met, but there are clues. The Workingmen's House was in the St. Vincent de Paul Parish, so Henry would have attended St. Vincent's Church. Most of the people he knew—including the Schloeders and Thomas Phelan—also attended St. Vincent's on a more or less regular basis, as church records show. Whillie's sisters, especially Lizzie, who attended Mass more often than the other Schloeders, might have brought Whillie with them on a day when Henry was there, and the two may have met during the coffee hour after Mass. It's also possible that the two had known each other before Henry was sent to the Asylum.

By the time he was eight years old, Henry had begun sneaking out of his father's apartment late at night to visit a night watchman at the factory where the man worked. Henry was in sore need of both money and affection and developed a relationship with the man. Whillie was born on January 14, 1879, thirteen years before Henry, and when Henry turned eight, Whillie would have been twenty-one. While the age difference is not enough to link Whillie to Henry's earlier paramour, Whillie's occupation may. Whillie was a night watchman for the Rinn Company on the southwest corner of West Division and Crosby. It would have taken Henry little effort to take the streetcar from the coach house apartment up Halsted to Rinn Company. Or he could have easily walked the distance of approximately a mile or so.

Regardless of how they met, Henry and Whillie clicked. Whillie was slim, much taller than Henry, and had similar dark hair and blue eyes. Neither of the two was matinee-idol handsome, but both were pleasing to the eye. In fact, Henry's boyishness would have been attractive to many.

It didn't take them long to discover that they had a number of important things in common. Both were unskilled laborers. Both were the sons of immigrant fathers from Germany. Both were Catholics. Whillie's father's death shortly after they met helped to draw them together, allowing Henry, whose father had died only a couple of years earlier, to show sympathy and support for what Whillie was going through. Whillie was older than Henry, and that allowed Henry to bask in the love and approval of an older man, something his father never gave him. At the same time, their age difference allowed Whillie to enjoy the attention and admiration of a younger man. As important, the Schloeder family grew fond of Henry, and he became a fixture in their home. Whillie's family embodied everything that Henry had missed during his childhood.

Whillie's parents were married on August 12, 1872. Michael was born in Germany, the son of Mathiae and Catharina. He moved to Chicago in 1864, the year before the American Civil War ended. Susanna, often called Susan, was born in Luxembourg, the daughter of Nicholas and Elizabeth Braun, and immigrated in 1871—the year of the Great Chicago Fire and a few years before Henry's father. Losing a bout with chronic bronchitis that had lasted two and a half months, Michael died on December 14, 1911 and was buried at St. Boniface Cemetery, a few blocks north of the much more famous Graceland Cemetery.

Whillie was nurturing and "did all he could to help" Henry when he needed it. Once, when Henry had "bad mysterious pains" in his face, Whillie took him to a neighborhood drugstore, and together they found medicine that took care of the problem. During another of Henry's illnesses, Whillie gave him a hot water bottle to help ease his pain. On November 21, 1927, Henry was stricken with a terrible toothache, and Whillie took him to Dr. P. A. Hielscher, the Schloeders' family dentist, who performed a root canal on Henry. Whillie was a gentle nurturer, concerned over the well-being and comfort of his beloved, so while the bill was made out to Henry, Whillie may have paid for the procedure.

Henry was proud to boast that "every evening and Sunday afternoons off" he "went visiting a special friend of mine"—"special friend" giving an important clue to their relationship. In the early 1900s, gay men often used "special friend" and similar phrases as codes for their mates, and with that phrase, Henry cast his and Whillie's liaison as romantic and almost certainly sexual. By also bragging that they were together "every evening and Sunday afternoons" that the two didn't work, Henry hinted at the intensity of their relationship. Like any couple in love, they spent every free minute that they had in each other's

St. Vincent's Church, which Henry attended off and on most of his adult life.

(Used by permission of Special Collections and Archives,
John T. Richardson Library, DePaul University, Chicago, IL.)

company. While courting, Henry and Whillie "often went to Riverview Park," and Henry bragged that "I did all the spending." Despite the fact that he lived virtually hand to mouth and that Whillie was affluent, he refused to taint his feeling for Whillie with even a hint of his being kept by the older, "well to do" man. It was Henry's way to show him that their relationship wasn't about money but love.

Located at Belmont and Western, Riverview Amusement Park was a short streetcar ride northwest of the Workingmen's House and Whillie's home. Or Henry and Whillie could take "any north side 'L' to Belmont Avenue, thence by surface lines to Western Avenue." Riverview was inexpensive entertainment for people of all ages, a con-

venience for married people with families, and a favorite fun spot for
dating couples. Riverview offered "roller skating and . . . mechanical
rides, including a roller coaster and chutes." Favorite amusements
among the park-goers were the House of Troubles, Crazytown, and
Bughouse, their names reminding Henry of the Asylum. By 1907, the
large section of the park where the ride called Shoot-the-Chutes was
located had been nicknamed Fairyland, as had one of the concessions.
The following year, a large carousel was installed in that section of
Riverview, and it was called Fairyland, too. By the time Henry returned to Chicago, one city-sponsored report claimed that the Windy
City's population included some "twenty thousand active homosexuals," and it's probable that many of them couldn't resist the amusement park's campy moniker. They would subtly cruise one another
in Fairyland exactly as they did on State Street in the Loop—but here
among picknicking families and strolling heterosexual couples, none
of whom had a clue about what was going on under their noses.

Although financially strapped families often brought picnic
lunches with them, the park had several restaurants, the most popular
of which was the Casino, a hot spot for dating couples like Henry and
Whillie or for those who could afford to eat there. It offered a large
menu, which included soups and relishes, as well as fish (halibut,
trout, and others for sixty cents), roasts (veal or pork for sixty cents),
and other entrees. For dessert, guests could order scoops of ice cream
or slices of cherry pie, both for twenty cents. While eating or just saun-
tering through the park's one hundred forty acres, Henry and Whillie
would have heard strands of the park's theme song, "Meet Me in
Riverview," wafting over the summer breezes:

> O meet me at Riverview Park, sweetheart,
> O meet me at Riverview Park, sweetheart,
> Where under the trees
> With the sweet balmy breeze,
> I have something to tell you, sweetheart.

The music so sweet and entertaining
Makes you feel with your sweetheart like dancing.
O meet me at Riverview Park, sweetheart.
O meet me at Riverview Park, sweetheart.

Depending on what part of the park Henry and Whillie happened to be in at any given time, they could hear all sorts of hit tunes. "Yes! We Have No Bananas" was then sweeping the nation with its jaunty tune and wonderfully silly lyrics. Ragtime and blues were hit genres of the day and would have been on steady rotation at the park. Besides the roller coaster, Ferris wheel, carousel, and similar family-oriented rides, Riverview offered other more risqué forms of entertainment. In the sweltering summer of 1909, for example, twenty- year-old George Quinn and twenty-one-year-old Quincy DeLang were arrested for performing an "immoral and lewd exhibition" there, a dance characterized by "sensuous movements," what devotees of the dance would later call "striptease." Both men, drag performers, were members of the well-known burlesque troupe Duncan Clark's Female Minstrels. Clark's troupe performed all over the East and Midwest and found an especially large fan base in the Windy City.

Put on trial, Quinn and DeLang were both found innocent of breaking any laws around the same time that Henry walked into Chicago on his long escape from the Asylum. DeLang continued to work for Duncan Clark's troupe to the end of the season, but Quinn disappeared almost immediately after their trial, shame-faced by his sudden and unwanted notoriety. Like hundreds of other Chicagoans before him, Henry decided to go see what the hubbub was all about. Besides, he knew from his childhood in West Madison Street that other queer men would be in the audience and on the prowl for sexual partners. DeLang and Quincy weren't the only drag performers to entertain audiences at Riverview, but they were the most notorious.

Not only were burlesque performances staged at Riverview, but nickelodeons along the penny arcade that showed reels of provocative movies were a big hit, too. Among the more scandalous, but very popular, titles were *The Queen of Sin*, *Strip Poker*, and *The Gay Deceiver*—all aimed at a male, heterosexual audience. Occasionally, the park administration received complaints about those and the arcades' other attractions, and a member of the staff wrote a note to the park's manager, explaining one of them: "There was a priest out here the other night who complained about certain of your pictures, especially the one called 'Forbidden Fruit.' I, therefore, have had them checked out and wish you would have the following removed at once." The season had just begun, and to keep from having a priest-led protest against Riverview's film policy disrupt attendance for the whole summer, the manager removed the objectionable titles.

Henry and Whillie also went to Lincoln Park, another hit among dating couples, where they took boat rides in the lagoons, sauntered along the shore of Lake Michigan, visited the zoo, and climbed the High Bridge—off which many rejected suitors, ex-lovers, and other dejected individuals had flung themselves to their deaths. After a day in the park, they went out for dinner. When the weather didn't allow them to go to Riverview or Lincoln Park, they stayed at Whillie's.

When Henry and Whillie saw that their relationship was more than casual dating, they decided to have their portrait taken together at Coultry Studio. William J. Coultry, who had opened his studio at Riverview in 1902, offered several studio settings in which his clients could choose to be photographed, but "the most popular of photo gallery props was the yellow crescent moon." The other sets that he provided were "new motor cars, the rear platform of an Overland train, surrey with pony, and later a western saloon bar." Henry and Whillie selected the Overland train caboose for each of the three portraits Coultry took of them over the course of several years for what were then called "Photo Postals"—postcards printed with an individual's unique images.

The caboose is virtually identical in all three portraits, and both Henry and Whillie are dressed in the current fashion in each, but the two men change physically over the years. One of the photos was taken not long after Henry and Whillie began dating. Henry appears to be in his late teens or perhaps twenty, so it would have been taken in late 1911 or perhaps in 1912. He's wearing a newsboy's cap, a suit, a white shirt, and a tie. His face is oval, his posture stiff, and his head is tilted defiantly chin up. This was the first time his picture had ever been taken, and he didn't know what to do. Whillie, on the other hand, appears relaxed. He's wearing a black fedora, a black suit, a white shirt, and a tie. He's leaning ever-so-slightly away from Henry. His face is narrow and long. Henry is very erect in his seat, obviously self-conscious about the difference in their heights and trying to appear to be as tall as Whillie. Neither is smiling, but people rarely smiled in photographs at this time. At thirty-two, Whillie is obviously much older than Henry.

Often in studio photographs like Henry and Whillie's, a sign was introduced somewhere as a caption, giving a hint about the person or persons in the photo and often adding a touch of humor to the scene. If Henry and Whillie had been a heterosexual couple, they might have chosen "Just Married," or "She Got Her Man," or some other romance-linked phrase since they'd already been together for a few years, but having to be circumspect about their relationship, they chose "We're on Our Way" for their first photo together. The caption suggests a journey to an actual destination, especially because of the train motif, but it also refers to a metaphoric journey—their relationship.

The second photo, like the other, used the Overland caboose as its setting, and its caption also suggests a journey. Henry and Whillie were "On Our Way to Cuba" this time. Whillie is in a dapper mood, his fedora cocked at a dashing tilt. They probably had it taken a few years after the first one, close to the 1920s, when Cuban culture came into vogue. In this photo, Whillie is on the left and is sitting farther away from the camera than Henry, making them appear to be approximately the same height. Whillie's features haven't changed much since the first photo, and his clothing is virtually identical to what he

Darger and William Schloeder/"We're on Our Way"
Photographer unidentified
Chicago
Mid-twentieth century
Paper photograph
8 x 10"
Collection American Folk Art Museum, New York
Gift of Kiyoko Lerner; photo by Gavin Ashworth

In the early years of their relationship, Henry and William Schloeder, whom Henry often referred to as "Whillie," had their portrait taken at the Coultry Studio at Riverview Amusement Park. The two met in 1911 and developed a relationship that continued until 1959, when Whillie died.

arger and William Schloeder/"Off to Frisco"
hotographer unidentified
hicago
Mid-twentieth century
aper photograph
3/8 x 3 1/2"
ollection American Folk Art Museum, New York
ift of Kiyoko Lerner; photo by Gavin Ashworth

Darger and William Schloeder/"On Our Way to Cuba"
Photographer unidentified
Chicago
Mid-twentieth century
Paper photograph
5 3/8 x 3 1/2"
Collection American Folk Art Museum, New York
Gift of Kiyoko Lerner; photo by Gavin Ashworth

wore in the first photo. Henry wears similar attire this time around, too, although his tie is a light color in this one and he's wearing a much flatter newsboy's cap of a dark color. His features have changed over the years. He's put on weight, and it shows in his face.

"We're Off to Frisco" is the caption on the third photograph, which was probably taken in the late 1920s or early '30s. Henry seems much more relaxed than he was in the first photo. He's wearing a straw boating hat, popular at the time, and a dark suit, dark shirt, and light tie. He has a mustache, which he will have the rest of his life, and it makes the difference in their ages less noticeable. Perhaps that's why he decided to grow it in the first place. All in all, Henry looks quite dapper. Whillie wears a black fedora and black suit coat, with a white shirt and a tie of a light color. The difference in their heights is obvious.

The caption is very revealing, the reference to San Francisco suggesting Henry and Whillie's involvement in Chicago's queer subculture. From at least the dawn of the 1900s and perhaps earlier, queer men in Chicago considered San Francisco, Hollywood, and indeed all of California a mecca of gay life, as interviews with many of them that were taken by graduate students in sociology at the University of Chicago from approximately 1900 to the mid-1930s reveal. One anonymous young gay man who called himself "Charles" claimed during his interview, "I determined to go to California where gay people were more accepted," while "David" told the graduate students, "I was going to California because I'd heard that there were many queer people there." The young men had heard correctly. By the early 1900s, San Francisco included gay bars among its many resorts, and in 1908, the Dash opened its doors for business, catering to queer men. Behind its walls, "female impersonators entertained customers, and homosexual sex could be purchased in booths for a dollar."

The photographs of Henry and Whillie were among Henry's most prized possessions, and the tiny holes in their corners show that he tacked them to his walls, making their happy times together something he could be reminded of frequently. In this, he and Whillie were no different than many gay couples of the nineteenth and twentieth century who often had their portraits taken together to signify their relationships in the same way that heterosexual couples did, as David Deitcher has revealed in his *Dear Friends: American Photographs of Men Together, 1840–1918*. In their portraits, Henry and Whillie's relationship is an open secret, frozen in time by the click of a camera, a loud flash, and a thick plume of smoke rising toward heaven.

PART II

ONE MAN'S ART

CHAPTER 5

I CAN'T BE AT ALL LEFT OUT

YOURS TRULY THE AUTHOR

ALTHOUGH HE WAS WORKING FULL-TIME AT ST. JOSEPH'S Hospital and dating Whillie whenever he had time off, Henry was also at work writing his first novel, to which he gave a nineteenth-century-styled title: *The Story of the Vivian Girls, in What Is Known as the Realms of the Unreal, of the Glandeco-Angelinian War Storm, Caused by the Child Slave Rebellion.* As Michael Bonesteel, who edited a selection of Henry's writings and paintings, recognized, page after page of *The Realms,* as its title may be shortened, are filled with long, rambling descriptions of battles between good Angelinian and evil Glandelinian forces "in encyclopedic detail, ushering in dozens of main characters, and recounting countless adventures. There is really no plot that moves toward a climax and then a resolution, but a succession of battles, ripping yarns, talking interludes, descriptions of cataclysms, ad infinitum."

In the opening pages of *The Realms*, Henry offered a summary of what will transpire in the next 15,000-plus pages:

> This description of the great war, and its following results, is perhaps the greatest ever written by an author, on the line of any fabulous war that could ever be entitled with such a name. The war lasted about four years and seven months in this story, and the author of this book has taken over eleven years in writing out the long and graphic details, and has fought on from day to day in order to win for the Christians' side this long and bloody war, and though the Christians had been threatened with defeat, on account of a strange Aronburg Mystery which cold not be solved by any one, not even myself, they finally won when they turned the tide against the enemy at the rightful battle of Aronburgs Run.

In *The Realms*, the heathen forces of the nation of Glandelinia overran the Christian nation Angelinia and kidnapped, then enslaved, Angelinian children. Henry calculated that, "for forty years" or so, "millions of children alone had been carried off" by the Glandelinians, and during that period, they "had lain bound and bleeding in these Glandelinian child slave prisons of horror; imploring for help from bondage seemingly in vain." The Glandelinians forced the child slaves to work naked and routinely crucified, strangled, and eviscerated them. While in captivity, they were also "tortured by flogging, suspensions, pouring boiling tar or water over their heads, suffocation, strangulation, amputation of their fingers, burning with hot irons, temporarily crucifying them." Some were used "for wicked purposes"—sexually—by the soldiers. After their usefulness as slave laborers was over, some of the "girls" became sex slaves for civilian Glandelinians, "sold to factories of ill fame."

Much of Henry's description of the child slaves' fate can be traced back to what he witnessed and experienced while living at the Asylum. The child slaves suffered "flogging," "boiling . . . water,"

"strangulation," and "amputation"—all of which were described in
the Special Investigating Committee's report on the Asylum. In the
novel, "the Glandelinians decided to throw" some of the Abbieannian
child slaves "into a tank of hot water . . . . Screaming frantically, they
furiously tried to get out of the tank of hot water, but the sides were
so high that they could not. Their sufferings were horrible, and . . .
the children died"—a scene that clearly recalls the tragic fate of Minnie Steritz. It's unlikely Henry actually saw her, but it's very probable
that he'd heard about her torturous death.

While in the Asylum, Henry had harbored fantasies about leading the "bright boys" in a rebellion against Dr. Hardt's evil forces, the
Asylum staff who strangled and beat the children and the men and
older boys who sexually abused them. The Asylum's caregivers were
the prototypes for Henry's Glandelinians. However, instead of depicting himself in his novel as the leader of the rebellion against the evil
Glandelinians, Henry created the Vivian girls, seven young sisters, and
their brother, Penrod, who come to the child slaves' rescue by engaging themselves as spies for the rebellion, devising military strategy
with the good Angelinians, and even occasionally joining with them
in battle.

Henry metamorphosed his commitment to the Asylum into
Angelinian children being stolen away by Glandelinians. His work at
the State Farm became children forced into slave labor. His escape
from the Asylum transformed into children rebelling against the evil
adults who'd enslaved them in the first place. He easily altered the
various abuses that he experienced—especially those at the Asylum
and its farm, but also at the Mission, Dunning, and the thoroughfares
of West Madison Street—into children being crucified, eviscerated, or
otherwise tortured. Ultimately, Henry converted nearly every struggle
he faced, from the time he was almost kidnapped by the "skidrow
bum" when he was playing on Adams Street to his escape from the
Asylum, into a battle of good against evil.

Henry also wrote a number of people he knew into the novel.

He depicted those who had been good to him, including Whillie, as members of the Christian Angelinians. In turn, he assigned those who were unkind or who had betrayed him roles among the evil Glandelinians.

Henry never forgave Phelan for his betrayal and held a grudge against him to "the bitter end." To get even with him, Henry wrote him into the novel, put him in the uniform of an especially blood-thirsty Glandelinian general, and depicted him as "monstrously evil." He called "General Phelan an Angelinian traitor," adding that he was "one of the worst men" of the Glandelinian army. In fact, in one of Henry's more graphic scenes, he pictured Phelan as a child murderer: "The brute seized her by the hair which was loose and flourishing a razor about her face . . . instantly began to choke her, tearing her nightie to tatters, then with one determined sweep of his muscular arm he nearly severed her chest open with his razor." When he drew the novel to a close some three decades after he first met Phelan, Henry killed him off—not without considerable satisfaction.

John Manley, who had been such a problem for Henry at the Mission, "was to play a powerful role" in *The Realms*. With two other men, he commanded the child-enslaving Glandelinians, and his role included being an "enemy of God" and "abuser of Our Lord," the worst roles Henry could assign to a character in *The Realms*. Because he blamed Mrs. Gannon, the Mission's matron, for being exiled to the Asylum—

If I had known at the time of the cause of me being sent to that Childrens nut house I surely would have never forgiven those at the Mercy of Our Lady Home and would have revenged it the very first chance I had. I a feeble minded kid. I knew more than the whole she-bang in that place.

I believe Mrs Gannon was really responsible.

—Henry depicted her son James in the novel's pages as a despicable Glandelinian king. Being completely aware of the ambiguity of human nature, he depicted a few characters, especially Whillie and himself, as both Glandelinians and Angelinians, as both bad and good.

Henry didn't stop at borrowing people from his past to serve as characters in *The Realms*. He also appropriated texts written by others into his novel without identifying their sources. In 1870, J. G. Wood wrote the following description of a brief encounter with a beautiful Hawaiian woman:

> I met just such a specimen as has often driven men mad, and whose possession has many a time paved the way to the subversion of empire on the part of monarchs.
>
> She was rather above the medium size of American women. Her finely chiseled chin, nose, and forehead were singularly Grecian. Her beautifully moulded neck and shoulders looked as though they might have been borrowed from Juno. The development of her entire form was as perfect as nature could make it. She was arrayed in a single loose robe, beneath which a pretty little nude foot was just peeping out. Her hair and eyebrows were as glossy as a raven's wing. Around her head was carelessly twined a wreath of the beautiful native ohelo flowers. Her lips seemed fragrant with the odor of countless and untiring kisses.
>
> Her complexion was very much fairer than the fairest of her country-women, and I was forced into the conclusion that she was the offshoot of some white father who had trampled on the seventh precept in the Decalogue, or taken to his embrace, by the marriage relation, some good-looking Hawaiian woman.
>
> But her eyes! I shall never forget those eyes! They retained something that spoke of an affection so deep, a spiritual existence so intense, a dreamy enchantment so inexpressibly beautiful, that they reminded one of the beautiful Greek girl Myrrha, in Byron's tragedy of 'Sardanapalus,' whose love clung to the old monarch when the flame of the funeral pile formed their winding-sheet.
>
> In no former period of my life had I ever raised my hat in the pres-

ence of beauty, but at this moment, and in such a presence, I took it off. I was entirely fascinated, charmed, spell-bound now. I stopped my horse; and there I sat, to take a fuller glance at the fair reality. And the girl stopped, and returned the glance, while a smile parted her lips, and partially revealed a set of teeth as white as snow, and of matchless perfection. I felt that smile to be an unsafe atmosphere for the nerves of a bachelor; so I bowed, replaced my hat, and passed on my way, feeling full assured that nothing but the chisel of Praxiteles could have copied her exquisite charms. And as I gently moved past her, she exclaimed, in the vocabulary of her country, 'Love to you!'

Henry doctored Wood's text to refer to a creature, a species called "Blengiglomenean serpents," or Blengins for short, that he invented for *The Realms*:

I met just such a specimen as has often driven men mad, and whose possession has many a time paved the way to the subversion of empire on the part of the Abbieannian monarchs. The Dortherean was rather above the medium size of the other kind of human headed Blengins. Her finely chiseled chin, nose, and forehead were singularly Grecian. Her beautifully moulded neck and shoulders and arms looked as though they might have been borrowed from Juno. The development of her entire form was as perfect as nature could make it. She was arrayed in the most beautiful wings ever seen on any Blengiglomenean creature, striped in the beautiful parts, and strewn with myriads of flowers in the form of pansies, roses, carnations and other kinds the artists have ever known. The hair and eyebrows of her beautiful girlish head were as glassy as shining gold. I was even surprised to see that around her head was carefully twined a wreath of the beautiful native flowers of those singular islands. Her lips seemed fragrant with the odor of her saliva. But her eyes. I never shall forget those lovely eyes. They retained something that spoke of affection so deep, a spiritual existence so intense, a dreamy enchantment so inexpressibly beautiful, that they reminded one of the beautiful Greek girl Myrrha, in Byron's tragedy of Sardanapalus, whose love clung to the old Monarch when the flame of the funeral pile formed their winding sheet. In no former period of my life had I ever raised my hat to beauty, but at this moment, in such a presence, I took it off. I was entirely fascinated, charmed, spell bound now. I stopped my horse and there I sat, to take a further glance at the fair reality. Half human being, half dragon. As the creature stopped, and I returned the glance while a sweet smile parted her lips, and partially revealed a set of teeth and two sharp pointed fangs as white as snow and of matchless perfection. I felt that smile to be an unsafe atmosphere for the nerves of an old bachelor like I was, so I bowed, replaced my hat, and passed on my way, feeling full assured that nothing but the chisel of Praxiteles could have copied her exquisite charms. And as I gently moved past her she exclaimed in the vocabulary of her one voice, 'Love and protection to you!'

When he changed "Love to you!" in Wood's text to "Love and protection to you" in his own, Henry underscored the chief attribute of the Blengins, feeling sympathy for suffering children:

> Children to the Blengiglomenean serpents seem to be beings more prettier than flowers, no matter whether the child is good looking or not. To see a child crying makes a Blengiglomenean serpent cry, to see a child injured by a Glandelinian seems to make a hell enter a Blengiglomenean serpent, and to see a child happy makes the creature work hard to increase the happiness of that child.

Blengins are what Henry thought adults should be but aren't. They also act the way Henry believed God and Christ should have acted in his life but didn't. Ultimately, they serve as instruments of retribution when, in a scene in *The Realms*, they slaughter Glandelinian soldiers in what can only be described as a bloodbath of revenge.

Also without identifying its source, Henry appropriated a lengthy scene from the writings of Roman Catholic mystic Anne Emmerich, whose disturbing texts revel in the blood and gore of Jesus's last hours on earth. Taking Emmerich's gruesome account of Jesus in the hands of the Romans, Henry "adds the remarkable 'detail' that the nude Jesus becomes sexually aroused" as the soldiers scourge him. Making Jesus's anguish even worse, Henry has Jesus's "tormentors turn his body so that his erect penis is exposed to his mother's gaze." This suggests that Henry may have put Jesus on display in *The Realms* as a sexual predator may have exhibited him in reality.

Henry's fear of fire also found its place in *The Realms*. He was faced with the problem of coming up with a force of mass destruction that he could put in the hands of the evil Glandelinian soldiers. It wasn't by chance that he selected fire. Adopting it for his novel was natural because it had been such a common and devastating force during his childhood. In fact, in one of his most vivid scenes, Henry described the aftermath of a forest fire, which was set by Glandelinians:

Where forests lately stood is a sea of smoulder and gray over whitened ashes. The scene was changed, all was over, but the sea of ashes and smoke is there, the air is shimmering in the heat, and the beautiful forests are no more. In their places are apparently desolated plains of smouldering ashes with a smoking tree standing here or there, or with even no tree visible, nothing to be seen . . . nothing but a great surface of white ashes or gray, smoking and smouldering read . . . . Not even the wild flowers in all their loveliness and beauty can be seen to hide the hideous tragedy of the 'red plague.' Nothing, but miles upon miles of smouldering ashes, as if a world is burned out and dead.

Because the battles between the godly Angelinians and the satanic Glandelinians so often take place in fields and forests, and not typically in urban settings, the fires ravage the countryside. One of Henry's soldiers tells the Vivians, "The enemy are even setting whole woods ablaze to drive back general Vivian's right. . . . Look, you can see the glow." Then the narrator reports,

> "There was also a strange roaring and humming sound which came from the direction of the fiery battle lines, and below in the valleys now a regular sea of fire from burning trees was lighting up the scene plainly, the roaring . . . fire making a sound as if the whole world was in an uproar, and hundreds of thousands of flashes were also seen undulating along the lines of batteries."

Fire as a weapon is essential to Henry's novel, and even takes up most of its fifth and sixth volumes.

To help himself visualize the scenes of fire that he included in his novel, Henry kept a scrapbook, *Pictures of Fires Big or Small in Which Firemen or Persons Lose Their Lives*, that "contains newspaper photographs and descriptions of fires" that had erupted in various cities. He'd clipped the items from different newspapers and magazines, and it served the same purpose as the pictures of children, his "models," did.

I'm an Artist, Been One for Years

As early as 1910, Henry began culling pictures of children, farms and plants, soldiers of both the Civil War and World War I, animals, buildings, locomotives, and other objects from magazines, newspapers, advertising circulars, children's coloring books, and other sources that he would use as models when he began illustrating his novel. Most of Henry's illustrations can't be dated with exactitude, although John MacGregor, who wrote the first critical book on Henry's art, believes he completed one painting, *An Inhuman Fiend Tormenting a Poor Child*, on or around August 13, 1918. Henry glued the painting to a piece of cardboard that had a label with that date on it. The scene it depicts—in which a "hun," a pejorative for German soldiers during World War I, menaces a terrified little girl— would be from that period, supporting MacGregor's assumption. If MacGregor is correct, it confirms that Henry was painting at least some illustrations for his first novel when he was living in the Workingmen's House and that he often painted them as he was writing his novels. At 8½ inches by 11¾ inches, it's small compared to the paintings he would undertake later.

Most of his paintings can be divided into two interrelated groups by their major themes. Those in one group depict battle scenes, with or without the Vivians, as well as portraits of various military men, maps of the battlefields and nearby terrain, and other related illustrations. The second group depicts either a sanctuary during wartime, a place far removed from battle and its evils, or a utopia gained after armistice. In this group, children are free from the threat of Glandelinian soldiers and live in a terrain lush and fecund with flowers that are so tall they stand treelike above the children.

Classifying Henry's paintings according to the process by which he created them is also revealing. The earliest category of Henry's art would then include his collages, the clippings of children and other individuals, including spies, soldiers, and royalty, that he scissored out of *Life*, *Saturday Evening Post*, *National Geographic*, and other sources and then doctored by adding color and, perhaps, facial hair, epaulets, hats, and other items before he glued them to cardboard. Henry sometimes also added lengthy captions to the portraits with information about the individual depicted, some of whom were the novel's most important characters, including the seven rebellious Vivian sisters. A large number became, under Henry's touch-ups, the generals on both sides of the Glandeco-Angelinian War. Interestingly, he painted Francis Viviana and General Nero romantically intwined in one another's arms.

Henry also depicted as adults some of the boys he'd once known at the Mission or the Asylum, including John Manley, John Johnson, and Donald Aurand. Donald, whose last name Henry changed to Aurandoco, was one of Henry's special friends at the Asylum. John E. Johnson, another of the Asylum boys, became Johnnie Johnston. Similarly, he painted scenes that were anchored in his experiences at the Asylum, but he often didn't bother to identify the experiences in the paintings. In *11. At Norma Catherine. Are captured Again by Glandelinian Calvary*, for example, Henry depicted three children lassoed by cowboys in what appears to be farmland. The scene recalls his own capture by Mr. West, "that farms cowboy," the first time he tried to escape the farm.

When focusing on battles and other cataclysmic events associated with war, Henry used his tried-and-true collage technique to produce illustrations that are so very complex and include so many details that they are extremely dense and overwhelming—unlike the portrait collages. What these lack in technique, such as perspective, they make up for in sheer emotional impact. Many of these illustrations contain images related to the American Civil War, which was still fresh in the minds and imaginations of many, and of World War I, which had already begun in Europe and could be seen brewing on the horizon from the United States. It appears that Henry was experimenting with both types of collage, the one cleanly focused on an individual or two, the other a mass of elements at the same time. Undoubtedly, one process informed the other as Henry worked to perfect his technique.

Henry developed his third type of illustration by combining many different images that he had clipped from sources and arranged together in a manner that gave the illustration perspective. Henry had always been concerned with depth of feeling and intense themes, but now he was also becoming aware of the need for perspective. After arranging all of the disparate pieces of the collages to underscore the illustration's theme and to attempt to suggest perspective, he painted them with his watercolors. These collages, which are larger than his earlier ones, measure up to fifteen inches high and nearly two feet long, paving the way for the very large canvases he would eventually create.

Henry then moved into a transitional phase during which he shifted away from relying solely on collage and to a slightly more complex process that also relied to varying degrees on tracing. Although he didn't abandon collage in this phase, tracing allowed Henry to remove individuals, animals, trees, and various other objects from their original context and place them into the context that the theme of the piece that he was working on dictated. For example, Henry traced the figure of Little Miss Muffet from a child's coloring book onto his canvas. In the original, she is running away from the spider that had frightened her while she was eating. Henry omitted the web, the spider, and the tuffet so that, with his manipulation, she became simply a little girl running with a terrified look on her face. She's no longer the subject of a child's nursery rhyme, but one of the Angelinian children threatened by Glandelinian soldiers who want to enslave her—or worse.

In the last stage of his creativity, Henry relied almost exclusively on tracing supplemented by photographic enlargements of the pictures he'd traced from original sources. He traced a specific image onto paper or took the original that he'd clipped from a source to local pharmacies that, at the time, had the technology to enlarge them to several different sizes. By using the enlarging process, Henry was able to add a variety of perspectives to his work. The enlarged images give viewers the sense that they are close to the object or person, while the images that haven't been enlarged seem to be in the distance. Henry enlarged at least 246 different figures to various sizes, which he then carefully filed away in envelopes that he labeled to identify who the figure was supposed to represent. He often used them over and over again in his illustrations.

Henry's depiction of the Vivian girls reveals more than anything else his ability to solve problems creatively. If he wanted to add one of the Vivian girls to a painting, he selected a drawing of an appropriate model from his collection and traced her form from the original source onto his canvas. If he needed her to be naked—he often depicted the Vivian girls; their brother, Penrod; and the child slaves nude—he simply ignored her clothing as he traced her. Using her outline as a guide, he drew the part of her body that would be covered by her clothing freehand. It's only when Henry depicted his figures nude that he ever actually drew. Otherwise, he traced.

By about 1932, he also began attaching different canvases together—end to end, top to bottom, bottom to top—to create diptychs, triptychs, and larger pieces. While we might assume that he glued together those paintings that shared, perhaps, theme or setting or some other common element, that wasn't always the case. Around this time he also began to paint on the reverse of finished paintings. Because art supplies were expensive, especially for the financially strapped artist, he painted on both sides to save money.

Henry never discussed his view on the painting process, but he did make some comments about it through Penrod, who, like Henry, was an untaught artist. At least once between battles in *The Realms*, Penrod mused on how to draw his sisters, something Henry must have spent hours pondering:

> Penrod after some considerable thoughts believed he could make a sketch of the faces of the Vivian Girls, and also their father's. . . . For about thirty minutes he worked steadily and succeeded on the face of Emperor Vivian [their father], but tore up five or six sketches of the Vivian Girls, that proved very unsatisfactory.

Penrod, Henry continues, is having difficulty capturing the Vivian girls'

> beautiful, queenly, subtile and innocent half frightened look, and a look which was not vanity, slyness, but something more pretty, holy lovable, dignified and important. Often he got the marked aristocratic features

or outlines of the features. . . . Soon to his relief, he observed that he was drawing the likeness to a clearer point but gradually. And it was not long before the features were clear enough to strike him "AS WELL DONE."

Satisfied with the results, Penrod shows his work to the Rattlesnake Boy, one of his compatriots, who responds to them enthusiastically. Rattlesnake Boy tells Penrod that his talent "is surely a great gift from God himself. It is the best gift of all. And it proves that it is absolute rely [really] true that your mind has got good and perfect training. The more you draw, the better you'll be able to draw." Rattlesnake Boy stroked Henry's ego and confirmed for him that his novel wasn't "trash," exactly what someone who'd once been branded as feeble-minded needed.

MARY PICKFORD AND THE PSYCHIC HERMAPHRODITES

Although they're children, the Vivian girls speak like adults; have adult abilities, talents, and intelligence; fight along with and usually better than adults; and command military forces of Angelinians, when necessary, as effectively as any five-star general. They are exceptional marksmen, excellent at swordplay, and brilliant equestrians. Only their ages and their small sizes differentiate them from adults. Angeline Vivian, the nominal leader of the sisters, recites the names and ages of the Vivians: "There's I Violet, Joy, Jennie, Catherine, Hettie Daisy and Penrod. Catherine is seven, Daisy also. Hettie is 8, I am nine, Violet nine and five months, Jennie and Joice ten. Penrod is the size of Violet but is eleven." Penrod is small for his age, as was Henry.

The Vivian sisters and their brother Penrod are the most important characters in *The Realms* and the figures who appear most often on his canvases. They aren't leaders during the war in the strictest sense of the word but rather spies who liberate child slaves and engage in other nefarious activities against the Glandelinians. With "exciting eagerness," the Vivian children

> do their noble daredevil work even when they do not need to. In order to help their generals, they obtain every piece of news and illustration from the sea of conflicts, escape enemy pursuers and save their generals and armies during battles, rescue friends in time of direst peril, and ace disasters during battles of extreme fury.

They're better than leaders. They're heroes. Best of all, the Vivian children never age, unlike their creator and the children for whom he wrote. Henry once complained, "Do you believe it, unlike most children, I hated to see the day come when I will be grown up. I never wanted to. I wished to be young always. I am grown up now and an old lame man, darn it." Yet, in a psychological sense, Henry never really grew up much, either, thanks to the powerful cocktail of childhood trauma and Catholic dogma.

The Vivians, including Penrod, are little more than pint-sized adults in word and act, but they aren't at all unique to Henry's art. Adultlike children were ubiquitous in American popular culture at the time and are exemplified in the roles of silent-screen actor Mary Pickford, among the most famous and beloved of all of the silent era's stars.

Pickford was born April 8, 1892, four days before Henry, and by the time he had escaped the Asylum and returned to Chicago, Pickford was well on her way to becoming "America's Sweetheart," as she would be nicknamed. By 1911, when Henry began the second version of *The Realms* (after Phelan had destroyed the first one), she had made nearly seventy films. Henry used a scene from one of Pickford's most popular movies, *Little Annie Rooney* (1925), in which Annie/Pickford is "peeking out from the inside of a sewer pipe," as a model for his illustration *At Jennie Ritchie. 2 of Story to Evans. They attempt to get away by rolling themselves in floor rugs.* In it, Henry paints all of the Vivian girls peeking out of carpets in which they've rolled themselves to escape a battalion of Glandelinians. He had probably seen *Little Annie Rooney* at the College Theatre, which ran all of Pickford's blockbusters. It was near the corner of Sheffield and Webster, a few blocks from his room and across the street from St. Vincent's Church.

Pickford "portrayed girls who were strong-minded and vigorous rather than silly and delicate," but "her masquerade of childishness undercut her potential for sexual subjectivity. It did not, however, undercut her potential to be a sexual object." As her fan base grew in the 1910s and '20s, she "appealed to and through a kind of cultural pedophilia that looked to the innocent child-woman to personify nostalgic ideals of femininity," as film scholar Gaylyn Studlar has revealed in her study of Pickford's place in early cinema. Consequently, Studlar continues,

> male fantasies were easily attached to her. She represented a dangerously attractive female whose masquerade of childishness appealed to adult men raised in the late Victorian period. Those men might find her enticing innocence a comforting alternative to the models of feminine sexual subjectivity offered by the flapper and the New Woman. On the other hand, Pickford's many child-woman heroines also could serve an identificatory function for women and girls who might read her as a comforting 'asexual' figure of freedom whose youth released her from the demands—including the sexual demands—of adult femininity.

In homage to Pickford, Henry named a site, Mary Pickford Junction, after her, and one of his alter egos, General Henry Darger, won a decisive battle against the Glandelinians there. More important, Henry created the rebellious, forceful Vivian girls with Mary Pickford's "child-woman" characters in mind, although he didn't realize the subtext of Pickford's roles, the "cultural pedophilia" that orbited her portrayal of the "child-woman."

Despite alluding to and appropriating the culture around him, Henry also gave the Vivian girls a characteristic that they share with a large number of the other girls on his canvases. When he depicted them naked, it's obvious that the Vivian girls aren't *girls* at all but hermaphrodites. Having the figures and the hairdos of girls (as traced from the models he'd accrued over the years), they also have penises, which he drew onto their bodies freehand. For Henry, they represent the psychic hermaphrodites that he, and many around him, associated with belles, fairies, pansies, queens, and queers. Sexologists of the time would have catalogued them as physical representations of the concept of "'*anima muliebris in corpore virili inclusa*'—a female soul enclosed in a male body."

A number of queer men in the earliest days of the twentieth century identified themselves as psychic hermaphrodites. In fact, for centuries, the figure of the hermaphrodite has played an important role in art, from *The Sleeping Hermaphrodite* (c. 200 B.C.) to Czanara's (i.e., Raymond Carrance's) drawing *The Hermaphrodite-Angel of Peladan* (c. 1960s–'70s) and beyond. In the preface to his autobiography, *The Story of a Life*, which was published in 1901, Claude Hartland prepared his readers for the truth of his life:

> In the following chapters, appears the history of a being who has the beard and the well-developed sexual organs of a man, who is, from almost every other point of view, a woman.
>
> He has the delicate, refined tastes of a woman, and what is worse, her sexual desires for men.

In his *Autobiography of an Androgyne*, Ralph Werther wrote in 1900 that "the fact that I was a boy—or rather that my body was that of a boy, because in mind I was thoroughly a girl—occasioned me an immense amount of regret and chagrin": "God has created . . . the woman with masculine genitals."

During the nineteenth century, gay men began theorizing about themselves, analyzing why they were men who were sexually attracted to other men and not to women, and some developed the belief that they were "a female soul enclosed in a male body," adopting the hermaphrodite—a physical emblem of the psychological combination of male and female—as a symbol for themselves in art and literature. This is not something that was typically known outside of the gay community at the time, and the few sexologists of the period who investigated it in their works—such as Karl Ulrichs, Richard von Krafft-Ebing, and Havelock Ellis—were closely associated with the gay subculture.

When Henry uses the phrase "Vivian Girls," it's not *girls* that he's actually thinking about but Vivian belles, fairies, pansies, queers, or queens. In fact, in Henry's second novel, which also stars the Vivians, the characters who come in contact with them refer to them as "fairies" more often than not. This allows Henry to give them an otherworldly cast as well as anchor them in a queer context. Such ambiguity has been a mainstay of gay art and literature for centuries, and Henry tapped into that strategy and made it his own.

When he depicted the Vivian *girls*, Henry was actually creating an image of homosexual boys running from adult men, leading troops against enemy battalions, and undertaking spy missions against the Glandelinians. If we're to understand Henry's vision as a novelist and as artist clearly and completely, we can't ever think "girls" when he writes or depicts the "Vivian girls." Instead, we have to substitute "girl-boys," "gay boys," or "imitation little girls"—which was Henry's term—for "girls." They are actually the "Vivian girl-boys." Henry revealed *who* Angeline, Violet, Joy, Jennie, Catherine, Hettie, and Daisy are in his novel, but he disclosed *what* they are in his illustrations for it.

IMITATION LITTLE GIRLS

At the same time that Henry revealed that what appear to be little girls are, in fact, girl-boys, his representation of gay boys, Henry also feminized himself in a variety of ways, both in his first novel and in its source materials. Midway through *The Realms*, Henry included a scene that he borrowed from his childhood, and in it, he depicted himself as "Marie," an adult woman recalling her mother's death when she was a child:

> While she was sitting here her mind went traveling back to her earliest memories. . . . She remembered standing beside the hospital bed on which her wounded and dying mother lay, and the mortally injured mother, gripping her hands fast in her burning ones, was telling her, over and over again, and finishing with—"Never forget how your dear mother and young cousin died Marie. Remember it and never forget." The frightened little girl had sworn, catching her words from her mother's lips. Since then she had remembered the whole thing or it had been engraved upon her memory forever. But it was long before she understood its meaning. Then she remembered her father's cruelty to her, not from pure senses, but that the loss of his wife so tragically had driven him insane and he knew not what he was doing. . . . The sight of her dying mother, and of her father's insanity, had inflicted a wound in the child's soul that never healed. . . . She never pretended to have forgotten as she might have done. She looked back on an early childhood that had because of this been a torture.

Clearly echoing the scene of his mother's deathbed, Henry depicted himself as a "frightened little girl" who had been "inflicted" with "a wound" in her "soul" that had "never healed." He also revealed that he understood why his father had abandoned him over and over: because Rosa's death had "driven" Henry Sr. "insane and he knew not what he was doing" when he threw Henry away. Despite the many times his father abandoned him, Henry, adopting the persona of the mature Marie, was tender and understanding toward his father's grief.

In the penultimate volume of *The Realms*, Henry added another scene that also gives eye-opening information about his father's reaction to Rosa's death. It's a memo written by two of his characters, Detectives Fox and West, and its tone is virtually the opposite of the earlier scene's:

> general Jack Evans himself received this note from a strange mysterious place; "It is requested that your excellency general Jack Evans, will look into the affair of said general Henry J. Darger that worked at St. Joseph's Hospital Abbieannia about seven years ago, whose wife died leaving him two little babies which through his foolish grief he has neglected and left them at your institution. They are as we have found out two little girl children of pretty style, and we advise you to notify the Sister Superior at St. Joseph's Hospital in Pandora, Abbieannia and see to it that he is made to take them back which if he will refuse, and returns them we'll see to his immediate arrest. If you do not know the children he does and you had better see to it that he sends for them, for he can describe them as he has their pictures. We are two detectives who are writing this. We'll give him about two months to recall them or he will go before the court."

Henry depicted himself in the memo as one of the "two little girl children of pretty style" who were his father's daughters. The second "little girl" was his sister, whom he never knew. Although Henry was playing with the facts, giving his father the job he had held, his anger over his father's "insanity" and his "foolish grief" that stemmed from "the loss of his wife" comes through loud and clear. In stark opposition to Marie's recollection, the detectives assert that the father wallowed in his grief and ignored his children, putting their emotional and physical welfare after his own.

Henry also transformed himself in other ways that were just as important to his creative process. Anna had taken Henry to be baptized when he was eight, but he didn't receive his first communion until his first winter at the Workingmen's House, when he decided to receive the sacrament in the chapel in St. Joseph's Hospital. The nuns wouldn't allow it until he showed them proof of his baptism. This would have been canon law and not an ad hoc rule that they created to keep Henry away from them. Either he asked the priest who presided over Mass for the sisters to get the information for him from St. Patrick's Church, or he contacted the offices at St. Patrick's himself. After showing them the proof, he received his first Holy Communion in their chapel during one "cold snowy" midnight Mass in December 1909.

To familiarize himself with Church doctrine before taking communion, Henry carefully copied a Roman Catholic catechism word for word from a published edition into a notebook that has been called his *Reference Ledger*. He wrote an introduction to the catechism that he copied, but he signed it with the name of one of his most important characters, Annie Aronburg, whom he named after his favorite aunt. This is not the only time that Annie had "authored" one of Henry's texts. Two pages into the introduction to the catechism, Annie makes an interesting claim: "I am the full writer of the manuscript as far as it goes of the battles raging with the Glandelinians and the rebels at the child labor places, and will have them published as soon as I can." She, according to Henry, wrote *The Realms*, and like General Viviana, she thinks it's good enough to publish.

Henry continued to use Annie as a persona, a resource, and a guide outside of the novel for decades. After Sister Rose left St. Joseph's in 1917, she and Henry corresponded for a short time. One of the things that makes their correspondence so important is the fact that Henry doctored her letters to him so that it appears that she was not writing to Henry at all but to Annie Aronburg. The original version of one, dated June 19, 1917, begins:

My dear Henry

Both of your letters reached me and I am grateful for your kind thought. I am glad that you are trying to be even a better boy since I left.

Henry's doctored version of her letter became:

My dear Aronburg

Both of your letters reached me and I am grateful for your kind thought. I am glad that you are trying to be even a better girl since I left.

He would also revise other documents, such as his discharge papers from the army, by crossing out specific words and inserting others so that the documents referred to Annie, again metaphorically transforming himself into her.

Others had feminized Henry long before he decided to adopt Annie as a stand-in for himself. As early as the discovery of his self-abuse, his father, the physician Schmidt, and anyone who had access to the Asylum application, in which Henry's self-abuse is mentioned three times in the three-and-a-half-page application—

16. *At what age and in what manner was any peculiarity first manifested?* self abuse for six years;

43. *State any peculiar habits the child may have.* self abuse;

56. *What cause has been assigned for its mental deficiency?* self abuse

—would have considered Henry female. Far into the twentieth century, it was still widely believed that self-abuse led a boy or man to invert his gender and become a fairy.

Just as important, each time Henry became a lamb to a wolf on the dark thoroughfares and the darker alleys of West Madison Street and each time he was sexually assaulted by one of the bigger, stronger boys or men at the institutions in which he lived, he was metaphorically turned into a female. Until late in the twentieth century, society didn't accept the fact that a man or boy could be raped, only a woman or girl could be, because the logic and the law of the time insisted that rape involved only a penis and a vagina. Any male who had been sexually victimized by another male kept it a secret because, if he didn't, he was opening himself up to ridicule of the worse kind. A raped man lost his claim to masculinity and the privileges that accompanied it, and anger over being powerless to guard his masculinity often consumed the male who had been raped.

Like many other survivors of sexual victimization, Henry was devoured by guilt and anger. Yet no one at the time would have recognized, much less acknowledged, any sort of problem that plagued him, or any other boy in Henry's situation. Physicians, social workers, and others might accept male-male rape as traumatic to its victim, but they would have speculated only on the physical trauma that it may have caused, such as rectal lesions, and would never have entertained the notion that the victim had been psychologically traumatized. In that regard, boys were on their own. As it turned out, "given the limited recognition of sexual dangers men posed to boys, and the lack of a sense that boys suffered anything more than physical injury as a result of such assaults," society's "concern" with the rape of "children led to the proviso of additional legal protection from sexual assault" in laws throughout the country, but the new laws were "only for girls."

Elsie Paroubek

Henry also found real little girls, not just pictures or film characterizations of them, on which to model his Vivian girl-boys. Whillie's parents, Michael and Susana, had seven children, but by the time Henry and Whillie began dating in 1911, only five were living: Elizabeth, aged thirty-six; William (called Bill), aged thirty; Henry, aged twenty-eight; Susan, aged twenty-three; and Katherine (or Catherine and sometimes Katheryn), the baby, aged twenty-one. Lucy, who was born in 1875, died between 1900 and 1910. What had happened to the seventh child?

As couples in the earliest days of their relationship typically do, Whillie and Henry would have shared all sorts of intimate details about their childhoods and family life with one another, although it was also likely that it was difficult for Henry to open up about his past because Whillie's life seemed so normal by comparison and because too many people had betrayed Henry too many times for him to reveal sensitive issues easily. Henry would also have been extremely circumspect about his childhood, not wanting Whillie to know about his victimization and the pain and shame that it caused him. Even when he was able to discuss his past, Henry would've been selective about what he revealed, and it probably took Henry a long time before he would mention the death of his mother and the birth and quick adoption of his younger sister. Whillie would have commiserated with the man he loved by revealing the death of his own sister. Born on December 11, 1876, she died before he was old enough to know her, just as Henry had never known his sister, but unlike Henry, Whillie knew his sister's name, Angeline. She was the first of his immediate family to have been buried in St. Boniface Cemetery.

Henry certainly would have liked the name Angeline because of its relationship to "angel," but it also meant a great deal to him personally. When Whillie revealed the loss of his sister, who was seven years older than he, to Henry—and when Henry revealed the loss of his sister, who was four years younger than he, to Whillie— a bond was created between them, one that at least Henry understood. In no time at all, Henry decided to give the leader of the Vivian girl-boys the name Angeline, Whillie's sister's name, to strengthen the bond between them exactly as the Coultry photographs did. He also gave Whillie's sister's name to the Christian nation Angelinia, whose generals fought against the evil Glandelini-ans. Similarly, he named one of the other Vivian girl-boys Catherine after the youngest of Whillie's sisters, Katherine. It's also likely that Henry borrowed the last name Vivian for his heroes from a nun, Sister Mary Vivian, who lived at St. Vincent's Convent, a block and a half from the church. She would've attended St. Vincent's Church, and he would've known her.

The inspiration for another of Henry's heroines came from a little girl he never knew. On Saturday, April 8, 1911, five-year-old Elsie Paroubek, a daughter of Bohemian immigrants, went missing. Her mother had left the little girl sitting on the front porch of their house at 2320 South Albany southwest of the Loop, as she had many times before. At around four, when Mrs. Paroubek checked on Elsie, the fifth of her six children, she discovered that Elsie was gone. Mrs. Paroubek assumed her daughter was visiting one of her playmates, so she didn't give it a second thought. Five hours later, when Mr. Paroubek retuned from work and Elsie was still not home, the Paroubeks reported her missing to the police. The next morning, Captain John Mahoney, commander of the Hinman Street Police Station, set out to find the blond, blue-eyed five-year-old, but the only clues he had to go on were two reports. One revealed that two different bands of gypsies, who had been camped in the area since before April 8, had pulled up stakes and left town around the time of Elsie's disappearance, and the other claimed that Elsie had last been seen following an Italian organ grinder as he made his way through her neighborhood.

The gypsies left their camp on Wednesday, April 12, the day that Elsie's story broke in local newspapers, including the *Chicago Daily News*, the *Chicago Evening Post*, and the *Chicago American*. That day also happened to be Henry's nineteenth birthday. Only the *Chicago American* ran her story on the front page. Its editors knew a blockbuster story when they saw one, so during the next six weeks, a report about the search for Elsie appeared in almost every edition of each day's *Chicago American*. Always eager to make a buck, its publisher was notorious for running the more salacious stories of the day: suicides, murders, rapes, kidnappings, extortions, embezzlements, famines, wars. The more blood and gore—or the more tugging at heartstrings—the better. Elsie's story was only one of hundreds to be splashed across its pages in the spring of 1911, but it was hers that thousands of readers ate up. Henry was among them.

Henry had access to an unlimited number of newspapers and magazines because, then as now, people who spent hours in hospital waiting rooms brought newspapers with them to help pass the time, then left them to those who followed. As a janitor at St. Joseph's, Henry had his pick. He followed Elsie's story in the newspapers and, in fact, saved at least one front-page article about her from the *Chicago Daily News* of May 9, 1911, "Paroubek Girl Slain," for the rest of his life.

Beginning Sunday, April 9, the police threw a dragnet over Chicago and the rest of northern Illinois, as well as across the northern parts of Indiana and Iowa and the southern section of Wisconsin. They and vigilantes—including Frank Paroubek, Elsie's father, and his brother-in-law, Frank Trampota, as well as friends, neighbors, and others interested in helping to find Elsie—routinely swept through the four-state area, tracking down and then raiding gypsy camps, wielding guns and other weapons, and terrorizing innocent men, women, and children. Nothing came of their efforts.

At the same time, detectives invaded the nearby Italian neighborhood centered around West Fourteenth and South Halsted Streets, to search every house for the organ grinder. Police eventually identified him as Tony Mangela, whom they finally found and arrested. While Mangela was in custody, police searched his apartment and questioned his three children who were there at the time. After hours of interrogating him, they decided Mangela was innocent and released him. Like the vigilantes who raided gypsy camps, they had come up empty-handed.

It wasn't long before others, wanting to help find the five-year-old, threw their hats into the ring. First, Elsie's six-year-old brother, Frank, offered to begin a search on his own. "I know I can find my sister," he told a reporter. "Some people are afraid of a policeman, and they would not tell him. But they would tell me." Four days later, twenty Bohemian businessmen agreed to devote their spare time to help in the search for Elsie. Not to be outdone by men, rich Bohemian women, members of Club Bohemia, the strongest Bohemian organization in the United States, offered money and the use of their cars to police to help find the girl. Then a group of five other women, all wives of wealthy Bohemian politicos, formed the Ladies' Auxiliary to help the police in their efforts. Carter Harrison Jr., mayor of Chicago, and Charles S. Deneen, the governor of Illinois, sponsored rewards leading to Elsie's discovery. The superintendent of Chicago's public school system, Ella Flagg Young, asked all of its 213,000 students to search for Elsie during their spring break, the second week of May:

> I want to ask the children to get up neighborhood searches. I believe they can greatly assist the police in this search. This is an admirable opportunity for the children. . . . Somehow I am sure little Elsie has not been taken out of Chicago. . . . I hope that every boy and girl will aid in this search.

Even convicted kidnapper William Birmingham, who claimed to have lived with gypsies and to know their ways, offered to help police from his cell in Joliet State Prison. He spoke with gypsy king Elijah George to extract Elsie's whereabouts from him, hoping that his effort would help to get his life sentence reduced. As it turned out, he discovered nothing at all about Elsie from George, and not a second was shaved off his life sentence.

The one volunteer in the search for Elsie Paroubek who most caught the public's attention—and Henry's imagination—wasn't a relative, a political figure, a wealthy person, or even an adult. Two weeks after Elsie's disappearance, eleven-year-old Lillian Wulff, who had been kidnapped by gypsies from her home at 3951 Armour Avenue on Saturday, December 7, 1907, and was then found alive, safe, and returned to her parents exactly one week later, told reporters that she was joining the search for Elsie because "detectives, police, sheriffs and even Governors"—all adults—"have failed." At the same time, "baffled at every point in the search," the reporter claimed, "the police authorities" were "ready to accept even the leadership of a child." The truth was that the authorities weren't at all interested in following the eleven-year-old, but that didn't stop the newspapers from pushing little Lillian into the spotlight as often as they could to sell papers.

"I am ready," she claimed from their pages:

> to lead a rescue party. I believe I could help a lot. I would advise the police to send circulars all around Chicago. That was what saved me. I understand that little Elsie never had her picture taken. Well, send descriptions to farm houses and country stores and post offices.
>
> You see, these people only take us little girls to beg for them. And they never like to have more than one little girl at a time because two little girls eat more than one, you see. Therefore, they should look for one of these closed canvas wagons that has only one little girl with it.
>
> She'll be afraid and crying, you can bet. If she doesn't get enough bacon and eggs for them at the farm houses they'll whip her. I know. They whipped me with a horsewhip.
>
> These country people should ask every strange little girl along the road: 'Are you Elsie?' then she'll begin to cry for her mamma and they'll know for sure it's her.

In a later edition on that same day, the *Chicago American* included more of Lillian's take on the situation. "Unless Elsie Paroubek is rescued in the next few days she will be killed and her body disposed of where it will never be found if she had fallen into the hands of gypsies," she said. Then she added a very personal note:

I am afraid, oh, so terribly afraid. I know the gypsies. I know how cruel they are to children, and they're cowards, too. That makes them commit murder or do any other crime if they think it will keep them from being captured and put in prison for kidnapping. I hate the sight of a gypsy, and even the sight of one of their covered wagons makes me want to scream, but I will lead the detectives to the camps if the police think I can help them any.

Eleven years old—Penrod's age—at the time of Elsie's disappearance, Lillian became yet another important model on which Henry based the Vivian girl-boys. Nothing had fired Henry's imagination as much as Lillian's moxie.

Lillian spoke with the same authority and type of language that we would typically associate with an adult—and a confident, powerful one at that. She also sounded like any one of Mary Pickford's characters. By the time newspapers were including Lillian's pronouncements in its pages, Henry had only been at work on the second version of *The Realms* for a little over a year. Already relying on Pickford's characters, Henry simply adopted Lillian's take-charge attitude for the little heroes, letting her bravado guide him in the choice of words he would put into their mouths and the poses in which he would paint them.

At approximately three p.m. on Monday, May 8, exactly a month to the day after she went missing, power plant employees found Elsie's body floating on the surface of the Illinois and Michigan Canal, a drainage ditch that was a mere seven blocks from her home. The reports that began surfacing immediately were at best contradictory. That day, Drs. E. A. Kingston and W. R. Paddock performed an autopsy on Elsie, and they determined that "death was due to drowning. There are no marks of violence other than would have been made by striking objects in the water." Then, later that same day, a second report from Kingston and Paddock appeared and contradicted the first. According to it, Elsie had suffered while in the hands of her kidnappers and evidence indicated that she was murdered, not accidentally drowned. Her lungs had no water in them, there were finger marks on her throat that indicated strangulation, and there was a mark near her temple where she had been struck. Amid the confusion, the Chicago police ordered a second autopsy, this one conducted by Drs. Warren Hunter and E. R. LeCount. They concluded that Elsie had been held captive for two weeks before being killed and that, during that time, she had been "attacked" by her kidnappers, a euphemism in use then to indicate rape.

Elsie's funeral was held at her home the morning of Thursday, May 11. Not only did relatives and friends show up to pay their last respects, but as many as five thousand sympathizers and gawkers crowded the street in front of the Paroubek house. In a tableau that caught Henry's attention, Elsie's six playmates were dressed in white with white flowers in their hair to attend Elsie's coffin. She and her friends were seven in number, the same as the Vivian girl-boys, and they ranged in age from six to ten—almost the exact range of the age of the Vivians. Two of Elsie's friends, Minnie Karel and Nellie Vetsnik, were nine years old, as were Henry's Angeline and Violet. The mystery of Elsie Paroubek's murder was never solved, but Henry was busy incorporating elements from the tragedy-laden case into his novel and responding to it in his life.

THE GEMINI

Henry understood Elsie's fear, her wanting to be back with her family, and what it meant to be raped and strangled. She became an emblem to him of his own abuse. They had suffered similarly, although Henry had escaped his abuse with his life. Henry knew that he hadn't been the only child in West Madison Street, the Mission, or the Asylum to experience sexual abuse and that all had been just as helpless to defend themselves as he had, but Elsie's story affected him intensely, exaggerating his own sense of guilt and shame. He began to think about ways he could protect children when he remembered something his uncles had told him about, the Masons, a secret society to which they belonged. That gave Henry an idea.

Henry began his own secret society called the Gemini, and he and Whillie led it as copresidents. He created a series of rites and ceremonies and even a certificate of membership to make the Gemini as official as other secret societies. In one of the documents that he created and later incorporated into *The Realms*, Henry claimed that someone named Thomas A. Newsome was one of the founders of the Gemini and that a number of other boys and men—"Vynne Marshall, Aldrich Bond, Henry Rich Littleton, Butler Noble Martindale, Simeon Binckney Woodring, Henry Walker Yeamann, Gerard Chambers, Johnstonia Fox"—had joined. None of these individuals appear in the census records or the city directories for the time in which the Gemini existed, suggesting the membership roll is a list of fictitious names, characters like those in his novel. To top it all off, Gemini members even created an altar, the centerpiece of their ritual-based meetings.

In March 1911, the Gemini convened for the first time in the Schloeders' barn that bordered the alley behind their house. They called the barn a "mimic chapel" and set about making it "neat and clean no matter how much work" it took them. They also constructed a "mimic altar" and began purchasing "material of all sorts" with which they would decorate it. "Chapel" and "altar" underscore the seriousness of their organization and add a decidedly religious overtone to it, a staple of all secret societies of the time. "Mimic" discloses that Henry and Whillie knew the chapel and altar weren't real, i.e., hadn't been consecrated by the Church.

Henry wasn't at all unique in creating a secret society, or club, as most would have called it. Many young men around his age and younger had been doing the same thing in Chicago since at least the end of the Civil War and perhaps earlier. Although some were decidedly gang-like in their focus, stealing from others and taking part in other illegal activities, many were simply the nexus of a group of friends who spent time together. All were, according to their members, *secret*, which added to the allure of them, making them and their members special.

Henry called his club the Gemini more often than not, but he also used at least two other names for it: the Black Brothers Lodge and the Child Protective Society. The Black Brothers Lodge recalls the Black Hand, which many consider a forerunner of the mafia, suggesting hidden agendas and lawlessness, but the Child Protective Society echoes the name of a real social agency in Chicago, the Juvenile Protective Association, which Henry knew about from his years in West Madison Street. In May, he put a photograph of Elsie that had been published in the *Chicago Daily News* on the altar to underscore the secret society's chief mission: to protect children.

The Gemini wasn't just a club for Henry and his friends; it also appears in *The Realms*, its members, especially Henry and Whillie, fighting side by side with the Vivian girl-boys and their brother, Penrod, against the Glandelinians. The Gemini was a force to be reckoned with in the novel, and Henry included its constitution, as well as its by-laws, in the novel's last volume. The Gemini are the "most dangerous persons" and are "spies and great thinkers," a "powerful society," and its rituals equal in drama to any the Masons had. One of its more important rituals began when

the Supreme Person with Solemn formality notified the other persons that on the following night a meeting will be held in the darkness of the Chamber. No details was necessary to convey the purpose of the main gathering.

A few minutes before the time set for the Destiny meeting, as the final Convention of the Chamber had come to be called, 11:30 o'clock, the Supreme Person entered the chamber. For a long time he is alone. . . . From the vault he took the Constitution and the laws of the Geminii and the Black Sack of Destiny. These he placed on a long black table which stood at the side of the first chair. After donning his official regalia, a long black robe with hood attached, he turned off the gas, and lighted a stub of candle, which he placed on the table. Precisely at 11 o'clock he opened the door leading to the room of rest, and standing on the Threshold in the full and Solemn dignity of his office, spoke in subdued tones, slowly and impressively:

Persons of the Geminii, it is the command of the Supreme Person that ye enter into the Chamber. There ye shall know more.

In a letter purportedly written by Thomas Newsome to Henry—but actually created, written, and signed by Henry in Newsome's name— Henry used arcane words and ornate language typically associated with secret societies to describe, in a somewhat disguised version, his experiences immediately after escaping the Asylum. As with similar texts based on his life, Henry fictionalized portions to suit his purpose:

For eight years from the last day of the Influence of the Sign of the Gemini of the Zodiac in the year 1919, ye have been absence from Lincoln Ill and at within that period had ye communicated by letter or telegraph with members of your Lincoln friends, or with anybody else of blood relationship. The first three months of the first year of your absence had been spent as a tramp.

When the period had begun ye had on your person not exceeding fifty cents or one dollar, as it was the will of the Supreme Person, Whom ye love, that ye earn your way and Sustenance.

After being a tramp for three months ye went to work in what capacity ye may elect, so long as ye defended solely up on the influence and fruits of your own ability. Within three months after ye had gone to farm work, ye had placed your feet on Hospital floors.

At all times thereafter ye had nothing more than that which ye have earned by your own hand and mind.

This document reveals that Henry/Newsome loved "the Supreme Person," who would have been either Henry himself, who was the main

Supreme Person, or more appropriately the "Assistant Supreme Person," who was Whillie.

In the document, Henry first wrote "1909" in the introductory phrase of the first sentence, but then to fictionalize his life, he stuck out the "0" and added a "1" over it to make the date "1919." Eight years before 1909 would roughly correspond with the date Anna took Henry to the Mission of Our Lady of Mercy. The document ends when Henry began working at St. Joseph's Hospital. Interestingly, Henry-as-Newsome seems to berate himself for not keeping in touch with his friends at the Asylum or his aunts and uncles.

The club's name, the Gemini, also reveals something about the relationship between Henry and Whillie, perhaps the only two members who actually existed. A constellation, Gemini had been important to queer men for centuries before Henry founded his club. In Greek mythology, Castor and Pollux were twins who had the same mother, Leda, but different fathers. Castor was the human king Tyndareus's son and therefore mortal. Pollux was the god Zeus's son and, like his father, immortal. When Castor was killed during a fight, Pollux was so overcome by grief that he begged the gods to let him share his immortality with Castor, and Zeus agreed, assigning them a place in the heavens, together forever. For queer men, the two young men, who are typically depicted in art as very handsome and nude, became the emblem of love shared eternally by two men. To nonqueers, the word "Gemini" would acknowledge the dual male leadership of the group, but queers would also have understood the eternal love that its two leaders shared.

Although *The Realms* is a metaphoric recounting of important episodes in his life, Henry was careful to cast all of his characters, especially himself, within a fictionalized framework. "Henry Darger" and the many other characters to whom he gave versions of his name (Captain Henry Darger, Hendro Dargar, Attorney General Darger, General Henry Darger Monterey, et al.) was not the Henry Darger who was born April 12, 1892. All were born after August 1909.

Henry, or rather a version of him, appears in the novel more than any other real person, closely followed by Whillie. Henry was linking himself to Whillie by including them both as heroes, and often as companions to each other.

Henry introduced Whillie to his readers early in the novel:

> "His friend's name is William Schloder. The two are regular hawks. They are the head presidents of the children's protective society—called the Gemini—a lodge of men congregated who are terrible enemies of all those who prove themselves child haters. They are both supreme heads of the Protective Society, and would bring the whole bunch down here to get the Glandelinians. . . . I have a picture of them both," and he produced a picture of two tall men, not handsome in looks or appearance, but nevertheless with a grim determination upon their faces.

The picture that the narrator refers to is probably the first of the three photos taken at the Coultry Studio and captioned "We're on Our Way."

Midway through *The Realms*, Henry's narrator describes Whillie:

> One of the members of the Gemini who came into the headquarters tent of Violet and her sisters to congratulate them, was the Assistant Supreme Person, Whilliam Schloder, the finest most successful secret service agent of the christian armies.
>
> . . .
>
> One of the things that had drawn them or him to them was his exceeding kindness and brotherliness to everyone that he knew and to those of the members who were under him. They loved to work for him, he loved to look out for their interest and direct them carefully in their missions. It had struck Violet and her sisters that his attitude tward those working under him was Christ like.

Henry even depicted a version of himself serving on the side of evil, as a Glandelinian officer. Evil Henry is eager to destroy the novel's chief protagonists, the Vivian girl-boys, and his commanding officer sends him to do exactly that:

> "Take a squad of men out and make a search for them. When you discover them, lure them in ambush and kill them. To prove of your success, bring their foul little bodies to me."
>
> "I'll do so your excellency," said Darger. "I hate them worse than the most dreaded disease, and I lust in their killing. If I succeed in getting them, I'll tear their bodies open alive."

Henry doesn't just present people and autobiographical tidbits from his past in the novel; he often stretches the truth, even mangling it as he does in this description of one of his alter egos, Captain Henry Darger, who is also one of the novel's heroes:

> A young man of sturdy built was on his way tward a three story house in the region of St. Joseph's Hospital on Garfield Avenue. He was alone in a uniform, the olive drab uniform of a soldier of the United States, but he wore the garb of a captain. He was a stern looking man, with a think brown beard, brownish complexion, herculean built, and tall enough to embrace six feet.

Henry was anything but "herculean" in build and was nearly a foot short of "six feet" tall, but that's not the point. Heroes can't be short, slim men in the type of novel Henry wrote. He worked within the rules of the genre he had selected for telling his story. In contrast to his depictions of real persons, Henry rarely altered the real places— "St. Joseph's Hospital," "Garfield Avenue," and the "three story house," which refers to the Schloeder residence on Garfield—that he included in the novel.

The Gemini had no real purpose except its foggy goal of "child protection" and working against those who would "tear their bodies open." Chances are it had no real members except for Whillie and Henry and perhaps one or two others. If that's the case, it was nothing more than a social club with high-minded goals and an ornate language in which to express them, and not much else. If it actually did have members, they had the opportunity to volunteer to help find the kidnapped Elsie Paroubek, but there's no evidence that anyone associated with a group called the Gemini ever did.

"WHAT IS RAPE?" ASKED PENROD

Midway through *The Realms*, General Viviana blames the massive destruction of the Glandeco-Angelinian war on "that Darger and his old picture," referring to the photograph of Elsie Paroubek that Henry had put on the "mimic altar." He had clipped it from the *Daily News* article that announced the discovery of her body. A few pages later, the general asks, "How, then, is it that the loss of the photograph of the plain picture also is responsible for the situation of this war?" General Darger, one of Henry's alter egos, replies, "That is a mystery, your excellency, even to me." Henry referred to the relationship of Elsie's picture to the Glandeco-Angelinian War as "the Aronburg Mystery" or "the Great Aronburg Mystery."

A year before Elsie was kidnapped and murdered, Thomas Phelan had destroyed Henry's first version of *The Realms* and, at the same time, trashed Henry's collection of "pictures of children," among them one he thought of as the model for Annie Aronburg, his persona. Almost as soon as he realized the pictures were gone, Henry began collecting new ones and would have been on the lookout specifically for one to replace the picture that had initially represented her. Annie was extremely important in the novel because she had been the "leader of the main army of child rebels." Ten years old, slightly younger than Lillian Wulff, Annie led an "army of 10,000 rebels," all of whom were "eighteen years old."

Henry, and the rest of Chicago, learned about Elsie's disappearance on his nineteenth birthday, making her story almost mystically important to him. As her story unfolded in the news, Henry saw in the five-year-old Elsie a representation of all children who'd been kidnapped, beaten, and raped, including himself, and he easily adopted a photo of Elsie for Annie's. "When the Child Labor Revolution broke out," General Darger explained to General Viviana, Annie's value to the cause increased. She had been "elected a leader by the child rebels and, by her gallantry, she made rapid progress, which enraged Phelan," the character, not the real man,

> who got permission from Federal to murder her in cold blood. I was a witness of the most bloodcurdling crime ever committed in Calverinia. Annie Aronburg, habited in her nighties, probably had been occupying her mind for some time by planning for victory, when the brute seized her by the hair, which was loose, and flourished a razor about her face. The screams and struggles of the poor child had the effect of changing, possibly, the guilty feeling of the rascal into those of wrath. Instantly, he began to choke her, tearing her nightie to tatters, then with one determined sweep of his muscular arm, he nearly severed her chest open with his razor. The sight of blood incensed his anger into frenzy. Gashing his teeth and flashing fire from his eyes, he flew upon the body of the unconscious child and imbedded his fearful talons in her throat, retaining his grasp until she expired.

Just as the real Phelan destroyed the photo that represented Annie, the character Phelan murdered the character Annie in Henry's novel. The passage also reveals that, in the novel, Phelan raped Annie. Henry defined rape with a metaphor he included in a conversation between Joice, one of the Vivian girl-boys, and her brother, Penrod:

"What is rape?" asked Penrod.

"According to the dictionary, it means to undress a girl and cut her open to see the insides," said Joice.

When the character Phelan "flourished a razor" and then "nearly severed" Annie's "chest open" so that the "sight of blood incensed his anger into frenzy," Henry is applying his metaphor for rape—the cutting open of someone "to see the insides"—to Annie. In that brief scene, Henry merged Annie with Elsie, who was strangled and "attacked," as well as with himself. Child sexual abuse—and Henry's empathy for other children who had faced the same victimization he had—is what connects the three and is extremely important to the novel and his illustrations for it. Henry wrote about a war fought against adults who strangle and rape children because *he* was strangled and raped, as was Elsie/Annie.

Beginning almost as soon as she was reported missing, photographs and drawings of Elsie had become plentiful, especially in the *Chicago American*, which had also included illustrations of her parents, her siblings, and other people involved in the case. A *Daily News* article for May 9 published one that fired up Henry's imagination more than any other, and it became Henry's prototypical "Annie Aronburg" photograph. The innocent-looking, strikingly androgynous waif who stared back from the front page of the *Daily News* would be perfect to represent Annie and, because of her androgyny, Henry himself. Henry had clipped the photo out of the newspaper when it appeared in May 1911, three months after the construction of the altar, and put it there along with other photographs of children who'd also been caught up in tragedies. In fact, he arranged them together in what he would call a "shrine." They reminded the Gemini's members that their goal was to protect children.

Later, Thomas Phelan, who was still living at the Workingmen's House, although no longer Henry's roommate, somehow found out about the "mimic altar" and the "shrine" of children. How he learned about them is a mystery complicated by the probability that only Whillie and Henry were the real members. One of them may have mentioned it to him or, more likely, to someone else who mentioned it to him. Regardless, Phelan decided the chapel and its altar were blasphemous. Not only had the altar not been consecrated, it also was covered with photographs of children and not the acceptable icons of the Church. In a fury of self-righteousness born in his days at the seminary and reminiscent of his reaction to *The Realms*, he tore it down and destroyed the children's pictures.

Phelan's irrational reaction caused Henry to disband the Gemini and abandon the "mimic chapel." It also devastated Henry, not only because he identified with Elsie and had linked her to his alter ego Annie but also because Phelan had betrayed him twice: by destroying his manuscript and his altar. Henry certainly felt as if Phelan was showing utter contempt not only for his creative endeavors but also, more to the point, for his sexual victimization.

Henry was never adept at analyzing his own motives or actions, much less his feelings, another of the many symptoms of childhood sexual victimization that he exhibited, so he never really understood the intensity of the link between Annie, Elsie, and himself. Although he recognized the fact that he had been extremely angry all of his life, he never understood where that anger had originated or why he had so much of it stored up in the first place. He once mentioned half-heartedly that it had something to do with his never having brothers or sisters, but at best, that was another example of his denial at work. Admitting that he had been victimized and unable to fend for himself would have been too painful for him to articulate, much less accept, so he buried his feeling about it deep down, beyond his consciousness. As his anger grew, so did his novel.

SELF-PORTRAIT WITH WHILLIE

The Gemini also makes an important appearance in one of Henry's paintings *At Jullo Callo, How They Were Rescued by Four Christian Spies and Three Secret Service Men and Two Members of The Gemini*, a virtually unknown work believed to have been painted in the 1930s. Henry glued it to three other paintings, two to its left and one to its right, making the set of four paintings 19 inches by 95 inches. The other three images depict children and the Vivians outside. In *Nude Children in Meadow with Clouds*, a large group of girls and girl-boys seem to be enjoying a rare peaceful moment, a lull in the "Glandeco-Angelinian War Storm." In *At Cedernine, Glandelinians Suspicious That Little Vivian Girls Are Among Child Slaves*, a Glandelinian soldier searches for a Vivian girl-boy, a spy believed to be hiding among a group of children. In the third, *At Norma Run, Later During the Battle, Evans Succeeds in Rescuing Them*, the Vivians are on horseback, galloping at top speed away from a fray that nearly cost them their lives. Wedged among the other paintings is the extremely important *How They Were Rescued by Four Christian Spies*. What makes it important is that it contains elements of Henry's life that are not at all camouflaged. The unabashed sexuality of the scene is shocking, even for a painting by Henry.

Unlike its three companion paintings, *How They Were Rescued by Four Christian Spies* depicts the interior of a room. Almost dead center are the four Christian spies who are mentioned in the title, taking a Glandelinian soldier into custody. The four surround him as he struggles to break free. To the left is a winding staircase. At the bottom of the stair, an adult man is escorting one of the Vivian girl-boys upstairs. There's no sign of struggle. The girl-boy is completely compliant, and the ease by which the adult leads the child should suggest that he is one of the rescuers, perhaps even one of the Secret Service men. However, he's not leading the child outside, away from the struggle and to safety, but upstairs—a place hidden from view—where there are undoubtedly sleeping quarters. The sexual tension in the scene is intense, and the obvious intention of the adult is disturbing.

Just as alarming is the scene to the right of the Christian spies and their captive. It appears that a man, who has been sitting in a chair, has been pushed backward. Although he's still in the chair, his back is now on the floor and his legs are up in the air. It would be a comical situation, perhaps even a skit on the burlesque stage, except for the fact that another man, perhaps the man who pushed him over in the first place, is approaching the man on his back, carrying what can only be described as a very large phallus. Is the man carrying the phallus about to rape the man whose spread legs are up in the air? Or is the man on the floor complying with the one approaching him, as the Vivian girl-boy on the left side of the painting complies with the adult man?

Making the entire scenario depicted in *How They Were Rescued by Four Christian Spies* even more interesting are the "two members of the Gemini" whom Henry depicted at the extreme right of the canvas. Standing very close together, they are leaning into one another, whispering, trading observations of the goings-on in front of them, specifically the two men in front of them. In direct contrast to the action in scenes elsewhere in the painting, the Gemini seem remarkably stationary. As members of a child protective agency, shouldn't they be doing something about the man leading the Vivian girl-boy up the stairs instead of focusing their attention on the adult men— one on his back with his legs in the air, the other slowly, deliberately approaching him with a giant phallus? They should be, but they're not. They're interested in the male-male sexual encounter about to take place in front of them.

Henry crowded many of his other illustrations for his novels with the images of children—girls, boys, and girl-boys—being raped by adult Glandelinian men. The children are never compliant. They run. They fight. More often than not, they don't succeed in escaping the predators. Only the Vivian girl-boys are that lucky. *How They Were Rescued by Four Christian Spies* is the only one of Henry's paintings in which he depicted a child accepting the advances of an adult. It's the only painting in which he depicted adults engaged in what will be sexual activity, and that the sexual activity will be between two men is especially important. This scene is also one of only two in which Henry depicted himself. The two Gemini are, it appears, Henry and Whillie, taking it all in, especially the engagement of the man on the floor with the one approaching him.

Henry used the very noticeable difference in his and Whillie's heights to suggest that two characters in *The Realms*, Mutt and Jeff, were his and Whillie's alter egos. Henry appropriated the two from Bud Fisher's comic strip *Mutt and Jeff*. Jeff was very short, as was Henry, while Mutt was very tall, like Whillie. As MacGregor has pointed out, to "those who knew" Henry and Whillie "as inseparable companions, they may well have come to be known as 'Mutt and Jeff.'" The link between the two is stronger, however. Like Henry, Jeff lived in a "bughouse," a slang word at the time for an insane asylum, where Mutt met and, later, adopted him, forming what scholar Michael Moon has called a "permanent partnership," echoing Henry and Whillie's relationship. For Henry, then, depicting two men—one short, one tall—pointed to him and Whillie, who lead the Gemini.

The other painting that includes Henry is *At Jennie Richee. The blunder of one of the Glandelinian rug carriers causes the others to fall with him, foiling the attempt of the Little Girls none too gently.* In it, Henry depicted the rug carrier tripping in a decidedly slapstick manner, and in *The Realms*, Henry identified a character bearing his name as a bumbling Glandelinian rug carrier.

CHAPTER 6

EVEN A BETTER BOY

THERE'S NO CALLING ON THE LORD—
HE NEVER HEARS

HENRY HAD ALREADY BEEN SPENDING A GREAT DEAL OF TIME AT Whillie's house when Susan, Whillie's sister, married Charles S. Macferran and moved into rooms on the top floor of the Schloeders' house. Two years later, their first child, a daughter, was born, followed by a son. Henry was able to watch Whillie's niece and nephew beginning to grow up: eating solid food, taking her first steps, saying her first words. Being around the two children evoked long-buried memories of the day that Mrs. Brown offered to adopt him, so he began to investigate how he and Whillie could adopt a child. He didn't care whether it was a boy or a girl; he just needed to help a child, to protect it, to give it all that he hadn't had growing up—exactly what he may have had if his father had only agreed to let Mrs. Brown adopt him.

A child would make Henry's life important in a way that his job could not. A child would make him feel like everyone else, erasing the horrific experiences of his childhood, something he couldn't do alone. A child would provide him and Whillie with the stability and focus that any heterosexual couple finds suddenly appearing in their lives when they become parents.

Not knowing how to go about it, Henry approached the priests at St. Vincent's Church to ask what he had to do to adopt a child. He wouldn't have mentioned Whillie to them because of the Church's homophobia. They answered that he should pray about it, which was their way of getting rid of him. Henry wanting to adopt a child would have struck them as ridiculous. After all, he was living in one room at the Workingmen's House. His income was meager, and his hours were long with little time off. He was single, only a janitor, and had once been locked up in a "nut house." As far as they were concerned, no one fit the bill for being a parent less than Henry, and yet, according to Henry, the priests at St. Vincent de Paul called his plan "one of the most worthy ones on record," probably another way to placate him and get him out of their hair.

Henry waited and prayed, prayed and waited, and yet God never answered his petition. He had to ask himself why. Was his prayer truly as "worthy" as the priests had assured him it was? Henry found himself in a very difficult situation. The nuns at St. Patrick's School and the priests at the Mission had filled Henry's mind with the notion that the prayers of good individuals were always answered, while God ignored the same prayer of a bad person. Henry had not grown beyond the nuns' and priests' indoctrination, and he quickly came to believe that he must be bad. That's why, as Henry prayed, God seemed to be looking in the opposite direction with his fingers in his ears.

Hopeful that a civil agency could help him when God was reluctant to, Henry went to an adoption agency in the Loop. A clerk there gave him a pamphlet with rudimentary information about adoption, but it did little to give him hope. According to it, he needed money in the bank to be a viable candidate to become an adoptive parent. Instead of giving him self-confidence, it simply aggravated his lingering self-doubt.

Henry outlined the situation he faced in a single, typed page that he called "Found on Sidewalk." Written in third person, he questioned himself about his desire and, more to the point, his suitability to adopt a child. He even answered several of the questions by hand, using a pencil for his reply. Like a number of other texts he created, such as the supposed letter from Thomas Newsome, Henry incorporated the questions into *The Realms*, copying them into its first and its last volumes.

In "Found on Sidewalk," Henry stated that because of "his small pay he never can in ten years save" enough money to adopt, then raise a child, especially because "prices go higher every year." That realization led him to a unique and virtually unprecedented moment of introspection in Henry's life. He asked himself, again in third person, "if it is through the cause that he has not the money he desires, is he afraid to try and look or a good paying job . . . or is it for the reason that he has not the ambition?" He scribbled a wobbly "both" beside the question. Henry was not only acutely aware that he had no money, he also painfully realized he had no job training and so no possibility for work other than menial jobs. Facing his situation—one of the few times in his life that he wouldn't rationalize or ignore it—made him decide to abandon his hope of adopting a child. Nevertheless, he also placed the blame for his situation on God. "There's no calling on the Lord," Henry decided, "he never hears." What Henry perceived as God's deafness to his pleas, which he understood as God's rejection of him, would haunt him the rest of his life.

SISTER ROSE

Of all Henry's relationships with people he met during his early years at St. Joseph's Hospital, his relationship with Sister Rose was the most complicated. In late 1916 or the early 1917, Henry admitted to her that he hadn't been released from the Asylum but had ran away from it just before coming to work at St. Joseph's, and went so far as to call the Asylum "Godless." Except for reciting "the Our Father" before and after meals and "Sunday school," Henry claimed there was "otherwise no sign of religion." He ended with "The way it was there . . . you'd think there was no God at all." She told him he was absolutely right to have run away from such a place.

Sister Rose left St. Joseph's by the summer of 1917 for the Marillac Seminary in Normandy, Missouri, just outside of St. Louis, and Henry tried to keep in touch with her, writing her twice before she answered him. In one letter, he revealed one of the most important things about himself, that he was a writer, showing that, despite their initial antagonist relationship, he sought her approval. It's likely that he'd found a mother figure in her, underscored by the fact that she and his mother shared virtually the same name.

Henry told Sister Rose he was writing something about a "Catholic Lodge"—an obvious reference to the Gemini in *The Realms*. While Whillie certainly knew he was writing a novel and illustrating it, mentioning his work to her was risky. Afraid she might damn it by calling his writing "trash," as Phelan had done, Henry paved the way for her to accept it by giving the organization a name that would resonate with her: not the pagan Gemini, not the threatening Black Brothers Lodge, not even the stilted Child Protective Society, but the suitable "Catholic Lodge." She responded in an odd combination of first and third person: "I was very much interested in your account of the Catholic Lodge, and, if your writing about it pleases you, be sure that Sr. Rose will also be interested." Whether Henry sent the manuscript to her is unknown, but her response to the "Catholic Lodge" was a small but important victory for Henry. Someone of authority from whom he sought approval had given it to him.

In one of his letters to Sister Rose, Henry asked if there were any jobs at the seminary that he could have. She didn't beat around the bush. "No," she told him firmly, "we have no duty here which you could perform so you will do better by remaining where you are." It's doubtful that he actually wanted to leave Chicago, though Henry probably did want to leave his job at St. Joseph's because, by 1917, he had become all too aware of the politics there.

This brief and quasi-friendly comment from Sister Rose's pen makes her relationship with Henry suspect. Certainly, she didn't really think of Henry as a friend, although he may have thought of her that way. In fact, at the beginning of the letter, she was patronizing to him. "I am glad that you are trying to be 'even a better boy' since I left," she told him. Henry wasn't a child, but a twenty-five-year-old adult. It's unlikely that she would have called any other man of Henry's age a "boy," but she knew Henry had been locked up at the "feeble-minded" asylum and that allowed her, at least in her mind, to treat Henry as if he had the mental capacity of a child.

THE DOUGHBOY

Europe was already in utter turmoil when, on April 6, 1917, the United States entered World War I, "the war to end all wars." A short time later, anticipating it would need more soldiers to beat back the powerful German army, the federal government began to draft young men into military service. Like thousands of others, Henry was excited by the prospect of adventurous travels in Europe, even if that meant being a solider on the battlefield. He obeyed the new conscription law, and on June 2, 1917, he arrived at the city clerk's office in Chicago, joined the long lines of hundreds of other young men in their underwear, and waited for what seemed like hours to be examined physically by a doctor.

The very brief registrar's report gives some of the twenty-five-year-old Henry's physical attributes. He was "short" and "slender" and had "blue" eyes and a full head of "light brown" hair. Henry underwent a vision test, and the doctor noted he had poor eyesight.

202 HENRY DARGER, THROWAWAY BOY

The examiner must have asked Henry where he'd lived most of his life. Henry knew he would have to swear to the validity of his answers at the end of his physical, so he felt obligated to disclose his secret— that he'd been institutionalized—to the examiner, who immediately added "mentality not normal" to the registration card.

After his draft notice, dated August 24, 1917, arrived, Henry was sent to Camp Grant in Rockford, Illinois, west of Chicago, for initial training. The following November he was herded up with hundreds of other draftees from the Chicago metropolitan area and northern Illinois and loaded onto a train bound for Camp Logan in Houston (now the site of Memorial Park), where he would remain until the end of December.

The train from Rockford to Houston was jam-packed with new recruits, and during the nearly two-day trip, parties full of cigar and cigarette smoke, dirty jokes, and dirtier French postcards sprung up car to car. Here and there during the festivities, a single soldier's voice would begin to sing the first few bars of one of the day's top tunes, soon joined by dozens of other voices. The flag-waving "Over There" was the most popular of all, followed closely by "For Me and My Gal" and "At the Darktown Strutters' Ball."

During the four and a half months that he was away at Camp Grant and Camp Logan, some of the staff at St. Joseph's kept in touch with Henry. Sister Camilla wrote to him, and although he was earning a salary from being in the military, she made sure he received his salary from St. Joseph's, too. In one of her letters, she mentioned that his friend Richard Logan, who also lived at the Workingmen's House, was remembering Henry in his prayers.

Despite his initial excitement about being in the army and seeing the world, Henry didn't take well to life in the armed services. He hated the strict authoritarianism. The regimentation there was worse than what he'd experienced at the Mission or even at the Asylum. The orders barked at him day and night surpassed anything Sister Rose had ever dished out. He also hated the many vaccinations that he received, one after another. He complained that "my arm or where I got the darn shots was so sore for days." On top of everything else, the constant drilling that his sergeant put Henry and the other men through caused his shoulder, the one he'd hurt in a fight when he was a child, to ache mercilessly night and day. As far as Henry was concerned, the only saving grace for being at Camp Logan was the fact that he could "buy all sorts of refreshments and other goodies" at the canteen to supplement the terrible military food.

Always a creative problem solver, he quickly figured out a way to escape his military obligation. He began complaining about his eyes. Henry had passed the eye examination at the city clerk's office, but because of his complaints his eyes were examined again at Camp Logan. This time, he failed the tests—on purpose. Although he'd had "real bad eye trouble" for years, he confessed much later that he also "greatly exaggerated" the problem so that he could go home.

He returned to his single room at the Workingmen's House and to his job pushing brooms, mopping floors, and taking out the trash at St. Joseph's. He had been at work for several weeks before his honorable discharge, dated December 28, 1917, arrived. It repeats some of the information from his draft card, but it also gives other data that wasn't on it: he had a "dark complexion" and stood a scant five feet one in his stocking feet.

Years later, Henry coyly hinted at another, deeper reason why he hated being in the military so much. He "had to leave behind" what he "so strongly yearned for." In other words, "I was forced to leave behind things I loved too much. That was almost unbearable."

What could Henry have missed and thought about so intensely and so constantly? Certainly not his job at St. Joseph's, where nuns and lay staff alike demeaned him. It could have been working on *The Realms*, which he'd been writing then for eight years, but he could always work on his novel, regardless of where he happened to be. Except for Anna, he had no family to speak of. The likeliest answer is also the most obvious: Whillie. Like any other draftee, Henry missed the person he loved almost unbearably.

LEAVING ST. JOSEPH'S HOSPITAL

The only thing that had changed at the hospital during Henry's brief foray into the military was Sister Rose had left and was eventually replaced by Sister Dorothy Clark, his new supervisor. Sister DuPaul Collins, who was already working at St. Joseph's and whom Henry mistakenly called Sister *De*Paul, immediately began flexing her muscles. There was bad blood between the two nuns, and Sister DuPaul began using Henry as a punching bag to show Sister Dorothy a thing or two.

"Sister DePaul had a bulldog like face," Henry recalled, adding that she "seemed to have the disposition of one," too. She cornered Henry one day while he was on his hands and knees, scrubbing the hospital floors as he'd been taught to do at the Asylum, and demanded that he stop what he was doing right then and there and clean the nuns' bathroom.

He had no time, he tried to tell her, to drop everything and do what she wanted him to do. He had to get his assigned work done first, but if he was able to finish it before he was scheduled to leave for the day, he'd be happy to begin on the sisters' quarters. But that didn't satisfy her. She bawled him out, and he was both embarrassed and angered by it.

Sister DuPaul began to interrupt his work on a regular basis to make demands of his time. Although he complained to Sister Dorothy and Sister Camilla, neither would stand up for him and curb Sister DuPaul. Sister Camilla even laughed it off, telling him to ignore her, but with DuPaul screaming in his face at the drop of a hat, it was easier said than done. And Sister Dorothy simply refused to "let me do it," Henry recalled, "until my work was done." To get Sister DuPaul off his back, he did the extra work for her on his own time without getting paid for it, extending his shift long beyond the scheduled ten hours. It didn't take Henry long to realize that the nuns were afraid of the bully, Sister DuPaul, a no-win position for him. Eventually, he admitted to himself that he "hated her" and "could not at all stand it any longer." He decided he had to quit his job.

After nearly a dozen years at St. Joseph's, Henry worked up enough nerve to tell Sister Dorothy he was leaving. He didn't tell her he was quitting because of Sister DuPaul. Instead, he claimed it was because he had never been given a vacation or paid sick leave. Sister Camilla wrote a letter of recommendation for him: "This is to certify that Mr. Henry Darger is a good, willing worker."

THE ANSCHUTZES' BOARDINGHOUSE

Once Henry decided he would quit his job at St. Joseph's Hospital, he had to move out of the Workingmen's House, where he'd lived for more than a decade. Only St. Joseph's employees—now 88 percent women, mostly nurses but some nonmedical staff—could live there. In the spring or summer of 1921, he found a room that he could afford in the back of the second floor of a boardinghouse at 1035 Webster across the street from St. Vincent's Church. Emil and Minnie Anschutz, a middle-aged couple from Germany, owned the building. During the eleven years that he boarded at the Anschutzes' house, a colorful array of characters lived under the same roof, arriving unexpectedly, living there only a short time, then leaving, only to be replaced by other transients. Henry witnessed the cycle close-up.

The police knocked on the boardinghouse door late one morning, looking for a swindler who was one of the Anschutzes' tenants, but the man and "all his belongings" had already vanished. Another roomer had an "in growing goiter that strangled him" slowly, and a third committed suicide. The suicide, Henry quickly added, hadn't killed himself in his room but somewhere else, but he willed some of his ashes to Emil and Minnie. Obviously, he felt a bond with them, as did Henry.

He ended up living with the Anschutzes longer than any of their other tenants and became their favorite. They gave Henry small Christmas presents: a handkerchief one year, a tie the next, each the sort of present one gives to a family member or a friend when it's impossible to figure out what he or she might actually want or need. Whether he wanted or could use the handkerchiefs and ties didn't matter to Henry. What was important was that the gifts acknowledged his importance to them. They meant so much to him that he never used them but preserved them in a box. It's doubtful Henry ever gave Emil and Minnie presents in return. He was far too poor. During the time he lived with Emil and Minnie, Prohibition was in full force, so "at New Years," Henry recalled, "we celebrated by seeing the old year out, and the new year in. We had ginger ale or other soft drinks," substitutes for champagne.

The slow deterioration of the U.S. economy caused the Anschutzes to cut corners to save money whenever possible. During one of Chicago's extremely cold winters, Minnie decided that, to save money, she wouldn't heat the house during the day, which was when most of her boarders were away at work. Angered by Minnie's frugality, one roomer moved out of the Anschutzes' boardinghouse and then immediately mailed a "complaint to the Health Department." It sent Minnie a warning in writing, threatening her with a hundred-dollar fine. She asked Henry to write a reply, probably because he had told the Anschutzes at some point during his time with them that he was a novelist, giving Minnie confidence in her tenant's prowess as a writer. As it turned out, his letter defending Minnie was successful, and the health department never bothered the Anschutzes again.

207 ENTRYEVEN A BETTER BOY

FROM THE FRYING PAN

The day after he quit his job at St. Joseph's, Henry began working as a dishwasher at Grant Hospital at 551 Grant Place, a few blocks northeast of St. Joseph's Hospital. Several weeks later, Sister Dorothy "sent the orderly" to the Anschutzes' to coax Henry into going back to work at St. Joseph's. Too late, she had come to realize that Henry was a responsible employee and regretted her cavalier attitude over his quitting. Because of his "fear of Sister DePaul," Henry didn't have to think twice about Sister Dorothy's invitation, and he was tickled pink to give the orderly a sharp *no* and shut the door in his face. His satisfaction over being needed at St. Joseph's was short-lived, however, because soon thereafter, Henry found himself caught up in Grant's staff politics, which seemed worse than those at St. Joseph's. As the politics threatened to engulf him, he felt as if he had "leaped from the frying pan into the fire," and yet some of his memories of working at Grant Hospital were happy, even positive.

Henry had made friends with a young woman, Johanna Kuback, who supervised the staff's "main dining room" located "on the ground floor." Each time that she had an afternoon off, either "winter or summer," clouds filled the sky and storms froze or drenched the city. Henry felt sorry for her bad luck with the weather. His afternoons off were usually sunny, and he offered to trade an afternoon with her so that she would have at least one good afternoon free.

With the supervising housekeeper's permission, they made an exchange. Johanna selected a Sunday in July, but unfortunately, Henry's luck with the weather didn't transfer to her. It rained that afternoon, too. "At Two Thirty it came," Henry later recalled, a "cloud as black as the color of Brown black and a very terrific cloud burst that lasted more than an hour." The storm was so bad that it flooded the kitchen in the area in which Henry worked.

When Johanna returned to work the next day, Henry apologized to her for her bad luck. He was, he said, "sorry for the debauchery of the weather." A man who knew about their exchange "made fun of her." Furious at the man, Henry "told him to shut his 'blanky blank' mouth." Shocked by Henry's outburst, the man backed off and "minded his own business after that." Although he allowed the nuns at St. Joseph's—and, for that matter, any person in a supervisory role—to walk all over him, Henry was more than ready to defend himself and his friends against coworkers at Grant.

AN EVENING WITH WHILLIE

Although they certainly spent much of their time together at Riverview Amusement Park, Lincoln Park, and other venues visited by couples for entertainment, Henry and Whillie most often spent time together at the Schloeders' home. Henry fondly remembered one such evening on October 31, 1923. Whillie's sisters Lizzie and Katherine and their mother, Susanna, were also there when they heard fire trucks blaring down Halsted Street. Henry peeked out the window and noticed a "glow" in the sky over DePaul University that was "very bright and getting brighter." At Mass at St. Vincent's Church the Sunday before, the priest had announced to the congregation that "on Halloween night the students" of DePaul University, which adjoined the church property and was administered by the church, "were to celebrate with a big halloween bonfire, with mostly wood that will make much more flame than smoke." He also told them that "all neighboring fire departments were notified that even if they did notice a rousing blare in the sky, they need not run out because theyll know what it is."

At first, Henry and the Schloeders thought nothing about it. They assumed the fire departments had forgotten about the celebration and, hearing that there was a fire at the church, sent fire trucks speeding to the bonfire, but then Lizzie reminded them that the priest had told them "the wood was not to make smoke." Because there was a con-

Henry Darger and his character Jack Evans shared a cool demeanor belying their boiling, ready-to-explode-at-any-second emotional state.

Untitled (Portrait of Colonel Jack Francis Evans)
Henry Darger (1892–1973)
Chicago
Mid-twentieth century
Watercolor, pencil, ink and collage on cardboard
13 3/4 x 11 1/2"
Collection American Folk Art Museum, New York
Museum purchase, 2002.22.5
© Kiyoko Lerner; photo by James Prinz

Darger depicted fire as a destructive force in many of his paintings as well as in his written works such as The Realms *and in the Sweetie Pie narrative of* The History of My Life. *The Blengiglomenean (or Blengin) creatures, which appear in many forms in his paintings, were protectors of children.*

53 At Jennie Richee Assuming nuded appearance by compulsion race ahead of coming storm to warn their father. (double-sided)

Henry Darger (1892–1973)
Chicago
Mid-twentieth century
Watercolor, pencil, and carbon tracing on pieced paper
19 x 70 1/4"
Collection American Folk Art Museum, New York
Gift of Ralph Esmerian in memory of Robert Bishop, 2000.25.3 a
© Kiyoko Lerner; photo by James Prinz

To escape forest fires they enter a volcanic cavern. Are helped out of cave, trap by Blengiglomenean Createns./ PERSUED BY FOREST FIRES, PROVING THE BIGNESS OF THE CONFLARRATION IT IS 40 MILES AWAY AND ADVANC-ING FAST./ How when they were put in a rat infested cell, they by using the rats and even a few mice they caught they managed to escape after being persued and hounded.

Henry Darger (1892–1973)
Chicago
Mid-twentieth century
Watercolor, pencil and carbon tracing on pieced paper;
19 x 70"
Collection American Folk Art Museum, New York
Museum purchase, 2000.25.1a
© Kiyoko Lerner; photo by James Prinz

The blonde children here are the Vivian girl-boys, a frequent feature of Henry's art.

Darger named a town and a vicious Glandelinian general after his roommate, Thomas Phelan, and probably based the tunnel in the middle panel on the one that joined the main building of the Asylum to its school building.

175 At Jennie Richee. Everything is allright though storm continues.

Henry Darger (1892–1973)
Chicago
Mid-twentieth century
Watercolor, pencil, carbon tracing and collage on pieced paper
24 x 108 1/4"
Collection American Folk Art Museum, New York
Museum purchase, 2001.16.2a
© Kiyoko Lerner; photo by James Prinz

At Phelantonburg. They raid a guardhouse / At Calmanrina Escape Through City Tunnel./ Last at Phelantonberg. They Witness a Massaacre of Children.

Henry Darger (1892–1973)
Chicago
Mid-twentieth century
Watercolor, pencil, and carbon tracing on pieced paper
19 x 70 1/4"
Collection American Folk Art Museum, New York
Museum purchase, 2000.25.3b
© Kiyoko Lerner; photo by James Prinz

Darger painted a number of scenes that include the Vivian girl-boys in idyllic, whimsical scenes away from violence that he so often depicted.

The roping of the Vivian girl-boys
together recalls the first time that young
Henry tried to escape from the Asylum's
farm, was roped by Mr. West, and led
back to the farmhouse like an animal.

At Jullo Callio via Norma They are captured by the
Glandelinians

Henry Darger (1892–1973)
Chicago
Mid-twentieth century
Watercolor, pencil, and carbon tracing on pieced paper
19 1/8 x 36 1/2"
Collection American Folk Art Museum, New York
Museum purchase, 2001.16.3
© Kiyoko Lerner; photo by James Prinz

The moxie of the Vivian girl-boys in this and other paintings probably reveals Mary Pickford's and Lillian Wolf's influence on Darger.

At battle of Drosabellamaximillan. Seeing Glandelinians re-treating Vivian girls grasp Christian banners, and lead charge against foe

Henry Darger (1892–1973)
Chicago
Mid-twentieth century
Watercolor, pencil, carbon tracing, and collage on pieced paper
19 x 47 3/4"
Collection American Folk Art Museum, New York
Museum purchase, 2002.22.1b
© Kiyoko Lerner; photo by James Prinz

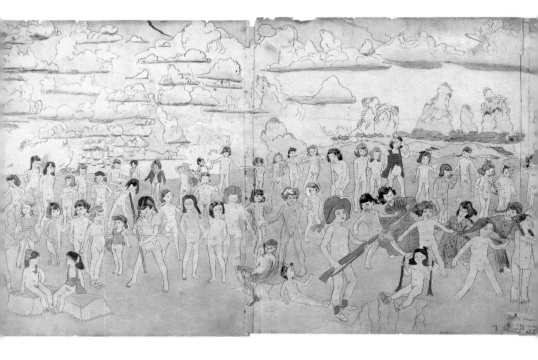

*The Vivians are not the only girl-boys in Darger's oeuvre, as this—
and many other paintings—reveals.*

(above) 3 Place not mentioned / Esposide 3 2 Escape
with great number of kids still fighting

Henry Darger (1892–1973)
Chicago
Mid-twentieth century
Watercolor, pencil, and carbon tracing on pieced
paper
24 x 76"
Collection American Folk Art Museum, New York
Museum purchase, 2002.22.6B
© Kiyoko Lerner; photo by James Prinz

(right) Fashion Illustration and Tracing

Henry Darger (1892–1973)
Chicago
Mid-twentieth century
Printed paper and pencil and carbon tracing on
paper
Illustration: 9 1/2 x 5 1/2"
Tracing 11 x 8 1/2"
Collection American Folk Art Museum, New York
Gift of Kiyoko Lerner, 2003.7.13a, b
© Kiyoko Lerner; photo by Gavin Ashworth

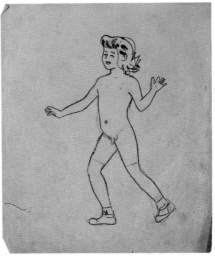

To draw a nude, Darger simply traced one of his "models" from
the source materials he collected and ignored the clothing.

The "cyclone like wind"—a trope Darger will
employ thoroughly in the Sweetie Pie portion
of his The History of My Life—responds to the
violence that adults perpetuate against children
in The Realms, *saving them, while in the Sweetie
Pie narrative, it helps to destroy the area where
the Asylum was located.*

(above) A Norma Catherine. But wild thunderstorm
with cyclone like wind saves them.

Henry Darger (1892–1973)
Chicago
Mid-twentieth century
Watercolor, pencil, colored pencil, and carbon
tracing on pieced paper
19 1/8 x 47 3/4"
Collection American Folk Art Museum, New York
Museum purchase, 2002.22.2a
© Kiyoko Lerner; photo by James Prinz

(right) Untitled (study of Vivian Girl with doll)

Henry Darger (1892–1973)
Chicago
Mid-twentieth century
Watercolor, carbon tracing, and pencil on paper
12 x 9"
Collection American Folk Art Museum, New York
Gift of Robert and Luise Kleinberg in celebration of
Granddaughter Cecelia Cooley, with Kiyoko Lerner,
2004.15.1
© Kiyoko Lerner; photo by Gavin Ashworth

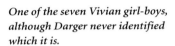
One of the seven Vivian girl-boys, although Darger never identified which it is.

172 At Jennie Richee. Storm continues. Lightning
strikes shelter but no one is injured.

Henry Darger (1892–1973)
Chicago
Mid-twentieth century
Watercolor, pencil, carbon tracing, and collage on
pieced paper
24 x 108 3/4"
Collection American Folk Art Museum, New York
Museum purchase, 2004.1.1a
© Kiyoko Lerner; photo by Gavin Ashworth

Another idyllic scene far removed from violence, this time with
a number of Blenglins with ram's horns and butterfly-like wings.
The boy in the center of the left half of the canvas—probably
Penrod, the Vivian girl-boys' brother—is mopping, recalling
Henry's job at the Asylum for Feeble-Minded Children.

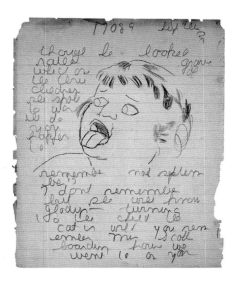

Male staff at the Asylum for Feeble-Minded Children often strangled the boys in their care to control them, the image of which Henry included in many of his paintings.

Untitled (study of strangled girl with surrounding text)

Henry Darger (1892–1973)
Chicago
Mid-twentieth century
Pencil and carbon tracing on paper
10 1/2 x 8"
Collection American Folk Art Museum, New York
Gift of Kiyoko Lerner, 2003.7.39
© Kiyoko Lerner; photo by Gavin Ashworth

One of Henry's characters in The Realms, *defines rape: "According to the dictionary, it means to undress a girl and cut her open to see the insides." Scenes of children being eviscerated—raped, according to Henry—are repeated throughout his oeuvre and reveal his experiences as a small, unprotected, and easily-victimized boy.*

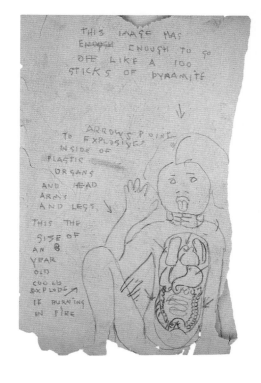

A 100 STICKS OF DYNAMITE (study of strangled girl with exposed organs)

Henry Darger (1892–1973)
Chicago
Mid-twentieth century
Pencil and carbon tracing on paper
12 x 7 1/2"
Collection American Folk Art Museum, New York
Gift of Kiyoko Lerner, 2003.7.16
© Kiyoko Lerner; photo by Gavin Ashworth

Authorities such John MacGregor consider This Human Fiend *as Darger's earliest painting.*

ADVANCING ABBIE-ANNIAN TROOPS/
THIS HUMAN FIEND

Henry Darger (1892–1973)
Chicago
Mid-twentieth century
Watercolor, ink, pencil, and collage on cardboard
11 5/8 x 16 1/8"
Collection American Folk Art Museum, New York
Gift of Kiyoko Lerner, 2003.7.63
© Kiyoko Lerner; photo by James Prinz

An early example of Darger's collage technique.

After M Whurther Run Glandelinians attack and
blow up train carrying children to refuge.

Henry Darger (1892–1973)
Chicago
Mid-twentieth century
Watercolor, pencil, carbon tracing and collage on
pieced paper
23 x 36 3/4"
Collection American Folk Art Museum, New York
Gift of Sam and Betsey Farber, 2003.8.1b
© Kiyoko Lerner; photo by Gavin Ashworth

siderable amount of smoke streaming into the sky, the women were sure the bonfire had gotten out of control and had spread to the university buildings. Henry and Whillie decided to investigate and walked toward the university. As they got close to the intersection of Fullerton and Sheffield Avenues, they discovered that a large broom factory at that corner was ablaze, and not the university at all. The broom factory stood directly across the street from St. Augustine's Home for the Aged, where Henry's father had lived out the last five years of his life.

Henry didn't admit to Whillie and the Schloeders his terrible fear of fire that had plagued him ever since he was a child. Afraid of fires or not, Henry, and many other people at the time, found them fascinating forms of entertainment. Smoke boiling skyward or sirens from fire trucks careening down Chicago's major streets often brought throes of gawkers to the neighborhoods in which fires were raging.

Henry and Whillie watched the broom factory blaze until about eleven that night, and then each went his separate way home to turn in for the evening. Once Henry got to the boardinghouse door, he realized he'd forgotten his keys. He knocked on the door several times, hoping someone would wake and let him in, but no one answered. Ten minutes later, Emil and Minnie arrived. They, too, had heard the sirens, seen the glow in the sky, and gone to check out the fire. There were so many gawkers from the neighborhood that Henry hadn't seen them there. After wishing his landlords good night, Henry crawled into bed. Deeply affected by the blaze, which reminded him of those he had witnessed as a child, Henry tossed and turned all night and got no sleep to speak of.

TO WHOM IT MAY CONCERN

By the mid-1920s, Henry's life began to change in small but important ways. On July 21, 1925, Henry's eighty-two-year-old uncle Charles, the last of the Darger brothers, died. Henry now had no immediate family alive, except for his aunt Anna. She had gotten word about Charles's death from his children and told Henry about it. It had been such a long time since they had seen each other, not since he'd returned from the Asylum in 1909, that he decided not to attend Charles's funeral.

Then, near the end of the decade, a shake-up in personnel at Grant Hospital threatened his job, and in late 1927, he decided to quit. Henry asked his supervisor, Miss Watson, to write a recommendation for him when he left. In a letter dated January 23, 1928, she told potential employers, "Henry Darger was employed at the Grant Hospital for a period of about five years. He was always prompt in his duties and he did his work well. He is honest." Henry knew that, to get a job, he would need more than one recommendation, and he was so desperate for a paycheck that he wrote one for himself and signed it with Whillie's name:

> To whom it may Concern.
>   I recommend Mr. Henry Darger of whom I spoke of yesterday morning as the man who is a good dishwasher.
>   He also has recommendations with him from other places he has worked at.
>   If you can use him I will appreciate it very much.
>
>   Whilliam Schloeder
>   Watchman at Phillip Rinn Company

Evidently, Whillie had put in a good word for Henry to wash dishes, probably at a restaurant or a lunchroom. Henry was following up with the letter, hoping to land the job.

In the meantime, Henry had also applied at a greasy spoon at the corner of Webster and Burling, a few blocks from the Anschutzes' house. The owner took one look at the thirty-six-year-old Henry and "insultingly told" him "to go to the poor farm at oak forest," referring to the Cook County Poor Farm. Henry was so desperate for a job that he even swallowed his pride and applied at St. Joseph's. He hoped that, if he was hired, Sister DuPaul would have moved on, perhaps following in Sister Rose's footsteps. The days passed and he heard nothing. Then Henry finally landed a job washing dishes in a café across the street from the Alexian Brothers Hospital at 1200 Belden Avenue. He worked for only a few days there when he got word that St. Joseph's wanted to rehire him, not as a janitor but as a dishwasher. He began his second stint at St. Joseph's in 1928, nearly six years after he'd quit because of the bully Sister DuPaul.

Anna Darger had been living with her daughter and son-in-law, Florence and Edward Nelson, and her two grandsons, Raymond and Frank, on Chicago's South Side since shortly after Augustine's death on January 27, 1916. The same year that Henry returned to work at St. Joseph's, she decided to move out on her own and into an apartment at 709 Garfield, the same block in which the Workingmen's House stood. Although Henry had already moved to the Anschutzes' by then, it's obvious that, with all of her children and their families living on the South Side, her move to the Near North Side signaled her desire to be near her nephew. For the next two years, they would spend as much time as Henry could spare with each other, but Henry was now thirty-six, had Whillie and his family on which to rely, and, when not with Whillie, spent his free time writing and illustrating his novels. He didn't have much time for her. By 1930, she had moved back to the South Side to live with her other daughter, Edna Feldkamp, whose husband had died several decades earlier. Anna lived there until her death on July 20, 1934.

During his second stint at St. Joseph's, Henry worked a thirteen-hour shift, from seven a.m. to eight thirty p.m. "and never got any time off," not even Sundays. He was under the thumb of Sister Rufina, "another prime and severe one," who treated him badly. He also found himself being sucked into the politics of the lay staff. It didn't take Henry long to realize that he'd made a huge mistake returning to St. Joseph's and wanted to quit, but he thought better of it. It was the mid-1930s, and "as there was then an awlfully severe depression on," what would later be referred to as the Great Depression, "it was utterly impossible to get a job with any place." Henry realized that he "had to stay there and go through a number of years of misery because of her [Sister Rufina's] nagging." Unless he wanted to end up on the streets like the "skidrow bum" or the hoboes of West Madison Street, he had to keep his job.

Through it all, Henry had learned to steer clear of as many people as often as possible. Otherwise, he had to deal with their egos, their threats, their all-around nastiness to him. He had already become something of "a loner," as his coworkers at the time believed, and at lunch, Henry wouldn't join others but "would sit in some little corner" and "wouldn't ever go out into the employees' dinning room to sit down." Still, he couldn't hide the soft spot he had in his heart for children. On his way home from his shift at St. Joseph's, he passed the playground down the street from the hospital that the DePaul Settlement House had created at the corner of Webster Avenue and Halsted Street. He would often stop for a little while during good weather to watch the "kids in the playground." Sometimes, he "waved to them and they waved back." When he turned his back to leave, the boys "made fun of him. They imitated his walk," but he "ignored them."

Then, after a few years, Henry's luck changed. A Miss Casey began working at the hospital and became Henry's supervisor. Unlike any of Henry's previous supervisors, she saw something in Henry that made her decide to give him supervisory responsibilities. She put him in charge of a group of girls who also worked in the kitchen. One of them continually misbehaved, and Henry tried over and over to ignore it. Eventually, he tired of her behavior and fired her on the spot. The other girls, who were friends of hers, walked out in protest, but Miss Casey agreed with Henry's decision. They weren't allowed to return. On May 1, 1937, Henry got a raise, a 10 percent increase in his salary, as well as a two-week vacation annually. Of course, it had taken the nuns twenty-eight years to reward Henry for his work.

CHAPTER 7

ANGRY AT GOD

WE HAVE A LOT OF LOVE FOR YOU

I N THE FALL OF 1932, ELEVEN YEARS AFTER HENRY MOVED INTO 1035 Webster, the Anschutzes decided to sell their house, which was falling into disrepair, and brought the devastating news to Henry. They had decided to trade properties with an Italian immigrant who lived at 2750 Logan Boulevard, a considerable distance west. It was a very large house, and they planned to rent many of its rooms to lodgers as they had at 1035 Webster. Minnie tried to put as good a spin on the news as possible, promising to invite him to their new home often.

Henry had developed a strong bond with the Anschutzes, especially Minnie, and he was panicked by the news. He'd grown comfortable in their home and fond of the two of them. Besides, he'd experienced an intense period of creativity under their roof. He was very close to finishing *The Realms*, and he'd also completed a substantial number of paintings there. Many were now considerably larger than when he initially began painting at the Workingmen's House, including *The Battle of Calverhine*, which he'd completed around August 28, 1929. It stretched to 9 feet 8 5/8 inches long and reached 3 feet 1 1/16 inches high. Because Henry reported that the Anschutzes were in his room on several occasions, it's unlikely that they didn't notice such a huge painting in his room. They must have been well aware of Henry's life as a painter.

Henry's attachment to the room and to his friends certainly caused him to question his immediate future. Would the new owner kick him out? Where would he be able to find a place that he could afford and move into easily? Would he find a room that would accommodate the extremely long manuscript to *The Realms* and his growing collection of source materials, while also providing him with enough space to work on his large canvases? His alarm lasted only a short time when he realized that, if he had to move, there were plenty of other rooming houses in the neighborhood with the same rent that he paid the Anschutzes, and he could have his pick of them.

When Henry moved from the Workingmen's House to Emil and Minnie's, he'd had only a few pages of a manuscript, a small collection of source materials, and a change or two of clothes. Now that *The Realms* was nearly done, it was enormous and heavy. Before moving out of the Anschutzes', Henry bound most of it into seven volumes. Even a quick look at the volumes reveals that he sewed the pages together in a professional manner, having probably learned bookbinding at the Mission, where Father Mahoney had begun a job training program in printing and bookbinding for his boys the year before Henry began living there. They printed a newsletter, *The Waif's Messenger*, to promote interest in the Mission among potential donors, as well as printing and binding *The Waif's Annual*, a book also meant to attract benefactors.

Henry and Margy Gehr owned 851 Webster, the building into which he moved, and were living there with their twenty-three-year-old son, Walter. Six or seven boarders besides Henry also lived there, and like Henry, they were all working class and single. The Gehrs never became close to Henry, as the Anschutzes had, but the room they rented to him was more than adequate for his needs.

At only 274 square feet, Henry's new room was no mansion, but it had three windows that faced south, giving him a considerable amount of direct sunlight in the summer and a steady, if not direct, light in the winter. The small middle window held stained glass and was set higher up the wall than the other two. Radiators meant to heat the room in the winter stood on either side of the two larger windows, but neither ever worked properly. Out his windows, Henry could see the tiny strip of yard in the back of the building, the alley, and farther away the Loop's skyscrapers.

Henry stored his library in a closet-like space beside the door to his room. His collection would include all the books in the Oz series, many of Dickens's novels, religious books (hymnals as well as catechisms), and various books on popular culture. In his copy of the Chicago Historical Society's *The Great Chicago Fire*, Henry had found a great deal of information and plenty of pictures to inspire much of his writing and many of his paintings. He also stored his 78s in the closet. He listened to the records late into the night as he wrote and painted.

He hung *The Battle of Calverhine* on the west wall, over his bed. It was so long that it almost took up the whole space. As time passed, he would add more of his own work to all four walls. These would include individual portraits of the Vivian girl-boys, many of his collages, such as *Child with Glass of Milk*, *Boys and Man*, *Twice*, and *Religious Collage with Madonna and Child*, and even a black-and-white headshot of a pope.

The previous roomer had left a large oval dining room table behind. Henry immediately scooted the wooden table to the center of the room so he could easily move around it to trace the models onto the paper, then color in the tracings with paint. A gas fireplace that hadn't worked in years took up most of the eastern wall, and he put knickknacks on its mantel. He shared a bathroom with the other third-floor tenants. There were no kitchen facilities, as had also been the case at the Anschutzes', so when he could afford it, he ate at the Seminary Restaurant, where Lincoln Avenue, Halsted Street, and Fullerton Avenue crisscrossed, or, more often, at Roma's Grill at the corner of Webster and Sheffield Avenues. When St. Vincent's Church opened its kitchen to the needy or when it had receptions or suppers for its parishioners, Henry would show up, first in line to eat. In time, he began to ignore as many people there as possible, even the priests.

Tellingly, it was Henry, not Minnie, who made the first move to safeguard their relationship. Right after they went their separate ways, Henry wrote Emil and Minnie a note, wishing them good luck with their new property and the new life that accompanied it and telling them how much he liked his new home. It was his way of making sure his friends wouldn't forget about him, not right away at least.

Minnie went out of her way to keep in touch with him, inviting him to her new home often. On September 10, 1932, she sent Henry a postcard:

> Dear Friend Henry
>   We received your wellcome Letter, and I am verry glad that you like your New Home. I wish you wouldt come this Friday coming in the afternoon, we will be Home and waiting for you.
>
>   With best Regards yours Friends
>   Emil & Minnie Anschutz

Henry didn't show up that Friday afternoon. Friday wasn't one of his scheduled days off.

Not to be deterred, she sent him other postcards, inviting him to their home. As part of their Christmas wishes for him, she included a snapshot of themselves. Taken in warm weather, Emil and Minnie are standing on the front porch of their new house, Emil looking snappy in a suit, Minnie all dolled up. She wrote "We wish you a Merry Christmas and a Happy New Year" on the back.

Then, on April 20, 1938, they invited him to an Easter party at their house, but instead of visiting, Henry sent them Easter cards. They responded with a thank-you note and another open-ended invitation:

> My Dear Friend!
>
> We received your welcome Letter and Easter Cards, so we thank you very well, we were waiting for you, and it is to bad that you could not come, we had a nice little Party here all good companie and people you now, but I see it could not be helped, but you come anytime you can get of, because your all ways welcomed so you take your time, and come wen ever you want to, we're having good Wetter now, and we're feeling good and healthy, and hoping your are the same. So don't forget to come, we have a lot of News for you.
>
> with best Wishes & Regards
> to you our best Friend from
> Emil & Minnie

On another postcard, this one undated, Emil and Minnie urged him, yet again, to visit them, but this time they add only if he's "healthy and the Wetter is nice." Minnie closed the note with "we have a lot of love for you." Like his aunt Anna, Mrs. Anderson, and Mrs. Brown, the Anschutzes, especially Minnie, saw something special in their former tenant and connected with him in a very real and meaningful way.

Henry's reluctance to visit the Anschutzes can easily be explained. Henry's long shifts at the hospital left little time for other activities. Whenever he and Whillie had time off from their jobs on the same day, they spent it together. Henry couldn't have brought Whillie along to the Anschutzes' parties because it would have raised more than a few eyebrows and, in fact, might have destroyed his relationship with them. What time he had to himself when Whillie was at work, Henry devoted to his novel and paintings. He simply prioritized his all-too-few hours away from the hospital, and that left no time for the Anschutzes.

INVESTMENTS

At least as early as the 1930s, and perhaps even earlier, while the rest of the country was sinking deeply into the economic morass that the Great Depression had created, Henry began investing large sums of money in the Marillac Seminary. For example, he invested $717 in 1933 and another $500 five years later. In today's money, the amounts would be about $12,652 and $8,134, respectively—in a period during which he worked as a dishwasher for less than $3,000 a year.

It's not difficult to figure out why Henry invested so much money in the nuns' seminary. He must have felt that, because the nuns had given him a job that came with a place to live, he owed them a favor. Or similarly, he may have felt that when he left Grant Hospital in a "huff" and the nuns rehired him at St. Joseph's, he was again deep in their debt. As important as anything else, investing in an organization run by the nuns would have been a way for Henry to assuage the guilt he felt over his sexual victimization as a child and for engaging in consensual homosexual activities as an adult, but why he invested in the seminary is less important in the long run than where he got so much money in the first place.

Henry made a remarkable comment only a few days before he was drafted in 1917 that hints at one possible source of the money he invested: "Graham's Bank went to smash. Great sums of savings lost or threatening to be lost. Loss incredible, inexcusable." For Henry to make such an emotional statement suggests that he was concerned over accounts he had opened there. Graham and Sons Bank, a well-known establishment at 661 West Madison Street, was only two blocks away from the coach house apartment he had shared with his father.

When the United States entered World War I, many of the bank's clients were in the throes of the patriotism then sweeping the nation and began to withdraw "large sums of money" to "purchase Liberty Bonds and make Red Cross contributions." The large number of withdrawals forced the bank to file for an "involuntary petition in bankruptcy" the afternoon of June 29, 1917, which eventually led to its closing down permanently. After closely examining its holdings, the Grahams realized they had enough money in the vaults to cover depositors' accounts, and no one would lose their money, despite the bankruptcy. Henry didn't lose a cent of whatever money he may have had in the bank, but he came uncomfortably close.

Sister Camilla sent Henry his very meager paychecks for the four months that he was in the army, but that plus his army pay, only $30 a month, wouldn't have been enough to give him the tidy nest egg that he invested. An inheritance was likely out of the question, too. His father was so destitute that Henry's uncles had to pay his way into St. Augustine's Home for the Aged, so it's unlikely that Henry got an inheritance from him. His uncle Augustine had died the year before the Graham and Sons fiasco, in 1916, but he wouldn't have left Henry an inheritance because his wife, Henry's aunt Anna, survived him. Augustine's money would have gone to her. His uncle Charles, who outlived his wife, would've left his money to his children.

It's most likely that someone Henry knew, someone who cared for him, gave him the money. That person could only have been Whillie. Henry wouldn't even allow him to pay for their dates at Riverview because he didn't want to appear to be a lamb, making it unlikely that he would have taken money from Whillie to invest. Yet that's probably the very reason why Henry paid for their dates. If Whillie had been giving Henry money to invest in his future, something we might expect in a loving relationship, Henry may have felt that paying their way during dates was the least he could do. Although we'll never know with any certainty, it seems logical that Whillie was Henry's benefactor.

Henry took another step that shows that he was all too aware of, and hoping to improve, his financial situation. In December 1935, now forty-three years old, Henry purchased a life insurance policy from Monumental Life for $500 with a "20 year endowment." His payments of $13.04 were due twice a year, on the tenth day of June and December. Henry kept a copy of his application for the policy, and Henry's answers to the third, fourth, and fifth questions on it reveal a great deal about the former inmate of the Illinois Asylum for Feeble-Minded Children. The third question asked the applicant, "Are you now in sound health?" to which Henry replied, "Yes." The fourth question asked him to list "all diseases . . . which" he had contracted, and he replied, "Scarlet fever when a little boy." When he reached the fifth question, "Does any physical or mental defect now exist . . . ?" he answered, "No."

Unlike on June 2, 1917, when he admitted to the draft registrar that he'd been an inmate in an asylum, he didn't offer a clue about his past to the insurance company, nor would anyone else in his shoes. He'd come to realize that his incarceration in the Asylum had nothing to do with a "mental defect" at all. In fact, he often railed that there had been nothing wrong with him and that he was, in fact, smarter than most of the other "bright boys" there. Besides, that was all behind him. By now, working his second stint at St. Joseph's, he was no longer feared by the nuns or called "Crazy." He'd out-lived the moniker.

QUEER THINGS HAPPEN IN THIS HELLISH NUT HOUSE

Henry had much more to say about the childhood experiences that he suffered than he was able to include in *The Realms*, and so, having finished his first novel in 1938 or early 1939, he began writing his second, *Further Adventures in Chicago: Crazy House*, or simply

Crazy House, in May 1939. In many ways it was a sequel to *The Realms*. Henry put the Vivian girl-boys and their brother, Penrod, at the center of *Crazy House*, too, but he set his new novel in West Madison Street, the vice district where he had lived as a child, where he was first and repeatedly thrown away, and where his sexual activities (forced, coerced, and consensual) had begun. Henry imported the Vivians from a make-believe world into a real one.

To tell his story, Henry wove three distinct but interrelated narratives into *Crazy House*, the most openly gay of all of his novels, which begins on September 18, 1911. In the first narrative, Henry introduced Webber George, a classmate of the Vivian girl-boys and their brother, Penrod, at the Skinner School, which Henry attended while living at the Mission. Ten-year-old Webber is filled with anger and strikes out violently at anyone who crosses him—adult or child—at the drop of a hat, just as Henry had done. Webber even slugs it out with Penrod at one point. More important is a note that Webber supposedly writes anonymously to a nun, accusing Angeline Vivian of performing a strip tease and then taking part in a sex circus:

> I found out that last night Angeline Vivian went to act in that big Vaudeville show on Halsted Street. She danced the Highland Fling on the stage with no clothes on at all with a strong light revealing her every motion.
>
> During intermissions she allowed naked boys to crowd around her, to take her into their arms, to sit on their laps and so on.

Instead of telling his readers what sexual activities take place between Angeline and the "naked boys," Henry used the phrase "and so on"—likely for the same reason he'd called his relationship with John Manley and the Scanlon brothers "other things." Angeline is, of course, one of Henry's "imitation little girls," making her involvement in a strip tease and a sex circus a decidedly homoerotic event.

Henry identified the theater where Angeline was accused of performing as the one standing at the northeast corner of Halsted and Madison, the threshold of the West Madison Street vice district. Although he never gives its name, the strip joint was probably the Haymarket Theater, a huge venue with enough seating on its main floor as well as its three balconies to accommodate an audience of 2,475, virtually all men. It opened in December 1887 and quickly became one of the most popular resorts in the area. An investigator who reported on the goings-on there revealed "that the shows being offered at this theater are as vulgar and sensuous as it is possible to find in any place save a house of prostitution. The vulgar jokes, the sensuous movements of young women and men performers have obviously only one purpose": to excite its male patrons. Once titillated, men in the audience could easily find a female prostitute or a fairy for a sexual liaison.

Although likely the Haymarket, the theater might also have been the Star and Garter, which was kitty-corner to and nearly as large as the Haymarket. Opening in February 1908, the year before Henry returned to Chicago, it was "famous for nude girlie shows and prostitution" and, like the Haymarket, had plenty of men-loving men in the audience cruising for sexual partners.

Belles, fairies, pansies, queens, and queers—and the "normal" men who enjoyed sex with them—not only made up a substantial percentage of the audiences at both establishments, they were also often an important topic for skits and comedians who performed there, showing how common and, at least in burlesque theaters, how visible they had become. One of the performers at the Star and Garter recalled,

When I first worked at the Star & Garter, skits pertaining to homosexuals were not infrequent and the term "fairy" or "pansy" was common, but in these last few years with the advent of commercialized homosexual haunts and the publicity of foreign political figures who indulged in degenerate activities, the subject of perverts has been a source of badinage in respectable vaudeville theaters, movies and night clubs. Since the burlesque theater has to follow the trends of obscenity offered on the various stages, in fact go them at least one better, I should have expected the amount of attention the comedians paid to homosexual situations in the dialogues at the latest Star & Garter show I saw. I have seen and heard plenty of filth on the stage, but that performance absolutely topped anything pervious.

Both theaters were open for business and were very popular resorts in 1911, the year in which Henry set *Crazy House*.

In the second narrative, Angeline is, like Henry, taken by a man named Tim Rooney by train to Arizona, where several different men—including Rooney—rape her. Rooney takes Angeline to Tucson on the same train line that the real Rooney took Henry to the Asylum at Lincoln, Illinois. While in the desert, Angeline realizes how much she misses her home—"To be torn away from those I love. That's unbearable"—using virtually the same language that Henry had used to express how he felt about being away from Whillie during the few months he was in the army in Texas, another desert state.

Angeline escapes her kidnapper and rapists and returns to Chicago, paralleling Henry's escape from the Asylum when he was seventeen. Like Henry, Angeline does everything she can to keep herself from remembering her sexual abuse—"the result was so terrible that I myself close my mind tightly against the memory," she confesses—but the strategy of denial fails her, as it did Henry. Although she can't bear to reveal what happened to her to anyone face-to-face, she writes about it in a letter to one of the novel's minor characters, Mrs. Red Eagle. It's likely that Henry also never spoke about his experiences to anyone, making it that much more imperative to him to write about them, as she did, albeit in disguised, metaphoric terms.

A subplot of the second narrative concerns the Vivian girl-boys and theology. Henry went to great lengths to identify the Vivian girl-

224 Henry Darger, Throwaway Boy

boys as being sinless, although he never claimed they were virgins. In fact, Angeline, who's been raped, couldn't be. The Vivian girl-boys refuse to go to confession before their first communion because confession cleanses the sinner, and the Vivians, who believe they are sinless, don't feel they need to be purified of anything. However, the priest who would be presiding over their first communion refuses to allow the Vivians to take communion unless they go to confession first.

In a larger context, their theological predicament is probably a moot point for most readers, but Henry was actually dealing with his own feelings of guilt. He didn't want to have to believe that victims of rape—as he and Angeline were—had committed sin when they were raped. It's likely that he'd heard people say, "She asked for it," in response to the rape of a woman. Given his own sexual abuse and his devout faith, it was very important for him to distinguish between consensual and nonconsensual sex and the Church's response to each. For him, it wasn't an abstract theological question at all but a very personal, and all-too-real, one.

Henry decided to consult a theologian he didn't know rather than the priests at St. Vincent's Church, probably because they hadn't been any help to him twenty years earlier when he wanted to adopt a child. He also knew that the priests would likely question him about why he was concerned over such an odd question and didn't want them prying into his business. On May 23, 1939, Henry wrote to the editors of *The Ave Maria*, a Catholic weekly newspaper, asking them whether a priest could, or should, allow children who had never committed a sin take communion without first going to confession.

Two days later, the magazine's associate editor, Father Charles M. Carey, sent a letter to Henry. He found Henry's "story"—evidently Henry shared at least some of the plot of *Crazy House* with him—to be "an unusual one" and then responded to Henry's question:

> As regards the practice of refusing Communion to those children, it seems to me that the priests in question should know the circum-

stances surrounding the case and be able to draw a proper conclusion more readily can could I. The Church's theology on the matter is simply this: you do not have to go to confession unless you are guilty of mortal sin.

Therefore, . . . the children should be allowed to receive Communion.

Father Carey continued to explain that there may be extenuating circumstances, situations, activities, etc., that the priest who is scheduled to preside over their first communion knows about and that may keep him from offering the children the Sacrament. He ends his letter, "I hope that my explanation may be of some help to you."

It was. Henry had gotten an answer that allowed him to continue with the manuscript. Eventually, the priest in *Crazy House* gives in, and the Vivian girl-boys receive communion without going to confession. They aren't simply happy about the turn of events; they're a little boastful that they've been right (and the priest has been wrong) all along. Unfortunately, Henry wasn't as confident. Father Carey's answer should have put Henry's concern to rest, but like his anger, his guilt over his own victimization was so intense that it continued to haunt him.

With the loose ends of the first two narratives tied up neatly, Henry then focused his attention on the crazy house itself in the last narrative. Owned by Michael Seseman—a name that sounds strikingly like "sissy man," suggesting that he's a fairy—the building has been cursed, and various demons haunt it. Henry's characters call it by a variety of names, among them "nut house" and "madhouse," although most simply refer to it as the "crazy house"—all synonyms for a mental institution. Henry even called the demon-ravaged Seseman's house "the house of a thousand troubles," an obvious reference to the name of a concession at Riverview Amusement Park, the House of Troubles

Henry is quick to tell readers that although the "crazy house" looks normal, even inviting, on the outside, inside it's "topsy-turvy."

It inverts its rooms—the ceiling becomes the floor, and the floor the ceiling—to kill whoever happens to be in them at the time, and as important, what readers might think of as normal is anything but. The crazy house is, in fact, a playground of oddities. The demons that haunt the house animate all sorts of otherwise innocuous household items—chairs, coat trees, Victrolas—that then become the demons' agents, attacking those who trespass into the house or onto its grounds. They even cause all sorts of "crazy phenomenon" to occur: "pervert phenomenon's," "fire phenomenon," "phenomenons of strangulation," "organ crash phenomenon," "immodest phenomenon," and "upside down phenomenon." Children's innocence incites the demons to rape and mutilate them, harkening back to the gory scenes on his canvases, which, in turn, harken even further back, to his experiences on the streets of West Madison and behind the walls of the Mission and the Asylum.

Beginning as early as the 1920s, but culminating in the mid- to late 1930s, the period in which Henry set out to write *Crazy House*, Chicagoans were in the throes of a paranoia that was sweeping the country. Stunned by a number of sexual assaults on girls and women who were then murdered, they saw crazed sex fiends lurking under every bed, stalking through every park, or sneaking down every street and alley—all after dark, of course. Henry tapped into that paranoia. Putting a new twist on the citywide terror, Henry wrote, "A little nine year old girl had been strangled raped and horribly murdered, not by a wicked sex man monster this time as at first suppose but by one of the fierce demons" haunting Seseman's house. In Henry's novel, little girls weren't being stalked and victimized by any of the usual suspects, what society had labeled sex fiends, but by the unexpected and even previously unknown invisible, indefinable demons.

Although *Crazy House* is set for the most part around Skinner School and in West Madison Street, Henry also included various places in his neighborhood on Chicago's Near North Side. Lincoln Park, St. Joseph's Hospital, and St. Augustine's Home for the Aged make appearances in the novel. On their way home from Mass one day, Penrod and Webber "paused" at the corner of Webster and Dayton "to improve a few gay dance steps." That corner happens to be a few feet from the building in which Henry was then living, 851 Webster.

He also populated the second novel with many characters from the first, not simply the Vivian girl-boys and Penrod but also, for example, Jack Evans and Hendro Dargar(the "famous Gemini Society leader") as well as some real individuals he knew, such as Sister Camilla and, of course, Whillie. However, Whillie is no longer just "Whillie" but is now often "Bill," the name his family called him, and his role in *Crazy House* is somewhat smaller than the one he had in *The Realms*.

THERE ARE LOTS OF QUEER PEOPLE IN THIS CITY

Walking down the street, Bill and another male character whom Henry never identified notice a girl whom they assume to be a prostitute because she's loitering at a street corner:

> 'Say Bill, look. Isn't that little girl a beautiful a young man, the scum sort one finds infesting corners where pedestrians are thickest . . .'
> 'She's a little peacherino all right' remarked Bill.

Bill's companion believes at first that the loiterer is a "girl," but suddenly, he realizes that she's really a "beautiful . . . young man." Having identified a fairy, the companion reacts as society in general would have, calling her "scum . . . infesting" the crowded streets of Chicago. She's "scum" not only because she's a girl-boy but also because she's either a prostitute or cruising for a sex partner. On the other hand, Bill acknowledges the attractiveness of the "peacherino" fairy, an obvious acceptance of her in direct contrast to his companion's rejection. Although both see the "peacherino" for what she is, neither of the men recognizes that she is actually Jennie, one of the Vivian girl-boys and one of the novel's heroes. With such accurate depictions of Chicago's gay scene, Henry obviously knew about queer cruising activities in a time when only the initiated would have had a clue.

At least as early as the mid-1930s, and probably much earlier, a favorite, very active place where Chicago queer men cruised one another was on State Street in the Loop, especially the block where Marshall Field's, a department store, stood. One young gay man admitted to sociology students at the University of Chicago that, when he was in his late teens, he "met a fellow" who told him, "if you ever want to make money come down to Randolph and State," which was at the store's northwest corner, "and stand with your arms crossed. This was a sign that you could and wanted to be picked up. You can make five or ten dollars easy that way."

In another part of *Crazy House*, two boys who are considerably older than Webber George pretend to be teachers at Skinner School and take Webber, who needs a place to spend the night, to the music teacher's room in what Henry called the "Teachers infirmary." It "is a long low but handsome structure two stories in height, with the windows of the first floor about nine feet above the ground." The teacher, Mr. Handel, is away, although he may return at any moment.

Henry described Mr. Handel's room as "exquisitely fitted up, a students lamp upon a table was alight . . . and threw a softened splendor upon the entire room. There were lidies [ladies'] silk hangings doilies lace pillowslips, silken curtains books selected seemingly for their pretty covers . . . and upon the toilet table a number of dainty articles." Just before leaving Webber alone in Mr. Handel's room, one of the older boys warns Webber not to let anyone else into the room, meaning Mr. Handel, because he might "impose on you." Seconds later, the boy repeats his warning: "Don't let him impose upon you." The boys are warning Webber against possible rape.

A few pages later, Henry described Mr. Handel, who's as effeminate in appearance as his room: "Mr Handel was a tall willowy young exquisite of 28 with a light mustache a delicate complexion and a dainty cane. He wore an abundance of wrings [rings]." Mr. Handel is the stereotype of an invert, a fairy. Despite the fact that Mr. Handel is queer, he's married to the female principal of Skinner School—a doppelgänger of the very strong-willed woman who'd expelled Henry decades earlier for making noises in Miss Dewey's classroom. Mr. Handel is one of many characters in *Crazy House* who leads a double life.

Father Casey, who is the chief priest of St. Patrick's Church, reveals that his secretary, Michael David, also has a secret life. Michael practices curtsying and has a "bosom-friend" named Jerry Monahan, a "janitor," which was Henry's first job. Jerry, who is married and a "normal" man, has a relationship not only with Michael but also with Webber's uncle, Henry George, another married, "normal" man. The relationship between Jerry and Henry George not only reveals that Henry knew that men who weren't fairies were attracted to one another but also parallels his and Whillie's—two "normal" men's—relationship.

Henry planted many other clues in *Crazy House* that reveal his firsthand knowledge of the gay subculture. At one point, the demons that haunt Seseman's house assault a priest, and another priest, Father Kelley, reveals that "there was a lot of dirty things they did to him." Father Kelley also admits, "There is another young priest" who's "a special friend of mine"—using the common code at the time, "special friend," for lover. Father Carney warns Jennie, who has been standing on street corners, trying to get picked up, about love. "I'm deathly afraid of it sometimes," he admits, because "if love gets into the wrong channels it means destruction." "Wrong channels" suggests an unnatural love, a perverse love, a queer love.

Henry reveals Penrod's sexual orientation in one sentence: "Penrod himself be it remembered was good or is an unusually good boy but even the most good boys have the passions of their own kind." Being an Abbieannian, Penrod's gay orientation is virtually a civic duty, according to Daisy, who claims that boys from Abbieannia "love each other well, too well." At one point, Webber and Penrod follow Angeline and Jennie to the Janet Theater in Towertown. After searching for them downstairs, the boys go to the balcony where the girl-boys are sitting with adult men. Henry described Jennie's date:

> He probably was over thirty years of age. His black glossy hair parted in the middle was very impressive.
> His eyes were large and dark, sharp and watchful as those of an owl, his forehead high and narrow, his features dark.
> He was dressed to accentuate his youthfulness.

Penrod is smitten by the handsome older man, and after a few seconds of staring at him through the darkened theater, he suddenly

> began to feel himself seized by a sort of fascination. He could not take his eyes off the fellow.
> He felt as though he were rooted to the spot. Suddenly the spell was broken The man as though Penrods gaze, made itself felt upon him suddenly turned his head.
> His eyes met Penrods eyes, and with the steadiness of an owl in that momentary gaze. He grinned.

Henry turns the plot away from the encounter we expect Penrod and the man may have and leaves Jennie the fairy alone to enjoy the company of her date, a "normal" man.

Interestingly, Penrod has a similar moment with his buddy James Mic-Givney "Rattlesnake Boy" Radcliffe, who's a "Calverinian boy scout," the first time they met. They are immediately attracted to one another, and after the two engage in small talk for a short time, Rattlesnake Boy asks Penrod,

"Do you want to join my company?"

"No," Penrod answered. "I am in command of a full regiment. I would rather you would join me."

He said it because in his own mind he had found a sort of response in the queer look in the Rattlesnake's eyes. He wanted to be with him if possible. He wanted to be with him for good. Strange as the Calverinian boy scout was, there was some kind of strong attraction in him.

Penrod isn't the only young gay man in Chicago who found himself attracted to older men, and Henry draws from his own experience to present such May-December romances. After all, he was well aware of the attraction a younger man might feel for an older one. As important, Henry was obviously aware that, in the early decades of the twentieth century, during the many ups and downs of the U.S. economy, young gay men often formed relationships with older ones for economic, as well as romantic, reasons.

One gay Chicagoan at the time, dubbed "Herman," recalled during his interview with University of Chicago sociology students that "his first homosexual relations were with a relative, who was twice his age." Another, who went by "Mr. D," engaged in sex with a number of adult men when he was a child and an adolescent, and a third, "Mr. R," developed a relationship with "an elderly man" when he was a young man. "H" had an affair when he was eighteen with a fifty-year-old executive at Mandel's, a large department store in the Loop, where "H" worked. "Harold" claimed, "I used to have an affair with a man much older than myself," although he didn't say how much older, and a student studying French in a Loop restaurant one afternoon allowed himself to be picked up by an executive with a Chicago-based South American company. Their affair lasted ten weeks.

To sate his "passions," Penrod has a number of sexual relationships with men and boys in *Crazy House*, including Jerry Monahan the janitor, Michael David's "bosom-friend." Like most of the other characters of *Crazy House*, Michael is a child, ten or eleven years old. Jerry, on the other hand, is "a pious dashing young Irishman of impulsive disposition having at that time a wife and a little boy and girl." Jerry enjoys Michael's company behind closed doors while, in the open, he's a doting father. Together, Jerry and Michael investigate Seseman's crazy house, and Henry includes in *Crazy House* an account of their investigation, called "The Wonderful Adventure of Michael the Office Boy and Jerry the Janitor in Sesemans House"—a story within a story told by Michael.

During their investigation, Jerry and Michael run into Penrod, who's conducting an investigation on his own. "What are you doing here?" Penrod asks Jerry, who responds, "I want to speak to you in private about this 'crazy house.'" Then

> Penrod stepped out [of the room they were in] and Jerry closed the door. "You're not a policeman are you?" says Penrod with a scowl.
> "Indeed I'm not" says Jerry. "Suppose Master Penrod we come up stairs and look things over."
> "Sure" says Penrod and up the steps they went arm in arm.

Penrod asks Jerry if he's a policeman because he's trying to protect himself, concerned that if Jerry's a member of the vice squad he'll arrest Penrod on morals charges. To keep from being arrested, queer men knew to ask a pick-up if he was a member of the police force before engaging in any sort of sexual activities. By law, the policeman had to answer that he was. If he didn't and arrested his quarry anyway, the judge had to dismiss the charges against the queer man as entrapment. This is an important lesson that all queer men who wanted to stay out of prison and to keep their names out of the newspapers had to learn—and one that Henry obviously knew. He could only have learned this important lesson of queer life through his connections with other queer men. Once Penrod hears Jerry's reply, "Indeed I'm not," he's willing to go "up the stairs" to have sex with Jerry.

A few pages later, Michael, who has observed their interactions, then watched them disappear upstairs together, ignores what has gone on between Penrod and Jerry and focuses "serenely" and without a hint of jealousy on the couple as they return. Jerry "walked down the second flight of stairs to the ground floor arm in arm with Penrod. The two of them looked like a pair of cooing doves." A "normal" man caught in the act of having had sex with a boy *and* being disloyal to his "bosom-friend," "Jerry glared at Michael and opened his mouth" as if "to say what he thought of him, but the proper words not coming," he only "remained open mouthed." Jerry's reaction to being caught in the act, an extreme surprise that leaves him speechless, underscores the sexual nature of his and Penrod's activities upstairs.

Although Henry never identified Penrod as a psychic hermaphrodite as his sisters are, Henry does occasionally give Penrod distinct, but temporary, feminine characteristics. The Vivian girl-boys are artists, and to help exorcise the haunted house, they paint the Sacred Heart of Jesus, just as Henry had done in real life. They use the picture of an actual heart that they have found in a biology book as a model, also as Henry had, and follow Father Casey's instructions. The Vivian girl-boys depict their brother in their version of the Sacred Heart as "the prettiest of the angels," and when Henry painted his version of the Sacred Heart, he went a step further. He portrayed Penrod in a girl's dress. In fact, Penrod had asked to be included—"In disguise make me one of the angels"—and Henry did.

At many points in the novel, Henry feminized Penrod, such as when he visits Webber George's aunt (the wife of one of the "normal" men, Henry George) in jail. She's shocked to learn that Penrod is a boy. He's so effeminate that she's sure he's actually a girl "dressed in boys clothes." Later in the novel, Henry wrote that "the little Vivians and their brother, all of them," were "dressed in taste that was like the little queens they were." "Queen" was then, and still is, gay argot that denotes effeminate gay men, a synonym for "fairy," and yet compared to his sisters, Penrod is far from being a psychic hermaphrodite.

Even some of the Vivian girl-boys' names point to their sexual orientation. Flowers played an important role in the lives of fairies of the early days of the twentieth century. Besides being called, and calling themselves, pansies and even "gardenia boys," they also adopted female names that were also the names of flowers, such as "Daisy" and "Violet," names Henry assigned two of the Vivian girl-boys. Interestingly, he didn't use "Rose," his mother's name and one that would have been an obvious choice for one of the Vivians.

Many of the characters in *Crazy House* describe the Vivian girl-boys, and when they do, they often call them "fairy," "fairies," or "fairy-like," terms that refer to both the creatures of legend and children's literature as well as to the most effeminate class of inverts. They also usually point out the Vivian girl-boys' blond or silver-colored hair. In the first three or so decades of the twentieth century, fairies often bleached their hair blond and wore it longer than most nonqueer men. Jennie says quite early in the novel, "There are lots of queer people in this city," and she was probably including the Vivian girl-boys.

WEBBER'S SECRET

Henry revealed other things about his life through his characters, especially Angeline, in *Crazy House*. At one point, she admits, "I've been going through all kinds of strange adventures and bad experiences all my life. . . . I've never hardly known a happy day"—something Henry repeated, but using a few different words, only a year and a half before he died. Like her creator, Angeline admits she "loved" storms and is disturbed by God's refusal to answer her prayers: "Why didn't our dear answer that prayer . . . ? What is the matter with me? Why am I so buffeted around? What have I done to deserve such handling? I don't know I don't know I've been ill treated everywhere since I was born." Her questions sound remarkably like those Henry asked himself in "Found on Sidewalk." Like Henry, the Vivians erect an altar, but they build theirs in Seseman's house, not in Whillie's barn.

Despite all the similarities between Henry and the Vivians, the character who represents Henry most strikingly is not any of the Vivians, neither the girl-boys nor Penrod, but Webber George. Once the Vivians' sworn enemy, Webber eventually becomes Penrod's special friend after another character, Alice Morrow, admits that she, not Webber, wrote the note that accused Angeline of taking part in a striptease and sex circus. The sexual attraction Penrod and Webber have for each other, and the romance that develops out of it, is very brief, both boys moving on to give their affections and bodies to other boys and men.

Webber shares more important attributes with Henry than any other character Henry ever created. Henry established the link between himself and Webber almost immediately. Webber claims that his "uncle . . . was once a mayor of a small city called Lincoln," the town in which the Illinois Asylum for Feeble-Minded Children was located. Webber "threw cool ashes" into Michael David's little sister's eyes, recalling the day decades earlier when Henry threw ashes into Francis Gillow's eyes. The narrator of *Crazy House* reveals that St. Patrick's School was not an appropriate place for Webber and suggests that the boy would be better off if he were sent to a reform school, recalling how the Mission's administration decided Henry didn't belong there but somewhere else more appropriate for someone who was "crazy." The narrator then reveals that Webber is so bad—"a thoroughly bad boy"—that he has been expelled, as Henry had been twice.

Of all the similarities between Webber and Henry, being a "thoroughly bad boy" is the most important and, ultimately, the most revealing. Henry admitted over and over again how "bad" he had been as a child and gave plenty of examples, but he could never bring himself to reveal why. After strongly linking himself to Webber, Henry made an amazing revelation about Webber and, by extension, about himself: "One cause mainly of the boy being bad, and a foolish one at that was because he was angry at God for not having created him into a girl which he wanted to be more than anything else." Henry's anger at God, which began when he was five or six years old and which he revealed by burning holy cards that depicted Jesus, was certainly caused by the physical and sexual abuse he suffered, by the jealousy he felt because other children's parents were taking care of them while his father ignored him, and by the general mistreatment that he experienced, usually at the hands of adults. Yet Henry was also angry—which became manifest in his "thoroughly bad" behavior—because he wanted to be female instead of male, just as his ten-year-old doppelgänger Webber did.

Many gay men in Chicago at the time also wished, like Webber, that they'd been born women instead of men. Initially this might seem as if they believed that they were transgendered, but the context in which they admitted dissatisfaction with their gender has nothing to do with feeling that their gender didn't match their bodies. Instead, it had everything to do with society and the sexual norms it had established and to which everyone was expected to adhere. Had they been born female instead of male, they could have expressed their desires for romantic and sexual relationships with men without any fear of interference from friends, family, church, or state. As it was, society had stripped them of their ability to express their desires honestly and completely unless they were willing to suffer the consequences: rejection by those whom they knew and loved, damnation by the church, and a prison term from the state.

Several gay men who were interviewed by graduate students in the University of Chicago's sociology program admitted they wished they'd been born women. "James" said that, when he was eighteen, he wanted to be a woman, and added, "Maybe this idea came to me because I thought that a woman can pick out whom she likes" for romance and sexual encounters. "Charles" echoed "James":

> From as far back as I can remember I have always wished I was a girl. About my attraction for Lew I was horribly shocked at myself. I didn't understand, I wished I was a woman so that we could do something about it. While I would liked to have touched him I never did.

"Lester" agreed with the other two: "Boys would tease me at five years of age, and would say you are a girl. I would say that I would rather be a girl than a boy because men would look upon girls before they would boys."

Webber's desire to have been born female rather than male was Henry's. Webber's anger was Henry's, too. Webber transferred his anger from God to those around him. He couldn't lash out at the Divine, so he lashed out at any little girl around him because a little girl "had many advantages which [a little] boy did not," echoing the comments made by "James," "Charles," and "Lester."

Henry pushed the envelope even further a few pages later. He actually entered the narrative and spoke directly to the reader as himself in nineteenth-century fashion. In the process, he essentially admitted that he was part of Chicago's queer subculture. "The reader may think this"—Webber's desire to have been born female—is "strange," Henry wrote, but "the writer knows quite a number of boys who would give anything to have been born a girl."

DEVIL'S ISLAND

Henry had loved to read ever since his father taught him how. Throughout his childhood, he read whenever books were available, and once he became an adult, he began buying them. His personal library would eventually contain more than a hundred volumes, and one of its most revealing books is a classic of gay literature, *Condemned to Devil's Island*. When Henry began writing *Crazy House*, he decided to borrow a number of details from it for the Vivian girl-boys' background.

Written by Blair Niles and published in 1928, *Condemned to Devil's Island* is supposedly a biography of a very handsome young Frenchman, Michel Oban, who, after being convicted of theft in France, was imprisoned on Devil's Island, a penal colony off the coast of French Guiana. Niles claimed to have visited the island and interviewed the convict thoroughly, and the book's subtitle, *The Biography of an Unknown Convict*, suggests exactly that, but the book is obviously fiction with the subtitle stuck on to protect it from the censor. It was a best seller and turned into a successful movie starring heartthrob Ronald Colman, who was nominated for an Academy Award for his performance as the "unknown convict" Michel.

Henry bought his copy in a secondhand bookstore for one dollar. Smudges on the upper corners of its pages show that he, and its two previous owners, had read it often, probably because the book is so amazingly frank for the time in its depictions of various male-male sexual relationships. A great deal of Niles's so-called observations of prison life would also have struck Henry as being virtually identical to his own experiences on West Madison Street and in the various institutions in which he lived.

Henry certainly would have also identified with Michel. Niles's "unknown convict" recalls early in the book that he has no family. His mother disappeared when he was very young, and he rarely sees his father—exactly what Henry could have said about his own childhood. Both Michel and Henry were convicted of crimes: Michel with theft, Henry with self-abuse. Both were exiled to institutions because of their crimes: Michel to Devil's Island, Henry to the Asylum. Once on Devil's Island, Michel can't help but become aware of, and take part in, a thriving homosocial, homoerotic culture, one in which men openly fight one another over the sexual favors of a younger, good-looking man and one in which men can even live together in marriage-like relationships. In the Asylum and on its farm, male-male romances and rapes were also common but were kept secret, unknown to all but those who lived or worked there.

Niles's characters often use the term "brat." Henry understood firsthand the meaning of it, a word synonymous with "kid" or "lamb," because of his childhood experiences. Niles explained "brat" to those unaware of its sexual connotation: "In the womanless world of the Guiana prisons the men who satisfy Adam's desire for Eve are called *mômes*. The English 'brat' is of course necessarily an inadequate rendering of the local significance of *môme*," but despite its being "an inadequate rendering" of the French, she uses it. Niles's narrator discloses early in the book that "whenever you see a young convict" on Devil's Island "who seems better fed and better dressed than the rest, put him down as somebody's brat." In fact, Michel quickly comes to the realization that "'There are only three sorts of men in prison' . . . 'the men who keep brats, those who become brats, and those that learn how to relieve themselves.'" While imprisoned, Michel witnesses male-male rapes and a fight sanctioned by guards between two wolves over Félix, a beautiful young lamb, and he even falls in love with another man.

As soon as he realized what the fate of good-looking young men at Devil's Island is, Michel says of himself, "Here's a boy who isn't going to be [a] brat to any of you," while, in response, another inmate counters, "While you," those who have recently arrived at Devil's Island, "have what you call croaker and fallen women, we have the 'brats' who are lost and fallen boys." Another new arrival reveals his plan for his future: "He'd drink or gamble, or keep a brat. Or perhaps all three." One of the more seasoned of the convicts "laughed at the notion that he would give up his brat." Any younger man who isn't a "good-looking fellow—one of those girly-boys,"a phrase that echoes "psychic hermaphrodite," might consider himself very unlucky. Those who keep brats give them food, clothing, even protection from others who might mistreat them—exactly what many wolves in West Madison Street had offered their lambs, including Henry.

Within a few pages of the opening of *Crazy House*, Henry wrote that the Vivian girl-boys have been kidnapped, then imprisoned on Devil's Island for four months, May through August 1910, when they escape. While they were there, the children not only witnessed men blatantly engaged in sexual activities with one another and even marriage-like relationships, they also were forced to live and work naked and were stricken with "awful fever horrors," a phrase fraught with sexual connotation. Angeline even acknowledges the intense sexual nature of life in the penal colony. Henry wrote that Father Casey, the priest in charge of St. Patrick's Church, "had a book on French Guiana," probably *Condemned to Devil's Island* and a hint of the priest's sexual orientation, which he loans to Angeline to read so that she can verify the sexual openness in the penal colony. After Angeline reads it, "she told him that everything that was printed in the book was true."

CHAPTER 8

I LOST ALL I HAD

THE OLD MAN'S DRAFT

O N SUNDAY, DECEMBER 7, 1941, THE JAPANESE AIR FORCE bombarded Pearl Harbor. The attack killed almost two and a half thousand U.S. civilians and military personnel. In response, the United States entered the fray that had already broken out across Europe and that would soon be called World War II. Desperate for soldiers by 1942, the U.S. government scheduled a draft registration for four different periods that year, and all men between the ages of eighteen and sixty-four had to register. At fifty-one years old, Henry registered for the draft a second time in his life, on April 27, in what has been called the "old man's draft registration." The last of the four different periods, it was established for men born between April 18, 1877, and February 16, 1897. Although Whillie was sixty-three, he didn't bother to register.

What little information that is available on Henry's draft card for World War II gives a sketch of a man in physical decline. He weighed only one hundred twenty-five pounds, a possible sign of malnourishment. His skin was "sallow," another probable indication of his poor eating habits and a symptom of general debilitation. His eyes were described as "hazel," although his draft card for the First World War claimed they were blue, and what was once dark brown hair had now turned "gray." The registrar also noted that his right leg had a noticeable limp, but he was still able to get around efficiently—for his purposes, although not for the army's.

Something very peculiar also appears on Henry draft card. When Henry registered for the draft just before the First World War, he was twenty-five years old and stood, according to his registration card, five feet one inch tall. Twenty-four years later, instead of shrinking as men typically do as they age, Henry sprouted an extra seven inches— growing to a remarkable five feet eight inches tall. There's no way to reconcile the discrepancy, except to conclude that one of these records is a mistake, and it must have been the later one. Although older men had to register for the draft, no one believed for a second they would ever be called to serve. Besides, even if some of the "old men" actually were inducted, Henry wouldn't have been because his limp would have guaranteed his exemption. The registrar would have been aware of this and probably couldn't have cared less if Henry's card contained accurate information.

The most important thing about his registration is neither his eye color nor his height but who Henry listed as the "Person Who Will Always Know Your Address." It wasn't a family member who would always know where Henry would be, of course. Only one, his aunt Anna, would have kept in touch with Henry and known his whereabouts, but she had died eight years earlier. His uncles and his other aunt were also dead, and his cousins were strangers. Only Whillie, with whom Henry had now had a relationship for more than thirty years, would know Henry's whereabouts, and that's who Henry designated as his contact person. While it served an obvious and acceptable official purpose, it was also another way he linked himself to his beloved in lieu of some other, more visible or legal union.

Obviously, Henry believed he and Whillie would be together for a very long time.

Henry's World War II draft card also reveals an interesting aspect of Henry's personality. He had begun using pseudonyms for important public documents. Although he signed his draft card for World War I with his real name, he signed his registration card for World War II "Henry Jose Dargarius," using a Spanish name for his middle name and a Latin-like version of his last name. This wasn't the first time that Henry's last name appeared on official documents incorrectly. In fact, inconsistencies about Henry's identity had begun when he was twelve years old and sent to the Asylum. Not only was his family name changed to "Dodger" in the Asylum's records, when he began working at St. Joseph's Hospital, he was known as Henry "Dagget" for at least his first year there. Eventually, the sisters corrected the mistake, but the Asylum administrators never bothered.

By the time he began writing *The Realms*, Henry had learned how easy it was to change his identity simply by altering his name. He took great pains to re-create himself in *The Realms*, metamorphosing himself into generals, journalists, and other characters with versions of his name. As Henry entered middle age, the pain he'd experienced during his abuse and the guilt he felt because of it became so relentless that he regularly used variations of Dagget to distance himself as much as possible from the little boy who'd been so inconsequential that his father abandoned him over and over again with little, if any, thought for his happiness or safety. What had happened to Henry *Dodger* at the Asylum had nothing to do with Henry *Darger*. His use of pseudonyms was simply another, albeit extreme, version of denial.

Henry first began using "Dargarius" when he began to fall ill and doctors examined him. Prescriptions that they wrote for him often identify him as "Henry Jose Dargarius," although one for "eye ointment" was issued simply to "Henry Dargarius." More often, he preferred to use "Dargarius." He even introduced himself to some of the other tenants in his building as Henry "Dargarius," and that was his name on his records of St. Vincent's Church. His withholding tax statements from his last employer were addressed to "Henry J. Dargarus," probably the name he'd used to apply for the job and the one under which he had been hired, and while his bank account at the Illinois Bank and Trust Company from 1934 to 1941 was Henry J. Darger's, he would later open accounts at Aetna Bank as "Henry J. Dargarus" and "Henry Vorger." The Bureau of the Census once even sent "Henry J. Darger" a letter inquiring about the whereabouts of "Henry J. Dargarus." There's no evidence to suggest that he ever told them.

WHILLIE IN SUBURBIA

When Whillie's mother, Susanna, died on August 9, 1931, she left the house at 634 Garfield to her children who had been living there with her at the time: Lizzie, Whillie, and Katherine. For the next ten years, Lizzie took her mother's place as the stay-at-home head of the household while Whillie continued to work as a night watchman at Philip Rinn Company and Katherine worked as a teller at various banks, including the National Bank of the Republic in the Loop. Then on February 26, 1941, "Lizzie died so mysteriously."

Henry had never really liked Lizzie. As far as he was concerned, Whillie's other sisters were enjoyable to be around, but Lizzie was "always contesting and fighting" with Whillie. And she always got her way. Henry didn't like it when anyone treated Whillie disrespectfully, but if truth be told, Whillie never stood up for himself against her, or against any of the women in the family for that matter. Lizzie had also kept Whillie and Katherine chained to the family house, quashing Katherine's life-long dream of living in Mexico. Although there were many obstacles that kept Whillie and Henry from living together, Lizzie would have been one of them.

Now freed of Lizzie's controlling ways, Whillie and Katherine decided to sell the house, which signaled their liberation. By then, the neighborhood, once solidly middle class, had fallen on hard times and was beginning to decline. In a very short time, the area would be considered in a less-than-standard condition or, in Henry's words, "the slums." However, Katherine didn't move to Mexico, and Whillie didn't move in with Henry. Instead, they decided to live together, probably at Katherine's insistence. She seems to have assumed control over Whillie when Lizzie died. After the sale, Whillie and Katherine packed up their clothing and the few pieces of furniture they wanted to keep and moved to Wilmette, a quiet, wealthy, northern suburb of Chicago.

Willie's sister Susan and her husband, Charles, had moved out of the Schloeders' house to Wilmette in the 1930s and added a third child, Jean, to their family. Charles had worked hard, rising from a clerk at the Loop branch of the National Bank of the Republic to vice president. He could afford to buy a very large home in that wealthy suburb and hire a live-in maid, Anna B. Brown, to manage the household. When Whillie and Katherine decided to move to Wilmette, Susan and Charles's children were thirty-one, twenty-five, and nineteen years old and were moving out of the house to pursue their own lives. It's probable that Charles and Susan had asked Katherine and Whillie to move into their home.

For the first time since they met over thirty years earlier, a substantial distance separated Henry and Whillie. Wilmette was a lengthy L ride away, two transfers and easily two hours one way. Henry was now forty-nine and Whillie sixty-two. They'd never lived together, so except for the distance that separated them, not much changed in their relationship. They made do. Henry could still visit Whillie, and Whillie could still visit him. Nevertheless, the separation caused Henry a great deal of inner turmoil.

With Whillie in suburbs, Henry continued to keep busy, busier now than ever, to try to squash the loneliness that threatened to overwhelm him. He was still working at St. Joseph's—his second round of employment there—trying to cope with the nuns and other employees as he had been for years. Writing his new novel, *Crazy House*, filled his evenings and days off for the next twenty-eight years or so, and he was still creating illustrations for it and *The Realms*.

At about the same time that Whillie moved out of Chicago, Henry began developing extreme pains in his legs. The pain would attack late at night, moving from one leg to the other and then back again and keeping him awake. He tried to ease the throbbing with heat pads, but nothing seemed to help. The pain became so intense at times that it caused Henry to yell blasphemies at God. It embarrassed him, but after a while, he was unable to stop.

During the few times that he discussed his blasphemy, he was typically contradictory: "I shook my fist twards heaven, meaning it for God" and "The knee pains at night I must confess and am not ashamed to tell of it, I actually shook my fist tward heaven. I didn't mean it for God though, though I felt like it." Henry also reacted with blasphemy during his shift in the dishwashing room when the work overwhelmed him by singing "awfully blasphemous words at God for hours without stopping." Henry was sure that God would strike him dead in retaliation, but that didn't happen. Instead, God ignored Henry's blasphemies exactly as he had ignored Henry's prayers to adopt a child. But the waves of pain continued as punishment for his sins, or so Henry believed.

Henry never overtly connected the onslaught of the pain with Whillie's move to Wilmette, which must have been a traumatic event. Instead, he recalled, "I got on me a very mean streak because of prayers not being answered on a question over the snow." It's certainly believable that another of Henry's prayers went unanswered, probably one concerning Whillie and probably one asking God to intervene and keep Whillie in Chicago or at least to keep Henry in Whillie's heart, but Henry was unable to articulate such personal matters. Instead, he disguised his real request with a trivial "question over snow."

It's interesting that Henry turned to the weather to camouflage his real concern because he'd been fascinated with clouds, storms, snow, and rain since he was a little boy:

> I was very interested in summer thunderstorms . . . and during winter could and would stand by the window all day, watching it snow, especially if there was a great big blizzard raging.
>
> I would watch it rain with great interest, also short or long showers.

In fact, the weather not only enthralled him, it also became a way for him to distract himself from his loneliness. Every day without exception, beginning the first day of 1958 and continuing until the last day of 1967, Henry kept a multivolume *Weather Report of Cold and Warm, Also Summer Heats and Cool Spells, Storms, and Fair or Cloudy Days, Contrary to What the Weatherman Says, and Also True Too* in which he logged the weather conditions and often added his own perspective and those of the meteorologists who, all too often, made mistakes:

> Weather for Monday before. Miserable. Almost impossible to walk because of ice on streets and sidewalks because of rain. Cold. Rain in morning. Morning from 3 to 4 a.m., 31. Afternoon at 5 p.m., 26. Tuesday another freeze rain, but walking less dangerous, or you at least could walk the streets

Another entry read:

> This is Christmas day. Weather report 50/50. It is report of clear skies. True. But it got much warmer than reported. Promise also for rain turning to snow, did not come true.

Tired of feeling he was God's whipping boy, Henry decided to retaliate. Although generally a steady church-goer, he swore off both

Mass and confession and cavalierly continued to sing "awfully blasphemous words" when his work became too intense or to shake his "fist twards heaven" when the pain in his legs became too severe for him to handle. In many ways, Henry was living out the conflict he depicted in *The Realms*, a battle between good and evil, but in this scenario, Henry was the paragon of good and God the exemplar of evil.

LEAVING THE NUNS FOR GOOD

In July 1946, Henry took what was probably his first vacation, three weeks away from his chores and the infighting at St. Joseph's. He had no money to speak of, so he stayed in Chicago, working on *Crazy House* and painting. Only days before he left, a new nun, Sister Alberta, had arrived at the hospital and taken over as mother superior. While he was gone, she and Henry's supervisor discussed him, and together they decided to fire him. The three-week vacation may also have been a ruse that, because they'd given him paid time off, allowed them not to feel guilty about firing him. As soon as he returned, Sister Alberta told him that she was dismissing him. Trying to make the bad news as easy on him as possible, she also told him he could eat for free at the employees' cafeteria until he found a new job. When she saw the hurt in his face, compounded by his sudden realization that, at fifty-four years old, he might not easily find work, she quickly added that she wasn't letting him go because of "any wrong doing," but because of the demands of the job itself: "the work was too much" for him, "the hours too long," and it was destroying his health.

That may have been at least partially true. If so, it was probably the first time in his working life that anyone showed any genuine concern for him. It's just as likely that Henry's "blasphemous" songs that he often sang aloud for hours nonstop in the dishwashing room prompted Sister Alberta's decision to get rid of him.

After thinking about it a little while, Henry decided that leaving St. Joseph's was a good idea. Because he had so much work to do, he was always exhausted and rarely had time to eat lunch. Sister Alberta had suggested that he try to get an "easier job," one with "much shorter hours," and he set out to do exactly that.

Almost immediately, Henry applied for work at Alexian Brothers Hospital, which was run by monks, at Belden and Racine, and he was offered a job there washing dishes a week after he was let go from St. Joseph's. The administrator had actually hired another man, but when he didn't show up on the first day he was scheduled to work, the administrator contacted Henry.

Although Henry hadn't had an easy time of it at St. Joseph's among the Daughters of Charity, working for Alexian Brothers wasn't perfect, either. He had two weekdays off each week, but only one Sunday off a month, and he had to work almost every holiday, including Christmas. He hated working on holidays and Sundays. "I know of a country where the employer would have to pay a thousand to 10,000 dollar fine to work himself, or work his employes on Sundays, holidays and holey days," he complained, but no one cared.

A man supervised him for the first time—in his adult life, anyway. He remembered the monk, Brother Fabian, as being "strict" but not "severe." Henry's job was to scrape food off dishes and utensils before putting them into the large dishwashing machine, and he did it for twelve years, from 1946 to 1959:

> The Brother stripped the dishes, I scraped off the refuse, and the machine operator loaded the dish trays and run them through.
>
> I never had the chance to run the machine though I worked at the receiving end once in a while, removing the clean dishes and loading the dish cart-wagons.
>
> I also took out the garbage and cleaned the cans. That was the only unpleasant job.

When the monks replaced the old dishwashing machine with a newer, more modern model, the administration decided that only women employees would run and work around it, and Henry's supervisor transferred him to the pot-washing room, where he scrubbed the industrial-size pans that the cooks used. He worked a ten-hour shift, from five thirty in the morning until three thirty in the afternoon. He was also responsible for collecting used dishes from the monks' dining room to be washed and then returning them to the dining room once they were clean.

All went well until the monks hired a new man to be in charge of their dining room. He refused to allow Henry to come in and do his job, probably because the man was being territorial. One day, Henry slipped in anyway, and when the new man discovered Henry, he forced him out physically. Henry became so angry that he told the man that, if he ever had the opportunity, he would "slash him with a knife"—as he had his teacher fifty years earlier. The man quit a short time later after getting into a "row with negro employes in the main kitchen."

After that, for the first time in his working life, Henry's relationships with his supervisors were free of the sort of pettiness that he'd experienced with the nuns at St. Joseph's and the laypersons at Grant. Perhaps as he matured, he was better able to negotiate work-related conflicts with his supervisors or, more probably, Alexian Brothers was just a much better place to work. His supervisors and coworkers dealt with Henry with far more respect and kindness than those at St. Joseph's or Grant had. At Alexian Brothers, Henry claimed that both the men *and* the women supervisors "were easy to get along with." After first working under Brother Fabian's direction, he was then supervised by Brother Hillery, whom Henry described as "all right." Miss Dalgiest replaced Brother Hillery, and Miss Sullivan, who was "good social and fair" and even friendly to those she supervised, replaced Miss Dalgiest. Henry "got along fine and dany [dandy]" with Miss Sullivan.

251 I Lost All I Had

However, Henry had a problem with another male employee. The man was jealous of Henry's ties to Miss Sullivan, and he claimed Henry "snitched" on him to her not once but twice. Henry never disclosed what he supposedly told Miss Sullivan, but he related this experience in the same way that he described his being accused of various transgressions during his childhood—with as few detailed as possible but with substantial pleas of innocence. He even claims that other employees stood up for him in the dispute. In defending himself, Henry explained, "I never had time to go hanging around Miss Sullivans apron strings." But then Henry revealed how easily his anger could be released: "I would have liked to find out who told him I snitched on him. Well? You can guess there were many knives around in the kitchen."

Although now a man in his fifties, Henry was reacting to problems with coworkers exactly as he had when, as a child in West Madison Street, bullies and other predators put him on the defense. His childhood experiences, especially the sexual victimization, had undercut his self-respect drastically, making him very defensive. He could cover up the brutality, but he couldn't camouflage his anger, steadily churning, consistently threatening to erupt without warning and at any time day or night.

ONE NIGHT I HAD A DREAM
THAT YOU WERE BACK AGAIN

After living in Wilmette for a few years, Katherine and Whillie began thinking about leaving the frigid Chicago winters behind and moving to Texas—San Antonio, to be exact. While San Antonio was not Mexico, it was the next best thing as far as Katherine was concerned. Besides, she was sure that a warmer, drier climate would be good for their health. Whillie was sixty-six and Katherine a decade younger. In 1945, they packed up a few belongings and made the move south.

As much as he hated to, Henry learned to accept the fact that Whillie now lived hundreds of miles away and would never be returning to Chicago. Shortly after Whillie's second move, Henry's pains became more intense, and he even developed excruciating pains on the right side of his abdomen. Different from the leg pains he had developed around the time that Whillie moved to Wilmette, the abdominal pains became so bad that he was bedridden for six days, and they aggravated his already developing lameness. After he got better, he occasionally had to use a cane to walk. Although his abdominal pains were physical, it's likely that they were brought on by the stress he experienced when Whillie moved to Texas. Whillie wasn't just Henry's partner in life. He was also the only person on whom Henry had depended for decades and was a sounding board for the problems he faced. When the pettiness at his jobs became overwhelming, he had complained about them to Whillie. When the novels or the paintings weren't working well—or when they were going smoothly—he had discussed them with Whillie. He discussed political events and the weather with Whillie. Once Whillie moved to Texas, Henry had no one on whom he could depend, and he must have been consumed by grief over the loss of the one person who'd remained steadfast in his life for thirty-five years, far longer than his father or even Anna. As when his father died, Henry held his grief over Whillie's move to Texas at bay, never expressing it, but it manifested itself as stress and impacted Henry's health.

Despite the distance between them, Henry made up his mind not to give up on their relationship. Instead, he did what he could to keep it intact. "I wrote to Whillie often," Henry remembered, "but as he could not write in English his sister wrote his answers for him." Henry was wrong. Whillie could read and write English. In fact, he was born in Chicago and went to school there. So why didn't he write letters in response to Henry's instead of allowing Katherine?

Being the baby of the family, Katherine had been spoiled by her parents and by her brothers and sisters. Once Lizzie died, she easily assumed Lizzie's mantle and became the decision-maker in the household. Like Lizzie before her, Katherine enjoyed controlling those around her, and besides, Whillie was a pushover, allowing practically anyone to run over him. And it wasn't just Lizzie and Katherine who controlled him. When Michael Schloeder died, all five of the children were in the house. Given the patriarchy of the time, it was Whillie's duty, and right, as the eldest son to assume the position of head of the household and report his father's death. Whillie didn't. His younger brother, Henry, stepped in and took care of everything instead. When Katherine wrote Whillie's so-called responses to Henry's letters and cards, she was controlling Whillie.

Besides, Whillie probably wasn't at all eager to write anything that Henry would read, including letters. When Whillie was a child, few children of the working class attended school for any substantial amount of time. What has been called the Long Depression struck the United States in 1873 and lasted until 1879, the year of Whillie's birth, but its wallop influenced the finances of U.S. citizens long into the 1890s. It was so devastating that all able-bodied male members of a family had to work, even if they were only able to bring home pennies, which was more often than not the case. Boys as young as six took any job they could find, often hawking papers as newsboys during the day and late into the night. The few who attended school didn't go on any regular schedule. Whillie was one of the children who should have been at school full-time but was already employed to help his family financially.

Whillie signed his draft registration card for the First World War, so it's obvious that he could write his name. Census records report that he could read and write English, so he was at least able to read basic, uncomplicated texts, such as newspaper articles, and to write brief notes. Nevertheless, being able to write a message and read the newspaper wouldn't necessarily have equipped Whillie with the tools necessary to write actual letters, especially if Henry's writing intimidated him. Whillie would have known Henry was a novelist and had already written thousands of pages of his own novels. He may not have had the confidence to write Henry, and rather than embarrass himself, he let Katherine have her way and write for him. Katherine's notes to Henry—she didn't write him a single letter—are quite distant, perfunctory, almost (but not quite) cold, and give no real information about her and Whillie's lives in San Antonio.

Terribly lonely, racked off and on by physical pains, Henry sent Whillie greeting cards of various types to keep himself in Whillie's thoughts. In 1954, he sent Easter cards to both Whillie and Katherine individually. On May 7, 1954, Katherine sent Henry a picture post-card that was several times larger in size than typical ones are, some-thing that tickled Henry's fancy. It contained a picture of the Sunken Garden in Brackenridge Park, San Antonio, which the card describes on its verso: "An abandoned stone quarry in the 363 acre Bracken-ridge Park, many years ago, was transformed as if by magic, into a floral fairyland that has since become famous as the Sunken Garden, one of the beauty spots of the Nation." "Fairyland" would have had special meaning to Henry, a subtle, quite reminder of a time when he and Whillie were together at Riverview and among the queer subcul-ture, and one that Katherine wouldn't have caught. The word suggests that Whillie probably picked the card out especially for Henry.

Not aware of the message embedded in the description, Katherine wrote on the postcard: "Bill & I wish to thank you for remembering us with the beautiful Easter Cards. We think you might enjoy these views of San Antonio. Hope you are well & happy. & Best wishes from Bill & Katherine." Henry also saved an Easter card that Katherine sent him. Below the card's Easter greetings, Katherine replied: "All good Wishes" and signed it "Bill & Katherine Schloeder." On the back, she wrote a brief message:

Your cards came today, & thank you very much.

It always makes Bill so happy to be remembered by you for he treasures your friendship very much Your gift is appreciated.

Hope you are well & do come to see us sometime soon.

At the same time that he was sending greeting cards to Whillie, Henry was also writing actual letters to him:

> My dear friend Bill
> I know it's a long long time since I wrote you last but I will tell the truth that I am not so good at writing letters I am well and hope you and your good sister are well and happy. To begin with I do not know whether Chicago or San Antonio was having the [wors]t wheather but [accor]ding to the papers Chicago [set] the record. Could you [s]ay it was true. I am still working at [t]he Alexian Brothers and I wish I had gone there sooner. St. Vincent Church last May had a $200000 fire and nothing has been done to repair the church yet Mass is said in the big show house across the [street?] I am not saying anyth[ing] but you ought to see th[e] yard of the house you used [to] live at at Dickens ave. It's a "beaut" From its appearance Im really sorry you had to sell it and move away. Now it looks like the [rest?] of the slums. And the old barn is gone and the building is not even taken care of.
>
> One night I had a dream that you were back again and I wish it were [true] so I could see you [...] to I still live at [851] Webster ave Chicago

Garfield, the name of the street on which the Schloeder house was located, had been renamed Dickens decades earlier, and the "big show house" would have been the College Theatre across the street from St. Vincent's Church, where Henry and Whillie would have seen Mary Pickford's films and perhaps even the film version of *Condemned to Devil's Island*. Henry closed the letter by signing it "Your best friend."

Written during the summer of 1955, the letter is full of chitchat that doesn't hide his deep sense of abandonment. After the gossipy first part of the letter, Henry focused on more personal matters and even let down his guard in a paragraph set off all by itself. He has dreamed of Whillie: "One night I had a dream that you were back again." He never says what the dream was about, but it might have been too inconsequential for him to bother to discuss or, perhaps, too romantic or too racy to describe in a letter that he knew Katherine would read. Having expressed his deep feelings as overtly as he dared, he returned to chitchat without missing a beat, reminding Whillie, "I still live at [851] Webster," probably a nudge to get Whillie to write him.

MR. LEONARD

In 1956, Nathan Lerner bought the buildings at 849 and 851 West Webster, the latter being Henry's building. It would become an extremely important event in Henry's life. Lerner was a renowned "photographer, painter and designer" and "professor of art and design." He lived in 849 and rented out the three apartments and the single room on the third floor of 851. Henry had lived in that room since 1932, longer than any of Lerner's other tenants.

When Lerner took possession of Henry's building, he became immediately aware that Henry was concerned about his home. Would Lerner let him stay or toss him out? Would Lerner raise his rent? If he did raise the rent, could he afford to stay? If not, how in the world would he move all of his tens of thousands of pages of manuscripts, his hundreds of paintings that illustrated his novels, and all of the source materials that he had now been collecting for more than three decades? Trying to find another place to live that he could afford and that would be close enough to Alexian Brothers so that he could walk to work would be extremely difficult, especially now that Whillie wasn't around to help him. It was a hugely traumatic time for Henry. Lerner must have intuited Henry's fears and fragility.

Lerner later recalled his and Henry's first meeting, during which he told Henry he didn't have to move:

> I remember Henry standing out on the porch and looking at me. I think he expected me to say, "You know, Henry, you are going to have to

move. The building now belongs to me." . . . I don't remember what I said to him, but he just turned around and went upstairs. I saw absolutely no reason why a man who was certainly neutral and harmless should have to move. I think he was very grateful. He wanted to buy me cigars.

This became the beginning of Henry's respect for, and reliance on, his new landlord, whom he called "Mr. Leonard."

That wasn't the end to Lerner's generosity to Henry. Henry approached Lerner to ask him to lower his rent from the forty dollars a month that he had been paying to thirty dollars, and he was able to cajole the good-natured Lerner into doing so. Lerner's purchase of the building afforded Henry a sense of security, something he needed badly because his health was beginning to fail drastically.

One morning in early November 1958, when he was at work at Alexian Brothers, Henry was doubled over by a pain that had erupted in his knees and then traveled to the right side of his abdomen. The pains were so bad that Miss Sullivan sent him to the doctor who was on call at the hospital. By the afternoon, the pain had intensified so much that Henry had to be put in bed and undergo a series of tests. Unfortunately, the tests "revealed nothing." By evening the pain had vanished, but the doctor kept him under observation and in bed for the next six days. Although the pain went undiagnosed, the doctor called it "a permanent strain," by which he may have been suggesting a hernia-like condition or stress. He prescribed medicine for Henry, warned him to "do no heavy lifting," and told the sixty-six-year-old that, if he didn't retire, he could be bedridden for the rest of his life. Henry conscientiously took the doctor's pills but ignored his advice.

At around the same time, the heat in the pot-washing room became too much for Henry. He developed what he called a "sort of heat sickness," a condition that recalls the one he'd read about in *Condemned to Devil's Island* and had assigned to the Vivian girl-boys in *Crazy House*, calling it "awful fever horrors." His condition was so bad that he had to go on sick leave for more than a week. While Henry was gone, Miss Sullivan, his supervisor, decided to help him out. When he returned, she transferred him to the vegetable room, where it was noticeably cooler and where he "peeled potatoes and cleaned and worked on all kinds of vegetables." He peeled some of the vegetables by hand but used a peeling machine for others. While the temperature was better for Henry, the length of his shift, a ten-hour workday, was just as demanding as ever.

LOST IN EMPTY SPACE

The following spring, the worst tragedy of his adult life struck Henry broadside and with devastating effect. "When in San Antonio three years," Henry recalled, "my friend Whillie died on the 5 of May (I forgot the year) of the Asian flu, and since that happened I am all alone." Henry was confused about the dates. Whillie and Katherine moved to Texas and lived there fourteen years before Whillie died on Saturday, May 2, 1959.

The next day, Katherine tried to contact Henry at work to tell him the bad news, but there was a mix-up, and he didn't learn about Whillie's death until the following Wednesday, May 6. Henry explained what happened in a letter to Katherine:

> You wrote that you phoned to me at the Alexian Brothers Hospital but you sure did not get me there.
>
> There is another Henry who is a Cook in the Main Kitchen there and it was as I found out that it was he that the colored girl called to the phone.
>
> I usually am through with work on Sunday at quarter after One, and leave for Home at Half past One.
>
> That I cannot hear is not so as I was not there when you called up. Why didnt you call where I live? Then I would have known, and if possible you could have me at the Funeral.

Then too I was off Monday and Tuesday, and therefore knew nothing what happened untill Henry and the colored girl told me Wednesday morning.

So you can see, at the Hospital I did not get the call on Sunday.

Whillie died of pneumonia, not influenza, at home shortly after midnight. Katherine was at his side. Whillie was cremated the day he died, and she had his body shipped back to Chicago, where he was buried on May 5 at St. Boniface Cemetery alongside his parents and sisters Lizzie, Lucy, and Angeline. Only his father has a tombstone. Michael Schloeder's wife and children lie north of him in unmarked graves.

In the same letter in which he explained the mix-up to Katherine, Henry revealed clearly and openly the depths of his feelings for Whillie for one of the few times in his life. "I feel as if lost in empty space," he wrote, adding, "Now nothing matters too me at all."

Then, after he pulled himself together, he thought of her, the pain she must have been feeling, and revealed his feelings to her one last time:

> As soon as I can I will have a Mass Said for Him and hope that He will be in Heaven before then. If you can will you send me something like a picture or something else to remember him by.
>
> And I hope you will soon receive consolation, because a loss is hard to take. It sure is too me to lose him for then too I lost all I had and had a hard time to stand it.

Katherine never sent Henry any mementos of Whillie.

Henry learned too late that the most important person in his life for forty-eight years had died, so he wasn't able to attend Whillie's funeral. Instead, he grieved the death of his beloved alone in the cool vegetable room as he peeled potatoes.

CHAPTER 9

THE SAINTS AND ALL
THE ANGELS WOULD BE
ASHAMED OF ME

THE PRODIGAL RETURNS

HENRY CONTINUED TO WORK IN THE VEGETABLE ROOM UNTIL the end of 1959 or early 1960, when it became obvious to Miss Sullivan that constantly standing on the uneven floor was undermining Henry's health. Because of the leg pains, he couldn't stand for any length of time now, and it wasn't possible for him to sit down to wash and slice the vegetables. To help him out, Miss Sullivan transferred Henry yet again, this time to the bandage room, where he could sit to work. Because it was in the attic, which had little or no insulation, it was the hottest department in the entire hospital in the summer and the coldest in the winter.

Joseph Harry was in charge of the bandage room and Henry's new supervisor. Harry lived on Montana Street, where he owned several houses that he rented and two guard dogs, one a German shepherd. Henry recalled that he and "joe got along fine, no troubles or nothing" and that he "missed him . . . when he left to retire" a few years later. At the same time that Joseph supervised Henry, Henry was in charge of another employee, "a helper by the first name of Jacob." Henry couldn't pronounce Jacob's last name, Feseri. He thought Jacob was "fussy," but also admitted that "he was absolutely peaceful, friendly and good natured."

The three men rolled strips of fabric fourteen feet long and six inches wide into what the staff called "hot packs," and the hospital charged patients fifty dollars each for them. Henry's shift was seven thirty to three, but if his work wasn't finished by three, he had to stay until it was. He was off on Thursdays and Sundays, as well as national holidays. Although there were occasional slack times for the three men who worked in the bandage room, they were overwhelmed by the work much of the time. If he had to stay late, he got a meal ticket for dinner, but Henry preferred to go home if he could rather than stay any longer than necessary at the hospital.

Working at Alexian Brothers ended up being the most pleasant of all of Henry's places of employment, especially because of his supervisors' many attempts to make his workday as easy on him as possible. Initially, the different jobs he was given seemed to help get rid of his various pains, but they eventually returned with a greater intensity than before. By early 1962, the pain had escalated so much that he had to reduce his work hours to part-time, and now he frequently had to use a cane to walk.

When not actually working, Henry, Joe, and Jacob relaxed a little, and often they would read the newspapers and magazines that people had left in the waiting rooms of the hospital. During a lull in work one day, Henry began reading the August 1961 issue of the *Saturday Evening Post* and came upon lyrics of a Civil War song, "The Vacant Chair," that spoke to him. Written by Henry S. Washburn and put to music by George F. Root, the lyrics focus on a dead soldier named Willie who had died a hero and whom the narrator loves:

> At our fireside, sad and lonely,
> Often will the bosom swell,
> At remembrance of the story
> How our noble Willie fell;
>
> How he strove to bear our banner
> Through the thickest of the fight,
> And uphold our country's honor
> In the strength of manhood's night.

The song was intended as an elegy to a dead Civil War soldier, but Henry would have thought of *his* Whillie, who'd died only two years earlier. He clipped out the page that contained the lyrics and saved it.

During another lull in work, Henry picked up a Catholic magazine and read a story in it about a wealthy man who'd turned to robbery and murder after "losing his fortune." He was captured, convicted, and sentenced to death, and in the afterlife, he "went to hell and was tormented horribly by fiends." Now in his early seventies, in ill health, and constantly reminded of his mortality by the various pains that erupted across his body, Henry was "scared . . . into repentance" and began attending Mass and confession again at St. Vincent's Church. During the week, he compulsively attended Mass at six, six thirty, seven, and seven thirty in the morning. On Sundays, he attended Mass at seven fifteen a.m. and eight thirty a.m. and again at five p.m. Every Monday evening at seven thirty, he also attended the Novena of the Miraculous Medal. Confession, which Henry took, was available at all the masses, too. Certainly, guilt over his sexual abuse and his attraction to men sent him into the pews, but church attendance also helped to fill the void that Whillie's death had created.

Henry was also driven back to the Church because he'd been blasphemous for so long and he felt the need to repent. The blasphemy he uttered in times of stress was a manifestation of his anger, and it allowed him to let off stream. He was nevertheless concerned that the rants might also seal his fate in the afterlife. Once, he even admitted to a priest during confession that he shook his fist "twards heaven," and the priest "was disturbed," "admonished" him for his blasphemy, and gave him an extra "severe" penance because of it.

Henry didn't want anyone to misunderstand the reason why he uncontrollably attended religious services, and once, pretending that someone had praised him for his piety, he said to the individual he imagined, "What did you say? I am being a saint? Ha. Ha. I am one, and a very sorry Saint I am. Ha. Ha. How can I be a saint when I won't stand for trials, bad luck, pains in my knees or otherwise." Henry didn't want others to think that he attended Mass because he was pious or even a relatively good person; he attended because his anger over the undeserved trials that he had faced all of his life had led him to act in a way that even he recognized as extreme and irrational. Henry would have agreed that shaking his fist at God or singing songs with blasphemous lyrics was odd, but his pent-up anger was so great he couldn't help himself.

Without Whillie as a sounding board, he had become even more of a victim to his emotions than he'd been as a child. "I firmly believe that there is no one," he once complained, who would "put up with such pains, my past severe toothaches, face pains, and side pains and other things I don't find time to mention here." In his typical fashion, Henry skipped over the most important trouble that vexed him, never clarifying what those "other things" he didn't have time to mention were. He would never admit that he had been sexually abused and that he suffered psychological pain because of it. Instead, he called that trauma "other things," the same phrase he'd used to camouflage his activities with John Manley and the Scanlon brothers, and ignored it as best as he could.

A LAZY LIFE

Henry recalled that, in the late spring or early summer of 1963, while he was still working in the bandage room, "my right leg began again while I was rolling hot packs, and it became so terribly severe, that I could not stand on it, and to add to my misery my right side acted up severely at the same time." Again, coworkers helped him to the doctor on call, who, Henry admitted, "examined my leg" and "advised me to retire."

Henry was already limping noticeably by 1945, when he registered for the "old man's draft," but now, at seventy-one years old, the pain that had attacked his legs and knees as well as his abdomen returned with a vengeance, sending him doubled over to the hospital's doctor yet again. This time, Henry took his doctor's advice and accepted what had become obvious to everyone else. He made plans to retire.

Having a job and being able to pay his own way had been a matter of pride for Henry since he landed his first job in 1909. When the Great Depression robbed millions of U.S. citizens of their jobs and their self-respect, Henry was employed. In fact, during his fifty-four years of working, from when he began work as a seventeen-year-old janitor at St. Joseph's Hospital until he was forced by his health into retirement from Alexian Brothers Hospital, Henry was unemployed less than a total of two weeks.

Henry once bragged that, while employed at the Alexian Brothers, he got three different raises in salary, something that was utterly amazing to him. He also mentioned that he held what we would call supervisory roles, albeit very small ones, during his second stint at St. Joseph's (overseeing the teenage girls in the dishwashing room) and at Alexian Brothers (guiding his "helper" Jacob Feseri). Yet Henry never made more than $3,000 any given year throughout his entire life. In 1956, for example, he earned $2,399.53, or only $197.46 a month. In that year, the mean income for men in Henry's age bracket and with his amount of elementary-school education was $6,462 or $538.50 a month. Two thirds of the men in the United States his age and in his educational bracket earned more than he.

Once he accepted the fact that he had no option but to retire, Henry knew he would barely be able to live on his Social Security. He'd made only $1,211 in 1962 because his health had forced him to reduce his hours to less than half-time. To get as much money as possible, he wrote the Social Security Administration in July 1963 to cancel his health insurance. He thought its cost was being deducted from his salary, and he didn't want the insurance if it meant he had to pay for it. On July 27, J. L. Fay replied to Henry's letter, explaining that his wages weren't being docked and the insurance was free. At about the same time that he was corresponding with the Social Security Administration, Henry applied for public aid from Cook County and received $15.66 a month from August 6, 1968, until at least August 6, 1972, to supplement his Social Security. He was also able to get medical insurance under Medicare at least as early as August 30, 1968.

Henry retired from Alexian Brothers Hospital on November 19, 1963, after doing virtually the same type of chore over and over again for fifty-four years. While many might have reveled in their release from a mind-numbing, assembly-line-like series of tasks for only cents an hour, Henry hated retirement. "I'll say it is a lazy life and I don't like it," he ranted, adding, "I suppose a real lazy person would enjoy it." But Henry was far from lazy. He continued to paint and write voluminously. He was winding up *Crazy House*. Shorter than *The Realms*, which logged in at well over 15,000 handwritten pages, it was nevertheless a whopping 10,000-plus pages. He kept a record of his work on his paintings that extends from 1958 through 1965. Although the log is sketchy, giving no painting's title but only the dates he began and then finished a particular one, it reveals that Henry was extraordinarily quick and that, except for the days on which he was ill, he worked constantly.

The entries of his painting log that cover 1960, for example, show Henry's rapid production as clearly as any year's entries do. He was able to begin and then finish each of the five paintings he produced that year in approximately three months, although some took far less time. He began one on December 11, 1959, and completed it on January 29, 1960, although illness interrupted his production. He was "delayed two days because of a severe cold." Nevertheless, Henry was extraordinarily dedicated to his creative work, allowing little to foil his mission.

The log also shows something of Henry's process. He traced the images he wanted onto the canvas first, and then later, he colored in the images just as he had done as a child with coloring books decades earlier.

Although at times Henry may have found children's tins of watercolors in the trash bins in his neighborhood and brought them home with him to use, he often bought paints and other items he needed for his art at Decorator's Paint and Wallpaper Company at 632 West North Avenue. Receipts from that store reveal a few of his purchases. Right after Christmas 1957, Henry spent $2.25 there for three sets of watercolors and 40¢ for tins of eight different colors. Two years later, he spent $4.86 for a set of watercolors and $1.10 for a "board," probably as backing for one of his paintings. Then, in 1962, he bought several more watercolor sets at $4.85 each. He also spent money on plywood, again presumably as backing for his paintings, at John Bader Lumber Company at 2020 Clybourn. In March 1956, he spent $2.68 for plywood, and in June 1959, he spent another $1.60 for it.

Several people actually report having seen Henry at work on his paintings, but no one took much note of it at the time. David Berglund, an art student who lived with his wife, Betsy, on the same floor as Henry, remembered that once, when he was in Henry's room, he "looked over his shoulder as he was doing one of his big paintings. He was very happy doing this, singing a song quietly to himself." At another time, when Lerner's wife happened to be in Henry's room, she noticed that he was "drawing on the table," the large oval one that stood in the middle of the room. Making small talk, she said, "Henry, you're a good artist." He replied without a shred of self-consciousness, "Yes, I am."

A CRANKY OLD FART

Because he was now retired and no longer working extraordinarily long hours with few days off, Henry had a great deal of free time, and neighbors report having seen the seventy-one-year-old roaming the neighborhood as far away as Belmont Avenue, several miles north. Although he devoted much of his extra time to his writings and paintings, Henry would hobble through the neighborhood in which he lived and pick through the garbage in alleys, looking for items he could use, especially source materials for his illustrations.

Henry had always been attentive to other people's castoffs. He was adept at salvaging them for his own use, and he had begun collecting as early as 1910 while living at the Workingmen's House. Initially, he collected to support his art in a direct way, and probably found most of the pictures and other items he would use for the illustrations of his novels in newspapers and magazines in hospital waiting rooms. He was very limited to what he could keep because there was virtually no privacy in the small, dorm-like room, and he didn't want to draw attention to himself. Besides, if Henry had begun collecting in any substantial way while living there, his neighbors would've easily noticed and rumors about his unorthodox activities would have quickly found their way to the nuns, just as his past in the Asylum had. The nuns were already ill at ease having someone who'd been in a "nut house" in their midst, and it would have been as good an excuse as any for them to give him the boot.

Everything changed when he moved into his room at the Anschutzes. At 1035 Webster, he had somewhat more room than he'd had at the Workingmen's House, but much more important, he had far more privacy. Both allowed him to write and illustrate *The Realms* in a far more substantial way. Just as important, he didn't have to worry that anyone would find his manuscript, his illustrations, or his small collection of source materials and chuck them out as Phelan had done twice.

After he moved into his new room at 851 Webster, Henry had much more room, and he began to fill it. On more than one occasion, his neighbor Mary Dillon, who lived at 851 Webster from 1961 until 1972 in the apartment under Henry's room, saw Henry lugging source materials into the building. Once it was "two big shopping bags of newspapers and stuff from the garbage." No sooner had he moved into his new home than he began decorating it with examples of his own artwork and other objects that he found, and over the years, Henry nailed a large number of his canvases and other objects onto his walls above the stacks of magazines and the piles of old shoes. He tacked a hand-painted sign, "No smoking under no conditions," onto the east wall to remind visitors—and probably himself—of the potential for fires in his room, which was filled nearly waist-deep with newspapers. The sign constantly reminded him of the time that he'd been caught setting fire to a stack of newspapers in his father's coach house apartment years earlier and the boxed ears he'd gotten from his father for doing it.

He displayed dozens of pictures—many of them little girls, but also little boys and adult men and women—that he'd cut out of *Life*, *Look*, *Ladies' Home Journal*, and many other magazines on the walls, too, and even tacked some of them on the doorjamb around the water closet door. One, a collage left untitled by Henry but usually referred to as *In Times Like These*, includes a photo of football sex symbol Joe "Broadway Joe" Namath in his uniform giving a sultry, over-the-shoulder, come-hither look to anyone who cared to notice. Henry obviously did.

Henry also exhibited on the fireplace mantel a considerable number of religious items, such as plaster statues of Jesus and Mary as well as Bibles, prayer books, and missals that he'd rescued from the neighborhood trash, found at rummage sales at St. Vincent's Church, or bought from shops specializing in religious items. At Benziger Brothers, Henry purchased several pictures that depicted the Virgin Mary and the child Jesus. He used the mantel as he'd used the mimic altar in Whillie's barn, but instead of photos of Elsie Paroubek, the pictures he placed on it were of nameless children whose stories he might imagine but never really know. He also added a calendar for 1955 that he got at May's Grocery & Delicatessen, a few doors away at 857 Webster, where he occasionally shopped.

Many of the notebooks and journals in which he wrote his novels and other texts had initially been someone else's property or were manufactured for purposes unrelated to writing. Beginning in the late 1960s, Henry kept a journal on the leaves of a 1932 desk calendar, an item he'd found around the time he moved away from the Anschutzes' house and saved for use later. He jotted notes or, less often, wrote paragraphs on its pages, ignoring the printed dates and adding those that designated the days on which he made the entries. Surprisingly, Henry's journals reveal his love of wordplay and his sense of humor. He would make a matter-of-fact statement—"Went on three walks to day"—and then follow it with a phrase in parentheses that had nothing to do with what he'd just written but that rhymed with it: "Went on three walks to day (Bales of hay)." They range from the off-color—"Went to after noon mass also 8:30 mass (not gas)"—to the silly—"More several tantrums especially over hazardous walking (not squaking)." In August 1967, he had X-rays for pain in his chest, and by the end of December 1968, Henry's pains overwhelmed his humor, and the rhymes all but disappear from the journals.

The 1932 calendar was only one of the many discarded items that he put to use. To organize his collection of source materials, he pasted pictures, cartoons, newspaper illustrations of fires, and other items onto the pages of telephone directories that he had found, covering the columns of names, addresses, and phone numbers to create huge, awkward scrapbooks. Henry also converted coloring books and other similar children's fare into scrapbooks. Henry dedicated one, *Playhouse Dolls*, a book of paper dolls and their clothing, to pictures of "Butterflies" and "small and big flowers and plants," as he wrote on its cover. Interestingly, the children on the front and back covers of *Playhouse Dolls* are so androgynous that, except for their gender-specific clothing and hairstyles (short for boys, long for girls), they are indistinguishable from one another.

Henry had once been virtually invisible to the other tenants around him, but his new neighbors couldn't help but notice him now. Far more educated than Henry, raised in solidly middle-class and reasonably well-off families, employed with decent wages, and able to rely on their friends and family for company, support, and love, many of them thought he was an oddball. The dapper young man who'd posed with his boyfriend for photographs at Coultry Studio in 1911 was by 1963 so poor that he had begun to dress peculiarly and so ill that he had begun to act strangely. Lerner, who was fifty in 1963 and had lived through the Great Depression and World War II, could relate to Henry far easier than the twentysomethings in his building.

To some of the tenants, Henry looked "filthy and homeless" like one of the hobos in West Madison Street. In the wintertime, the coat was "navy-blue" and had probably been issued to him when he was in the army. Had he remained in the army, he would've been sent to the European theater of the war during winter 1917. When the Chicago winters were especially brutal, Henry wore "a kind of fisherman's cap with earflaps" to and from work. Indoors, Henry typically wore "dark green or gray cotton work shirts and trousers" that he bought at Sears and Roebuck and wore "until they fell apart." In the summer, he often "ripped the sleeves off his shirts at the shoulder," although the rips were "never straight."

But Henry's clothing wasn't the only out-of-the-ordinary thing about him. Mary Dillon "heard him talking to himself all the time," even when he was outside. Betsy Berglund, now Betsy Fuchs, remembered that he talked aloud to himself: "We would hear two different voices. . . . I know that we could hear conversations. . . . It wasn't very loud. It seemed like there were two voices; a high voice and a low voice, an answer and a refrain. I'm sure I heard conversations, but I don't remember what they were about." Lerner also recalled Henry's "conversations" because he actually performed them for Lerner. "He was a wonderful mimic," Lerner remembered. "I would listen to him. He would mimic the nuns at the hospital. He hated some of his superiors." Betsy may have been overhearing Henry's rehearsals for his performances for Lerner. David Berglund agreed with Nathan Lerner: "I think he was reliving the arguments he had with the nuns."

When he ran into other tenants going up or down the stairs from one floor to the next or out on the street, he often responded to their hello with a weather report—"A tornado is coming from Kansas tomorrow"—if he answered them at all, because "he did not want to speak to anybody. He didn't want anybody speaking to him." In fact, "if he seen you on the street, he would just pass you by. He would just look the other way." If they pushed him to respond, he might snap at them angrily: "'Leave me alone.' He would say that. 'Just leave me alone.'" David Berglund recalled that, when he ran into Henry in the building or on the sidewalks, Henry responded to his "greeting with 'Okay,' and then grunt, 'Gotta be going.'" It's no wonder that, to many of the other tenants, "Henry seemed funny and different."

Dillon remembered him in a slightly more favorable light. She said that, during the eleven years she lived at 851 Webster, "Henry was living above my apartment. He was a pleasant man. He was very quiet. He didn't make any noise. Nobody ever came to see him. He'd say hello, how are you, thank you, or goodbye, but little else. He wasn't talkative, and seemed very private. We weren't sure he was 'all there.'" Andrew J. Epstein, then an art student who lived in Henry's neighborhood and occasionally ran into Henry on the sidewalk, gave perhaps the most damning of all pronouncements about Henry's behavior. "He mumbled a lot," Epstein remembered, and so he thought Henry "was definitely talking to someone who wasn't there, but then also to me. I just figured he was probably schizophrenic. He was very weird, very strange."

Henry knew he didn't fit in with the other tenants. Although he was about the same age as the other lodgers when he'd first moved into the building decades earlier, he was now so much older, far poorer, and less educated than they that being around them only intensified his awareness of being different, something he'd been forced to deal with since he was first nicknamed "Crazy" at the Mission. He chose not to be around them any more than he absolutely had to, leading him to use the alleys instead of sidewalks to get to and from, for example, Roma's Grill, where he often ate. When he couldn't escape their notice, as when he ran into one of them on the stairwell or the street, he made his interaction with them as short as possible.

Still, there were some things that Henry couldn't escape or hide from the others. As Henry's problem with his leg intensified, he had difficulties climbing up or walking down steps. He was so wobbly, even when using his cane, which he now depended on all the time, that he had to lean against the wall when he used the stairs, and after a few years, his shoulder rubbed a smudge on it. Everyone in the building was aware of the trail that Henry left behind.

As some older persons tend to do, Henry complained about his pains, bragged about how he could stand them despite how debilitating they were, and challenged those who were in better health than he to spend some time in his shoes:

> Yet despite that pain even bothering me severely in the morning I went to and stayed through three Holy Masses a week on Thursday Saturday and Sunday.
>
> And also to work on the working days. Yet I stood it.
>
> Would you have done it?

Still, Henry was completely aware of how others perceived him. In another, all-too-rare moment of objectivity, Henry once admitted that "people who do suffer are usually crabby or hard to get along with." Those around him, particularly the other tenants, remembered that he was "crabby" much of the time, but no one knew how much he suffered both physically and emotionally.

On top of everything else, Henry stopped bathing, just as some elderly men and women living alone and in utter poverty do. "One time," Mary Dillon complained to Lerner "about water leaking from the upstairs bathroom" through her ceiling. Lerner thought that Henry may have let the bathtub overflow in the shared bathroom, but when he approached Henry about the leak, Henry claimed he had nothing to do with it, looked at Lerner "with shock and dismay," and said, "'I never take baths in the wintertime.'" One spring, Lerner recalled, "two weeks after" Ash Wednesday, Henry still had ash on his forehead because he hadn't washed his face during that entire time. Berglund recalled that he and Betsy once went into Henry's room behind his back and nabbed his clothing. They held the clothes hostage until he agreed to bathe.

Berglund also remembered that he was worried over Henry's debilitating pains and set up a doctor's appointment for him, but "Henry refused to bathe" before going to the appointment. Once there, the "doctor took one look at him and said" to Berglund, "'You are to take him home, bathe him, and bring him back in three days.' We went home and I bathed him. . . . He did not like a bath at all." In the process of bathing his friend, Berglund discovered that "Henry suffered from a serious hernia," undoubtedly the cause of at least some of the pain in the right side of his abdomen.

Late in the night of January 26, 1967, the pain in Henry's abdomen returned so viciously that it gave him a bad case of chills, and once that passed, he felt as if he needed to vomit but couldn't. Henry admitted, "because of the pain I shook my fist towards heaven, meaning it for God" and added, "I am afraid I was a sort of devil if I may call myself one." However, it wasn't just in the dead of night that the pains struck. During Mass the following spring, it became virtually impossible for him to stand or kneel at appropriate moments during the liturgy because of the pains in his legs, and once, while Henry was attending an afternoon Mass, the abdominal pain returned, and he had to hurry outside, where he vomited "green stuff" at the church's west wall.

Making matters worse, on June 27, 1968, a car struck Henry in the crosswalk near his building. His left leg and the left side of his hip were so badly injured that he was laid up in bed for two and a half months. The accident aggravated the condition that had been causing his pains for years. While walking outside after a bad snow and ice storm during the following December, he slipped on the slush-covered ice and fell, and five weeks later, he fell again, this time at the bottom of the steps in front of his building. Then, eight days after that, he nearly fell a third time but caught himself as he was going down. His health was rapidly declining, and his ability to take care of himself had become a huge question mark. He knew it, and the other tenants were aware of it, too.

A CHILD IN BRAZIL

The neighborhood in which Henry lived had seen better days. When he moved into the Anschutzes' boardinghouse, the area had been somewhat prosperous. It had become a favorite among German immigrants, some of whom, like the Anschutzes, owned rooming houses and rented to the overflow from Towertown, mostly young men and women who were employed in semiprofessional or clerical roles. It was full of cheap but clean and safe lodgings. By the time Nathan Lerner bought the two buildings on Webster, the area was verging on the seedy. Younger persons—"art students" who attended DePaul University only a stone's throw away and "models, photographers, and musicians" who were looking for inexpensive places to rent—were attracted to the building at 851 Webster.

A man now nearly eighty years old among a group of twenty- or thirtysomethings, Henry stood out like a sore thumb. "Henry didn't really fit in," his neighbor David Berglund recalled years later. "He kept his door locked. He was gone during the day. You'd hear him unlocking and locking his door. We'd say 'hello' on the stairs. . . . Henry was kind of like a mystery, he just came in and out of the room."

Mary Dillon recalled her time in the building fondly. It was a "sort of a community in the four apartments," she recalled, describing it as "a wonderful place." She "had the most fun in [her] life" there. She summed it up as "a lovely happy place, a playground." Her version of life there stands in direct contrast to Henry's. He stayed away from his young neighbors and their "playground" as much as he could. Theirs was the freewheeling life of bohemians and university students. His was the daily grind of a poverty-stricken dishwasher, bandage roller, and retired man. Henry lived hand to mouth. They had barbecues in the backyard. Although he didn't care to socialize with them, the young people would "send him up plates of food" after their get-togethers because they were concerned about their misfit neighbor. Henry was so angry over his lot in life by then that he probably never appreciated their kindnesses. At least, none ever mentioned he thanked them.

Despite the differences in their ages, backgrounds, and day-to-day experiences, the Berglunds and the other tenants empathized with Henry and did what they could to help him out. "A lot of us in the building looked out for him," Dillon recalled. "I remember when he retired, we were all concerned about his retiring." In the winters, when she knew Henry was cold—the steam radiators in his room failed to work properly—Dillon "used to go up and offer him food, tea, cookies."

After falling several times, Henry knew that, at his age, he had to depend on others' help, and he wasn't ashamed to ask for it. Henry would come to the Lerners' home when he needed a light bulb in the ceiling changed, and Lerner's wife would climb up a ladder to reach the ceiling ten feet above the floor to change the bulb for him. Henry once included a note in a Valentine's Day card for Berglund. He addressed the note to "My friend David" and wrote, "I would like you to do me a short time favor when I come back from Church at nine of clock or sooner. It needs climbing the ladder which I dare not do."

The Berglunds did far more to help Henry than anyone else in the building. Beginning in the early 1970s, they rented the front four-room apartment on the third floor, and Henry's room was behind their apartment. When he was ill and bedridden, Betsy made Henry a breakfast of two slices of buttered toast. His bed was along the west wall, so she crossed his room from the front door to his bed every morning for several weeks. She remembered that "he wore layers of clothes," perhaps several shirts at a time. When David gave him a bath in the large, claw-foot tub the three of them shared, she was shocked at how tiny he was. "My God," she thought to herself, "he's skinny underneath all that!"

Despite being one of the few people with whom Henry had interactions during his last years and someone who'd worked to make his last days as easy as possible, Betsy remembered him as "not talkative at all" around her, and yet, unlike some of the other tenants in the building, she never felt even remotely threatened or uneasy around him. "When you got close to him, he was very benign. The only creepy part was his room." Despite the fact that Henry usually kept his shades up so that the room was well lit, its stacks of trash, its smell and grime, its walls cluttered with various forms of art—from calendar pictures and his original art to images of saints and children—disturbed her. "He was an unknown," she said. "We didn't know anything about the strangled girls" in his paintings yet, so as far as she was concerned, Henry was simply "an older gentleman" who lived on the same floor as they did among a considerable amount of "junk."

One Christmas, Betsy invited Henry to the dinner that she was making for her parents. He showed up, but he wasn't at all willing to talk to anyone. He ate the meal in silence and left after it was over without speaking to a soul. During another Christmas season, either Betsy or David asked Henry to let them know what he'd like for a Christmas present. Henry answered in a note he included in a St. Valentine's Day card, which he probably had found and decided to use in lieu of a traditional Christmas card, which he couldn't afford: "For Christmas presents I would like what I need most a bar of Ivory soap and a large tupe [tube] of palm olive brushless shaving cram and something to eat Christmas afternoon. Chicken no Turkey. I hate it."

Other people in the neighborhood who knew Henry, and not just the other tenants, also kept an eye out for him, including the proprietor of Roma's, where Henry regularly ate "hot dog sandwiches." Roma's was located only a couple of blocks west, at the corner of Webster and Sheffield Avenues, and once, when its owner became concerned about not seeing Henry for a few days, he went to Henry's apartment to check on him. The priests from St. Vincent's Church visited him in his room about every six months to make sure he was all right. They knew he'd had problems getting around and was living with a variety of ailments.

One, Father Thomas J. Murphy, even sent Berglund a note about Henry. Henry had undergone outpatient procedures at Illinois Masonic Medical Center in June 1971, and in the note, the priest gave Berglund the information the Church had on Henry. Berglund was probably trying to help get Henry's bills paid because he had begun receiving past-due notices from the center.

According to St. Vincent's Church records, Henry's last name was Dargarus, he was born in Brazil, and his birthdate was 1903. None of the information was true. At the end of his note, Father Murphy thanked Berglund for watching out for the infirm seventy-nine-year-old. "Sure is wonderful of you and Mrs.," Murphy wrote, "to keep your eye on him. He is more helpless than I presumed."

During the last few years of Henry's life, the Berglunds threw him two birthday parties, the first in their apartment, which the Lerners attended, and the second in the backyard of the Lerners' building next door. At the first one, the hosts wanted to bring Henry out of his shell and, because most of those present had heard him singing in his room at one time or another, they asked him to sing for them. Surprising them all, Henry said, "I can sing some children's marching songs" that he claimed he'd learned as a child in Brazil. Berglund recalled that "it sounded like real Portuguese. He sang in a foreign language. It sounded so genuine, we believed him." It was at times like these, when Henry seemed to open up to those around him, that David Berglund could admit, "I used to think he was a cranky old fart," but these moments "showed another side of him."

The others who lived in the building also seemed to see Henry in a different light. As he sang lyrics that certainly seemed "foreign" to them, he revealed himself to be a small, harmless old man who, despite his gruff exterior and his eccentricities, was no one to fear. What they didn't know, of course, was that pain, both psychological and physical, filled Henry's life, day and night, causing him to be a "crabby," distant loner. They had no idea about the trauma that he had faced as a child, the day-to-day struggle he had to overcome to survive at his menial jobs, the depths of loneliness that he had endured after Whillie's move to Texas and then his death, and the guilt—as intense as anything else he experienced—that haunted him his entire life. He was certainly odd, as they believed. He was unmistakably lax in his personal hygiene. He was obviously different from them in every way imaginable, but they cared for him and did all that they could to help him anyway.

FALLING DOWN ANGRY TEMPER SPELLS

Henry could only express his built-up anger metaphorically, through his novels and paintings. The children whom he depicted as psychic hermaphrodites and whom adults abused horrifically spoke on his behalf, although no one heard. As an old man in his mid-seventies, emotionally exhausted from struggling to keep his anger locked up, Henry finally lost his ability to hold it at bay, and he surrendered to it.

Of course, he'd slipped up on several occasions in the past, as when he slashed his teacher in grade school and when he lost his temper with coworkers, but the slips weren't occasional anymore. They were daily. Tiny, insignificant mistakes, missteps, and disappointments in his day-to-day life—making ink blotches on his manuscript as he was writing, the sun's heat or the lack of cooling rains in the summers, misplacing his glasses in his cluttered room and having to take all morning to find them—took on overwhelming significance, and his fury transformed itself into vocalized ranting and raving.

Counseling for victims of sexual abuse, especially for men, wasn't available when he was a child and wouldn't be available for many decades. Even if it had been available, Henry was too poor to afford it. Instead, he suffered it in silence, as one of his characters, Jack Evans, suffered over his own experiences. Meant to be a stand-in for Henry at various moments in *The Realms*, but less so in *Crazy House*, Henry depicted Evans as having experienced a great deal of horror during the war between Glandelinia and Angelinia, not the least of which was witnessing the way the evil Glandelinians enslaved, tortured, and murdered the children whom they captured. Like Henry, Evans is incapable of dealing with his feelings and shoves them beneath the surface of his consciousness:

Jack Evans, who had heard all, saw most of it, and saw their condition many a time, is so cool and quiet that it seems as if he cared nothing about it. But in his heart there is burning a fierce anger, an anger that is extremely dangerous, and . . . someday he is going to explode like a mighty volcano.

Henry created Evans as a key to his own predicament and even once admitted, "I am a spitting growling if not thundering volcano," echoing his description of Evans. Other tenants in Henry's building and his neighbors may have described him in various ways, but none would ever have a clue that he was filled with a "fierce anger" that threatened to explode at any moment. Interestingly, when he was working on a novel and its illustrations, Henry wasn't as likely to blow up. Creative activity seems to have kept the "volcano" from exploding, and that may be one reason for his huge manuscripts and the hundreds of illustrations. Creative activity quelled his rage.

Occasionally, Henry was able to divert his attention from problems by engaging himself in other activities, defusing his anger in the process, as an entry in his journal suggests: "Did singing instead of tantrum and swearing." Henry's neighbors didn't just report that Henry spoke to himself when alone. They also mentioned that they heard him singing to himself late into the night, another one of his ways of taming his fury at God, at priests and nuns, and at the predators who had prowled the sidewalks and alleys of West Madison Street and the hallways and dormitories of the Mission and the Asylum.

During the early 1910s, Henry kept a journal as a way of tracking the plot twists and turns, the numbers of casualties on both sides, and the names of generals and battles in *The Realms*. It contains only a few references to his personal life, and many of those have some direct connection to writing the novel. However, Henry's later journals, which he began in the late 1960s, are very personal, recording Henry's anger, highlighting the days when it ran rampant and those when he was able to keep it corralled.

At least as early as 1932, Henry began collecting string of various

types and lengths that he found on the street, tying the pieces end to
end to create balls ten to twelve inches in diameter. He used the twine
for binding the pages of *The Realms* into volumes, for bundling the
magazines and newspapers in which he found source material, and for
other practical purposes, but the twine also became the cause of many
of his tirades. "Threaten ball throwing at Sacred image. Always
threaten but don't do it," Henry wrote in his journal when he had trouble tying the ends of the twine together. "Sacred image" refers to the
religious statues and pictures—Christs hanging from crosses, Madon-
nas and their children—on the mantel of the fireplace, the metal
shelves against the eastern wall, or elsewhere in his room that he targeted. On Saturday, April 6, 1968, six days before his seventy-sixth
birthday, Henry jotted down in his journal, "Over cords falling down
angry temper spell with some blasphemies. Almost about to throw
the ball at Christ statue. I blame them"—by which Henry meant God
and Jesus—"for my bad luck in things Im sorry to say so. I'll always
be this way Always was and I don't give a damn." This wasn't the
only time Henry targeted the Divine with his anger. He also wrote
"Threaten to throw ball at some sacred image because things go
wrong" and "Tantrums over difficulty with twin and cord. Defied
heaven to make things worse Threaten to throw ball."

In old age, Henry was reverting to behaviors that he'd first
begun as a child. In his "younger days," Henry recalled, "when angry
over something I burned holy pictures and hit the face of Christ in
pictures with my fist." Now as an old man, he flew into "tantrums,"
a child's, not a mature adult's, behavior. "Tantrum" even suggests
that Henry recognized his own immaturity. Institutionalized children
don't typically or easily grow into mature adults, retaining adolescent
(or younger) ideas, motivations, concerns, and responses. Henry was
no exception.

He superstitiously wondered if God wasn't about to strike him
dead for his blasphemous actions: "I was all right till twards evening
then . . . threw a tantrum tantrum and defied defied Heaven to make

my Cross worse and cursed at Heaven and God I believe. Will anything happen to me." His repetition of "tantrum" and "defied" shows that Henry's outbursts and defiance were intense. The question "Will anything happen to me"—that is, will God punish Henry for the flare-ups—not only reveals the depth of Henry's religious indoctrination but also adds a pointed pathos to his situation.

Henry dutifully recorded the number of times each day he attended Mass or other liturgical events at St. Vincent's Church—all in all, at least thirty-three services each week—while, at the same time, engaging in "severe tantrums and bad words." The interplay of blasphemy and church attendance continued day after day virtually until the journal's last entry.

As he began to attend church obsessively, Henry also began to question the culture in which he now lived as well as his own past experiences. In December 1965, he wrote to Father Charles E. Lannon, a priest at St. Vincent's Church, to complain about how women were beginning to dress when they attended Mass. Vatican II and the consequent liberalization of the Roman Catholic Church was now underway, and Henry was angry that "woman's dress" was "completely out of line." The priest, obviously conservative in his views, agreed with Henry: "They are absolutely wrong to enter Church in such outfits," perhaps referring to pantsuits, which were becoming popular among women. However, while he had Father Lannon's ear, Henry had also questioned the priest about "Scripture" and cross-dressing, probably referring to Deuteronomy 22:5: "The woman shall not wear that which pertaineth unto a man, neither shall a man put on a woman's garment: for all that do so are abomination unto the Lord thy God." Father Lannon responded, "As for the Scripture it is referring to those who for sinful reasons dress contrary to their sex—e.g., a man dressing as a woman, etc." Now seventy-three years old, Henry was trying to get the Church's stance on homosexuality: "a man dressing as a woman" for "sinful reasons."

Henry's Vivian girl-boys cross-dressed, as did several of his other characters. On occasion—as when the "peacherino" Jennie was hanging out on the street corner or when Jennie and Angeline were on dates with older, "normal" men at the Janet Theater—they cross-dressed for potentially "sinful reasons." Henry, as he mentioned, had known plenty of boys who wanted to be girls and who, if they were fairies as he suggested, probably even cross-dressed, again for "sinful reasons." Interestingly, Father Lannon doesn't overtly condemn those who "dress contrary to their sex," but it's obvious that they're sinful in his eyes and so can't be afforded salvation—another reason for Henry's obsession with Mass and confession.

Occasionally, Henry came close to admitting what the root cause of his anger was. On June 2, 1969, he confessed in his journal, he "got angry at some things." Typical of Henry, he was vague when facing real issues, disguising the source of his anger with "some things." Had it been the usual "things" that got him riled up—twine or even pain—he would've been explicit. He'd mentioned both many times in the journals before June 2, and he had no reason not to mention them again if they had been the causes. His omission hints that dark, shameful "things" may have been responsible for his anger because "some things" echoes the "other things" Henry once mentioned that had caused him so many problems between him, John Manley, and the Scanlon brothers.

Henry thought long and hard about his tantrums, and he summarized two principal reasons for his sudden and violent outbursts, seeing a slight, but important, difference between the two: "I am a real enemy of the cross or a very very Sorry Saint." Given Henry's faith, to be an "enemy" of Christianity was to be the worst type of human being, an infidel perhaps or a heretic. He was probably referring as much to his blasphemies as his sexual experiences, both the coerced and the consensual ones. To be a "Sorry Saint" was to be a lapsed believer, one who acknowledged Catholicism's tenets but who nevertheless ignored them. An "enemy of the cross" would have been damned, usually with no hope of salvation, unless he or she converted, while a "Sorry Saint" was a believer who could be assured of salvation by changing his or her ways and attending confession and Mass regularly. Henry saw himself as being both simultaneously. He believed that going to confession and attending Mass and other liturgical events saved him from the fate that would've awaited him because of his blasphemies: "Priest who I confess to said it was a serious sin for what I said at God. Good thing I received Communion," which cleansed his soul.

Neither confession, nor communion, nor Mass ever lessened Henry's belief that, because God controlled all in the universe, the problems he faced beginning on the day that he was born were God's fault. Henry wasn't the only one who was angry at God and blaspheming against him. Webber George skipped Mass one Sunday and filled the day with "bad words about God." Webber, like Henry, was outraged by God, who had failed him by creating him male instead of female, but Henry's anger was more wide-ranging than Webber's. He was also outraged by God's consistent failure to protect him.

God didn't stop Henry's father from packing him off to the Mission and, when that didn't change him for the better, to the Asylum. He didn't protect Henry against the sexual abuse he suffered. God took both of his parents away from him long before their time: his mother when Henry was four, his father when he was sixteen. God caused his legs to throb with pain and the pain to slice through his abdomen. God created Henry as the wrong sex, as he had Webber. Because he was attracted to men, he should've been born female, not male. For all of the years he and Whillie were together, their relationship was never complete. They could never live together, and he and Whillie couldn't adopt children. Then God sent Whillie away, first to Wilmette, then to San Antonio. After that, he sent what Henry thought was the "Asian flu" to kill Whillie. God had made Henry's life a rosary of miseries and tragedies without end, despite what the priests and nuns had promised. God deserved Henry's curses.

Mark Waters, who grew up a few doors from Henry's building and was an altar boy at St. Vincent's Church when Henry attended Mass there, saw something in Henry that few others had taken the time to notice:

> The altar boy holds a shield that protects the communion Host from dropping to the floor. So I was always right there [when Henry took communion], and he always looked me in the eye [when he took the Host]. And he had a sort of sweet look, actually. I would say that he felt very concerned to do things right. He wanted to be an obedient, faithful one.

Regardless of how diligently Henry worked to stop the tantrums, they beleaguered him. Sometimes the tantrums were small, inconsequential outbursts that were over almost as soon as they'd begun, but generally, they consumed him: "Tantrums a plenty," "Tatrums Galore," "Sever Tantrums." Page after page of his journals reveal his "disrespectful words against Heaven and God."

On the few days that he was able to control himself and not explode, he called himself a "good boy."

WRITE LIFE HISTORY (NOT MYSTERY)

Henry had loved dogs since he first read about Dorothy's little dog, Toto, in *The Wonderful Wizard of Oz*, and when he worked with Joe Harry in the bandage room at Alexian Brothers, Henry learned that Harry had two. Henry wanted his own. After Lerner married in 1967 and his wife moved into 849 Webster with him, the couple had a dog named Yuki. Henry had a great deal of affection for Yuki, who would jump on him and lick his nose. While her affection for Henry sprang from the food he often gave her, she was also simply responding to his gentleness.

287 THE SAINTS AND ALL THE ANGELS WOULD BE ASHAMED OF ME

Wanting to ease his loneliness, Henry asked Lerner's wife how much it would cost him to take care of a dog properly. When she gave him an approximate cost for food and other items the dog would need, Henry realized he couldn't afford one and gave up on the idea, although that didn't stop him from having substitutes in his room. Henry put statuettes of a Great Dane and of a spaniel, as well as a photo of a little girl holding two puppies, on the mantel of his fireplace among the religious icons. Unable to afford a pet to keep him company, Henry set out to write his third book to occupy his time.

Although in physical pain much of the time, Henry began his autobiography *The History of My Life*, his last book, in 1968, a few months before his seventy-sixth birthday. It opens with a mysterious, extremely brief, first paragraph: "In the month of April, on the 12, in the year of 1892, of what week day I never knew as I was never told, nor did I seek the information." For some reason, perhaps because he was in a hurry to get his autobiography underway, perhaps because he was momentarily distracted, Henry forgot to reveal what April 12 was and why it was important to his life. It was the day he was born.

Making matters worse, Henry was often self-censorious. He whitewashed any number of experiences rather than presenting them honestly, and far too often, when Henry was about to reveal something that had the potential to embarrass him, that might put him in a bad light, or that could reveal something related to sex, he claimed he couldn't remember what really happened. Of course, because of his advanced age, he really might not have been able to recall some events as they actually happened sixty or seventy years earlier, but it was only with those situations that would somehow reflect negatively on him that he suddenly drew a blank about specifics. Otherwise, he was clear more often than not. Henry camouflaged his strategy of denial into forgetfulness to give a confused, patchwork version of his life. Nevertheless, at least two major themes emerge from *The History of My Life*. First, Henry was thrown away—ignored, lied to, cheated, betrayed, left, abandoned, exiled—by everyone important in his life.

Second, from his earliest years, he was filled with an anger that, by the time he'd begun his autobiography, had all but consumed him.

The second section of the autobiography begins on page 206 and extends through the remaining 4,878 pages. Henry had been describing an accident that had happened to one of his coworkers while he was employed at Grant Hospital when, out of the blue, he announced, "There is one really important thing I must write which I have forgotten."

At the top of the next page, Henry wrote, "Now I will come to what I intend to write." With that, he began to recount the journey undertaken by a character named Henry Darger to track down a tornado, called Sweetie Pie, that has devastated much of Central Illinois. Obviously, the Sweetie Pie section is as much an integral part of his life story as the first 206 are. To underscore exactly that, he included the running head "My Life History" from the beginning of the manuscript to its end, some 5,000-plus pages. As in *The Realms* and *Crazy House*, Henry's heavily camouflaged life is the focus of the narrative of Sweetie Pie. This time, however, Henry doesn't disguise himself as a Vivian girl-boy or a general, not as an angry little boy who wishes he'd been born a girl or as the leader of a secret society devoted to the well-being of children, but as Sweetie Pie itself while, at the same time, remaining the narrator, Henry Darger.

Fifteen years old, the character Henry Darger is unaccountably walking in Missouri with "two companions," when they notice the distant eastern sky turning black. Without explanation, he and his friends are suddenly transported to the area of Illinois that surrounded the Asylum, at a siding of the Illinois Central Railroad that ran along the northern boundary of its property. They watch "a very wide cloud," which turns out to be Sweetie Pie, "hurling a frightful storm of everything from the ground in all directions as it moved along" accompanied by an indescribable "bedlam of sound." The tornado devastates the site. It "turned bottom up-

289 THE SAINTS AND ALL THE ANGELS WOULD BE ASHAMED OF ME

wards" dozens of railroad cars: "passenger cars, pullmans," and "flat cars, which had been loaded with . . . big stone slabs." Although shaken by the scene, the boys continue to follow the swath of destruction Sweetie Pie leaves behind. It is August 15, a little after four thirty in the afternoon, and the odd trek that the character Henry Darger is on is reminiscent of the real Henry Darger's escape from the Asylum in July 1909, when he was seventeen and accompanied by his two buddies.

From the railroad siding, Henry Darger and his friends walk to Chesterbrown, a nearby town that the tornado has destroyed, where Henry Darger becomes "head of the Relief Committee," recording in extreme detail for thousands of pages the destruction Sweetie Pie has wrecked: the crumbled buildings, the uprooted trees, the deaths of thousands of men, women, and children. The swirling winds aren't the only destructive force that besets the towns and lands near where the Asylum stood. A huge fire mysteriously comes to life in Sweetie Pie's wake, fans across the wasteland that the twister has created, and burns to ash whatever it has left behind. Later, after the fire has been extinguished, Henry Darger continues his journey through the area, describing the fire's and the tornado's destruction and gathering the testimonies from those few who have been left alive.

As in his other books, Henry scattered individuals from his past throughout the plot. Whillie shows up in various guises, and as himself as well, along with his sister Angeline, Jim and John Scanlon, Donald Aurand, Daniel Jones, Sister Rose, and Thomas Phelan. Dorothy Gale and other characters from the Oz books also make an appearance. By borrowing the trope of a tornado from *The Wonderful Wizard of Oz*, he acknowledged his love of Baum's novels. Interestingly, Henry even created a character named Henry Schloeder, uniting himself with his beloved, who'd died a decade earlier, and feminizing himself—because he took Whillie's last name as brides traditionally have done—in a make-believe marriage. Henry didn't add persons from his past to the narrative to get back at them as he had in *The*

Realms. Regardless of whether they had been good or not to him in real life, all work along with the character Henry Darger as part of the Relief Committee's efforts.

Nevertheless, Sweetie Pie's story is a revenge narrative. The Angel Guardian Orphanage, where the tornado kills hundred of children and from which hundreds of others disappear, perhaps blown away by the tornado's terrible wind, is a stand-in for the Illinois Asylum for Feeble-Minded Children. The Child Refuge Settlement also represents the Asylum and is devastated, along with its child refugees—as also happens to the Gleason Orphanage, another version of the Asylum. The Sacred Heart Convent is a thinly disguised St. Joseph's Hospital. Henry wrote that one of the survivors of Sweetie Pie's rampage had been employed as a dishwasher there by the head nun, who is now dead, sounding remarkably like Henry's employment at St. Joseph's. Sweetie Pie flattens the convent and kills all of the nuns who lived there.

Eventually, Henry Darger learns that four soldiers, who have been part of the efforts of the Relief Committee, set the fire that followed Sweetie Pie. They're put on military trial, are found guilty of arson, and are sentenced to be drummed out of every town, one after another, in Central Illinois. "In their own town they were so disgraced," Henry Darger states, "that no one would have anything to do with them, they could buy nothing and had to go far away elsewhere. Even their best friends or nearest relations would not associate with they, they were not even allowed to enter a church of any kind." The arsonists' exile from all they knew and loved is reminiscent of Henry's disgraceful exile to the Asylum, after no one in his family would step forward to help him.

Unable to get back at the adults who harmed him in life, Henry used the Sweetie Pie narrative to placate at least some of his anger. On March 16, 1968, an especially bad day for him, Henry wrote in his journal, "Mad enough to wish I was a bad tornado," and in the Sweetie Pie narrative, he made his wish come true. When he depicted a tornado destroying the countryside and all who lived where he had been institutionalized for five years, Henry was metaphorically wrecking vengeance on the Asylum and all the people associated with it. In the most imaginative strategy he'd ever undertaken in his writing, Henry metamorphosed himself into both the character he named after himself and the tornado Sweetie Pie, becoming both the hero and the villain of his own life story, the savior of refugees and the murderer of those who had harmed him.

Although Sweetie Pie levels towns, tears up train tracks and upsets the train cars, strews debris all over the countryside for hundreds of miles, murders thousands and makes thousands more homeless, she also steals a record book from the Gleason Orphanage called "the great book of Records." Dr. Henry Gale was "the head administrator" of the Gleason Orphanage, and "he wrote into it all that happened anywhere in the home and what the children received from rich relatives and friends." It is a "five hundred fifty pound book" that represents the records kept about Henry and other children at the Asylum. The relief workers eventually find the book among wreckage in a town called Laneville. Henry's desire to wipe out any evidence that he'd been in the Asylum, as represented by the huge book, comes through loud and clear, although he recognized the fact that the past can't be erased. Someone always discovers it.

In fact, many of Henry's characters who actually see Sweetie Pie in action swear that its shape reminds them of "a little girl childs head turned side ways with clouds form like hands around the neck in a strangling grip with the tongue stretching out and mouth wide open." With that, Henry also links Sweetie Pie to the children at the Asylum who were strangled in order to make them pliant for whatever caretakers wanted to do to them. Making the link even stronger, Henry has another eyewitness claim that the child is not only being strangled but her body has also been ripped open, like those of so many of the children on his canvases. Sweetie Pie represents the physically and sexually abused children of Henry's childhood, Henry among them.

All the attempts by Henry Darger and his men to extinguish the conflagration engulfing Central Illinois fail, so they decide to "coax God to send . . . rain." Henry Darger suggests that they "talk this over with God in a friendly manner. But will he grant it." He continues, "I've been very angry with Him because of this tornado disaster." Although they say "the Rosary and the Litany of the Mother of God" not once but three times, God ignores their prayer as he had ignored Henry's petitions to adopt a child.

One of the more minor characters, Mr. Cigarover, asks Henry, "Why were you mad at God? He didn't make or will the tornado. Though for some cause he let it happen." Henry answered, "To me its the same as doing it." For Henry and his character Henry Darger, God's allowing evil to happen is the same as creating it.

Henry decided to intrude into the Sweetie Pie narrative in nineteenth-century fashion as he had in *Crazy House* and, in doing so, revealed where he got at least some of the information about tornadoes and fires that he had used in it. "As of now," he confessed, "I've got a book with photographs of what the tornado in Easter Sunday March 23 1913 did, and now have photos of the twister horror of Oak lawn . . . of April 21 1967." The book he referred to is Frederick E. Drinker's *Horrors of Tornado, Flood, and Fire*. What Henry didn't mention was that he appropriated some of Drinker's text for his own without acknowledging its source. Drinker wrote, "Bravery lacked neither rank nor station. It may thrill the soul of a Napoleon or a Wellington," which Henry doctored: "Bravery lacked neither rank nor station or leadership among the thousands of fire fighters. It may thrill the soul of a Napoleon Bonapart, or a Duke of Wellington." Also without acknowledging the source, Henry took a few sentences from a song that the Knight, a character in *The Royal Book of Oz*, sings:

Up, up, my lieges and away!
We take the field again—
For Ladies fair we fight today
And KING! Up, up, my merry men!
. . .
Avaunt! Be off! Be gone—Methinks
We'll be asleep in forty winks!

Henry changed the original slightly for his own purposes:

Up up my lieges and away
We take the field again
For our country fair we fight to night
Up up my merry men with all your might
. . .
Avaunt Be off Be gone methinks
We'll have you whipped
In forty winks.

His change of "For Ladies fair we fight today" to "For our country fair we fight to night" nullifies its original heterosexual context.

Henry's choice of Sweetie Pie as a name for the agent of his revenge is also interesting, at once a term of endearment and a type of doll popular in the early decades of the twentieth century. The survivors of the tornado's devastation don't take well to the sentiment the name suggests. Looking around at the destroyed buildings and corpses, they think it has been sardonically named.

The actual manuscript of *The History of My Life* also coincidentally reveals some important aspects of Henry's life. First, it clearly shows that Henry was working on his art as late as at least 1968 to 1969, when he was seventy-seven or so years old. He always had so much piled on his table that he had to write on top of his paintings or draw and paint on top of his writings. In several places in the manu-

294 HENRY DARGER, THROWAWAY BOY

script, Henry had been tracing images from a source onto his canvas but didn't realize that there was a sheet of carbon paper upside-down under it. Beneath the carbon paper, his manuscript lay open. As he traced the image onto the canvas, he also traced it onto the manuscript. Unfortunately, the images that show up on his manuscript are generic plants, not the Vivian girl-boys or any unique figure, so they can't help in dating the canvases on which they appear.

He wrote some of the manuscript of the Sweetie Pie section of *The History of My Life* on paper from interesting sources. Henry discovered in the garbage a cache of stationery from the office of Chicago Alderman George B. McCutcheon, on which he wrote several sections of the book, and he also found a composition notebook that Norma Pietri, a sixth-grader at Waller School, had once owned and some of her graded assignments. He used a few of the assignments of several other Waller sixth-graders—Ana Delia González, Sandra Hughes, and Wendy Kimbrell—too.

The single most captivating of Norma's assignments that Henry preserved is the one on which he wrote nothing about Sweetie Pie. It's a mimeographed line drawing of the male reproductive system in cross section. Obviously, the assignment was for the children in Norma's classroom to identify the system's various parts. Unfortunately, she failed to identify anything correctly and received an F- as her grade. Regardless, Henry slipped it into his manuscript, writing "not to be covered" across the top of the page and adding page number 4,716 to it as if it were somehow a part of Sweetie Pie's story. There's no discernible reason for him to have included the clinical drawing to his manuscript at that point in the novel's plot, and why he did is a mystery.

CHAPTER 10

AFTERLIFE

I WANT TO DIE HERE

ONE DAY IN THE LATE 1960S OR THE EARLY '70S, HENRY RUSHED to the house next door where the Lerners lived and, between gasps for air, told "Mr. Leonard," "I was raped by a beautiful 17-year-old in the vestibule of the building, and she cut the strings to my wallet and took all of the money I had." Henry wasn't at all concerned about what he claimed to be a sexual attack but rather about the theft of his money. He asked Mr. Leonard if he could lend him some money until the following month, promising to pay him back. Lerner gave Henry the loan he asked for, and sure enough, he repaid Lerner the day he said he would.

It's highly unlikely that Henry was raped that day, but it's very possible that Henry—a small old man close to his eighties and an easy target—was mugged by a young woman (or a long-haired young man) in the entrance of his own building. If he was mugged, his sudden lack of control—something he'd experienced over and over again during his sexual victimization as a child and adolescent—was so traumatic that the rapes of the past and the mugging of the present merged in his mind into one event.

Some of the other tenants, such as the Berglunds, had realized that Henry's health was failing, but no one knew he was suffering from arteriosclerotic heart disease and senility—the first wracking his body, the second attacking his mind.

Arteriosclerosis harasses the body slowly, and often over many years. In its earliest stages, it isn't necessarily detectable. For some who have been stricken with it, it can focus on specific body parts, concentrating on, for example, the arteries of the legs, causing extreme pain that eventually leaves the individual unable to walk. This—and the stress caused by Whillie's moves to Wilmette and San Antonio, and then his death—was probably causing Henry's intense leg pains.

Henry had also shown symptoms of senility for several years before he died, although the people whom he knew chalked the symptoms up to his being an eccentric old man. The medical literature reveals that his inability to control his "tantrums" is also easily attributed to senility, as is his confusing the sexual abuse he'd experienced as a child with being mugged by a young woman. Similarly, his fantasy of having been born and raised in Brazil, the country closest to Devil's Island, where, if the inmates were lucky enough to escape the penal colony, they could live free, and his use of pseudonyms may also have been prompted by his senility.

Despite his mental decline, Henry never once forgot Whillie. He continued to include him in his writings, although often referring to him as *a* or *the* "tall man":

> I remember when I and a tall man were walking down Webster ave homeward bound at dark in late fall we saw an auto driver without head lights on strike a dog nearly killing the animal right there and then nearly being hit by a car coming from the west.
>
> I wish we had been motorcycle cops then, We would have arrested him.

The lovers were walking west, down the street on which Henry lived, "homeward bound" suggesting they'll spend the night together at Henry's.

Entries of Henry's journals show his chief concerns and preoccupations during the last years of his life:

> Three Masses and Holy Communion in the morning. Mass also in the afternoon.
> No tantrums
> Life History.
> . . .
> The same as above.
> One bad word. No tantrums.
> Life History.
> . . .
> The same as above.
> Confession in the morning
> Life history

Henry wrote the same message with virtually the same words over and over again until, in one of the last entries of the journals, he made a lengthier comment:

> Not much history until October when I had an eye operation of the left one because of a serious infection and was in bed at home until a little before Christmas because I could not dare go out because of an unusual eye covering for protection placed by the doctor. I had a poor a very poor nothing life Christmas. Never had a good Christmas all my life nor a good new good year and now reviewing it I am very bitter but fortunately not revengeful though I feel I should be. Now I am I am walking the streets and again going to Mass as usual What will it be for me for New Years 1972 God only knows. . . .

Tantrums (his anger), church attendance (his guilt), and *The History of My Life* (his art) consumed him.

Lerner and some of his tenants began to be aware that, now in his eighties, Henry needed daily care. Concerned over his friend's well-being, Lerner began suggesting to him that he might want to move into a nursing home where he'd be looked after properly. Lerner recited a list of the advantages to being in a home: help on a daily basis, three meals a day, even companionship. Henry wasn't buying it, however. He'd had his fill of institutional life, a total of ten years of his childhood, and how so-called caregivers could become predators in the blink of an eye. "I want to live here," he told his friend. "I want to die here."

Henry still wasn't interested when Lerner approached him again to suggest that he enter St. Augustine's Home for the Aged only a little more than five blocks away. He didn't know that Henry's father had died in St. Augustine's more than seventy years earlier, leaving Henry unprotected and abandoned to the whims of strangers. The thought of living there would have chilled Henry. He couldn't help not wanting to go, but he couldn't stay in his room. Henry knew that he couldn't take care of himself much longer and that he didn't want to become a burden to anyone.

In the meantime, concerned over Henry's health and future, Lerner went to the priests at St. Vincent's Church to see if they might be able to help Henry out, and in an effort to see that Henry had around-the-clock supervision, the priests "made arrangements for Henry to move" in with them. Once it was settled, Mr. Leonard told Henry about his good fortune, but despite his ever-increasing ill health and his awareness that he couldn't hold out much longer, Henry still couldn't bring himself to move.

In his entry for February 1971 to December 1971, the next-to-the-last statement in his journals, he hinted about a possible outcome for his situation. It reads, "This year was a very bad one, hope not to repeat" it. Then he added what seems to be the beginning of a resolution: "If so—." The blank invites a question: If the new year was going to be another "very bad" one full of physical and psychological pains, loneliness, and bitterness over his lot in life, would he rather be dead? Henry's last comment in the journals suggests his concern, especially over forces that he couldn't control. On the first page of his first journal for "January 1 1972 To January 1973," Henry considered his future and wondered, "What will it be?—"

ONE LAST INSTITUTION

Henry turned eighty years old on April 12, 1972. The pains in his legs left him barely able to walk on good days and bedridden on the bed. In October, he asked his friend Lerner to find him a "Catholic home" where he could go to live out his days. Lerner returned to the priests at St. Vincent's Church for their help. They'd thought it over since Lerner's last contact with them and had changed their minds. They didn't want to bother with Henry after all. Because Henry had attended services at St. Vincent's Church so often, all the priests would have been aware of him—and his eccentricities. Undoubtedly, they thought he was "retarded" or "schizophrenic" or, at the very least, "very weird, very strange," as others did. They didn't know that Henry was quickly slipping into senility. Regardless, they pawned him off on the Little Sisters of the Poor, the group of nuns who founded and ran St. Augustine's Home for the Aged.

Although they wrote down his personal information for their records, the Little Sisters of the Poor didn't want Henry to move in immediately and suggested a trial run. They wanted to make sure Henry would be happy with them. They also wanted to make sure that they would be happy having him among their other clients. The priests at St. Vincent's had likely warned the nuns about Henry's eccentricities and the problems that they foresaw in bringing him to St. Augustine's.

Henry agreed to a trial run. He would spend a long weekend at the Home, Friday to Monday, and see how it went. If things worked out, he'd move there for good. If not, he wouldn't.

The morning of Friday, November 17, 1972, Lerner's wife walked Henry the five and a half blocks from his building to St. Augustine's Home for the Aged. It was a cold but clear day, and their breath turned white and wafted skyward. The streets and sidewalks were icy, making it especially difficult for Henry to walk. He held his cane in one hand and her hand in his other one. When the sidewalks became impassable, they walked in the street where the cars had worn the ice away in patches, giving them a path. When they got to St. Augustine's, Henry easily maneuvered the two small steps up to the glass double doors of the Home.

She dropped Henry off in the nuns' care and went home. The days passed. Henry sat in a wheelchair by himself in the lobby each day. Around noon, an attendant wheeled Henry into the dining room and across its black-and-white linoleum floor to a table for lunch. After lunch, the attendant wheeled him back to the lobby, where he sat, still alone, in the wheelchair until dinner. Later each night, another attendant wheeled him to one of the rooms upstairs. All the rooms were identical, and because the building had been constructed nearly ninety years earlier with only minimal upkeep since then, all were dingy and needed painting. Nevertheless, the Home's staff kept everything spick-and-span. Most of the rooms had religious iconography of one type or another—crucifixes, statues and prints of Mary or of Mary and Child, pictures of the venerable St. Augustine and of St. Elizabeth Ann Seton, the order's founder—in the rooms and hallways.

The following Monday, the ice wasn't quite as bad as it had been the Friday before, and Lerner's wife walked back to the Home to pick up Henry. When he appeared, it was obvious to her that he'd had a bath and that the nuns had given him a completely new wardrobe.

Henry on the front steps of 851 West Webster a few years before his death.

(Photo by David Berglund)

During the next week, Henry argued with himself over the pros and cons of going into the nursing home in much the same way that he'd argued with himself about running away from the Asylum when he was seventeen. He came a conclusion, and a week after his trial run, Lerner's wife walked him to St. Augustine's once more, this time for good. She helped Henry carry the few clothes and the towels and washcloths he wanted to bring with him. Henry was admitted as a resident of St. Augustine's Home for the Aged on Friday, November 24, exactly sixty-nine years to the day after Tim Rooney had picked Henry up at the Mission of Our Lady of Mercy and taken him to the Illinois Asylum for Feeble-Minded Children.

An Archeological Dig

Lerner's wife left Henry to the care of the nuns and went home as she had a week earlier. Henry had filled out the paperwork to admit him into the Home during the trial run, but as with the priests of St. Vincent's Church, he gave the nun in charge of admissions incorrect information. His name, he told her, was Henry Dargarius, as was his father's. He told her the truth when he said he was born in Illinois—not in Brazil, as he was so fond of telling the tenants at 851 Webster—but he claimed his mother was "Emma," not Rosa. At least, that's what the nun heard. It's possible that Henry's senility caused him to confuse his real mother with his aunt Anna, who was as much of a mother to him as he had ever experienced, and that the nun heard "Emma" when Henry said "Anna." He also claimed he was a janitor for "commercial realty," although he stopped being a janitor when he became employed at Grant Hospital in 1921 and had worked in hospitals almost exclusively, never in real estate.

Henry turned the clothing and linens that he'd brought with him over to the nuns. They embroidered his name or initials onto all of the items.

Dr. Michael Marchi, the Home's physician, examined Henry as a matter of routine. Whether that examination gave the doctor any clues about Henry's physical and mental condition is unknown. He was assigned a room, one as dingy as all the others in the Home, and a wheelchair. A member of the staff wheeled Henry into the lobby, where he would spend each day, sitting alone on one side of the room and staring into space while the other inmates sat together on the other side of the lobby, watching TV.

At the same time, Lerner was beginning to make plans for renovating the top floor of 851 Webster. The neighborhood was now at the beginning of a period of gentrification brought about by the influx of young, urban professionals. When Henry moved into the area sixty-four years earlier, it was full of boardinghouses, like the Anschutzes', that offered single rooms to rent, but now the owners were converting their boardinghouses into three-flat apartment buildings. Stable renters—those who wanted a place to live for years, not weeks—were replacing transient lodgers. With Henry now gone, Lerner planned to take care of the plumbing, which had been a problem for their upstairs tenants for years, to clean out Henry's room, and then to combine it with the Berglunds' to create a larger apartment that they could rent to yuppies for considerably more money than the total that the Berglunds and Henry had paid.

Henry's room had not been painted or even cleaned thoroughly since Lerner purchased the building in 1956, and probably not since Henry first moved there in 1932. It was "filthy," and the "floor was covered with two or three layers of carpet, nailed down" to the floor. Not long after buying the building, Lerner had "offered to paint it or," at least, to "clean the wallpaper" for Henry, but Henry would have none of it: "I don't want anyone to work on my room."

Henry was concerned that, if workers were allowed into his room, one might steal or destroy his manuscripts, art, and source material, as Phelan had done decades earlier. It was better to live in dinginess on mildewed carpets than to lose his life's work, which was extremely valuable to him and irreplaceable. So Henry's room remained "filthy" and, as time progressed, more and more cluttered.

Lerner hadn't just dumped Henry onto the Little Sisters of the Poor and then forgotten all about him but often came to the Home to see him. Lerner recalled, "We used to go downtown by 'El,' and everytime we stopped to say hello to Henry." During one of his visits, he told his former tenant, "'Henry, we'd like to clean up your room, is there anything you'd like us to bring you?' Henry said, 'No, I don't want anything, they're of no use to me anymore. You can throw them away.'"

Initially, Lerner thought Henry was referring to the "junk" that littered the place, but then, after what seemed like an archeological dig, what Henry was really thinking about became crystal clear.

Henry had turned his room into a gallery of his own work and of the art he collected. His paintings and pictures from magazines and other sources covered the walls, the fireplace mantel, and even the doors. It seemed as if every inch was occupied by something. The huge *The Battle of Calverhine*, a panorama of the horrors of war, stretched across the west wall, and his portraits of each of the individual Vivian girl-boys stared from their frames on the east wall around the fireplace at anyone who entered the room. The fireplace mantel held various knickknacks, both religious and secular. Among the many pictures of the Virgin Mary, Henry had placed various photos of children that he'd clipped out of newspapers and often framed. Henry's collection suggested an odd series of Madonna and Child. (He had also included several traditional representations of the Virgin and Jesus.) Because he exhibited images in his room of children in both dangerous and safe-and-sound situations, a strange juxtaposing of evil and good—an almost before-and-after scenario—also crowded his room, reminding him daily that good *is* possible alongside and in response to evil.

Many of the images of children with which Henry decorated his room were girls or boys, their gender obvious. Yet a number were so androgynous that their sex wasn't at all immediately apparent. An example is a framed "portrait" of St. John as a child, his gender so unascertainable that he would be mistaken for a saintly little girl, perhaps even Angeline Vivian, one of the "imitation little girls," if it weren't for the caption below the picture that identifies him.

Henry had draped rosaries on the chandelier that hung from the center of his ceiling over the oval table where he worked. And the door to his "water closet," where he had a sink but no toilet or tub, was decorated with the covers of various Catholic magazines, illustrations from calendars produced by religious publishers, and even a photo of a pope.

Henry also packed his room with "several dozen empty Pepto-Bismol bottles; about 80 pairs of broken eyeglasses mended with tape; 88 pairs of old shoes, most with holes in them and in different sizes," and "a few dozen brand-new handkerchiefs in boxes" that Minnie and Emil Anschutz had given him decades earlier as Christmas presents. There were also stacks and stacks of newspapers and magazines, most bundled up with the twine Henry saved. Henry also saved specific articles out of newspapers. Their titles and subjects are revealing: "Girl Injured, Stepdad Held"; "War Cost This Lad Daddy and Home"; "'He's a Brute,'" which is about a brutal father; and several about kidnapped girls and boys. One, "Girl, 11, Under Porch Five Days," had been published forty years earlier, in 1923.

The items often overwhelmed anyone who entered Henry's room. Mary Dillon once visited him there and later recalled, "It smelled bad in the room. . . . You could hardly go into the room and turn around. He had quite a collection of stuff. In the room it was piled to the ceiling. There was no place to sit unless you sat on the bed. . . . The table was so covered with stuff you couldn't tell where anything was." Along with the "stuff" on his oval table, Henry had placed a single print block—the letter *W*, for "Whillie"—where he could always see it.

When Betsy Fuchs (then Betsy Berglund) gave Henry breakfast during the time he was bedridden, she was in his room daily, and her impression of it remained with her for decades afterward. She described it simply as "dusty" and noted that his bedding was "gray with grime."

David Berglund remembered,

> The feeling you got when you went into the room was that the clutter was overwhelming! It wasn't anything you would expect . . . there was a tremendous amount of stuff. Things were layered. Newspapers and magazines piled in bundles up to the ceiling. If there was one pair of glasses there must have been two hundred. Rubber bands, boxes of rubber bands. Shoes, lots of shoes. But you went into the room and it was organized. There was this path through the room. It led from the door, to the desk, to the bed, and around in back. Everything was just piled and piled and piled. The table was cluttered to a depth of two to three feet, except for a working area. He had all these drawings and pictures across the top.

There were "many telephone directories," "several boxes filled with balls of twine," "children's coloring books," "quite a few large aluminum disks from music boxes; an old Victrola and many one-sided records of music of Tchaikovsky, Chopin, and Rachmanioff; bundles of old *National Geographic* magazines that had turned green" with mold and mildew, and stacks and stacks of newspapers one on top of the other. His room appeared to many as a hoarder's paradise.

Researchers who've delved into the lives of hoarders have come up with a number of important theories about the psychological reasons that cause it, and most of their conclusions apply directly and emphatically to Henry. They "have suggested that hoarding behaviors may develop from experiences of emotional deprivation," an inescapable fact of Henry's early life. His mother's death, his father's lack of interest in and eventual abandonment of him, and his life in three different institutions underscores the huge "emotional deprivation" that characterized Henry's childhood. People with "emotional deprivation" may hoard to fill in the emotional holes that the deprivation created.

The same theorists also assert that "the types of traumas that occurred more frequently in hoarding populations include witnessing a crime, having something taken by threat or force, being handled roughly, physical abuse, sexual abuse, rape, and forced sexual activity," all of which were also part and parcel of Henry's early years. At least from the time he was six and began masturbating until he escaped the Illinois Asylum for Feeble-Minded Children when he was seventeen, he constantly witnessed crimes, was "handled roughly," experienced physical and sexual abuse, and was certainly raped or coerced into sexual activities of various types. By the time he was sent to the Asylum in 1904, he had already been programmed by his experiences to become a hoarder. By the time he escaped from it in 1909, he had experienced so much trauma that he became a hoarder almost immediately at the Workingmen's House, although he would have been limited in how much he could collect because of his small room and the lack of privacy in the dormitory-like building. By the time he moved into 851 Webster, he began hoarding newspapers and magazines, twine, empty Pepto-Bismol bottles, shoes, broken and scratched eyeglasses, and other items. And yet, while Henry can be easily labeled a hoarder, he collected items with specific purposes in mind. The items didn't simply fill the emotional holes of his life. They were things he could put to use in his everyday life or his creative activities.

In fact, despite the clutter, there was little chaos in Henry's room. He cataloged and filed away many of the pictures he'd used as source material and the enlargements he'd made from them. He also carefully labeled his various paints and kept them in order. Henry even tied up his scores of newspapers and magazines into bundles, using the twine

*North wall of Darger's room, water closet (left)
and entrance (right).*

*Close-up of the water closet, which
had a sink but no toilet or tub.*

East wall of Darger's room.

South wall of Darger's room.

West wall of Darger's room.

Henry lived in the upstairs, back room at 851 West Webster Street in Chicago for 42 years, writing some of The Realms and all of Crazy House and The History of My Life there, as well as completing a large percentage of his paintings under its roof.

(Photos by Michael Boruch)

he found on the street and tied end to end to organize them. Most of the items Henry collected were "junk" only to those who didn't know their purpose in Henry's life.

Besides the large, oval table on which he worked, he owned two or three large trunks in which he stored his manuscripts and clothing. He also had two smaller tables, on which he kept his two typewriters, and a bed that "was covered with newspapers, telephone books, and phonograph records." Because the bed was piled high, Henry often slept on a cane-bottom chair. He loved music and owned "an old upright wind-up Edison phonograph" on which he played his phonograph records and "a music box with large metal music disks."

Berglund also found items in the room that give an insight into Henry's creative process. For example, the wandering, difficult-to-follow plots of Henry's books suggest that he simply sat down and wrote spontaneously, without plan. He was, in fact, far more organized than is immediately apparent. A five-page sheaf of papers, which has been given the title "Jennie Ritchie Notations," outlines a part of the plot of *The Realms* at a place that Henry called Jennie Ritchie. Another text that Henry had typed single-spaced in blue ink has the title "Confirmed" and gives information about the war that engulfs the inhabitants of Angelinia. A third manuscript, "[One of the most terrible forest fires on record]," is a three-page plot summary that Henry composed for *The Realms*. In it, Henry identifies General John Manley as the arsonist who started a devastating forest fire as a weapon against the Angelinians. Formatted like a letter with a date—August 18, 1928—at the top, it bears his signature, "By H.J. Darger," followed by his address: the Anschutzes' house. Another short manuscript, referred to as "From a French Guiana to Little Princess Jennie," is material meant to help him compose *Crazy House*. A number of scraps, too, show that he kept notes to guide him through the writing of his lengthy books. On one, he reminds himself of the devastation that Sweetie Pie brings to central Illinois: "a building destroyed in Howe town by Sweetie

Pie all the money in the world or the material made for it cannot never be replaced or paid."

Although Lerner had been in Henry's room numerous times in the sixteen years between the day he bought the building and the day Henry went into the Home, he could now inspect it thoroughly, and without Henry, the reality of the room's condition and the crowd of the items Henry stored in it stared him in the face. To move forward on the renovation of the upstairs of the building, Lerner asked David Berglund to clean out Henry's room, and the first step in the process was to rent a Dumpster that they would use to haul Henry's "junk" away to the dump.

At first, Berglund spent most of his time carrying armfuls of Henry's things to the Dumpster, but almost immediately, he tired of having to make dozens of trips up and down the stairs and began throwing the "junk" out one of Henry's windows into the backyard. In very late November or early December 1972, Berglund found something that he couldn't have imagined even in his wildest dreams. He discovered three bound, homemade albums of Henry's illustrations stacked on top of the large oval table. Each of them measured approximately twelve feet long and two feet high and con-tained as many as forty sheets of Henry's illustrations. To save money, Henry had painted on both sides of the sheets. Then, in one of Henry's trunks, Berglund also came across several of Henry's small collages along with his various novel manuscripts, journals, reference materials, and other writings. Although Berglund had seen Henry painting on at least one occasion, accidentally coming across a huge collection of art left him stunned. He immediately told Lerner of his discovery.

Lerner was as astounded by the find as Berglund had been, and probably even more so. He hadn't had a clue about his tenant's talent. As an artist himself, Lerner was immediately drawn to the paintings. All were beautiful, many horrifying. Each was engaging, yet a number were repelling. Some were full of pain; others were Edenic, with children (and strange, mythological-like creatures) at play among flowers that had grown as tall as buildings. Their color was exquisite, their themes often murderous and always mysterious. He couldn't believe that his tenant, the quiet little man who was cranky most of the time and who had little to do with him or his tenants unless he needed something, could have created the vibrant watercolors. And then there were the writings that, he would discover, were actually novels and what was probably an autobiography and journals and . . . *How did Henry come up with all of this, the paintings, the writings? Why? Why on earth* would *he?* There were many questions lurking among the boxes and stacks of Henry's possessions, but not a single answer that Lerner could find.

THROW IT ALL AWAY/PLEASE KEEP IT

After discovering Henry's paintings and manuscripts, Berglund dropped by St. Augustine's Home to tell Henry that they'd found his work and to ask Henry what he wanted him to do with it. Berglund recalled that Henry responded to the news as if "I had punched him in the stomach, taken the wind out of him, and he said 'It's too late now.' He didn't want to talk about it." Yet Berglund couldn't drop the subject. He had to know what Henry wanted to do with his manuscripts and paintings. When pushed, Henry replied with a no-nonsense "Throw it all away." Shortly afterward, during one of his many visits with Henry, Lerner also asked Henry what he should do with Henry's work. His reply was "It's all yours, please keep it."

Henry's opposite and conflicting reactions to Berglund's and Lerner's questions can be explained by his mental condition. When the men approached him, Henry's senility had all but taken over. Lerner recalled that, when he first visited him, Henry recognized him, but that soon began to change, and he recognized Lerner "less and less" over the weeks that followed. Finally, after a few months,

Lerner would find him "in a big hall, in the corner sitting by himself, head down." Henry seemed "catatonic" to him. It's no wonder that Henry responded with contradicting instructions to Lerner and Berglund.

Michael Boruch was a friend of David Berglund and visited him during the time that Berglund and Betsy were Henry's neighbors. Occasionally, Boruch would pass Henry on the stairs or see him walking to or from the bathroom that he shared with the Berglunds. Boruch recalled that Henry, who was nearly eighty by the time that he became aware of him, made a "shuffling sound" as he walked. Boruch took a number of black-and-white and color photos of Henry's room not long after Berglund cleaned up the place and recalled that, when he was in the room, it had a "dusty, musty smell." He was also present when Lerner moved one of the bound volumes of Henry's paintings off Henry's oval table that, by then, had been pushed to the west wall. Because they were so large and fragile, moving them was very awkward. It ended up taking "two or three people to move them carefully."

Henry lived at St. Augustine's for four and a half months. He sank deeper and deeper into silence as time passed, and during his last visit, Lerner realized that Henry had become little more than a "shell." In fact, Henry's condition had deteriorated so badly that on April 6, Dr. Marchi decided to examine him. Then on April 13, 1973, a Friday, one day after his eighty-first birthday, Henry Joseph Darger died in his bed at 1:50 in the afternoon. A nun, Sister Madeline Parks, who was also a registered nurse, was at Henry's side. His death certificate, which Dr. Marchi filled out and signed, states that Henry died of "arteriosclerotic heart disease" and "senility," which had been so prevalent and controlling during the last decades of his life. Although no one tracked them down, many members of Henry's family were alive when he died. They include Dorothy Backe, Valarie Cloghessy, Elaine A. Balling, Florence Klein, Charleen Sadowski, and Margaret J. Sleeper—all descendents of Henry's cousin Annie, his uncle

Charles's daughter. Dorothy had seven children, Valarie six children, and Charleen five.

The Little Sisters of the Poor looked after their poverty-stricken clients even in death. They sent Henry's body to Barr Funeral Home at 6222 North Broadway on the day that he died, and on April 16, he was buried at All Saints Cemetery in Des Plaines, a suburb northwest of Chicago. The nuns gave him a no-frills pauper's grave (Section 6, Block 13, Grave 19) in the older part of the cemetery called All Saints East. While they donated graves to the indigent who died in their care, they didn't bother to place any sort of marker on them because of the added cost.

Nine days after his death, the priests at St. Vincent's Church added Henry's name—actually, one of his pseudonyms, "Henry Dargarus"—to the "Rest in Peace" column of the parish bulletin to announce his death to the other parishioners, and on Wednesday, May 30, a priest said Mass for the soul of "Henry Dargarus."

For the next few years, Lerner scrutinized the watercolors closely. He also skimmed the manuscripts. As an artist himself, Lerner easily discerned a unique talent at work in the paintings, and the more he examined them, the more he knew that his former tenant had created something distinctive and valuable. Four years after his tenant's death, he helped to oversee the first exhibit of Henry's work at the Hyde Park Art Center in Chicago. The exhibit "was intended to display just the paintings, but at [Lerner's] insistence, the exhibition ended up showing many aspects of Henry's life in order to put everything into context. The exhibition displayed some personal effects from the room, his chair, his typewriter, diaries, the *Realms of the Unreal*, enlargements, comic strips and many other source materials."

Henry's debut exhibit was quickly followed by another show the following year, this time with other artists, at the Museum of Contemporary Art in Chicago. In the 1990s, Henry's work appeared across the country, from Baltimore's American Visionary Art Museum to the Los Angeles County Museum of Art, with stops in between at the Museum of American Folk Art in New York, the High Museum of Art in Atlanta, and the Philadelphia Museum of Art. His first international exhibit was held at the Collection de l'Art Brut in Lausanne, Switzerland, in 1996.

As his art was finding its place in the world, Henry was becoming very well known among aficionados of what is often called "outsider art." Michel Thévoz, curator of the Collection de l'Art Brut, which is devoted to that genre, described it as drawings, paintings, sculpture, and other works produced by people who for various reasons have not been culturally indoctrinated or socially conditioned. They are all kinds of dwellers on the fringes of society. Working outside fine art system (schools, galleries, museums and so on), these people have produced, from the depths of their own personalities and for themselves and no one else, works of outstanding originality in concept, subject and techniques. They are works which owe nothing to tradition or fashion. A number of very important outsider artists, including Adolf Wölfli and Martín Ramírez, have a history of mental illness that necessitated their spending time in institutions. Henry, who spent five years of his adolescence in the Asylum, seamlessly fit the bill as an outsider artist despite the fact that he was not mentally ill. His brand had been created.

In the meantime, as Lerner was exhibiting Darger's paintings, he also began selling some of them for about $1,000 each. A report published by *Artfact* reveals that, between 1989 and 1997, the Lerners sold sixteen of Henry's paintings through auction houses such as Christie's and Sotheby's.

After Lerner's death in 1997, his widow continued to sell Henry's paintings—the prices of some had risen to as much as $100,000 each by now—and began copyrighting all of Henry's paintings and other visual texts in her name. According to a report in the *Chicago Tribune*, in 2000 she also sold "much of his work"—more than sixty paintings of various sizes—to an unidentified "New York museum," probably the American Folk Art Museum, for "$2 million." She included Henry's writings, source materials, library, and many other items in the sale, and these became the core of the American Folk Art Museum's Henry Darger Study Center, a mecca for anyone interested in Henry, his writings, and his paintings. A lengthy article in *Chicago* magazine revealed that Lerner's widow announced "that she would stop selling" Henry's paintings after the last day of 2004, which caused "dealers and investors" to clamor to "buy her Dargers." According to Andrew Edlin, a well-known New York gallery owner who had sold a number of Henry's paintings for her, "in some cases, prices rose as much as 40 percent in the span of a few months."

By the time the twentieth century slipped into the twenty-first, Henry's paintings had gained a great deal of attention internationally, with exhibits being held at the Irish Museum of Modern Art in Dublin, the KW Institute for Contemporary Art in Berlin, the Watari Museum of Contemporary Art in Tokyo, and the Magasin 3 Stockholm Konsthall. Henry's work also became the subject of several scholarly books and numerous reviews, articles, and essays and the inspiration for poet John Ashbery's book-length poem *Girls on the Run*, a play by Mac Wellman, and a dance presentation by the Pat Graney Company. In 2004, Academy Award winner Jessica Yu brought Darger to the general public's attention virtually single-handedly with her beautifully crafted documentary *In the Realms of the Unreal*, and shortly thereafter, Henry was deemed "the most bankable of outsider artists, with his works bringing up to $150,000." By 2009, sales of Henry's small watercolors began "at $25,000" with his "large-scale, important works selling for more than $200,000" each.

In the meantime, Henry was being lionized by the popular culture world, with an all-female rock-and-roll band calling itself the Vivian Girls and singer-songwriter Natalie Merchant recording her song "Henry Darger." Punk-rock icon Patti Smith performed at an American Folk Art Museum benefit billed as a birthday party for the artist, in May 2010. Most recently, Lerner's widow sold or donated—

which is unclear—thirteen of Henry's paintings to the Museum of Modern Art.

Such a wide public awareness of him probably would have shocked Henry, who worked unknown during his entire life—while also pleasing him. The large prices for which the Lerners sold his paintings likely would have left Henry, who never made more that $3,000 or so during any year of his entire life, speechless.

But fame has its costs.

Those who were first to write about Henry in the many reviews and notices of his exhibits responded to his paintings in knee-jerk fashion, beginning with Henry's very first show. C. F. Morrison, its curator, took photos of the exhibit, and through her record, it's apparent that Henry's debut was very balanced in terms of the paintings' chief themes and techniques, from the early collages and tracings of children to those obviously influenced by popular culture to those depicting the evisceration, crucifixion, and strangulation of children. It's just as obvious why his work became the target of suspicion among his earliest reviewers. The paintings that were spring-clipped to the center's walls included some of Henry's most violent images, among them *They are almost murdered themselves though they fight for their lives, Typhoon saves them* and *At Jennie Richee again escape*. Several of the pieces in the exhibit depicted Henry's little girls with penises.

Reviewers zeroed in on the images of the little girls with penises and the torture Henry depicted them enduring: strangulation, crucifixion, vivisection. Because of these images, a number of the exhibit reviewers and art critics immediately labeled Henry a serial killer, a sadist, a pedophile, or some combination of the three. Pulitzer Prize-winning critic Holland Cotter argued that "sexual sadism is unmistakable" in the paintings, while Richard Vine, the managing editor of the influential *Art in America*, mused that Darger "may have been, in sensibility if not in documented fact, a pedophile." In *Time*, Robert Hughes wondered if Henry might not be considered "the Poussin of pedophilia," and artist E. Tage Larsen likened the paintings to "collectable kiddie-porn." Many of those who've written about Henry have quoted from John MacGregor. In his review for the *San Francisco Bay Guardian*, author Stewart Lee Allen claimed that MacGregor declared that "Darger 'possessed the mind of a serial killer'" and speculated that he was also a "child-murderer," and in his piece for the *Village Voice*, Ed Park revealed that MacGregor also identified him as "a serial killer" and a "murderer and pedophile." Even the unidentified author of the online essay "Henry Darger: Desperate and Terrible Questions" said MacGregor described Henry as "posed on the edge of violent and irrational sadistic and murderous activity" and summarized the effect of the paintings as "the ongoing fantasies of a serial killer."

Although he could do nothing about Henry's reputation, Lerner did save Henry's life's work from the garbage heap and bought a marker for Henry's grave. A small group of those who knew Henry gathered at his grave on Tuesday, November 19, 1996, to remember their friend and to witness the stone's installation. Besides Henry's name and birth and death dates, Lerner had it inscribed with "Artist, Protector of Children" as a tribute to his friend. Obviously, he hadn't believed the reviewers for a second.

Lerner also devised one other tribute for Henry. He decided to scrap his plans for renovating the top floor of 851 Webster Avenue and, instead, to preserve the room and its contents— Henry's furniture, his collection of books and music recordings, his two typewriters, his hundreds of bottles and tins of paints, his religious statuary and prints, his clothing, and other personal items—virtually as he had left them. While Henry's paintings found new homes across the globe, his room, where he'd created a majority of them, stood unoccupied and frozen in time for twenty-eight years. Its stillness was interrupted only when visitors interested in Henry stopped by to ask Lerner to show them the room or when John MacGregor was at work on his book there. In 2000, Lerner's widow saw to it that the room and everything preserved in it went to Intuit: The Center for Intuitive and Outsider Art. The room was reconstructed there, outfitted with Henry's possessions, and put on permanent display.

Coincidentally, the day on which Henry's room and personal items left the building—April 13, 2000—was the twenty-seventh anniversary of his death.

NOTES

Epigraph

p. 7   "Every picture seems": MacGregor 22.

Introduction

p. 22   "junk": Biesenbach 19.

Part I: One Boy's Life

CHAPTER 1: THE THROWAWAY BOY

Throwing Henry Away

p. 30   "kept by charity": Illinois Asylum for Feeble-Minded Children, "Application for Admission" 4.

p. 30   "president of the Illinois State": Hoffmann 237.

p. 31   "self abuse": Illinois Asylum for Feeble-Minded Children, "Application for Admission" 1.

p. 31   "Acquired": Illinois Asylum for Feeble-Minded Children, "Application for Admission" 3.

p. 32   "children's nut house": Darger, *The History of My Life* 43.

Vice

p. 32   "a kind and easy": Darger, *The History of My Life* 3.

p. 33   "Fullman": Illinois, Cook County, Vital Statistics, Clerk's Office, Return of a Birth [Birth Certificate], Henry Darger, 6 May 1892.

p. 33   "tailor": Illlinois, Cook County, Vital Statistics, Clerk's Office, Return of a Birth [Birth Certificate], Henry Darger, 6 May 1892.

p. 33   "established to provide": Phelps.

p. 33   "unknown": Illlinois, Cook County, Vital Statistics, Clerk's Office, Return of a Birth [Birth Certificate], Henry Darger, 28 May 1894.

p. 34   "West Madison Street": Civil Service Commission 17.

p. 34   "Halsted street to Hoyne avenue": Civil Service Commission 17.

p. 34   "cheap burlesque shows": Reckless 252.

Tragedies

p. 36   "Nursed by mother": Illinois Asylum for Feeble-Minded Children, "Application for Admission" 4.

p. 36   "typhoid, measles, and mumps": Illinois Asylum for Feeble-Minded Children, "Application for Admission" 3.

p. 36   "whipped": Illinois Asylum for Feeble-Minded Children, "Application for Admission" 3.

p. 36   "childbed fever": Leavitt.

It was also known as puerperal septicemia, puerperal sepsis, and puerperal fever. Childbed fever was "the largest single cause of maternal mortality" from the time it was identified in the 1700s until the 1940s, and the thought of it terrorized all women of childbearing age. (Harmon 633.) Severe fever, intense flu-like symptoms, sharp and unrelenting abdominal pain, foul-smelling vaginal discharge, and abnormal, heavy vaginal bleeding accompanied it. Neither statistics nor symptoms reveal the emotional trauma that most women faced because of the threat of the disease. It ran rampant among those families who, like Henry Sr. and Rosa, couldn't afford hospital care during childbirth.

Twelve years later, Henry's father claimed that Rosa Darger had died from "typhoid fever" (Illinois Asylum for Feeble-Minded Children, "Application for Admission" 1).

p. 37   "I do not remember the day": Darger, *The History of My Life* 1.

p. 37   "I lost my sister": Darger, *The History of My Life* 8.

A Very Dangerous Kid

p. 39   "besides being a tailor": Darger, *The History of My Life* 5.

p. 39   "our meals were not scant": Darger, *The History of My Life* 4.

p. 39   "mostly always got": Darger, *The History of My Life* 7.

p. 39   "bought the food coffee milk": Darger, *The History of My Life* 5–6.

p. 40   "easy going people": Darger, *The History of My Life* 4.

p. 40   "a kitchen with a large stove": Darger, *The History of My Life* 2.

p. 40   "living quarters": Darger, *The History of My Life* 3.

p. 40   "watching it snow": Darger, *The History of My Life* 10.

p. 40   "it rain with great interest": Darger, *The History of My Life* 10.

p. 41   "What he looked like": Darger, *The History of My Life* 30.

Henry's father's parents, who remained in Germany although their sons moved to the United States, were Henry and Annie (née Breslaw).

p. 41   "girls' school": MacGregor 674, note 60.

p. 41   "strict severe, and prime": Darger, *The History of My Life* 6.

p. 41   "on the nose": Darger, *The History of My Life* 120.

p. 41   "in a hospital for a long time": Darger, *The History of My Life* 118–119.

p. 41   "much bigger boy": Darger, *The History of My Life* 120.

p. 42   "a half brick": Darger, *The History of My Life* 120.

p. 42   "in a hospital for a year": Darger, *The History of My Life* 68.

p. 42   "hated baby kids": Darger, *The History of My Life* 7–8.

p. 42   "third floor porch": Darger, *The History of My Life* 19.

p. 42   "was a meany one day": Darger, *The History of My Life* 4.

p. 42   "ashes in the eyes": Darger, *The History of My Life* 8.

p. 42   "a very dangerous kid": Darger, *The History of My Life* 120.

p. 43   "love them": Darger, *The History of My Life* 9A.

p. 43   "more to me": Darger, *The History of My Life* 9A.

p. 43   "would take no scouldings": Darger, *The History of My Life* 6.

p. 43   "cutting up in class": Darger, *The History of My Life* 117.

p. 43   "slashed her on face": Darger, *The History of My Life* 118.

Having a large amount of bottled-up anger was not unique to Henry. Other children who've been abused sexually, who never get the psychological help that they need to cope with their victimization, are full of anger. Joey Almeida was one such little boy. Locked up in a state institution for the mentally ill, Joey suffered many of the same experiences that Henry had. Other inmates and caregivers sexually abused him, the first time when he was eleven when an attendant performed fellatio on him. He suffered sexual abuse for years after that first incident, and he "seethed with anger" for years because of it. When a female caregiver slapped him for a minor infraction of the rules, Joey "impulsively wheeled and hit her back, right across the face"—the same impulsive act as Henry's when he slashed his teacher (D'Antonio 93). Both boys' violent outbursts were responses to the sexual abuse they experienced, and only tangential reactions to their being punished.

Being sexually victimized left them feeling angry because they were helpless to defend themselves. It also left them facing huge amounts of guilt. Boys who've been sexually victimized often blame themselves for their victimization because, being male, they've been socialized into believing they should have been capable of defending themselves, but because they're only children, they can't fend off adult predators. Regardless, they call their own masculinity into question, blaming themselves for allowing the assault to happen and, in fact, internalizing their anger. In Henry's cases, his well of anger deepened more and more as the years passed and the internalization continued.

p. 43   "Once on a late summer": Darger, *The History of My Life* 12–12B.

p. 43   "I was scared of burning buildings": Darger, *The History of My Life* 12.

p. 44   "raged all night": Darger, *The History of My Life* 12A.

p. 44   "put lots of newspaper": Darger, *The History of My Life* 10–11.

p. 44   "boxed": Darger, *The History of My Life* 10.

p. 44   "every 4 of July": Darger, *The History of My Life* 11.

p. 44   "crazy about making bonfires": Darger, *The History of My Life* 11.

p. 44   "both noticed a light": Darger, *The History of My Life* 16.

p. 44   "the shebang including the side": Darger, *The History of My Life* 16.

p. 45   "the few crates": Darger, *The History of My Life* 16.

p. 45   "in an old wooden three story house": Darger, *The History of My Life* 34.

p. 45   "a Salvation Army Sunday School": Darger, *The History of My Life* 35.

p. 46   "very busy every day": Darger, *The History of My Life* 6.

p. 46   "as long as there were any 'punks'": Anderson, "Chronic Drinker" 3.

p. 46   "Give me a clean boy": Anderson, "Chronic Drinker" 4.

p. 46   "hundreds of them": Anderson, "Chronic Drinker" 4.

p. 47   "front side window": Darger, *The History of My Life* 79.

Be Good, or I'll Pack You Off to Dunning!

p. 48   "small boys home": Darger, *The History of My Life* 30.

p. 48   "haven": Shaw, *The Jack-Roller* 93.

p. 49   "West Madison Street and vicinity": Shaw, *The Jack-Roller* 97.

p. 49   "invariably come in contact": Shaw, *The Jack-Roller* 185.

p. 49   "cases of 'jack-rolling'": Shaw, *The Jack-Roller* 38.

p. 49   "As I'd walk along Madison Street": Shaw, *The Jack-Roller* 85–86.

p. 50   "One day my partner": Shaw, *The Jack-Roller* 86.

p. 50   "to do immoral sex acts": Shaw, *The Jack-Roller* 89.

p. 50   "older boys": Shaw, *The Jack-Roller* 25.

p. 51   "Be good, or I'll pack you": Loerzel.

p. 51   "crazy train": Perry.

p. 51   "long knife": Darger, *The History of My Life* 118.

p. 51   "longstick": Darger, *The History of My Life* 32.

p. 52   "cried once when snow": Darger, *The History of My Life* 165.

p. 52   "I was like a little devil": Darger, *The History of My Life* 14.

p. 53   "paint boxes": Darger, *The History of My Life* 7.

p. 53   "I used to go": Darger, *The History of My Life* 36–37.

p. 54   "sad remembrance": Darger, *The History of My Life* 37.

p. 54   "white slave trade": Territo 153, note 2.

p. 54   "young men": Territo 153, note 2.

p. 55   "The usual procedure": Oien 1.

p. 55   "utterly filthy": Oien 4.

p. 55   "skidrow bum": Darger, *The History of My Life* 78.

p. 55   "as vulgar and sensuous": Cressey 14.

p. 55   "taking in a burlesque show": Friedman 48–49.

p. 56   "most of his soliciting": Nels Anderson, "Young Man, Twenty-Two" 3–4.

p. 56   "stretched between the Water Tower": Duis, *Challenging* 151.

p. 56   "general price": Nels Anderson, "Young Man, Twenty-Two" 3.

p. 56   "W.B.P. seems to have contempt": Nels Anderson, "Young Man, Twenty-Two" 2.

p. 56   "picked me up": Vollmer 3.

p. 57   "grownups, and especially": Darger, *The History of My Life* 13.

p. 57   "tempted to run away": Darger, *The History of My Life* 37.

p. 57   "If I knew where to go": Darger, *The History of My Life* 38.

Chapter 2: Mercy

Anna Darger

p. 60   "prostitutes near their homes": Vice Commission of Chicago 237.

p. 60   "Court records show": Vice Commission of Chicago 240.

The Mission of Our Lady of Mercy

p. 64   "street arabs": Baldwin 601.

p. 64   "sleep in one dormitory": "Good News for Boys."

p. 65   "He knows": "Home for Boys Who Work."

p. 65   "in all his advices and corrections": "Home for Boys Who Work."

p. 65   "saved thousands of homeless boys": MacGregor 41.

p. 67   "Our large sleeping room": Darger, *The History of My Life* 22.

Class Clown

p. 68   "excelled in spelling": Darger, *The History of My Life* 19.

p. 68   "almost knew by heart": Darger, *The History of My Life* 19.

p. 68   "three histories that told": Darger, *The History of My Life* 19–20.

p. 69   "was a little too funny": Darger, *The History of My Life* 31.

p. 69   "saucy and hateful looks": Darger, *The History of My Life* 31.

p. 69   "very sharply and angrily": Darger, *The History of My Life* 33.

p. 69   "one of the best behaving boys": Darger, *The History of My Life* 34.

p. 70   "often, in the winter": Darger, *The History of My Life* 40.

p. 70   "wacking": Darger, *The History of My Life* 23.

p. 71   "Fr. Meaney": Darger, *The History of My Life* 26.

p. 71   "prime": Darger, *The History of My Life* 27.

p. 71   "whacked": Darger, *The History of My Life* 38.

p. 71   "climb to the top": Darger, *The History of My Life* 27.

p. 71   "to tell on them once": Darger, *The History of My Life* 27.

p. 71   "of the bigger boys": Darger, *The History of My Life* 27.

p. 71   "let out a big whopper": Darger, *The History of My Life* 24.

p. 71   "oldest one there": Darger, *The History of My Life* 24.

p. 71   "If he is crazy": Darger, *The History of My Life* 24.

p. 71   "It was you": Darger, *The History of My Life* 24.

p. 72   "not know any better": Darger, *The History of My Life* 24.

p. 72   "she wanted to adopt": Darger, *The History of My Life* 27.

p. 72   "good woman": Darger, *The History of My Life* 25.

p. 73   "Once my father brought": Darger, *The History of My Life* 40–41.

Something

p. 73   "There was one boy": Darger, *The History of My Life* 27–28.

p. 74   "He wanted my company": Darger, *The History of My Life* 28.

p. 74   "He wanted my company but": Darger, *The History of My Life* 28.

p. 74   "He wanted my company always": Darger, *The History of My Life* 28.

p. 74   "into a younger or smaller boy's": D'Antonio 108.

p. 75   "the younger boy would receive": D'Antonio 108.

p. 75   "retreated into a fog": D'Antonio 51.

p. 75   "so traumatized that they": D'Antonio 159.

p. 76   "overseer": Darger, *The History of My Life* 37.

p. 76   "did not have the brains": Darger, *The History of My Life* 38.

p. 76   "pretending it was snowing": Darger, *The History of My Life* 38–39.

p. 76   "raining": Darger, *The History of My Life* 11.

p. 77   "her son and Otto Zink": Darger, *The History of My Life* 39.

p. 77   "strange things": Darger, *The History of My Life* 38.

p. 77   "The boys there all": Darger, *The History of My Life* 28.

p. 77   "Crazy": Darger, *The History of My Life* 24.

The Masturbator's Heart

p. 78   "I was taken several times": Darger, *The History of My Life* 41.

p. 78   "Where was it supposed": Darger, *The History of My Life* 41.

p. 80   "The seminal fluid is the most": Melody 7.

The masturbation belt and other devices were widely available to anyone who could afford them. They and various potions that claimed to restore "vigor" were advertised in the classified sections of newspapers throughout the country and could even be ordered from Sears and Roebuck catalogs.

p. 81   "excessive masturbation": Melody 15.

p. 82   "trade": "Glossary of Homosexual Terms" 1.

p. 82   "dirt": "Passengers will please refrain."

p. 83   "weak, pale, and feeble": Melody 12.

p. 83   "A search in any insane asylum": Stall 141.

p. 83   "who had masturbated a lot": Bachus 205.

p. 84   "such an enlargement": Bachus 206.

p. 84   "the masturbator's heart": Hall 445.

p. 84   "masturbatic insanity": Spitzka 57.

p. 84   "in a more or less casual way": Hall 445.

p. 85   "feeble-minded or crazy": Darger, *The History of My Life* 42.

p. 85   "cold windy threatening": Darger, *The History of My Life* 42.

p. 85   "Had I known what was going": Darger, *The History of My Life* 42.

p. 95   "got to like the place and the meals": Darger, *The History of My Life* 56.

p. 96   "bonded cases": Department of Poor Relief 56.

p. 96   "replaced by a watchman": Royal Commission 121.

p. 97   "better suited to the feeble-minded": Board of State Commissioners of Public Charities 88.

p. 97   "arts, manual training, physical culture": Board of State Commissioners of Public Charities 88.

p. 97   "Is the child capable": Illinois Asylum for Feeble-Minded Children, "Application for Admission" 3.

p. 97   "awakened at 5:00 a.m.": Trent 100.

p. 97   "'younger boys and girls'": Trent 100.

p. 97   "breakfast consisted of fried": Trent 101.

p. 98   "soup, in-season vegetables": Trent 101.

p. 98   "plus an occasional sweet": Trent 101.

p. 98   "the meals were good": Darger, *The History of My Life* 56.

p. 98   "wormy prunes": Illinois General Assembly 935.

p. 98   "On typical weekday evenings": Trent 100.

p. 98   "put with a company of boys": Darger, *The History of My Life* 55.

p. 98   "American institutions": Trent 100.

p. 99   "The rural setting": Trent 100.

p. 99   "an outlet for restless boys": Trent 105.

p. 99   "hard work and fresh air": Trent 105.

p. 99   "often newly admitted to the institution": Trent 105.

p. 99   "planted and tended the fields": Trent 106.

p. 99   "institutional authorities": Trent 106.

p. 100   "State Farm": Darger, *The History of My Life* 56.

p. 100   "earliest teens": Darger, *The History of My Life* 56.

p. 100   "in a two storey building": Royal Commission 117.

p. 100   "the bughouse": Darger, *The History of My Life* 61.

p. 100   "the work": Darger, *The History of My Life* 56–57.

p. 100   "at eight in the morning": Darger, *The History of My Life* 56.

p. 100   "Saturday afternoons and Sundays": Darger, *The History of My Life* 57.

p. 100   "splendid": Darger, *The History of My Life* 57.

p. 100   "loved to work in the fields": Darger, *The History of My Life* 59.

p. 100   "that plant is used by": Darger, *The History of My Life* 58.

p. 100   "had to wear protective gloves": Darger,,*The History of My Life* 58.

p. 100   "It is a strange but very beautiful": Darger, *The History of My Life* 58.

p. 100   "It really was a most beautiful plant": Darger, *The History of My Life* 58–59.

Special Friends

p. 102   "a perfect storm": Darger, *The History of My Life* 46.

p. 102   "What if the asylum had a fire?": Darger, *The History of My Life* 50.

p. 103   "marvelous": Darger, *The History of My Life* 53.

p. 103   "I was not ever the talking back kind": Darger, *The History of My Life* 97.

p. 103   "Who ever talked back": Darger, *The History of My Life* 97.

p. 103   "special friends": Darger, *The History of My Life* 50.

p. 103   "was no bully or exactly bossy": Darger, *The History of My Life* 56.

p. 103   "had to obey": Darger, *The History of My Life* 56.

An Uncovering of Horrors

p. 104   "an uncovered radiator": Trent 119.

p. 104   "on his left ear, neck, and face": Trent 119.

p. 104   "the institution's matron": Trent 119.

p. 104   "it is nothing serious": Illinois General Assembly 224.

p. 104   "serious": Illinois General Assembly 932.

p. 104   "very extensive": Illinois General Assembly 932.

p. 105   "on the back part": Illinois General Assembly 932.

p. 105   "The hair was matted": Illinois General Assembly 932.

p. 105   "a seething mass of pus": Illinois General Assembly 932.

p. 105   "destroyed the middle ear": Illinois General Assembly 932.

p. 105   "Anybody that would dress": Illinois General Assembly 932.

p. 105   "a friend": "Inquiry Is Urged for State Asylum."

p. 106   "looked as if she had been": Illinois General Assembly 245.

p. 106   "Her finger was just": Illinois General Assembly 245.

p. 106	"was severely burned": Trent 121.
p. 106	"had been badly scalded": Illinois General Assembly 932.
p. 106	"The child was of such a kind": Illinois General Assembly 933.
p. 106	"it would have been painful": Illinois General Assembly 933.
p. 106	"sexual indiscretion": Trent 121.
p. 107	"With such horror was masturbation": Hamowy 260, note 124.
p. 107	"several years": Ball.
p. 107	"made efforts to overcome": Ball.
p. 107	"before retiring": Ball.
p. 108	"doing very well": Ball.
p. 108	"guilt-ridden": Hamowy 260, note 124.
p. 108	"entered the dorsal surface": Hamowy 260, note 124.
p. 108	"9 o'clock on Saturday morning": Illinois General Assembly 15.
p. 108	"hospital wards": Illinois General Assembly 15.
p. 108	"physician's Memo book": Illinois General Assembly 63.
p. 108	"John Morthland died": Illinois General Assembly 65.
p. 108	"When Harry Hardt's new baker": Trent 101.
p. 109	"some of the injuries": MacGregor 701, note 43.
p. 109	"the house of a thousand troubles": Darger, *Crazy House* 7,387.
p. 109	"one of the brightest children": Illinois General Assembly 15.
p. 109	"put his right hand": Illinois General Assembly 15.
p. 109	"ground to pieces": Illinois General Assembly 237.
p. 109	"it was clearly": Illinois General Assembly 15.
p. 110	"I never dreamed for one minute": Illinois General Assembly 237.
p. 110	"When I got down to St. Clair's": Illinois General Assembly 237.
p. 110	"Walter was one": Illinois General Assembly 237.
p. 110	"he was kicked": Illinois General Assembly 237.
p. 110	"I don't like to have any kind": Illinois General Assembly 237.
p. 110	"two weeks": Illinois General Assembly 240.
p. 110	"Dr. Hardt": Illinois General Assembly 240.
p. 111	"I thought it wouldn't": Illinois General Assembly 241.
p. 111	"all over the side": Illinois General Assembly 241.
p. 111	"Now, how are those boys": Illinois General Assembly 558.

p. 111   "That is done under Dr. Hardt's": Illinois General Assembly 558.

p. 111   "Mr. Miller, I understand, had taken": Illinois General Assembly 558.

p. 111   "Is that laundry work": Illinois General Assembly 558.

p. 111   "No, sir": Illinois General Assembly 558.

p. 111   "Why is it, then, doctor": Illinois General Assembly 558.

p. 111   "I don't know": Illinois General Assembly 558.

p. 111   "Is the child given": Illinois General Assembly 60.

p. 112   "I fear he is": Illinois General Assembly 60.

p. 112   "were permitted to spank": Trent 127.

p. 112   "one of the brighter boys": Illinois General Assembly 246.

p. 112   "face was beaten up": Illinois General Assembly 246.

p. 112   "25 or 26 years old": Illinois General Assembly 246.

p. 112   "*Chairman Hill*: Ever see one": Illinois General Assembly 260.

p. 113   "When you choke anybody": Illinois General Assembly 261.

p. 113   "uncovering of horrors": "Children Suffer in State Asylum" 1.

p. 113   "cruel or brutal conduct": Illinois General Assembly 935.

p. 113   "the record of the injuries": Illinois General Assembly 931.

p. 113   "a want of co-ordination": Illinois General Assembly 931.

p. 113   "the careless and unprofessional treatment": Illinois General Assembly 932.

p. 114   "It is also the opinion of the Committee": Illinois General Assembly 933.

p. 114   "The Committee": Illinois General Assembly 936.

p. 114   "Asylum for Feeble-Minded Children": Illinois General Assembly 936.

p. 114   "Apparently the screams": Illinois General Assembly 933.

A State of Ugliness

p. 114   "once in a while catholic prayer books": Darger, *The History of My Life* 44.

p. 115   "I did not cry or weep": Darger, *The History of My Life* 61–62.

p. 115   "I was even very dangerous": Darger, *The History of My Life* 62.

p. 116   "boys": Trent 106.

p. 116   "night crawlers": D'Antonio 108.

p. 116   "lights were turned off": D'Antonio 108.

p. 117   "Inquiries into the subnormal condition": Vice Commission of Chicago 229.

p. 117   "that farms cowboy": Darger, *The History of My Life* 62–63.

p. 119   "a wagon load of something": Darger, *The History of My Life* 64.

p. 119   "At meal times": Darger, *The History of My Life* 64.

p. 119   "kept the other boy": Darger, *The History of My Life* 65.

p. 119   "the Illinois Central to Decator": Darger, *The History of My Life* 65.

p. 119   "walked from Decator Ill to Chicago": Darger, *The History of My Life* 65.

Fool Enough To Run Away from Heaven

p. 120   "liked the work": Darger, *The History of My Life* 57.

p. 120   "loved": Darger, *The History of My Life* 61.

p. 120   "Yet the asylum was home": Darger, *The History of My Life* 61.

p. 120   "I can't say whether": Darger, *The History of My Life* 74–75.

p. 120   "sort of heaven": Darger: *The History of My Life* 75.

p. 121   "I liked the work": Darger, *The History of My Life* 57.

p. 121   "uneventful but busy": Darger, *The History of My Life* 44.

CHAPTER 4: TWENTY THOUSAND ACTIVE HOMOSEXUALS
Refuge

p. 126   "hardly able to sleep": Darger, *The History of My Life* 65.

p. 126   "refuge": Darger, *The History of My Life* 65.

p. 128   "crazy": Darger, *The History of My Life* 69.

p. 128   "old injury": Darger, *The History of My Life* 67.

p. 129   "back to the Lincoln Asylum": Darger, *The History of My Life* 72.

p. 129   "I was of the kind that only": Darger, *The History of My Life* 6.

p. 130   "dared not take off": Darger, *The History of My Life* 82.

p. 130   "should have been in bed": Darger, *The History of My Life* 82.

p. 130   "from unprotected machinery": U.S. Department of Labor.

p. 130   "sawmill worker": U.S. Department of Labor.

p. 130   "a worker got caught": U.S. Department of Labor.

Thomas M. Phelan

p. 135   "a sort of shaking sickness": Darger, *The History of My Life* 168.

p. 135   "took charge": Darger, *The History of My Life* 168.

p. 135   "old man": Darger, *The History of My Life* 167.

p. 135   "the adventures of seven sisters": Kevin Miller.

p. 136   "story books": Darger, *The History of My Life* 7.

p. 136   "Trash": Darger, *Journal* 1:24.

p. 137   "slanders": Darger, *Journal* 1:25.

Whillie

p. 137   "Whillie": Darger, *The History of My Life* 109.

Interestingly, Henry called Schloeder "Whillie" with an *h* only in his autobiography. In the one letter he wrote to Whillie that still survives, Henry addressed him as "Bill." This suggests that "Whillie" was one of Henry's creations, a persona he devised for Bill that was meant to perform a role in the autobiography that, like his first novel, he dreamed of publishing one day.

p. 138   "went seeing Whillie": Darger, *The History of My Life* 123.

p. 138   "well to do": Darger, *The History of My Life* 124.

p. 138   "very charitable": Darger, *The History of My Life* 124.

p. 140   "did all he could to help": Darger, *The History of My Life* 124.

p. 140   "bad mysterious pains": Darger, *The History of My Life* 124.

p. 140   "every evening and Sunday": Darger, *The History of My Life* 122.

p. 141   "often went to Riverview Park": Darger *The History of My Life* 122.

p. 141   "any north side 'L'": Building Good Will.

p. 142   "roller skating and": Duis, *Challenging* 216.

p. 142   "twenty thousand active homosexuals": Sprague, "On the Gay Side" 11.

p. 142   "O meet me at Riverview Park": Newberry Library, "1920s: Correspondence, etc."

p. 143   "immoral and lewd exhibition": "2 Park Arrests."

p. 144   "There was a priest out here": Newberry Library, "Rides and Concessions. Casino Arcade—Correspondence, etc."

p. 144   "the most popular of photo gallery": Haugh 36.

For an interesting exploration of photographs of gay couples, see Russell

Bush's *Affectionate Men: A Photographic History of Male Couples (1850s to 1950s)*, New York: St. Martin's Griffin, 1998.

p. 144   "new motor cars": Haugh 36.

p. 148   "I determined to go to California": "Charles, Aged Twenty-Three" 8.

p. 148   "I was going to California": "David—Age Twenty-One" 9.

p. 148   "female impersonators entertained": Boyd 27.

Part II: One Man's Art
CHAPTER 5: I CAN'T BE AT ALL LEFT OUT
Yours Truly the Author

p. 153   "yours truly the author": Darger, *Journal* 16.

p. 153   "in encyclopedic detail": Bonesteel 19.

p. 154   "This description of the great war": Darger, *The Realms* 1:1.

In actuality, Angelinia and Glandelinia are the two largest countries engaged in the war. Angelinian forces include soldiers from other Roman Catholic, and therefore good, nations.

It's obvious that Darger derived the name of the evil soldiers, "Glandelinian," from the word "gland," as he developed "Angelinian" from "angel," but the question of why demands an answer.

Beginning in the early 1900s and culminating in the late 1920s and early '30s, doctors explained cases of rape and other sexual assault to "endocrine malfunction" in the accused, and in fact, the phrase "over-active glands" was often used to explain rape. Medical authorities explained rape as a state of hypersexuality in a man who was, therefore, unable to control his lust and was forced to commit rapes in order to curb his medical condition. These individuals were also called "sex fiends." Although the community would ultimately and officially abandon this earlier theory of why men rape, popular imagination held to it long into the 1960s. Darger adopted the "gland" theory to his Glandelinians, whose chief characteristic is assaulting—often, but not always, sexually—the Angelinian children, both female and male, whom they capture.

p. 154   "for forty years": Darger, *The Realms* 1:2.

p. 154   "had lain bound": Bonesteel 19.

p. 154   "tortured by flogging, suspensions": Darger, *The Realms* 5:481.

p. 154   "for wicked purposes": Darger, *The Realms* 5:481.

p. 154   "girls": Darger, *The Realms* 5:481.

p. 155   "the Glandelinians decided": MacGregor 563.

p. 156   "the bitter end": Darger, *Journal* 1:25.

p. 156   "monstrously evil": MacGregor 58.

Phelan was seventy-four when he died at 11:25 a.m. on August 21, 1919. An Irish immigrant, he died of myocarditis arteriosclerosis in this room at St. Joseph's Hospital. He was buried at Calvary Catholic Cemetery two days later.

p. 156   "General Phelan": MacGregor 62.

p. 156   "The brute seized": MacGregor 504.

p. 156   "was to play": MacGregor 43.

p. 156   "enemy of God": MacGregor 227.

p. 156   "If I had known at the time": Darger, *The History of My Life* 43.

p. 157   "I met just such a specimen": Wood 1082–1083.

The passage also appears in the same piece published in *Monthly Magazine* 52 (Oct. 1880): 309. It's impossible to know in which of Woods's publications Henry initially discovered the passage.

p. 158   "I met just such a specimen": Darger, *The Realms* 1:169.

p. 159   "Children to the Blengiglomenean serpents": Darger, *The Realms* 1:43.

p. 160   "adds the remarkable 'detail'": Moon 114.

Moon includes excellent analyses of Darger's reliance on various popular culture sources for his paintings and states, "Those recurrent scenes in Darger's work in which girl warriors are captured, stripped of their clothing, beaten, maimed, and executed by Glandelinian soldiers" . . . "may . . . disturb us, but they look less anomalous, and considerably less like evidence of extreme personal pathology, when we discover that similar scenes were not at all uncommon in a wide range of male-authored" popular and often pulp "fiction of the 1920s and 1930s" (116).

p. 160   "tormentors turn": Moon 114.

p. 160   "Where forests lately stood": Darger, *The Realms* 6:393–394.

p. 160   "The enemy are even setting whole woods": Darger, *The Realms* 9:757.

p. 161   "There was also a strange": ": Darger, *The Realms* 9:757.

p. 161   "contains newspaper photographs": MacGregor 120.

I'm an Artist, Been One for Years

p. 161 "I'm an artist": Darger, *The History of My Life* 163.

p. 165 "Penrod after some considerable": Darger, *The Realms* 3:129–130.

p. 165 "beautiful, queenly, subtle": Darger, *The Realms* 3:129–130.

p. 166 "is surely a great gift": MacGregor 684, note 53.

Mary Pickford and the Psychic Hermaphrodites

p. 166 "There's I Violet, Joy, Jennie": Darger, *Crazy House* 26.

p. 167 "exciting eagerness": Darger, *The Realms* 2:[1].

p. 167 "Do you believe it, unlike most children": Darger, *The History of My Life* 14.

p. 167 "peeking out from the inside": Bonesteel 30.

Darger was also a fan of Charlie Chaplin and Ben Turpin, alluding to both in *The Realms*.

p. 168 "portrayed girls who were strong-minded": Studlar 209.

p. 168 "appealed to and through a kind": Studlar 209.

p. 168 "male fantasies were easily attached": Studlar 211.

p. 169 "'anima muliebris in corpore'": Silverman 340.

I've used the phrase "psychic hermaphrodites" to refer to those whom Brill claimed exhibited "psychic hermaphroditism" (Brill 336).

p. 169 "In the following chapters": Hartland.

p. 169 "the fact that I was a boy": Werther, *Autobiography* 41.

p. 170 "God has created": Werther, *Autobiography* 156.

p. 170 "imitation little girls": Darger, *The Realms* 13:3,094.

Imitation Little Girls

p. 171 "While she was sitting here": Darger, *The Realms* 8:386.

p. 172 "general Jack Evans himself": MacGregor 42.

p. 173 "cold snowy": Darger, *The History of My Life* 72.

p. 173 "I am the full writer": Darger, "Copied Catechism" 274.

In the early 1920s, Darger sought publication with two New York song publishers, the Simplex Company and Lennox Company Music Publishers. He'd written several songs that he included in *The Realms*, and it's likely that these were what he'd hoped to have published. Unfortunately, neither company was interested in Darger's songs.

p. 174 "My dear Henry": MacGregor 506. I've used MacGregor's text but have clarified it.

p. 174 "My dear Aronburg": Rose 1.

p. 174 "*16. At what age*": Illinois Asylum for Feeble-Minded Children, "Application for Admission" 1, 2, and 3.

p. 175 "given the limited recognition": Stephen 360–361.

Elsie Paroubek

p. 179 "I know I can find my sister": "Where Is Elsie Paroubek?"

p. 179 "Some people are afraid": "Where Is Elsie Paroubek?"

p. 179 "I want to ask the children": "213,000 Children Asked to Help Hunt Elsie Paroubek."

p. 180 "detectives, police, sheriffs": "Child Once Stolen Aid in Search."

   Lillian was wrong about this. A number of photographs and drawings of Elsie appeared in the *Chicago American* and, at the end of the search for her, in the *Chicago Daily News*.

p. 180 "baffled at every point": "Child Once Stolen Aid in Search."

p. 180 "I am ready": "Child Once Stolen Aid in Search."

p. 180 "Unless Elsie Paroubek is rescued": "Wulff Girl Leads Lost Child Hunt."

   The doctors who undertook the second of Elsie's two autopsies reported that she was killed at the end of her second week of captivity, at about the same time that Lillian was making this statement.

p. 181 "I am afraid, oh, so": "Wulff Girl Leads Lost Child Hunt."

p. 181 "death was due to drowning": "Kidnapped Girl Found in Canal."

p. 182 "attacked": "Funeral of Slain Girl Is Stopped."

The Gemini

p. 183 "Vynne Marshall, Aldrich Bond": MacGregor 678, note 249.

p. 183 "mimic chapel": Darger, *Journal* March 1, 1911.

p. 183 "mimic altar": Darger, *Journal* March 1, 1911.

p. 184 "most dangerous persons": MacGregor 239.

p. 184 "the Supreme Person with Solemn": Darger, *The Realms* 13:3,048–3,049.

p. 185 "For eight years from the last day": Darger [as Newsome] 1.

p. 186   "Assistant Supreme Person": Darger, *The Realms* 7:551–552.

p. 186   "1909": Darger [as Newsome] 1.

p. 187   "'His friend's name is William Schloder'": MacGregor 62.

p. 187   "We're on Our Way": Coultry, "We're on Our Way."

p. 187   "One of the members of the Gemini": MacGregor 242.

p. 188   "Take a squad of men out": MacGregor 238.

p. 188   "A young man of sturdy built": MacGregor 96.

p. 189   "tear their bodies open": MacGregor 238.

"What Is Rape?" Asked Penrod

p. 189   "that Darger and his old picture": Bonesteel 201.

p. 189   "How, then, is it that the loss": Bonesteel 204.

p. 189   "That is a mystery": Bonesteel 204.

p. 189   "the Aronburg Mystery": Bonesteel 204.

p. 189   "the Great Aronburg Mystery": Bonesteel 195.

p. 189   "pictures of children": Darger, *Journal* March 11, 1911.

p. 189   "leader of the main army of child rebels": MacGregor 505.

p. 190   "army of 10,000 rebels": Darger, Planning Journal 274.

p. 190   "When the Child Labor Revolution": Bonesteel 201.

p. 190   "elected a leader by the child": Bonesteel 201.

p. 191   "'What is rape?' asked Penrod": Bonesteel 34, note 19.

p. 191   "shrine": Darger, *Journal* 1:1 March 1911

Self-Portrait with Whillie

p. 195   "those who knew": MacGregor 251–250.

p. 195   "bughouse": Moon 94.

CHAPTER 6: EVEN A BETTER BOY
There's No Calling on the Lord—He Never Hears

p. 198   "one of the most worthy ones": Darger, "Found on Sidewalk."

p. 199   "his small pay he never can": Darger, "Found on Sidewalk."

p. 199   "if it is through the cause that": Darger, "Found on Sidewalk."

p. 199   "There's no calling on the Lord": MacGregor 627.

Sister Rose

p. 200 "Godless": Darger, *The History of My Life* 73.

p. 200 "the Our Father": Darger, *The History of My Life* 73.

p. 200 "otherwise no sign of religion": Darger, *The History of My Life* 74.

p. 200 "The way it was there": Darger, *The History of My Life* 74.

p. 200 "Catholic Lodge": Rose 2.

p. 200 "I was very much interested": Rose 2.

p. 200 "No": Rose 2.

p. 201 "I am glad that you are trying": Rose 1.

The Doughboy

p. 201 "short": "Registration Card" June 2, 1917.

p. 202 "mentality not normal": "Registration Card" June 2, 1917.

p. 203 "my arm or where I got": Darger, *The History of My Life* 172.

p. 203 "buy all sorts of refreshments": Darger, *The History of My Life* 172.

p. 203 "real bad eye trouble": Darger, *The History of My Life* 158A.

p. 203 "dark complexion": U.S. Army.

p. 203 "had to leave behind": Darger, *The History of My Life* 172.

p. 203 "I was forced": Darger, *The History of My Life* 170.

Leaving St. Joseph's Hospital

p. 204 "Sister DePaul had a bulldog": Darger, *The History of My Life* 86.

p. 204 "let me do it": Darger, *The History of My Life* 85.

p. 205 "hated her": Darger, *The History of My Life* 84.

p. 205 "could not at all stand it": Darger, *The History of My Life* 87.

The Anschutzes' Boardinghouse

p. 205 "all his belongings": Darger, *The History of My Life* 101.

p. 205 "in growing goiter": Darger, *The History of My Life* 101.

p. 206 "at New Years": Darger, *The History of My Life* 103.

p. 206 "complaint to the Health": Darger, *The History of My Life* 174.

From the Frying Pan

p. 207   "sent the orderly": Darger, *The History of My Life* 87.

p. 207   "fear of Sister DePaul": Darger, *The History of My Life* 87.

p. 207   "leaped from the frying pan": Darger, *The History of My Life* 88.

p. 207   "main dining room": Darger, *The History of My Life* 90.

p. 207   "winter or summer": Darger, *The History of My Life* 91.

p. 207   "At Two Thirty it came": Darger, *The History of My Life* 91–92.

p. 208   "sorry for the debauchery": Darger, *The History of My Life* 93.

p. 208   "made fun of her": Darger, *The History of My Life* 94.

p. 208   "told him to shut his 'blanky blank'": Darger, *The History of My Life* 94.

p. 208   "minded his own business after that": Darger, *The History of My Life* 94.

An Evening with Whillie

p. 208   "glow": Darger, *The History of My Life* 108.

p. 208   "on Halloween night the students": Darger, *The History of My Life* 107.

p. 208   "all neighboring fire departments": Darger, *The History of My Life* 107.

p. 208   "the wood was not to make smoke": Darger, *The History of My Life* 108.

To Whom It May Concern

p. 210   "Henry Darger was employed": Wilson.

p. 210   "To Whom It May Concern": Darger [as William Schloeder].

p. 210   "insultingly told": Darger, *The History of My Life* 95.

p. 211   "and never got any time off": Darger, *The History of My Life* 103.

p. 211   "another prime and severe": Darger, *The History of My Life* 96.

p. 212   "as there was then an awlfully": Darger, *The History of My Life* 98.

p. 212   "had to stay": Darger, *The History of My Life* 98.

p. 212   "a loner": McDonough.

p. 212   "kids in the playground": McDonough.

p. 212   "waved to them": McDonough.

p. 212   "made fun of him": McDonough.

Chapter 7: Angry at God

We Have a Lot of Love for You

p. 216   "Dear Friend Henry": Anschutz, Postcard.

p. 217   "We wish you a Merry Christmas": Anschutz, Photograph.

p. 217   "My Dear Friend!": Anschutz, Letter.

p. 217   "healthy and the Wetter": Anschutz, Postcard n.d.

p. 217   "we have a lot of love": Anschutz, Postcard n.d.

Investments

p. 218   "huff": Darger, *The History of My Life* 95.

p. 218   "Graham's Bank went to smash": Darger, *Journal* August 1917.

p. 219   "large sums of money": "A Chicago Bank Closed."

p. 219   "involuntary petition in bankruptcy": "Business Records."

p. 220   "20 year endowment": Monumental Life.

p. 220   "Are you now in sound health?": Monumental Life.

p. 220   "all diseases ... which": Monumental Life.

p. 220   "Does any physical or mental defect": Monumental Life.

Queer Things Happen in This Hellish Nut House

p. 221   "I found out that last night Angeline": Darger, *Crazy House* 833.

p. 222   "that the shows being offered": Cressey 14.

p. 222   "famous for nude girlie": Rodkin.

These weren't the only establishments to offer such fare: "On December 27, 1934, acting on orders from Mayor Ed Kelly, police closed the Star and Garter (815 West Madison St.), an old burlesque house famous for nude girlie shows and prostitution. That same day, they also shut down two women's cross-dressing clubs: the Rosal (1251 N. Clark St.) and the 1230 (1230 N. Clybourn Ave.)" (Rodkin).

p. 222   "When I first worked": "Degeneracy" 1.

p. 223   "To be torn away": Darger, *Crazy House* 1,624.

p. 223   "the result was so terrible": Darger, *Crazy House* 1,876.

p. 224   "story": Carey.

p. 225 "I hope that my explanation": Carey.

p. 225 "nut house": Darger, *Crazy House* 7,373.

p. 225 "madhouse": Darger, *Crazy House* 7,537.

p. 225 "crazy house": Darger, *Crazy House* 7,368.

p. 225 "the house of a thousand troubles": Darger, *Crazy House* 7,387.

p. 225 "topsy-turvy": Darger, *Crazy House* 7,109.

p. 226 "crazy phenomenon": Darger, *Crazy House* 7,411.

p. 226 "pervert phenomenon's": Darger, *Crazy House* 7,158.

p. 226 "fire phenomenon": Darger, *Crazy House* 6,869.

p. 226 "phenomenons of strangulation": Darger, *Crazy House* 7,324.

p. 226 "organ crash phenomenon": Darger, *Crazy House* 8,044.

p. 226 "immodest phenomenon": Darger, *Crazy House* 6,390.

p. 226 "upside down phenomenon": Darger, *Crazy House* 6,389–6,390.

p. 226 "A little nine year old girl": Darger, *Crazy House* 5,433.

p. 227 "paused": Darger, *Crazy House* 8,635.

p. 227 "famous Gemini Society leader": Darger, *Crazy House* 10,491.

There Are Lots of Queer People in This City

p. 227 "'Say Bill, look'": Darger, *Crazy House* 8,312-8,313.

p. 228 "met a fellow": "Three Children" 6.

p. 228 "Teachers infirmary": Darger, *Crazy House* 1,237.

p. 228 "is a long low": Darger, *Crazy House* 1,237.

p. 228 "exquisitely fitted up": Darger, *Crazy House* 1,238.

p. 228 "impose on you": Darger, *Crazy House* 1,240.

p. 228 "Don't let him impose upon you": Darger, *Crazy House* 1241.

p. 229 "Mr Handel was a tall willowy": Darger, *Crazy House* 1241.

p. 229 "bosom-friend": Darger, *Crazy House* 7,757.

p. 229 "there was a lot of dirty things": Darger, *Crazy House* 8,941.

p. 229 "There is another young priest": Darger, *Crazy House* 8,005.

p. 229 "I'm deathly afraid of it": Darger, *Crazy House* 8,353.

p. 229 "Penrod himself be it remembered": Darger, *Crazy House* 1,063.

p. 230 "love each other well": Darger, *Crazy House* 8,734.

p. 230 "He probably was over thirty": Darger, *Crazy House* 8,515.

p. 230   "began to feel himself seized": Darger, *Crazy House* 8,517–8,518.

p. 230   "Calverian boy scout": Bonesteel 109.

p. 231   "'Do you want to join'": Bonesteel 109.

p. 231   "his first homosexual relations": "Case of Herman."

p. 231   "an elderly man": "Case of Mr. R."

p. 231   "I used to have an affair": "Harold, Age Twenty One" 5.

p. 232   "a pious dashing young Irishman": Darger, *Crazy House* 7,418–7,419.

p. 232   "'What are you doing here?'": Darger, *Crazy House* 7,431–7,432.

p. 232   "Penrod stepped out": Darger, *Crazy House* 7,432.

p. 233   "serenely": Darger, *Crazy House* 7,446.

p. 233   "walked down the second": Darger, *Crazy House* 7,446.

p. 233   "Jerry glared at Michael": Darger, *Crazy House* 7,446.

p. 233   "the prettiest": Darger, *Crazy House* 6,373.

p. 233   "In disguise make me": Darger. *Crazy House* 6,373.

p. 233   "dressed in boys clothes": Darger, *Crazy House* 2,586.

p. 233   "the little Vivians and their brother": Darger, *Crazy House* 6,463.

p. 234   "gardenia boys": Chauncey 415, note 47.

p. 234   "There are lots of queer people": Darger, *Crazy House* 1,817.

Webber's Secret

p. 234   "I've been going through": Darger, *Crazy House* 1,617.

p. 234   "loved": Darger, *Crazy House* 2,380A.

p. 234   "Why didn't our dear answer": Darger, *Crazy House* 2,184A–2,185.

p. 235   "uncle . . . was once a mayor": Darger, *Crazy House* 1,220.

p. 235   "threw cool ashes": Darger, *Crazy House* 645.

p. 235   "a thoroughly bad boy": Darger, *Crazy House* 1,042.

p. 235   "One cause mainly of the boy": Darger, *Crazy House* 1,116.

p. 236   "Maybe this idea": "Case of James" 1.

p. 236   "From as far back": "Charles, Age Twenty-Three" 4–5.

p. 237   "Boys would tease me": "Lester, Negro" 3.

p. 237   "had many advantages": Darger, *Crazy House* 1,117.

p. 237   "The reader may think this": Darger, *Crazy House* 1,117.

Devil's Island

p. 238   "In the womanless world": Niles 53, footnote.

p. 239   "whenever you see a young convict": Niles 53.

p. 239   "There are only three sorts of men": Niles 133.

p. 239   "Here's a boy who isn't": Niles 54.

p. 239   "While you": Niles 133.

p. 239   "He'd drink or gamble": Niles 167.

p. 239   "laughed at the notion": Niles 164.

p. 239   "good-looking fellow": Niles 330.

p. 240   "awful fever horrors": Darger, *Crazy House* 22.

p. 240   "had a book on French Guiana": Darger, *Crazy House* 72.

p. 240   "she told him that everything": Darger, *Crazy House* 72.

CHAPTER 8: I LOST ALL I HAD
The Old Man's Draft

p. 241   "old man's draft registration": "Find Your Folks."

p. 242   "sallow": "Registration Card" April 27, 1943.

p. 242   "hazel": "Registration Card" April 27, 1943.

p. 243   "Henry Jose Dargarius": "Registration Card" April 27, 1943.

p. 243   "eye ointment": Pharmacy.

Whillie in Suburbia

p. 244   "Lizzie died so mysteriously": Darger, *The History of My Life* 125.

p. 244   "always contesting and fighting": Darger, *The History of My Life* 123.

p. 245   "the slums": Darger, Letter to William Schloeder 2.

p. 246   "I shook my fist twards": Darger, *The History of My Life* 155.

p. 246   "The knee pains at night": Darger, *The History of My Life* 160.

p. 246   "awfully blasphemous words": Darger, *The History of My Life* 155.

p. 246   "I got on me a very mean streak": Darger: *The History of My Life* 139.

p. 247   "I was very interested in summer": Darger, *The History of My Life* 10.

p. 247   "Weather for Monday before": Bonesteel 246.

p. 247   "This is Christmas day": Bonesteel 246.

Leaving the Nuns for Good

p. 248   "any wrong doing": Darger, *The History of My Life* 104.

p. 248   "the work was too much": Darger, *The History of My Life* 104.

p. 249   "easier job": Darger, *The History of My Life* 104.

p. 249   "I know of a country where": Darger, *The History of My Life* 148.

p. 249   "strict": Darger, *The History of My Life* 105.

p. 249   "The Brother stripped the dishes": Darger, *The History of My Life* 194.

p. 250   "slash him with a knife": Darger, *The History of My Life* 121.

p. 250   "row with negro employes": Darger, *The History of My Life* 122.

p. 250   "were easy to get along with": Darger, *The History of My Life* 193.

p. 250   "all right": Darger, *The History of My Life* 151.

p. 250   "good social and fair": Darger, *The History of My Life* 152.

p. 250   "got along fine": Darger, *The History of My Life* 152.

p. 251   "snitched": Darger *The History of My Life* 177.

p. 251   "I never had time to go hanging": Darger, *The History of My Life* 177.

p. 251   "I would have liked to find out": Darger, *The History of My Life* 177.

One Night I Had a Dream That You Were Back Again

p. 252   "I wrote to Whillie often": Darger, *The History of My Life* 125.

p. 254   "An abandoned stone quarry in the 363 acre": Schloeder, Postcard.

p. 254   "Bill & I wish to thank you": Schloeder, Postcard.

p. 254   "All good Wishes": Schloeder, Greeting Card/Easter.

p. 254   "Your cards came today": Schloeder, Postcard.

p. 255   "My dear friend Bill": Darger, Letter to William Schloeder.

p. 255   "Your best friend": Darger, Letter to William Schloeder.

Mr. Leonard

p. 256 "photographer, painter and designer": MacGregor 9.

p. 256 "I remember Henry standing": Lerner, "Henry Darger" 4.

p. 257 "Mr. Leonard": MacGregor 672, note 4.

p. 257 "revealed nothing": Darger, *The History of My Life* 142.

p. 257 "a permanent strain": Darger, *The History of My Life* 150.

p. 257 "do no heavy lifting": Darger, *The History of My Life* 150.

p. 257 "sort of heat sickness": Darger, *The History of My Life* 135.

p. 258 "peeled potatoes and cleaned": Darger, *The History of My Life* 135.

Lost in Empty Space

p. 258 "When in San Antonio three years": Darger, *The History of My Life* 125.

p. 258 "You wrote that you phoned": Darger, Letter to Katherine Schloeder.

p. 259 "As soon as I can": Darger, Letter to Katherine Schloeder.

CHAPTER 9: THE SAINTS AND ALL THE ANGELS WOULD BE ASHAMED OF ME
The Prodigal Returns

p. 261 "joe got along fine": Darger, *The History of My Life* 150.

p. 262 "missed him": Darger, *The History of My Life* 145.

p. 262 "a helper by the first name": Darger, *The History of My Life* 144.

p. 262 "fussy": Darger, *The History of My Life* 144.

p. 262 "he was absolutely peaceful": Darger, *The History of My Life* 145.

p. 262 "hot packs": Darger, *The History of My Life* 105.

p. 263 "At our fireside, sad and lonely": Washburn.

p. 263 "losing his fortune": Darger, *The History of My Life* 140.

p. 263 "went to hell and was tormented": Darger, *The History of My Life* 140.

p. 263 "scared . . . into repentance": Darger, *The History of My Life* 141.

p. 264 "was disturbed": Darger, *The History of My Life* 160.

p. 264 "What did you say?": Darger, *The History of My Life* 158.

p. 264 "I firmly believe": Darger, *The History of My Life* 159–160.

A Lazy Life

p. 265   "my right leg began": Darger, *The History of My Life* 162,

p. 265   "examined my leg": Darger, *The History of My Life* 162.

p. 266   "I'll say it is a lazy life": Darger, *The History of My Life* 162.

p. 267   "delayed two days": Darger, "Painting Log/Diary" 3.

p. 267   "board": Decorator's Paint October 9, 1959.

p. 267   "looked over his shoulder": Bonesteel 13.

p. 268   "drawing on the table": Bonesteel 13.

p. 268   "Henry, you're a good artist": Bonesteel 13.

A Cranky Old Fart

p. 269   "two big shopping bags": Dillon.

p. 269   "No smoking": Darger, "No smoking under no conditions."

p. 270   "Went on three walks to day": Darger, *Journal* April 18, 1968.

p. 270   "Went to after noon mass": Darger, *Journal* April 11, 1968.

p. 270   "More several tantrums": Darger, *Journal* December 22, 1968.

p. 271   "Butterflies": *Playhouse Dolls.*

p. 271   "filthy and homeless": Biesenbach 15.

p. 271   "he wore a World War I": Biesenbach 15.

p. 271   "navy-blue": Bonesteel 11.

p. 271   "a kind of fisherman's cap": Bonesteel 11.

p. 271   "dark green or gray cotton": Bonesteel 11.

p. 271   "ripped the sleeves off": Bonesteel 11

p. 271   "never straight": Biesenbach 15.

p. 271   "heard him talking": Dillon.

p. 272   "We would hear two different voices": MacGregor 78.

p. 272   "He was a wonderful mimic": MacGregor 78.

p. 272   "I would listen": MacGregor 78.

p. 272   "I think he was reliving": MacGregor 78.

p. 272   "A tornado is coming": Biesenbach 13.

p. 272   "he did not want": O'Donnell, *In the Realms.*

p. 272   "if he seen you": Rooney, *In the Realms.*

p. 272   "'Leave me alone'": O'Donnell, *In the Realms.*

p. 272   "greeting with 'Okay'": Bonesteel 13.

p. 272   "Henry seemed funny": O'Donnell, *In the Realms*.

p. 272   "Henry was living above": MacGregor 78.

p. 273   "He mumbled a lot": MacGregor 79.

p. 274   "Yet despite that pain": Darger, *The History of My Life* 162.

p. 274   "people who do suffer": Darger, *The History of My Life* 161.

p. 274   "One time": Bonesteel 13.

p. 274   "with shock": Bonesteel 13.

p. 274   "two weeks after": Bonesteel 13.

p. 274   "Henry refused to bathe": MacGregor 79.

p. 274   "doctor took one look": MacGregor 79.

p. 274   "Henry suffered from": MacGregor 679, note 314.

p. 274   "because of the pain": Darger, *The History of My Life* 155.

p. 274   "I am afraid I was a sort of devil": Darger, *The History of My Life* 158–158A.

p. 275   "green stuff": Darger, *The History of My Life* 155.

A Child in Brazil

p. 275   "art students": MacGregor 78.

p. 276   "Henry didn't really fit in": MacGregor 78.

p. 276   "sort of a community": MacGregor 78.

p. 276   "had the most fun": MacGregor 78.

p. 276   "a lovely happy place": MacGregor 78.

p. 276   "send him up plates of food": MacGregor 78.

p. 276   "A lot of us in the building": MacGregor 78.

p. 276   "I remember when he": MacGregor 78.

p. 276   "used to go up and offer him": MacGregor 78.

p. 277   "My friend David": Darger, Letter to David Berglund "[My Friend David]."

p. 277   "he wore layers": Fuchs.

p. 277   "My God": Fuchs.

p. 277   "not talkative": Fuchs.

p. 277   "When you got close": Fuchs.

p. 277   "He was an unknown": Fuchs.

p. 277   "We didn't know": Fuchs.

p. 278   "For Christmas presents": Darger, Letter to David Berglund "[For My Dear ~~Mrs.~~]."

p. 278   "hot dog sandwiches": MacGregor 679, note 297.

p. 279   "Sure is wonderful of you and Mrs.": Thomas J. Murphy.

p. 279   "I can sing some children's marching songs": MacGregor 83.

p. 279   "it sounded like real Portuguese": MacGregor 83.

p. 279   "I used to think": Bonesteel 13.

Falling Down Angry Temper Spells

p. 280   "Jack Evans, who had heard all": MacGregor 277.

p. 281   "I am a spitting growling": Darger, The *History of My Life* 196.

p. 281   "Did singing instead of tantrum": Darger, *Journal* April 17, 1968.

p. 282   "Threaten ball throwing": Darger, Journal April 6, 1968.

p. 282   "Over cords falling down angry": Darger, *Journal* April 6, 1968.

p. 282   "Threaten to throw ball": Darger, *Journal* March 27, 1968.

p. 282   "Tantrums over difficulty with twin": Darger, *Journal* April 10, 1968.

p. 282   "younger days": Darger, *The History of My Life* 69.

p. 282   "I was all right till twards evening": Darger, *Journal* April 26, 1968.

p. 283   "severe tantrums and bad words": Darger, *Journal* March 2, 1969.

p. 283   "woman's dress": Lannon.

p. 283   "They are absolutely": Lannon.

p. 283   "As for the Scripture": Lannon.

p. 284   "got angry at some things": Darger, *Journal* June 2, 1969.

p. 284   "I am a real enemy of the cross": Darger, *Journal* April 16, 1968.

p. 285   "Priest who I confess to": Darger, *Journal* August 4, 1968.

p. 285   "bad words about God": Darger, *Crazy House* 138.

p. 286   "The altar boy": Waters.

p. 286   "Tantrums a plenty": Darger, *Journal* Novembr 5, 1968.

p. 286   "Tatrums Galore": Darger, *Journal* November 6, 1968.

p. 286   "Sever Tantrums": Darger, *Journal* November 26, 1968.

p. 286 "disrespectful words against Heaven": Darger, *Journal* October 12, 1968.

p. 286 "good boy": Darger, *Journal* July 12, 1968.

Write Life History (Not Mystery)

p. 286 "Write Life History (Not Mystery)": Darger, *Journal* August 1,1968.

p. 287 "In the month of April": Darger, *The History of My Life* 1.

p. 288 "There is one really important thing": Darger, *The History of My Life* 206.

p. 288 "Now I will come": Darger, *The History of My Life* 207.

p. 288 "two companions": Darger, *The History of My Life* 222.

p. 288 "a very wide cloud": Darger, *The History of My Life* 211.

p. 288 "bedlam of sound": Darger, *The History of My Life* 212.

p. 288 "turned bottom upwards": Darger, *The History of My Life* 213..

p. 289 "head of the Relief Committee": Darger, *The History of My Life* 4,958.

p. 290 "In their own town": Darger, *The History of My Life* 2,577.

p. 290 "Mad enough to wish": Darger, *Journal* March 16, 1968.

p. 291 "the great book of Records": Darger, *The History of My Life* 1,679.

p. 291 "the head administrator": Darger, *The History of My Life* 1,708.

p. 291 "five hundred fifty pound book": Darger, *The History of My Life* 1,702.

p. 291 "a little girl childs head": Darger, *The History of My Life* 3,111.

p. 292 "coax God to send . . . rain": Darger, *The History of My Life* 1,826.

p. 292 "talk this over with God": Darger, *The History of My Life* 1,826.

p. 292 "I've been very angry": Darger, *The History of My Life* 1,826.

p. 292 "the Rosary and the Litany": Darger, *The History of My Life* 1,826.

p. 292 "Why were you mad": Darger, *The History of My Life* 1,827.

p. 292 "To me its the same": Darger, *The History of My Life* 1,827.

p. 292 "As of now": Darger, *The History of My Life* 249.

p. 292 "Bravery lacked neither rank": Drinker 273.

p. 292 "Bravery lacked neither rank nor station": Darger, *The History of My Life* 2,589.

p. 293 "Up, up, my lieges": Baum.

p. 293   "Up up my lieges and away": Darger, *The History of My Life* 2,054.

p. 294   "not to be covered": Darger, *The History of My Life* 4,716.

CHAPTER 10: AFTERLIFE

I Want to Die Here

p. 295   "I was raped by a beautiful": Biesenbach 17.

p. 296   "tall man": Darger, *The History of My Life* 163.

p. 297   "Three Masses and Holy Communion": Darger, *Journal* June 24, 1969.

p. 297   "The same as above": Darger, *Journal* June 25, 1969.

p. 297   "The same as above": Darger, *Journal* June 26, 1969.

p. 297   "Not much history": Darger, *Journal* February–December 1971.

p. 298   "I want to live here": MacGregor 84.

p. 298   "made arrangements for Henry": Biesenbach 19.

p. 298   "This year was a very bad": Darger, *Journal* February–December 1971.

p. 299   "If so—": Darger, *Journal* February–December 1971.

p. 299   "What will it be?": Darger, *Journal* January 1, 1972–January 1973.

One Last Institution

p. 299   "Catholic home": Biesenbach 19.

An Archeological Dig

p. 302   "Emma": Darger, Illinois Department of Public Health.

p. 302   "commercial realty": Darger, Illinois Department of Public Health.

p. 303   "filthy": Biesenbach 19.

p. 303   "offered to paint it or": Biesenbach 19.

p. 303   "'I don't want anyone'": Biesenbach 19.

p. 304   "We used to go downtown": MacGregor 680, note 343.

p. 304   "'Henry, we'd like to clean up'": Biesenbach 19.

p. 305   "several dozen empty Pepto-Bismol": Biesenbach 21.

Brooke Davis Anderson, former director and curator of the Contemporary Center of the American Folk Art Museum, once mentioned to me that Darger likely bought bottles of Pepto-Bismol to soothe the abdominal pain that attacked him, an idea shared by others who've studied him.

p. 305   "It smelled bad in the room": MacGregor 78.

p. 306   "dusty": Fuchs.

p. 306   "The feeling you got": MacGregor 79.

p. 306   "many telephone directories": Biesenbach 21.

p. 306   "have suggested that hoarding": Meunier 738.

p. 307   "emotional deprivation": Meunier 738.

p. 307   "the types of traumas that occurred": Meunier 728.

p. 310   "was covered with newspapers": Bonesteel 13.

p. 310   "an old upright wind-up Edison": Bonesteel 13.

p. 310   "By H.J. Darger": Darger, "[One of the most terrible]."

p. 310   "a building destroyed": Darger, "[Note for *Crazy House*]."

Throw It All Away/Please Keep It

p. 312   "I had punched him": MacGregor 19.

p. 312   "Throw it all away": MacGregor 19.

p. 312   "It's all yours": MacGregor 680, note 341.

p. 312   "less and less": MacGregor 680, note 343.

p. 313   "in a big hall, in the corner": MacGregor 680, note 343.

p. 313   "catatonic": MacGregor 84.

p. 313   "shuffling sound": Boruch, Interview.

p. 313   "dusty, musty smell": Boruch, Interview.

p. 314   "two or three people": Boruch, Interview.

p. 314   "shell": MacGregor 84.

p. 314   "Henry Dargarus": "Rest in Peace."

p. 314   "Henry Dargarus": "[Masses]."

p. 314   "was intended to display": Biesenbach 23.

p. 315   "outsider art": "What Is Outsider Art?"

p. 315   "much of his work:" Eskin.

p. 316   "that she would stop": Holst.

p. 316   "in some cases": Holst.

p. 316   "the most bankable": Holst.

p. 316   "at $25,000": Shaw-Williamson

p. 317   "sexual sadism is unmistakable": Cotter.

p. 317   "may have been, in sensibility": Vine.

p. 317   "the Poussin of pedophilia": Steinke.

p. 317   "collectable kiddie-porn": E. Tage Larson.

p. 318   "Darger 'possessed the mind'": Steward Lee Allen.

p. 318   "a serial killer": Park.

p. 318   "posed on the edge": "Henry Darger: Desperate and Terrible Questions."

BIBLIOGRAPHY

BP   Burgess Papers, Special Collections, Regenstein Library, University of Chicago, Chicago, Illinois

CCR   Crane Company Records, Midwest MS Crane, Newberry Library, Chicago, Illinois

DH   Dolores Haugh Riverview Amusement Park Collection, 1904–1975, Newberry Library, Chicago, Illinois

GAS   Gregory A. Sprague Papers, Chicago History Museum, Chicago, Illinois

HDA   Henry Darger Archives, Henry Darger Study Center, American Folk Art Museum, New York, New York

HDM   Henry Darger Materials, Robert A. Roth Study Center, Intuit: The Center for Intuitive and Outsider Art, Chicago, Illinois

L/AFAM Library, American Folk Art Museum, New York, New York

SVCP   St. Vincent's Church Papers, Special Collections and Archives, John T. Richardson Library, DePaul University, Chicago, Illinois

Abbott, Edith. *The Tenements of Chicago 1908–1935*. 1936. Reprint. New York: Arno, 1970.

Abelove, Henry. "Freud, Male Homosexuality, and the Americans." *Dissent* 33 (1986): 59–69.

Adam, Barry D. "Where Did Gay People Come From?" *Christopher Street* 64 (1982): 50–53.

Adams, Myron E. "Children in American Street Trades." *Annals of the American Academy of Political and Social Science* 25 (1905): 23–44.

Adler, Alfred. "The Homosexual Problem." *Alienist and Neurologist* 38 (1917): 268–287.

Adler, Jeffrey S. *First in Violence, Deepest in Dirt: Homicide in Chicago, 1875–1920*. Cambridge, MA: Harvard UP, 2006.

Aetna Bank, Chicago, IL. Savings Account Books. [Henry J. Dargarius]. HDA, Box 49, Folder 49.15.

————. Savings Account Books. [Henry J. Dargarus]. HDA, Box 49, Folder 49.15.

————. Savings Account Books. [Henry Vorger]. HDA, Box 49, Folder 49.15.

"[After falling in the experience]." n.d. BP, Box 98, Folder 11.

Aldrich, Robert, ed. *Gay Life and Culture: A World History*. New York: Universe, 2006.

————. "Homosexuality and the City." *Urban Studies* 41 (Aug. 2004): 1719–1737.

"Alexander Stahl." n.d. MS. BP, Box 98, Folder 5.

Alexian Brothers Hospital Pharmacy. Receipt. 4 Oct. 1965. HDA, Box 49, Folder 49.23.

————. Receipt. 3 Dec. 1965. HDA, Box 49, Folder 49.23.

Allen, Robert C. *Horrible Prettiness: Burlesque and American Culture*. Chapel Hill, NC: U of North Carolina P, 1991.

Allen, Stewart Lee. "The Selling of Henry Darger." *San Francisco Bay Guardian*, 8 Sept. 1998. Web. henrydarger.tripod.com/sfbg.htm. 15 April 2004.

Anderson, Nels. "Chronic Drinker, Stockyards Worker, Seldom Migrates, Many Arrests, Away from Wife Twelve Years: 'Shorty.'" n.d. TS. BP, Box 127, Folder 1.

————. "College Man, Twenty-Seven, Ex-Salesman, Left Wife, Homosexual Experience, Avoids Work." n.d. TS. BP, Box 127, Folder 1.

————. "An Evening Spent on the Benches of Grant Park." n.d. TS. BP, Box 127, Folder 4.

————. *The Hobo: The Sociology of the Homeless Man*. 1923. Reprint. Chicago: U of Chicago P, 1961.

————. "The Juvenile and the Tramp." *Journal of Criminal Law and Criminality* 14 (1923–1924): 290–312.

————. "The Milk and Honey Route (1930)." Web. 28 August 2005.

————. *On Hobos and Homelessness*. Ed. Raffaele Rauty. Chicago: U of Chicago P, 1998.

————. "Young Man, Twenty-Two, Well Dressed, Homosexual Prostitute, Loafs in Grant Park. " n.d. TS. BP, Box 127, Folder 4.

"Another Patient Scalded at Lincoln." *Daily Review* [Decatur, IL], 20 Feb. 1908: 1.

Anschutz, Emil and Minnie. Letter to Henry Darger. 20 Apr. 1938. MS. HDA, Box 48, Folder 48.22.

————. Photograph of Emil and Minnie Anschutz. n.d. HDA, Box 48, Folder 48.23.

————. Postcard to Henry Darger. n.d. HDA, Box 48, Folder 48.23.

————. Postcard to Henry Darger. 10 Sept. 1932. HDA, Box 48, Folder 48.23.

Anthony, Francis. "The Question of Responsibility in Cases of Sexual Perversion." *Boston Medical and Surgical Journal* 139 (1898): 288–291.

"Archbishop Likes the Homely Lad." *Chicago Daily Tribune*, 23 Aug. 1909: 16.

"As Told to Laury by Harold About Max." n.d. MS. BP, Box 128, Folder 7.

"As Told to Me by Harry." n.d. MS. BP, Box 98, Folder 5.

"As Told to Me by Mr. H. Who Now Hustles." n.d. MS. BP, Box 98, Folder 5.

"Asylum for Feeble-Minded Children." *Historical Encyclopedia of Illinois* (1901). Web. genealogytrails.com/ill/institution.htm. 23 Dec. 2009.

"[At the age of six]." n.d. MS. BP, Box 98, Folder 4.

"At the Lake-Front Music Halls." *Chicago Daily Tribune*, 24 Sept. 1893: 28.

"At Thompson's Restaurant Randolph St." n.d. .MS. BP, Box 98, Folder 11.

"'Attractions' Go Into Court Today." *Chicago Daily Tribune*, 14 June 1909: 3.

Auditor's Office, Illinois. *Biennial Report of the Auditor of Public Accounts to the Governor of Illinois: December 31, 1914.* Springfield, IL: 1914.

"Bachelors and Dudes Take Notice." n.d. MS. HDA, Box 47, Folder 47.4.

Bachus, G. "Ueber Herzerkrankungen bei Masturbanten." *Deutches Archiv fur Klinische Medizin* (1895): 201–208.

"Bad Park Show to Go." *Chicago Record-Herald*, 7 July 1909: 10.

Baldwin, Peter C. "'Nocturnal Habits and Dark Wisdom': The American Response to Children in the Streets at Night, 1880–1930." *Journal of Social History* 35.3 (2002): 593–611.

Ball, B. A. "Auto-Surgical Operation." *Boston Medical and Surgical Journal*, 28 Feb. 1844: 82–83.

"Band Programme." Photocopy. DH, Box 1, Folder: "Chicago Riverview Exposition, 1910–11."

Barbosa, L. Letter to Henry Darger. n.d. HDA, Box 48, Folder 48.17.

Barker, William S. "Two Cases of Sexual Contrariety." *St. Louis Courier of Medicine* 28 (1903): 269–271.

Barker-Benfield, G. J. *The Horrors of the Half-Known Life: Male Attitudes Toward Women and Sexuality in Nineteenth-Century America*. New York: Routledge, 2000.

Barlow, Damien. "'Oh, You're Cutting My Bowels Out!': Sexual Unspeakability in Marcus Clarke's *His Natural Life*. *Journal of the Association for the Study of Australian Literature* 6 (2007): 33-48.

Bauer, Joseph L. "The Treatment of Some of the Effects of Sexual Excesses." *Medical and Surgical Journal*, 17 May 1884: 614–616.

Baum, L. Frank, et al. *The Royal Book of Oz*. Web. 15 Dec. 2011.

Beck, Frank O. *Hobohemia*. Rindge, NH: Smith, 1956.

Beirut, Julia. "Senile Dementia Symptoms." Web. 20 Dec. 2011.

Bekken, Jon. "Crumbs from the Publishers' Golden Tables: The Plight of the Chicago Newsboy." *Media History* 6.1 (2000): 45–57.

Benjamin, M. Letter to Henry J. Dargarus. 15 July 1963. HDA, Box 48, Folder 15.

Bentzen, Conrad. "Notes on the Homosexual in Chicago." 14 Mar. 1938. Paper for Sociology 270. Department of Sociology, University of Chicago. TS. BP, Unpublished ms., Box 146, Folder 10.

Benziger Brothers. Receipt. HDA, Box 49, Folder 49.24.

———. Receipt. HDA, Box 73, Folder 73.20.

Berglund, David and Betsy. Birthday Greeting Card to Henry Darger. n.d. HDA, Box 48, Folder 26.

Biesenbach, Klaus. "Henry Darger: A Conversation Between Klaus Biesenbach and Kiyoko Lerner." *Henry Darger: Disasters of War*. Berlin: KW Institute for Contemporary Art, n.d. 11–23.

Bill. Letter to Jimmie. n.d. MS. BP, Box 98, Folder 5.

"Billy." n.d. MS. BP, Box 128, Folder 8.

Bolton, Frank G., Jr.; Larry A. Morris; and Ann E. MacEachron. "Whatever Happened to Baby John? The Aftermath." *Males at Risk: The Other Side of Child Sexual Abuse*. Newbury Park, CA: Sage, 1989: 68–111.

Bonesteel, Michael, ed. *Henry Darger: Art and Selected Writings*. New York: Rizzoli, 2000.

Boruch, Michael. Personal Interview. 5 March 2012.

———. "Project on Henry Dargarus: *The Realms of the Unreal*." TS. Proposal for an independent study. School of the Art Institute. Fall 1973. HDA, Box 48, Folder 47.7.

Boswell, John. *Christianity, Social Tolerance, and Homosexuality*. Chicago: U of Chicago P, 1980: 375–376, note 50.

"Bound in Straight-Jacket in Cellar." *Daily Review* [Decatur, IL], 3 Feb. 1908: 2.

Boyd, Nan Alamilla. "Transgender and Gay Male Cultures from the 1890s Through the 1960s." *Wide-Open Town: A History of Queer San Francisco*. Ed. Nan Alamilla Boyd. Berkeley: U California P, 2003.

"Boys, Girls, Vice, Police, Sloth and Hypocrisy." *Chicago Record-Herald*, 5 Aug. 1909: 8.

"Boys' School Is Not Reformatory." *Juvenile Court Record* 7 (March 1907): 23–24.

Breckinridge, Sophonisba P., and Edith Abbott. *The Delinquent Child and the Home*. 1916. Reprint. New York: Arno and New York Times, 1970.

Brill, A. A. "The Conception of Homosexuality." *Journal of the American Medical Association*, 2 Aug. 1913: 335–340.

Bruce, Earle Wesley. "Comparison of Traits of the Homosexual from Tests and from Life History Materials." Diss. Department of Sociology, University of Chicago, 1942.

Building Good Will. Chicago: Riverview Press, [1936]. DH, Box 1, Folder: "Riverview Press."

Bullough, Vern L. "Challenges to Societal Attitudes Toward Homosexuality in the Late Nineteenth and Early Twentieth Centuries." *Social Science Quarterly* 58 (1977): 29–44.

Bullough, Vern L., and Martha Voght. "Homosexuality and Its Confusion with the 'Secret Sin' in Pre-Freudian America." *Journal of the History of Medicine* 28 (Apr. 1973): 143–155.

Burnham, John. "Early References to Homosexual Communities in American Medical Writings." *Medical Aspects of Human Sexuality* 7 (Aug. 1973): 34, 40–41, 46–49.

Burt, A., Jr. "Onanism and Masturbation." *Medical and Surgical Reporter*, 17 Mar. 1888: 11.

"Business Records." *New York Times*, 30 June 1917: 15.

Camilla, Sister. Letter to Henry Darger. n.d. Henry J. Darger Study Center Archives, Box 48, Folder 36. American Folk Art Museum. New York, NY.

"Canal Yields Up Body of Missing Elsie Paroubek." *Chicago Daily Tribune*, 9 May 1911: 1–2.

Capps, Donald. "From Masturbation to Homosexuality: A Case of Displaced Moral Disapproval." *Pastoral Psychology* 51 (Mar. 2003): 249–272.

Carey, Charles M. Letter to Henry J. Darger. 25 May 1939. TS. HDA, Box 48, Folder 24. American Folk Art Museum. New York, NY.

"Carl's Experience." n.d. MS. BP, Box 98, Folder 2.

Carpenter, Edward. *The Intermediate Sex: A Study of Some Transitional Types of Men and Women.* London: Allen, 1903.

"Case of Herman [One of Herman's early childhood]." n.d. MS. BP, Box 98, Folder 2.

"Case of James." n.d. MS. BP, Box 98, Folder 11.

"Case of Mr. R." n.d. MS. BP, Box 98, Folder 2.

Cauldwell, D. O. "Psychopathia Transexualis." *Sexology* (Dec. 1949): 274–280.

"Charles, Age Twenty-Three." n.d. MS. BP, Box 128, Folder 9.

"Charlie." n.d. MS. BP, Box 98, Folder 2.

Chauncey, George. *Gay New York: Gender, Urban Culture, and the Making of the Gay Male World, 1890–1940.* New York: Basic, 1994.

Chicago, *Civil Service Commission Final Report: Police Investiation, 1911–1912,* Chicago: 1912.

"A Chicago Bank Closed." *New York Times,* 30 June 1917: 19.

Chicago Census Report . . . [and] Complete Directory of the City. Chicago: Edwards, 1871.

Chicago Census Report and Statistical Review. Chicago: Richard Edwards, 1871.

Chicago History Society. "Century of Progress." Web. 1 Nov. 2010.

———. "The Great Chicago Fire and the Web of Memory." Web. 1 Oct. 2011.

"Child Once Stolen Aid in Search." *Chicago American,* 24 Apr. 1911: 1.

"Children Suffer in State Asylum." *Chicago Daily Tribune,* 18 Jan. 1908: 1–2.

Chipley, W. S. "A Warning to Fathers, Teachers, and Young Men, in Relation to a Fruitful Cause of Insanity, and Other Serious Disorders of Youth." *American Journal of Insanity* 17 (Apr. 1861): 69–77.

Chudacoff, Howard P. *The Age of the Bachelor: Creating an American Subculture.* Princeton, NJ: Princeton UP, 1999.

Clopper, Edward N. *Child Labor in City Streets*. New York: Macmillan, 1912.

"Close Parks, Demand." *Chicago Record Herald*, 12 July 1909: 2.

Continental Illinois Bank, Chicago, IL. Savings Account Books. [Henry Darger]. HDA, Box 49, Folder 49.15.

"A Conversation with Edwin Teeter." n.d. TS. BP, Box 187, Folder 6.

Conzen, Michael P. "Progress of the Chicago Fire of 1871." *Electronic Encyclopedia of Chicago*. Web. 1 June 2009.

Cornell, William M. "Cause of Epilepsy." *Medical and Surgical Reporter*, 7 June 1862: 254–255.

Cotter, Holland. "A Life's Work in Word and Image, Secret Until Death." *New York Times*, 24 Jan. 1997. Web. 15 Mar. 2005.

Cotton, Wayne L. "Role-Playing Substitutions Among Homosexuals." *Journal of Sex Research* 8 (1972): 310–323.

Coultry Studio, Riverview Amusement Park, Chicago. Photograph of Henry Darger and William Schloeder "[Off to Frisco]." n.d. HDA, Box 85, Folder 85.15.

———. Photograph of Henry Darger and William Schloeder "[On Our Way to Cuba]". n.d. HDA, Box 85, Folder 85.15.

———. Photograph of Henry Darger and William Schloeder "[We're on Our Way]." n.d. HDA, Box 85, Folder 85.15.

Cressey, Paul G. "Report on Summer's Work with the Juvenile Protective Association of Chicago." 26 Oct. 1925. TS. Local Community Studies. BP, Box 130, Folder 5.

———. *The Taxi-Dance Hall: A Sociological Study in Commercialized Recreation and City Life*. 1932. Reprint. Montclair, NJ: Patterson Smith, 1969.

Crosby, Josiah. "Seminal Weakness—Castration." *Boston Medical and Surgical Journal*, 9 Aug 1843: 10–11.

Crozier, Ivan. "James Kiernan and the Responsible Pervert." *International Journal of Law and Psychiatry* 25 (2002): 331–350.

"Curlies First Experience." n.d. MS. BP, Box 98, Folder 3.

Curon, L. O. *Chicago: Satan's Sanctum*. Chicago: Phillips, 1899.

Dana, Charles L. "On Certain Sexual Neuroses." *Medical and Surgical Reporter*, 15 Aug. 1891: 241–245.

D'Antonio, Michael. *The State Boys Rebellion*. New York: Simon and Schuster, 2004.

Darger, Henry. "Black Brothers Lodge." n.d. MS. HDA, Box 48, Folder 48.1.

362 Henry Darger, Throwaway Boy

———. "Certificate No. 19967." n.d. MS. HDA, Box 48, Folder 48.2.

———. "Certificate No. 27573." n.d. MS. HDA, Box 48, Folder 48.2.

———. "Confirmed." n.d. TS. HDA, Box 49, Folder 49.32.

———. "[Copied Catechism of Christian Doctrine]." [*Reference Ledger*]. n.d. MS. HDA, Box 46, Folder 46.4.

———. "Found on Sidewalk." n.d. MS & TS. HDA, Box 47, Folder 47.5.

———. "[From a French Guiana to Little Princess Jennie]." n.d. MS. HDA, Box 49, Folder 49.30.

———. *Further Adventures in Chicago: Crazy House*. n.d. MS. n.d. Microfilm version. L/AFAM.

———. *The History of My Life*. n.d. MS. Microfilm version. L/AFAM.

———. "[It was the will of the Supreme Person]." n.d. MS. HDA, Box 47, Folder 47.3.

———. "[Jennie Ritchie Notations]." n.d. MS. HDA,

———. *Journal*. June 1911–Dec. 1917. MS. Microfilm version. L/AFAM.

———. *Journal*. 27 Feb. 1965–1 Jan. 1972. MS. Microfilm version. L/AFAM.

———. Letter [as F. J. P. Mery] to Annie Aronburg. 19 June 1911. HDA, Box 48, Folder 48.32.

———. Letter [as Thomas Newsome] to Henry Darger. n.d. HDA, Box 47, Folder 47.3.

———. Letter [as William Schloeder] "To Whom It May Concern." n.d. HDA, Box 48, Folder 48.20.

———. Letter to Katherine Schloeder. 1 June 1959. HDA, Box 48, Folder 48.30.

———. Letter to William Schloeder. n.d. HDA, Box 48, Folder 48.32.

———. "List of Paintings Beginning and End." n.d. MS. HDA, Box 50, Folder 50.2.

———. "No Smoking Under No Conditions" [Signage]. n.d. MS. "The Henry Darger Room" [Installation]. Intuit: The Center for Intuitive and Outsider Art. Chicago, IL.

———. "[Note for *Crazy House*]." n.d. MS. HDA, Box 50, Folder 50.3.

———. Note to David Berglund "[For Christmas presents]." Greeting Card. n.d. MS. HDA, Box 48, Folder 48.27.

———. Note to David Berglund "[My friend David]." Greeting Card. n.d. MS. HDA, Box 48, Folder 48.29.

————. "[One of the most terrible forest fires on record]." 18 Aug. 1928. MS. HDA, Box 50, Folder 50.5.

————. "[Painting Log/Diary]." 1955–65. MS. HDA, Box 50, Folder 50.6.

————. "Society of Black Brothers." n.d. MS. HDA, Box 48, Folder 48.3.

————. *The Story of the Vivian Girls, in What Is Known as the Realms of the Unreal, of the Glandeco-Angelinian War Storm, Caused by the Child Slave Rebellion*. n.d. MS. Microfilm version. L/AFAM.

"Dark Alone & Quiet." n.d. MS. BP, Box 98, Folder 3.

Darves-Bornoz, J. M., et al. "Gender Differences in Symptoms of Adolescents Reporting Sexual Assault." *Social Psychiatry and Psychiatric Epidemiology* 33 (Mar. 1998): 111–117.

"David—Age Twenty-One." n.d. MS. BP, Box 128, Folder 9.

Davies, Marcus. "On Outsider Art and the Margins of the Mainstream." Web. 30 Mar. 2010.

De Armand, J. A. "Sexual Perversion in Its Relation to Domestic Infelicity." *American Journal of Dermatology and Genito-Urinary Diseases* 3 (1899): 24–26.

Dean, Dawson F. "Significant Characteristics of the Homosexual Personality." PhD diss., School of Education, New York University, 1936.

Decorator's Paint and Wallpaper Company. Receipt. 30 Dec. 1957. HDA, Box 49, Folder 49.24.

————. Receipt. 9 Oct. 1959. HDA, Box 49, Folder 49.24.

————. Receipt. 11 Feb. 1962. HDA, Box 49, Folder 49.24.

"Dedicate Working Boys' Home." *Chicago Daily Tribune*, 22 Aug. 1909: 3.

"Degeneracy." n.d. MS. BP, Box 265, Folder 27.

D'Emilio, John. "Gay Politics and Community in San Francisco Since World War II." *Hidden from History: Reclaiming the Gay and Lesbian Past*. Ed. Martin Bauml Duberman, Martha Vincus, and George Chauncey Jr. New York: New American Library, 1989: 456–473.

————. "The Stuff of History: First-Person Accounts of Gay Male Lives." *Journal of the History of Sexuality* 3 (1992): 314–319.

Deneen, Charles S. *Governor's Message to the Forty-Fifth General Assembly Discussing the Report of the Special Committee of the House of Representatives to Investigate State Institutions*. Springfield, IL: 1908.

"Deneen Criticized in Asylum Report." *Daily Review* [Decatur, IL], 6 May 1908: 1.

"Deneen's Defense Scorches Saloons." *Chicago Daily Tribune*, 24 May 1908: 5.

"Describe Orgy of New Year Eve as Blow to City." *Chicago Daily Tribune*, 2 Jan. 1913: 1–2.

Dexter, George T. "Singular Case of Hiccough Caused by Masturbation." *Boston Medical and Surgical Journal*, 9 Apr. 1845: 195–197.

Diamond, Nicola. "Sexual Abuse: The Bodily Aftermath." *Free Associations* 3, Part 1 (1992): 71–83.

DiGirolamo, Vincent. "Crying the News: Children, Street Work, and the American Press, 1830s–1920s." Diss. Department of History, Princeton University, 1997.

———. "Newsboy Funerals: Tales of Sorrow and Solidarity in Urban America." *Journal of Social History* 36 (2002): 5–30.

Dillon, Mary. Interview. *In the Realms of the Unreal: The Mystery of Henry Darger*. Dir. Jessica Yu. 2004. Wellspring. DVD.

———. Interview. *Revolutions of the Night: The Enigma of Henry Darger*. Dir. Mark Stokes. 2011. Quale. DVD.

Ditcher, David. *Dear Friends: American Photographs of Men Together, 1840–1918*. New York: Abrams, 2001.

Doll, E. A. "On the Use of the Term 'Feeble-Minded.'" *Journal of the American Institute of Criminal Law and Criminology* 8 (July 1917): 216–221.

"Dr. H. G. Hardt Makes Statement." *Daily Review* [Decatur, IL], 1 Feb. 1908: 1.

Dreger, Alice Domurat. *Hermaphrodites and the Medical Invention of Sex*. Cambridge: Harvard UP, 1998.

Dressler, David. "Burlesque as a Cultural Phenomenon." PhD diss., School of Education, New York University, 1937.

Driever, Juliana. "In the Realms of the Unreal: The Process, Paintings, and Pertinence of Henry Darger." *Research, Writing, and Culture: The Best Undergraduate Thesis Essays, 2002–2003 [No. 4]*. Chicago: School of the Art Institute of Chicago, 2003: 18–31. Web. 10 Sept. 2010.

Drinker, Frederick E. *Horrors of Tornado, Flood, and Fire*. Harrisburg, PA.: Minter, 1913. Google Books. Web. 23 Oct. 2010.

Drucker, A. P. *On the Trail of the Juvenile-Adult Offender: An Intensive Study of 100 County Jail Cases*. Chicago: Juvenile Protective Association, 1912.

Dublin, Louis I. "Vital Statistics." *American Journal of Public Health* 18 (Oct. 1928): 1300–1303.

Duis, Perry R. *Challenging Chicago: Coping with Everyday Life, 1837–1920*. Chicago: U of Illinois P, 1998.

———. "Whose City? Public and Private Places in Nineteenth-Century Chicago." *Chicago History* 7 (Spring 1983): 4–27.

Dunn, F. Roger. "Formative Years of the Chicago Y.M.C.A.: A Study in Urban History." *Journal of the Illinois State Historical Society* 37 (1944): 329–350.

Durden, Michelle. "Not Just a Leg Show: Gayness and Male Homoeroticism in Burlesque, 1868 to 1877." *Thirdspace*. Web. 15 Nov. 2007.

East, W. Norwood. "The Interpretation of Some Sexual Offences." *Journal of Mental Science* 71 (July 1925): 410–424.

Edwards' Annual Directory to the Inhabitants . . . of Chicago for 1870–71. Chicago: Edwards, 1870.

Edwards' Chicago, Illinois General and Business Directory for 1873. Chicago: Edwards, 1873.

Edwards, Irving. Letter to H. J. Darger. 10 Oct. 1923. HDA, Box 48, Folder 48.25.

Ellenzweig, Allen. "Picturing the Homoerotic." *Queer Representations: Reading Lives, Reading Cultures*. Ed. Martin Duberman. New York: New York UP, 1997: 57–68.

Ellis, Havelock. "Sexual Inversion in Relation to Society and the Law." *Medico-Legal Journal* 14 (1896–97): 279–288.

———. "Sexual Inversion with an Analysis of Thirty-Three New Cases." *Medico-Legal Journal* 13 (1895–96): 255–267.

———. *Studies in the Psychology of Sex. Vol. 2: Sexual Inversion*. Philadelphia: Davis, 1906.

———. "The Study of Sexual Inversion." *Medico-Legal Journal* 12 (1894–95): 148–151.

Ellis, Havelock, and John Addington Symonds. "From Sexual Inversion, 1897." *Nineteenth-Century Writings on Homosexuality*. Ed. Chris White. London: Routledge, 1999: 94–103.

"Elsie Paroubek Lost 4 Weeks; Police to Hunt for Dead Body." *Chicago Daily Tribune*, 7 May 1911: 2.

Engelhardt, H. Tristram, Jr. "The Disease of Masturbation: Values and the Concept of Disease." *Bulletin of the History of Medicine* 48 (1974): 234–248.

"Erogenous Zones." *Chicago Magazine*, July 2009. Web. 2 Apr. 2010.

Eskin, Leah. "Henry Darger Moves Out." *Chicago Tribune*, 17 Dec. 2000. Web. 16 Apr. 2008.

Evans, T. H. "The Problem of Sexual Variants." *St. Louis Medical Review* 8 Sept. 1906: 213–215.

"Even Though I Do Not Suck or Brown, I Am Queer, Temperamental." n.d. MS. BP, Box 98, Folder 4.

"The Eyewitnesses." *The Great Chicago Fire and the Web of Memory*. Web. 3 June 2011.

Fay, J. L. Letter to Henry J. Dargarus. 27 July 1963. HDA, Box 48, Folder 15.

Feray, Jean-Claude, and Manfred Herzer. "Homosexual Studies and Politics in the Nineteenth Century: Karl Maria Kertbeny." *Journal of Homosexuality* 19 (1990): 23–47.

"Fired Asylum Workers Heard." *Chicago Daily Tribune*, 15 Mar. 1908: 6.

"1st Experience." n.d. MS. BP, Box 98, Folder 2.

Fleeson, Lucinda. "The Gay '30s." *Chicago Magazine*. Web. 18 Dec. 2009.

Flint, Austin. "A Case of Sexual Inversion, Probably with Complete Sexual Anaesthesia." *New York Medical Journal* 94 (1911): 1111–1112.

Flood, Everett. "An Appliance to Prevent Masturbation." *Medical Age*, 25 July 1888: 332–333.

———. "Notes on the Castration of Idiot Children." *American Journal of Psychology* 10 (Jan. 1899): 296–301.

Flynt, Josiah. "Homosexuality Among Tramps." *Studies in the Psychology of Sex. Vol. 2: Sexual Inversion*. By Havelock Ellis. 3rd ed., rev. and enl. Philadelphia: Davis, 1915: 359–367.

"Four Sisters Who Are." n.d. MS. BP, Box 98, Folder 11.

Frassler, Barbara. "Theories of Homosexuality as Sources of Bloomsbury's Androgyny." *Signs* 5 (1979): 237–251.

Freedman, Estelle B. "'Uncontrolled Desires': The Response to the Sexual Psychopath, 1920-1960." *Passion and Power: Sexuality in History*. Eds. Kathy Peiss and Christina Summons. Philadelphia: Temple UP, 1989: 199–225.

Friedman, Andrea. "'The Habitats of Sex-Crazed Perverts': Campaigns Against Burlesque in Depression-Era New York City." *Journal of the History of Sexuality* 7 (1996): 203–238.

————. *Prurient Interests: Gender, Democracy, and Obscenity in New York City, 1909–1945*. New York: Columbia UP, 2000.

Friedman, Mack. *Strapped for Cash: A History of American Hustler Culture*. Los Angeles: Alyson, 2003: 48–49.

Fuchs, Betsy [Betsy Berglund]. Personal Interview. 6 Mar. 2012.

"Funeral of Slain Girl Is Stopped." *Chicago American*, 10 May 1911: 1.

Gee, Derek, and Ralph Lopez. *Laugh Your Troubles Away: The Complete History of Riverview Park*. Chicago: Sharpshooters, 2000.

Gilbert, Arthur N. "Conceptions of Homosexuality and Sodomy in Western History." *Historical Perspectives on Homosexuality*. Ed. Salvatore J. Licata and Robert P. Petersen. New York: Haworth/Stein and Day, 1981: 57–68.

————. "Doctor, Patient, and Onanist Diseases in the Nineteenth Century." *Journal of the History of Medicine* (July 1975): 217–234.

Gilbert, J. Allen. "Homo-Sexuality and Its Treatment." *Journal of Nervous and Mental Disease* 52 (1920): 297–322.

Gilfoyle, Timothy J. *City of Eros: New York City, Prostitution, and the Commercialization of Sex, 1790–1920*. New York: Norton, 1992.

"Girl Is Missing; Gypsies Sought." *Chicago Daily Tribune*, 13 Apr. 1911: 7.

"Girl Once Stolen Is Sleuth." *Chicago Daily Tribune*, 24 Apr. 1911: 3.

Gittens, Joan. *Poor Relations: The Children of the State in Illinois, 1818–1990*. Urbana, IL: U Illinois P, 1994.

Glasscock, Jennifer. *Striptease: From Gaslight to Spotlight*. New York: Abrams, 2003.

Glendinning, Gene V. *The Chicago and Alton Railroad: The Only Way*. DeKalb, IL: Northern Illinois UP, 2002.

Glenn, W. Frank. "Hygiene of Circumcision." *Medical and Surgical Reporter*, 25 May 1895: 733–7352–74.

"Glossary of Homosexual Terms." n.d. TS. BP, Box 145, Folder 8.

Goldberg, Harriet L. *Child Offenders: A Study in Diagnosis and Treatment*. 1948. Montclair, NJ: Patterson Smith, 1969.

"Good News for Boys." *Chicago Daily Tribune*, 2 Feb. 1884: 13.

Goodner, Ralph A. "The Relation of Masturbation to Insanity, with Report of Cases." *Medical News*, 27 Feb. 1897: 272–273.

"Gov. Deneen Turns Accuser in Illinois Asylum Investigation." *Chicago Daily Tribune*, 12 Feb. 1908: 2.

Graham, Sylvester. *A Lecture to Young Men*. 1838. Reprint. New York: Arno, 1974.

"Graham's Lecture to Young Men." *Graham Journal of Health and Longevity*, 21 July 1838: 237–238.

Grant, Julia. "A 'Real Boy' and Not a Sissy: Gender, Childhood, and Masculinity, 1890–1940." *Journal of Social History* 37 (2004): 829–851.

Greenberg, David F. *The Construction of Homosexuality*. Chicago: U of Chicago P, 1988.

"H." n.d. MS. BP, Box 98, Folder 2.

"H. 28." n.d. MS. BP, Box 98, Folder 3.

Hafferkamp, Jack. "Penises, Pain and the Progressives: How America Prepared for the 20th-Century by Cutting Off Its Foreskins." *Libido*. Web. May 1, 2010.

Hagenbach, Allen W. "Masturbation as a Cause of Insanity." *Journal of Nervous and Mental Disease* 6 (1879): 603–612.

Hall, G. Stanley. *Adolescence: Its Psychology and Its Relations to Physiology, Anthropology, Sociology, Sex, Crime, Religion, and Education*. 2 vols. New York: Appleton, 1904.

Haller, Mark. "Urban Vice and Civic Reform." *Cities in American History*. Ed. Kenneth T. Jackson and Stanley K. Schultz. New York: Knopf, 1972.

Hamowy, Ronald. "Medicine and the Crimination of Sin: 'Self-Abuse' in 19th Century America." *Journal of Libertarian Studies* 1 (1977): 229–270.

Hansen, Bert. "American Physicians' 'Discovery' of Homosexuals, 1880–1900: A New Diagnosis in a Changing Society." *Framing Disease: Studies in Cultural History*. Ed. Charles E. Rosenberg and Janet Golden. New Brunswick, NJ: Rutgers UP, 1992. 104–133.

———. "American Physicians' Earliest Writings About Homosexuals, 1880–1900." *Milbank Quarterly* 67 (1989): 92–106.

Harmon, G. E. "Mortality from Puerperal Septicemia in the United States." *American Journal of Public Health* 21 (June 1931): 633–636

"Harold, Age Twenty One." n.d. MS. BP, Box 128, Folder 9.

Hartland, Claude. *The Story of a Life*. 1901. Reprint. San Francisco: Grey Fox, 1985.

Hash, Phillip M. "Music at the Illinois Asylum for Feeble-Minded Children: 1865–1920." n.d. TS.

Haugh, Dolores. *Riverview Amusement Park*. Chicago: Arcadia, 2004.

"Haymarket Theater." *Cinema Treasures*. Web. 10 Dec. 2011.

Heap, Chad. "The City as a Sexual Laboratory: The Queer Heritage of the Chicago School." *Quantitative Sociology* 26 (Winter 2003): 457–487.

———. *Homosexuality in the City: A Century of Research at the University of Chicago*. Chicago: U of Chicago Library, 2000.

Held, William. *Crime, Habit or Disease? A Question of Sex from the Standpoint of Psycho-Pathology*. Chicago: Privately Printed, 1905: 72.

Henry, George. "Psychogenic Factors in Overt Homosexuality." *American Journal of Psychiatry* 93 (1937): 880–908.

———. "Social Factors in the Case Histories of One Hundred Underprivileged Homosexuals." *Mental Hygiene* 22 (1938): 591–611.

"Henry Darger." *ABCD: Art Brut*. Web. 25 Oct. 2011.

"Henry Darger." *Art +Culture*. Web. 9 Jan. 2003.

"Henry Darger: Art and Myth." Exhibit Catalog. 15 Jan.–Mar. 2004. Galerie St. Etienne, New York, NY.

"Henry Darger: Desperate and Terrible Questions." *Interesting Ideas: Outsider Pages*. Web. 26 June 2003.

"Henry Darger Auction Price Results." *Artfact*. n.d. Web. 20 Aug. 2010.

"Henry Darger Room" [Installation]. Intuit: The Center for Intuitive and Outsider Art. Chicago, IL.

Herdt, Gilbert. "Representations of Homosexuality: An Essay on Cultural Ontology and Historical Comparison." *Journal of the History of Sexuality* Part 1:1 (Jan. 1991): 481–504; Part 2:1 (Apr. 1991): 603–632.

"Herman [I liked my mother best]." n.d. MS. BP, Box 98, Folder 2.

"Herman's Diary. Age 28." n.d. MS. BP, Box 98, Folder 11.

Herring, Scott. "Introduction." *Autobiography of an Androgyne*, by Ralph Werther. Ed. Scott Herring. New Brunswick, NJ: Rutgers UP, 2008.

Hielscher, P. A. Receipt. 21 Nov. 1927. HDA, Box 49, Folder 49.23.

"History of Hospitals in Cook County." *Illinois Trails: History and Genealogy*. Web. 21 Aug. 2010.

History of Medicine and Surgery and Physicians and Surgeons of Chicago. Chicago: Biographical, 1922.

Hitchcock, Alfred. "Insanity and Death from Masturbation." *Boston Medical and Surgical Journal*, 8 July 1842: 283–286.

Hoffmann, John, ed. *A Guide to the History of Illinois*. New York: Greenwood, 1991.

Holden, G. P. "Adolescence." *New York Observer and Chronicle*, 22 Apr. 1909: 496.

Holst, Amber. "The Lost World." *Chicago Magazine*, Nov. 2005. Web. 20 Aug. 2010.

"Home for Boys Who Work." *Chicago Daily Tribune*, 31 July 1893: 3.

"How many people died in the attack on Pearl Harbor?" Web. 7 October 2010.

Howard, William Lee. "Psychical Hermaphroditism." *Alienist and Neurologist* 18 (Apr. 1897): 111–118.

———. "Sexual Perversion in America." *American Journal of Dermatology and Genito-Urinary Disease* 8 (1904): 9–14.

———. "The Sexual Pervert in Life Insurance." *Glances Backward: An Anthology of American Homosexual Writing, 1830–1920*. Ed. James Gifford. Peterborough, Ont.: Broadview P, 2006: 329–333.

Huey, Edmund Burke. *Backward and Feeble-Minded Children*. Baltimore: Warwick, 1912. Google Books. Web. 29 Oct. 2011.

Hughes, C. H. "Erotopathia: Morbid Eroticism." *Alienist and Neurologist* 14 (1893): 531–578.

Hughes, Robert. "A Life of Bizarre Obsession." *Time*, 24 Feb. 1997. Web. 15 Mar. 2005.

Hull, William I. "The Children of the Other Half." *Arena* 17 (June 1897): 1039–1051.

Hunt, Alan. "The Great Masturbation Panic and the Discourses of Moral Regulation in Nineteenth- and Early Twentieth-Century Britain." *Journal of the History of Sexuality* 8 (Apr. 1998): 575–615.

Hunt, Milton B. "The Housing of Non-Family Groups of Men in Chicago." *American Journal of Sociology* 16 (1910): 145–170.

Hyde Park Protective Association and Chicago Law and Order League. *A Quarter of a Century of War on Vice in the City of Chicago*. Chicago: 1918.

"I Don't Like to Hang Around Chickie." n.d. MS. BP, Box 98, Folder 4.

"I Like 69 Best." n.d. MS. BP, Box 98, Folder 4.

"I Was Sitting in Thompson's." n.d. MS. BP, Box 98, Folder 2.

Illinois Asylum for Feeble-Minded Children. "Application for Admission." 5007 [Henry J. Dodger (Darger)]. 16 Nov. 1904. Record Group 254.004. Illinois State Archives, Springfield, IL.

———. 5007 [Henry J. Darger]. *Case Histories*, 7 May 1865–27 Sept. 1930. Record Group 254.011. Illinois State Archives, Springfield, IL.

———. Henry Dodger [Henry Darger]. *Register of Applications*, 1865–1908. Record Group 254.005. Illinois State Archives, Springfield, IL.

———. Henry J. Dodger [Henry Darger]. *Register of Admissions*, 1881–1910. Record Group 254.006. Illinois State Archives, Springfield, IL.

Illinois Board of State Commissioners of Public Charities. *Twenty-First Fractional Biennial Report*. Springfield, IL: 1911.

Illinois, State Civil Service Commission.

———. *First Annual Report to the Governor for the Period from August 3, 1905 to December 21, 1906*. Springfield, IL: 1906. Web. 20 March 2010.

———. *Fourth Annual Report to the Governor for the Period from January 1, 1909 to December 31, 1909*. Springfield, IL: 1910. Web. 20 March 2010.

Illinois, Cook County. Marriage License for Henry Darger and Rosa Ronalds. 18 Aug. 1890. Web. Ancestry.com. 28 Aug. 2009.

Illinois, Cook County, Chicago, City Board of Health. Death Certificate for Elisabeth Darger. 15 Sept. 1883.

Illinois, Cook County, Chicago, Department of Health, Bureau of Statistics. Death Certificate for Henry Darger [Sr.]. 2 March 1908. Web. Ancestry.com. 28 Aug. 2009.

Illinois, Cook County, Chicago, Department of Health, Bureau of Vital Statistics. Death Certificate for Margaret Darger. 9 July 1896.

Illinois, Cook County, Chicago, Department of Public Health, Division of Vital Statistics. Death Certificate for Thomas Phelan. 21 Aug. 1919.

Illinois, Cook County, Vital Statistics Department, Clerk's Office. Return of a Birth, Henry Darger. 6 May 1892. Web. Ancestry.com. 28 Aug. 2009.

Illinois, Cook County, Vital Statistics Department, Clerk's Office. Return of a Birth, Henry Darger. 31 May 1894. Web. Ancestry.com. 28 Aug. 2009.

Illinois, Department of Poor Relief, County Hospital Institutions at Dunning, Juvenile Court and Detention Home. *Charity Service Reports, Cook County, Illinois*. Chicago: 1908.

Illinois, Department of Public Aid. Case Identification Card for Henry Dargarus. n.d. HDA, Box 48, Folder 5.

Illinois, Department of Public Health, Office of Vital Records, Chicago Board of Health. "Medical Certificate of Death," Henry Dargarius [Henry Darger]. 15 Apr. 1973.

Illinois General Assembly. *Laws of the State of Illinois Enacted by the Forty-Eighth General Assembly at the Regular Biennial Session*. Springfield, IL: Illinois State Journal, 1913.

Illinois General Assembly, House of Representatives, Special Committee to Investigate State Institutions. *Investigation of Illinois State Institutions 45th General Assembly: 1908; Testimony, Findings and Debates*. Chicago: Regan, 1908.

Illinois Masonic Medical Center. Outpatient Bill for Henry Dargarus. June 1971. HDA, Box 49, Folder 49.23.

"Illinois Probe Is Condemned." *Daily Review* [Decatur, IL], 4 June 1908: 2.

Illinois, Superintendent of Public Instruction. *Biennial Report: July 1, 1898–June 30, 1900*. Springfield, IL: 1901.

"Impersonator in Chorus." *Variety*, 30 Mar. 1927: 40.

"Inquiry Is Urged for State Asylum." *Chicago Daily Tribune*, 10 Jan. 1908: 4.

"Items." *Medical and Surgical Reporter*, 19 May 1877: 453.

Jablonski, Joseph. "Henry Darger: Homer of the Mad." Web. 9 Jan. 2003.

Jamison, Eleanor. "Skinner Public School, Chicago." *Chicago Genealogist* 35 (Winter 2002–03): 42–43.

"Jimmy—Age." n.d. MS. BP, Box 128, Folder 8.

John Bader Lumber Company. Receipt. 12 Mar. 1956. HDA, Box 49, Folder 49.24.

———. Receipt. 12 June 1959. HDA, Box 49, Folder 49.24.

Johnson, David K. "The Kids of Fairytown: Gay Male Culture on Chicago's Near North Side in the 1930s." *Creating a Place for Ourselves: Lesbian, Gay, and Bisexual Community Histories*. Ed. Brett Beemyn. New York: Routledge, 1997: 97–118.

"Judge Opens Fund to Find Girl." *Chicago Daily Tribune*, 21 Apr. 1911: 1.

"Katy Flier." Web. 1 June 2010.

Katz, Jonathan Ned. "Coming to Terms: Conceptualizing Men's Erotic and Affectional Relations with Men in the United States, 1820–1892." *A Queer World*. Ed. Martin Duberman. New York: New York UP, 1997: 216–235.

———. "'Homosexual' and 'Heterosexual': Questioning the Terms." *A Queer World*. Ed. Martin Duberman. New York: New York UP, 1997: 177–180

———. *Love Stories: Sex Between Men Before Homosexuality*. Chicago: U of Chicago P, 2001.

Kerow, Wratsch Djelo. "Heterotransplantation in Homosexuality." *Archives of Neurology and Psychiatry* 23 (1930): 819.

"Kidnapped Girl Found in Canal." *Chicago American*, 9 May 1911: 1.

Kiernan, James G. "Bisexuality." *Urologic and Cutaneous Review* 18 (1914): 372–376.

———. "Classifications of Homosexuality (1916)." *American Queer, Now and Then*. Ed. David Shneer and Cryn Aviv. Boulder, CO: Paradigm, 2006: 8–10.

———. "Increase of American Inversion." *Urologic and Cutaneous Review* 20 (1916): 44–46.

Kimmel, Michael. *Manhood in America: A Cultural History*. New York: Free Press, 1996.

Kneale, James. "Modernity, Pleasure, and the Metropolis." *Journal of Urban History* 28 (July 2002): 647–657.

Krafft-Ebing, Richard von. *Psychopathia Sexualis: A Medico-Forensic Study*. New York: Pioneer, 1953.

Kunzel, Regina G. "Prison Sexual Culture in the Mid-Twentieth-Century United States." *GLQ* 8 (2002): 253–270.

Lakeside Chicago, Illinois General and Business Directory. 1881, 1890, 1910, 1917.

Lakeside Directory of the City of Chicago. 1874–1907, 1909–1917.

Lannon, Charles E. Letter to Henry Dargarius. 4 December 1965. HDA, Box 48, Folder 48.37.

Laqueur, Thomas W. *Solitary Sex: A Cultural History of Masturbation*. New York: Zone, 2004.

Larsen, E. Tage. "The Unrequited Henry Darger." *Zing Magazine*. n.d. Web. 5 Aug. 2006.

"Last Engagement Here of Evans and Hoey." *Chicago Daily Tribune*, 22 Oct. 1893: 38

Lazarus. "Sex." n.d. TS. Hughes Papers, Box 92, Folder 1. Special Collections, Regenstein Library, University of Chicago, Chicago, IL.

Leavitt, Judith Walzer. Rev. of *The Tragedy of Childbed Fever*, by Irvine Loudon. *New England Journal of Medicine* 343 (2000): 587. Web. 6 June 2010.

Leidy, Philip and Charles K. Mills. "Reports of Cases from the Insane Department of the Philadelphia Hospital: Case III, Sexual Perversion." *Journal of Nervous and Mental Disease* 13 (1886): 712–713.

Lelar, Henry, Jr. "Address to the Young Men of Pennsylvania." *Episcopal Recorder*, 12 May 1838: 25.

Lennox, Co. Envelope. 7 July 1922. HDA, Box 49, Folder 49.7.

"Leo. Age 18. Colored." n.d. MS. BP, Box 98, Folder 11.

"Leonard. Age 32." n.d. MS. BP, Box 98, Folder 11.

Lerner, Kiyoko. "Henry's Room." *Henry's Room: 851 Webster*. Ed. Yukiko Koide and Kyoichi Tsuzuki. Tokyo: Imperial Press, 2007: 4–5.

———. Personal Interview. 16 May 2012.

Lerner, Nathan. "Henry Darger: Artist, Protector of Children." *Henry Darger: In the Realms of the Unreal*. John M. MacGregor. New York: Delano Greenidge, 2002: 4–6.

"Lester, Negro. Age 16. Only Child." n.d. MS. BP, Box 98, Folder 11.

Letter to Charlie. DH, Box 1, Folder: "Rides and concessions. Casino Arcade—Correspondence, etc."

Lewis, James R. "Images of Captive Rape in the Nineteenth Century." *Journal of American Culture* 15 (June 1992): 69–77.

Lichtenstein, Perry M. "The 'Fairy' and the Lady Lover." *Medical Review of Reviews* 27 (Aug. 1921): 369–374.

Lieber, Katherine Rook. "Henry Darger: Connecting the Realms of Beauty and Horror." Rev. of exhibit, Carl Hammer Gallery, 25 Apr.–31 May 2003. Web. 25 Nov. 2003.

"Life Expectancy at Birth by Race and Sex, 1930–2007." *Infoplease*. Web. 3 May 2010.

"Light on Dark Minds." *Chicago Daily Tribune*, 21 Jan. 1894: 29.

"Lincoln State School." *Our Times* 5 (Winter 2000): 1–3.

Little Sisters of the Poor. "St. Joseph's Home." Web. 8 Mar. 2010.

Loerzel, Robert. "Be Careful, or You're Going to Dunning!" *Alchemy of Bones*. Web. 1 June 2010.

Loughery, John. *Other Side of Silence: Men's Lives and Gay Identities; A Twentieth-Century History*. New York: Holt, 1998.

Lutz, Tom. *American Nervousness, 1903: An Anecdotal History*. Ithaca, NY: Cornell UP, 1991.

Lydston, G. Frank. "Sexual Perversion, Satyriasis and Nymphomania." *Medical and Surgical Reporter*, 7 Sept. 1889: 253–258; 14 Sept 1889: 281–285.

"M. A. Donohue." *The Lucille Project*. Web. 3 June 2010.

"Ma Was My Living God." n.d. MS. BP, Box 98, Folder 4.

MacDonald, Martha Wilson. "Criminally Aggressive Behavior in Passive, Effeminate Boys." *American Journal of Orthopsychiatry* 8 (1938): 70–78.

MacFarquhar, Larissa. "Thank Heaven for Little Girls: The Lubricious Fantasies of Henry Darger." Rev. of exhibit "Henry Darger: The Unreality of Being," Museum of American Folk Art, 13 Feb.–24 Apr. 1997. *Slate.* Web. 20 Dec. 2005.

MacGregor, John. "Art by Adoption." *Raw Vision* 13 (Winter 1995–96): 26–35.

———. "Further Adventures of the Vivian Girls in Chicago." *Raw Vision.* n.d. Web. 23 Nov. 2004.

———. *Henry Darger: In the Realms of the Unreal.* New York: Delano Greenidge, 2002.

———. "Henry Darger's Room: On the Evolution of an Outsider Environment." *Henry Darger's Room: 851 Webster.* Ed. Yukiko Koide and Kyoichi Tsuzuki. Tokyo: Imperial, 2007: 76–88.

MacQueary, T. H. "Schools for Dependent, Delinquent, and Truant Children in Illinois." *American Journal of Sociology* 9 (July 1903): 1–23.

Mae's Grocery. Receipts. 31 May -6. HDA, Box 49, Folder 49.24.

Maggio, Alice. "Who Died in the Chicago Fire?" *Gapers Block.* Web. 20 Feb. 2011.

Marillac Seminary, Normandy, MO. "Interest Report on Investment." 1933. HDA, Box 49, Folder 49.17.

———. "Interest Report on Investment." 1938. HDA, Box 49, Folder 49.17.

———. "Interest Report on Investment." 1 Dec. 1962. HDA, Box 49, Folder 49.17.

Marshall, J. "Emasculation for Seminal Weakness." Letter. *Boston Medical and Surgical Journal,* 6 Sept. 1843: 96–97.

Marshall, J. H. "Insanity Cured by Castration." *Medical and Surgical Reporter,* 2 Dec. 1865: 363–364.

Martin, Karin A. "Gender and Sexuality: Medical Opinion on Homosexuality, 1900–1950." *Gender and Society* 7 (1993): 246–260.

"[Masses]." *St. Vincent de Paul Parish Bulletin,* 27 May 1973: 2. SVCP. Box 21.

"Masturbation." *Liberator,* 16 Jan. 1846: 11, 16.

"Masturbation and Insanity." *Medical and Surgical Reporter,* 2 May 1874: 415.

"Masturbation and Its Effect on Health." *Graham Journal of Health and Longevity*, 20 Jan. 1838: 23-26.

Mayne, Xavier. *The Intersexes: A History of Similisexualism as a Problem in Social Life*. 1908. Reprint. New York: Arno, 1975.

Mayo Clinic. "Arteriosclerosis/Atherosclerosis." Web. 23 Oct. 2012.

"Mayor Aids Lost Girl Hunt." *Chicago Daily Tribune*, 28 Apr. 1911: 3.

McAndrew, Tara McClellan. "An Illinois Artist's Amazing Life After Death." *Illinois Times*, 16 July 2009.

McDonough, Della. Interview. *Revolutions of the Night: The Enigma of Henry Darger*. Dir. Mark Stokes. 2011. Quale. DVD.

Meagher, John F. W. "Homosexuality: Its Psychobiological and Psychopathological Significance." *Urologic and Cutaneous Review* 33 (1929): 505–518.

"Meet Me in Riverview." 1908. MS. DH, Box 1, Folder: "1920s Correspondence, etc."

Melody, M. E., and Linda M. Peterson. *Teaching America About Sex: Marriage Guides and Sex Manuals from the Late Victorians to Dr. Ruth*. New York: New York UP, 1999.

"Menu." Riverview Park Casino. 19 July 1924. DH, Box 1, Folder: "1920s: Correspondence, etc."

Meunier, Suzanne A., Nicholas A. Maltby, and David F. Tollin. "Compulsive Hoarding." *Handbook of Psychological Assessment, Case Conceptualization, and Treatment*. Eds. Michel Hersen and Johan Rosqvist. Vol. 1: *Adults*. Hoboken, NJ: Wiley, 2008.

Meyerowitz, Joanne. "Sexual Geography and Gender Economy: The Furnished Room Districts of Chicago, 1890-1930." *Gender and History* 2 (1990): 274–296.

Miller, Kevin. *Henry Darger: The Certainties of War*. Curator's Statements. American Folk Art Museum. 4 Nov. 2010–8 July 2011.

Miller, Toby. "A Short History of the Penis." *Social Text* 43 (1995): 1–26.

Milstein, Phil. "Henry Darger: Outsider Artist . . . Song-Poet?" Web. 17 Jan. 2009.

Minton, Henry L. "Community Empowerment and the Medicalization of Homosexuality: Constructing Sexual Identities in the 19230s." *Journal of the History of Sexuality* 6 (1996): 435–458.

"Mr. C." n.d. MS. BP, Box 98, Folder 11.

"Mr. H. Age 19." n.d. MS. BP, Box 128, Folder 7.

"Mr. Joe. Age 32." n.d. MS. BP, Box 98, Folder 11.

"Mr. P." n.d. MS. BP, Box 128, Folder 7.

"Mr. X. 27 Also Has 2 Brothers. 30 and 32." n.d. MS. BP, Box 128, Folder 8.

Monumental Life Insurance Co. Application. December 10, 1935. HDA, Box 47, folder 47.1

Moon, Michael. *Darger's Resources*. Durham, NC: Duke UP, 2012.

Moss, Frank. "Ignorance, Perversion and Degeneracy." *Medical News*, 24 June 1905: 1180–1181 [abstract].

Moss, Jessica. "The Henry Darger Room Collection." Curator's Statement. Chicago: Intuit: The Center for Intuitive and Outsider Art, n.d.: 6–9.

Mumford, Kevin J. "Homosex Changes: Race, Cultural Geography, and the Emergence of the Gay." *American Quarterly* 48 (1996): 395–414.

———. *Interzones: Black/White Sex Districts in Chicago and New York in the Early Twentieth Century*. New York: Columbia UP, 1997.

Murphy, Lawrence R. "Defining the Crime Against Nature: Sodomy in the United States Appeals Courts, 1810–1940." *Journal of Homosexuality* 19 (1990): 49–66.

Murphy, Thomas J. Letter to David Berglund. n.d. HDA, Box 48, Folder 32.

———. Letter to Henry J. Dargarus. 19 Nov. 1965. HDA, Box 48, Folder 48.33.

"'Mutoscope' Presents Over 400 New Reels." DH, Box 1, Folder: "Miscellaneous."

"My First Meeting of the Homo—Sept. 1927." MS. BP, Box 98, Folder 4.

"My Mother Told Me Very Little." n.d. MS. BP, Box 98, Folder 4.

"Nature and Man Unkind to These." *Daily Review* [Decatur, IL], 12 Mar. 1908: 6.

"Neglect Children in Large Families." *Chicago Daily Tribune*, 1 Nov. 1903: 22.

Neuman, B. Paul. "Take Care of the Boys." *Eclectic Magazine and Monthly Edition of the Living Age* (Jan. 1899): 50.

Neumann, R. P. "Masturbation, Madness and the Modern Concepts of Childhood and Adolescence." *Journal of Social History* 8 (1975): 1–27.

"The New Remedy for Seminal Weakness." *Boston Medical and Surgical Journal* 29 (1843): 97–98.

Neyman, E. H. " A Case of Masturbation, with Remarks." *Chicago Medical Examiner* (Sept. 1862): 523–531.

Niles, Blair. *Condemned to Devil's Island: The Biography of an Unknown Convict.* New York: Grosset and Dunlap, 1928.

O'Donnell, Mary. Interview. *In the Realms of the Unreal: The Mystery of Henry Darger.* Dir. Jessica Yu. 2004. Wellspring. DVD.

Ohi, Kevin. "Molestation 101." *GLQ* 6 (2000): 195–248.

Oien, [Paul]. "West Madison Street." n.d. TS. BP, Box 135, Folder 2.

"$100,000 Fire Routs 500 in St. Vincent's." Photocopy. *Chicago Sun-Times,* 6 May 1955: 3. SVCP. Box 1, Folder: "Newspaper Articles—Church Files."

Osborne, A.E. "Castrating to Cure Masturbation." *Pacific Medical Journal* 38 (1895): 151–153.

Otis, Margaret. "A Perversion Not Commonly Noted." *Journal of Abnormal Psychology* 8 (1913): 113–116.

"Oz Park." Web. 17 Nov. 2010.

"Paraplegia from Masturbation." *Medical and Surgical Reporter,* 8 Dec. 1860: 249.

Park, Ed. "The Outsiders." *Village Voice,* 23 April 2002: 92, 94, 96.

"Park Reform Is Only a Spasm." *Chicago Daily Tribune,* 5 Aug. 1909: 38.

"Pay Tables for 1917." *Field Service Pocket Book, United States Army, 1917.* Washington: GPO, 1917. *Couvi's Blog,* Web. Dec. 1, 2010.

Peiss, Kathy. *Cheap Amusements: Working Women and Leisure in Turn-of-the-Century New York.* Philadelphia: Temple UP, 1986.

Perry, Mary Elizabeth. "Dunning." *Encyclopedia of Chicago.* Web. Aug. 21, 2011.

Phelps, Margaret Dorsey. "Almshouses." *Encyclopedia of Chicago.* Web. Aug. 21, 2011.

Picard, Caroline. "Reflections from the World of Darger." Web. 20 June 2011.

"Plan Strong Plea for State Colony." *Chicago Daily Tribune,* 13 Dec. 1908: 6.

Playhouse Dolls. Sandusky, OH: 1949. HDM. Box 41.

Polanski, G. Jurek. "Henry Darger: Realms of the Unreal." 11 Oct.–11 Nov., 2000. Rev. of exhibit, Carl Hammer Gallery, Chicago, IL. ArtScope.net. Web. 1 Sept. 2003.

Polk's Chicago City Directory, 1923, 1928.

Poole, Ernest. "The Little Arabs of the Night." *Collier's*, 7 March 1903: 11.

———. "Waifs of the Street." *McClure's*, May 1903: 40–48.

"Prison Discipline Society." *New York Evangelist*, 5 Jun. 1841: 90.

Prokopoff, Stephen. "Realms of the Unreal." Rev. of exhibit, 11 Oct.–11 Nov. 2000, Carl Hammer Gallery. Chicago, IL. Web. 20 Sept. 2005.

Purple, William D. "On the Morbid Condition of the Generative Organs." *New York Journal of Medicine and Collateral Sciences* (Sept. 1849): 207–218.

Rabinovitz, Lauren. *For the Love of Pleasure: Women, Movies, and Culture in Turn-of-the-Century Chicago*. New Brunswick, NJ: Rutgers UP, 1998.

Raffalovich, Marc Andre. "Uranism, Congenital Sexual Inversion: Observations and Recommendations." *Journal of Comparative Neurology 5* (1895): 33–65.

Reckless, Walter C. *Vice in Chicago*. Montclair, NJ: Patterson Smith, 1969.

Reckless, Walter Cade. "Natural History of Vice Areas in Chicago." Diss., University of Chicago, 1925.

Reed, Lawrence W. "A History of Depressions in America: The Business Cycle." Web. 1 June 2010.

"Reform of Parks Is Only a Spasm." *Chicago Daily Tribune*, 5 Aug. 1909: 38.

"Registration Card." Henry J. Darger. 2 June 1917. Chicago, IL. Web. 28 Aug. 2009.

"Registration Card." Henry Jose Dargerius. 27 April 1943. Chicago, IL. Web. 28 Aug. 2009.

"Rescuing Henry Darger." Rev. of *Henry Darger: Art and Selected Writings*, by Michael Bonesteel. *Interesting Ideas*. n.d. Web. 9 Jan. 2003.

"Rest in Peace." *St. Vincent de Paul Parish Bulletin*, 22 Apr. 1973: 2. SVCR, Box 21.

"Reward for Slayer $1,000." *Chicago Daily Tribune*, 11 May 1911: 2.

Reynolds, H. "Causation and Prevention of Insanity." *Phrenological Journal and Science of Health* (Apr. 1884): 212–217.

Richards, James B. "Causes and Treatment of Idiocy." *New York Journal of Medicine*, ser. 3, 1 (1856): 378–87.

"Riverview Park." *Jazz Age Chicago*. Web. 5 May 2005.

Robb, Graham. *Strangers: Homosexual Love in the Nineteenth Century*. New York: Norton, 2003.

"Robert—Age 33 Years." n.d. MS. BP, Box 128, Folder 9.

Robertson, Stephen. "Signs, Marks, and Private Parts: Doctors, Legal Discourses, and Evidence of Rape in the United States, 1823-1930." *Journal of the History of Sexuality* 8 (Jan. 1998): 345–388.

Robinson, William J. "My Views on Homosexuality." *American Journal of Urology* 10 (1914): 550–552.

———. "Nature's Sex Stepchildren." *Medical Critic and Guide* 25 (1925): 475–477.

Rodkin, Dennis. "Erogenous Zones: Local Landmarks from Chicago's Rich History of Sexual Adventurers, Revolutionaries, Misfits, and Crackpots." *Chicago Magazine*, July 2009. Web. 18 Dec. 2009.

Rogers, S. "Masturbation: Its Consequences." *Water-Cure Journal*, 1 Feb. 1849: 51–52.

Romesburg, Don. "'Wouldn't a Boy Do?': Placing Early-Twentieth-Century Male Youth Sex Work Into Histories of Sexuality." *Journal of the History of Sexuality* 5 (1994): 207–242.

Rooney, Mary. Interview. *In the Realms of the Unreal: The Mystery of Henry Darger*. Dir. Jessica Yu. 2004. Wellspring. DVD.

Rose, Sister. Letter to Henry Darger. 19 June 1917. HDA, Box 48, Folder 48.38.

———. Package for Henry Darger. n.d. HDA, Box 48, Folder 48.37.

Royal Commission. *Report on the Care and Control of the Feeble-Minded Upon Their Visit to American Institutions*. Vol. 7. London, 1908. 117.

"St. Joseph's Hospital." *History of Medicine and Surgery and Physicians and Surgeons of Chicago*. Chicago: Biographical, 1922: 274.

St. Joseph's Hospital Pharmacy. Prescription. n.d. HDA, Box 49, Folder 49.23.

St. Vincent DePaul Parish Bulletin, 5 March 1967: 2. SVCR, Box 21.

St. Vincent's Church. Petition for Remembering the Dead on All Souls' Day. n.d. HDA, Box 73, Folder 73.18.

Sanderson, Lisa. "The Financial Crisis of the 1870s: The Long Depression." Suite101.com. Web. 20 Nov. 2010.

"Says Bad Shows Gain by Public Exposure." *Chicago Record Herald*, 18 July 1909: 9.

Schilder, Paul. "On Homosexuality." *Psychoanalytical Review* 16 (1929): 377–389.

Schloeder, Bill and Katherine. Greeting Card to Henry Darger "[Happy

Easter to a Special Friend]." n.d. HDA, Box 48, Folder 48.28.

———. Greeting Card to Henry Darger "[The Christmas Star Is in the Sky]." n.d. HDA, Box 48, Folder 48.28.

———. Postcard to Henry Darger "[Sunken Garden]." 7 May 1954. HDA, Box 48, Folder 48.28.

"School Children Hunt Girl." *Chicago Daily Tribune*, 30 Apr. 1911: 6.

"See Need of Home for Weak Minded." *Chicago Daily Tribune*, 12 July 1908: 16.

Seguin, E.C. "Sexual Excesses and Masturbation as Exciting Causes of Insanity." *Medical and Surgical Reporter*, 23 Nov. 1878: 450–451.

Sellar, Tom. "Realms of the Unreal." *Theater* 32 (Winter 2002): 100–109.

"Sept 30, 1932." MS. BP, Box 98, Folder 3.

Seton Music Company. Receipt. 9 June 1921. HDA, Box 49, Folder 49.24.

———. Receipt. 1 Mar. 1922. HDA, Box 49, Folder 49.24.

"1745 Larrabee Kroch Halls." n.d. MS. BP, Box 98, Folder 11.

"Seventieth Anniversary Picnic of the Crane Company." 16 May 1925. "Riverview Amusement Park Company Picnic, 1925." CCR Box 1, Folder 11.

Shaw, Clifford. *The Jack-Roller: A Delinquent Boy's Own Story*. 1930. Reprint. Chicago: U of Chicago P, 1966.

———. *The Natural History of a Delinquent Career*. 1931. Reprint. New York: Greenwood, 1968.

Shaw, Lytle. "The Moral Storm: Henry Darger's *Book of Weather Reports*." *Cabinet* 3 (Summer 2001): 99–103.

Shaw-Williamson, Victoria. "Eccentric Visions: Collecting Outsider Art." *Chubb Collectors*, 19 Feb. 2009. Web. 30 Dec. 2012.

"She Becomes Hysterical, Then Rushes Down Lockport Street." Photocopy. HDM, Box 12.

Shrady, George F. "Perverted Sexual Instinct." *Medical Record*, 19 July 1884: 70–71.

Shteir, Rachel. *Striptease: The Untold History of the Girlie Show*. Oxford: Oxford UP, 2004.

"Shut 2 Night Clubs, with Girls Garbed as Men, and Theater." Photocopy. GAS, Box 22, Folder 3.

Sibalis, Michael. "Male Homosexuality in the Age of Enlightenment and Revolution, 1680–1850." *Gay Life and Culture: A World History*. Ed. Robert Aldrich. New York: Universe, 2006: 102–123.

Silverman, Kaja. "A Woman's Soul Enclosed in a Man's Body: Femininity in Male Homosexuality." *Male Subjectivity at the Margins*. New York: Routledge, 1992: 339–389.

Sisters of St. Joseph Hospital. Letter of Recommendation for Henry Darger. n.d. HDA, Box 48, Folder 19.

Sivakumaran, Sandesh. "Male/Male Rape and the 'Taint' of Homosexuality." *Human Rights Quarterly* 27 (2005): 1274–1306.

"6/29." MS. BP, Box 98, Folder 2.

Smith, Alison J. *Chicago's Left Bank*. Chicago: Regnery, 1953.

Smith, Roberta. "Nathan Lerner, 83, Innovator in Techniques of Photography." *New York Times*, 15 Feb. 1977. Web. 25 Oct. 2011.

Spargo, John. *The Bitter Cry of the Children*. 1906. Reprint. Chicago: Quadrangle, 1968.

Spitzka, E.C. "Cases of Masturbation (Masturbatic Insanity.)" *Journal of Mental Science* 33 (1887): Part I, Apr.: 57–78; Part II, July: 238–247.

———. "A Historical Case of Sexual Perversion." *Chicago Medical Review* 4 (1881): 378–379.

———. "Self Abuse in Its Relation to Insanity." *Medical and Surgical Reporter*, 8 Jan. 1887: 42–45.

Sprague, Gregory A. "Chicago Past: A Rich Gay History." *Advocate*, 18 Aug. 1963: 28–31, 58.

———. "Chicago Sociologists and the Social Control of Urban 'Illicit' Sexuality, 1892–1918." n.d. TS. GAS, Box 6, Folder 5.

———. "Discovering the Thriving Gay Male Subculture of Chicago During 1920s & 1930s." n.d. MS. GAS, Box 13, Folder 4.

———. "Gay Balls: An Old Chicago Tradition." *Gay Life*, 14 Nov. 1980: 3, 8.

———. "Male Homosexuality in Western Culture: The Dilemma of Identity and Subculture in Historical Research." *Journal of Homosexuality* 10 (Winter 1984): 29–43.

———. "On the 'Gay Side' of Town: The Nature and Structure of Male Homosexuality in Chicago, 1890–1935." n.d. TS. GAS, Box 5, Folder 12.

———. "Urban Male Homosexuality in Transition: The Characteristics and Structure of Gay Identities in Chicago, 1920–1940." n.d. TS. GAS, Box 5, Folder 7.

Stall, Sylvanus. *What a Young Man Ought to Know*. Rev. ed. Philadelphia: Vir, 1904.

"Star & Garter Theater." *Jazz Age Chicago*. Web. 19 Dec. 2009.

"Start Big Search for Girl's Slayer." *Chicago Daily Tribune*, 10 May 1911: 3.

Stekel, Wilhelm. "Masked Homosexuality." *American Medicine* (Aug. 1914): 530–537.

Stencell, A. W. *Girl Show: Into the Canvas World of Bump and Grind*. Toronto: ECW, 1999.

Stephen, Robert. "'Boys, of Course, Cannot Be Raped': Age, Homosexuality and the Redefinition of Sexual Violence in New York City, 1880–1955." *Gender and History* 18 (Aug. 2006): 357–379.

Stone, Lisa. "From 851 West Webster to Intuit." Curator's Statement. Chicago: Intuit: The Center for Intuitive and Outsider Art, n.d.: 1–5.

Studlar, Gaylyn. "Oh, 'Doll Divine': Mary Pickford, Masquerade, and the Pedophilic Gaze." *Camera Obscura* 16 (2001): 196–227.

Sullivan, Gerard. "Discrimination and Self-Concept of Homosexuals Before the Gay Liberation Movement: A Biographical Analysis Examining Social Contest and Identity." *Biography* 13 (1990): 203–221.

Sylvanus Stall, *What a Young Man Ought to Know*. New rev. ed. Philadelphia: Vir, 1904. 141.

Talbot, E. S., and Havelock Ellis. "A Case of Developmental Degenerative Insanity, with Sexual Inversion, Melancholia Following Removal of Testicles." *Journal of Mental Science* 42 [1896]: 340–346.

Tamagne, Florence. "The Homosexual Age, 1870–1940." *Gay Life and Culture: A World History*. Ed. Robert Aldrich. New York: Universe, 2006: 166–195.

Taylor, Kristin. "The History of Riverview Amusement Park." Web. 27 July 2009.

Territo, Leonard, and George Kirkham. *International Sex Trafficking of Women and Children: Understanding the Global Epidemic*. Flushing, NY: Looseleaf Law, 2010.

Terry, Jennifer. "Anxious Slippages Between 'Us' and 'Them': A Brief History of the Scientific Search for Homosexual Bodies." *Deviant Bodies: Critical Perspectives on Difference in Science and Popular Culture*. Ed. Jennifer Terry and Jacqueline Urla. Bloomington: Indiana UP, 1995: 129–169.

"They Did Not Talk Dirty." n.d. MS. BP, Box 98, Folder 3.

Thrasher, Frederic. *The Gang: A Study of 1,313 Gangs in Chicago*. Chicago: U of Chicago P, 1927.

"Three Children." n.d. MS. BP, Box 98, Folder 2.

"Told to Me by M.G." n.d. MS. BP, Box 98, Folder 11.

"Told to Me by Sandy." n.d. MS. BP, Box 98, Folder 11.

"Transplantation of Testes in Relation to Homosexuality." *Journal of the American Medical Association*, 12 Aug. 1922: 598.

Trent, James W., Jr. *Inventing the Feeble Mind: A History of Mental Retardation in the United States*. Berkeley: U of California P, 1994.

Turner, George Kibbe. "The City of Chicago: A Study of the Great Immoralities." *McClure's Magazine*, Apr. 1907: 575–592.

"2 Park Arrests Made." Photocopy. Davison Papers. Clippings on Vice in Chicago (Crerar Ms. 234): Vol. 4, Special Collections, Regenstein Library, University of Chicago, Chicago, IL.

"213,000 Children Asked to Help Hunt Elsie Paroubek." *Chicago American*, 29 April 1911: 2.

"Tying the Spermatic Artery." *Boston Medical and Surgical Journal*, 22 June 1842: 321.

"Under Hypnosis Sept. 24, 32." MS. BP, Box 98, Folder 4.

U.S. Army. "Honorable Discharge from the Army of the United States." 28 Dec. 1917. HDA, Box 48, Folder 48.4.

U.S. Bureau of the Census. "Annual Mean Income, Lifetime Income, and Educational Attainment of Men in the United States, for Selected Years, 1956 to 1972." *Current Population Reports*. Series P-60, No. 92. U.S. Washington, D.C.: GPO, 1974.

U.S. Department of Commerce, Bureau of the Census. Tenth Census of the United States. Schedule 1—Inhabitants. Illinois. Washington, D.C.: GPO, 1880. Web. 20 Feb. 2011.

———. Twelfth Census of the United States. Schedule No. 1—Population. Illinois. Washington, D.C.: GPO, 1900. Web. 20 Feb. 2011.

———. Thirteenth Census of the United States. 1910—Population. Illinois. Washington, D.C.: GPO, 1910. Web. 20 Feb. 2011.

———. Fourteenth Census of the United States. 1920—Population. Illinois. Washington, D.C.: GPO, 1920. Web. 20 Feb. 2011.

———. Fifteenth Census of the United States. 1930 Population Schedule. Illinois. Washington, D.C.: GPO, 1930. Web. 20 Feb. 2011.

———. Sixteenth Census of the United States. 1940 Population Schedule. Illinois. Washington, D.C.: GPO, 1940. Web. 20 Feb. 2011.

U.S. Department of Labor, Office of the Assistant Secretary for Administration and Management. "Progressive Era Investigations." n.d. Web. 15 Jan. 2010.

"Urges Reform in Insane Asylums." *Chicago Daily Tribune*, 18 Aug. 1906: 7.

Vice Commission of Chicago. *The Social Evil in Chicago*. Chicago: 1911.

Vicinus, Martha. "The Adolescent Boy: Fin-de-Siècle Femme Fatale?" *Journal of the History of Sexuality* 5 (1994): 90–114.

Vine, Richard. "Thank Heaven for Little Girls." *Art in America*, Jan. 1998. Web. 15 March 2005.

Vollmer, Myles. "Boy Hustler—Chicago." n.d. MS. BP, Box 145, Folder 8.

W. "Insanity, Produced by Masturbation." *Boston Medical and Surgical Journal*, 25 Mar. 1835: 109–111.

Washburn, Henry S. "The Vacant Chair." *Saturday Evening Post*, August 1961. HDA, Box 48, Folder 48.12.

Waters, Mark. Interview. *In the Realms of the Unreal: The Mystery of Henry Darger*. Dir. Jessica Yu. 2004. Wellspring. DVD.

Watson, Mary. Letter of Recommendation for Henry Darger. 23 Jan. 1928. HDA, Box 48, Folder 18.

Weeks, Jeffrey. "Inverts, Perverts, and Mary-Annes: Male Prostitution and the Regulation of Homosexuality in England in the Nineteenth and Early Twentieth Centuries." *Hidden from History: Reclaiming the Gay and Lesbian Past*. Ed. Duberman, Martin Bauml, Martha Vicinus, and George Chauncey Jr. New York: New American Library, 1989: 195–211.

———. "'Sins and Diseases': Some Notes on Homosexuality in the Nineteenth Century." *History Workshop* 1 (1976): 211–219.

Wertheim, Elsa. *Chicago Children in the Street Trades*. Chicago: Juvenile Protective Association of Chicago, 1917.

Werther, Ralph. *Autobiography of an Androgyne*. 1918. Reprint. New York: Arno, 1975.

———. *Autobiography of an Androgyne*. Ed. Scott Herring. New Brunswick: Rutgers UP, 2008.

———. *The Female Impersonators*. 1922. Reprint. New York: Arno, 1975.

———. "Studies in Androgynism." *Medical Life* 27 (1920): 235–246.

"West Madison Street's Claims to Fame." *Chicago Daily Tribune*, 2 Apr. 1911: 11.

Wey, Hamilton D. "Morbid Sensuality in a Reformatory." *Chicago Medical Recorder* 10 (1896): 143–145.

"What Is Outsider Art?" *Raw Vision*. Web. 25 October 2011.

"What of the Newsboy of the Second Cities?" *Charities*, 11 Apr. 1903: 368–371.

"When I Really Love the Person." n.d. MS. BP, Box 98, Folder 3.

"When I Was a Youngster." n.d. MS. BP, Box 98, Folder 4.

"Where Is Elsie Paroubek?" *Chicago American* 21 April 1911: 2.

White, Kevin. *The First Sexual Revolution: The Emergence of Male Hetero-sexuality in Modern America*. New York: New York UP, 1993.

White, W. H. "Insanity Cured by Castration." *Medical and Surgical Reporter*, 6 Jan. 1866: 17–18.

"Will Indecency Win?" *Chicago Record-Herald*, 19 July 1909: 6.

Williams, Mornay. "The Street Boy: Who He Is, and What To Do with Him." *Proceedings of the National Conference of Charities and Corrections . . .* (1903): 238–244.

Williams, Stephen W. "Imaginary Diseases." *New Jersey Medical Reporter and Transactions of the New Jersey Medical Society*, July 1854: 7.

Winslow, Randolph. "Report of an Epidemic of Gonnorrhoea Contracted from Rectal Coition." *Medical News*, 14 Aug. 1886: 180–182.

Wlodarczyk, Chuck. *Riverview: Gone but Not Forgotten, 1904–1967*. Rev. ed. Chicago: Riverview, 1977.

Wolcott, David Bryan. "Cops and Kids: The Police and Juvenile Delinquency in Three American Cities: 1890–1940." Diss., Carnegie Mellon University, 2000.

Wood, J. G. *Uncivilized Races of Men in All Countries of the World*. Vol. 2. Hartford, CT: Burr, 1870.

Wright, Clifford A. "The Sex Offender's Endocrines." *Medical Record*, 21 July 1939: 399–402.

"The Writer Attended a Party Last Summer." n.d. MS. BP, Box 98, Folder 11.

"Wulff Girl Leads Lost Child Hunt." *Chicago American*, 23 April 1911: 1.

"WWII 'Old Man's Draft' Registration Cards." *Fold 3*. Web. 7 October 2010.

Zorbaugh, Harvey Warren. *The Gold Coast and the Slum: A Sociological Study of Chicago's Near North Side*. 1929. Reprint. Chicago: U of Chicago P, 1976.

INDEX

vestments, 218; and journals,
297; and "kid," 52–53; leg
pains, 246, 252, 265; and letters from Sister Rose, 173; Library of, 215, 237; and life
insurance policy, 220; and
Marillac Seminary, 218; and
masturbation, 31, 111–12,
52, 174; and military service,
201–4, 241–42; and mother,
36–37, 171; mugging of, 295;
and Newsom/Henry letter,
185–86; and night watchman,
53–55, 57, 61, 139; and nuns
at St. Joseph's, 128–31; paintings, classification of, 162;
paintings, price of, 316; portraits of with Whillie, 144–45;
posthumous exhibits of, 314;
and pseudonyms, 243–44,
278, 296, 302, 314; reputation of, 21–24; retirement, financial situation during,
265–66; retirement, output
during, 266–67; room, de-
scription of, 304–10; and Sister Rose, 128–29; and school,
trouble in, 41–43; scrapbooks
of, 161, 271; and self-trans-
formation in The Realms,
172–73; and senility, 296; and
sister, 37; and smaller children, moment of empathy,
42–43; and St. Augustine's
Home for the Aged, 299–300,
302; and St. Joseph's Hospital, 126–27; St. Joseph's, firing from, 248; St. Joseph's,
promotion and raise, 212; St.
Joseph's, quitting of, 204–5;
St. Joseph's, second stint at,
211; taken from home, 47–

48; and tantrums, 270, 281,
282, 283, 284, 286, 296, 297,
298; The History of My Life,
40; and tornado, 288–92;
tracings, 164; and vacation,
248; and vegetable room,
258; and weather, 52, 89,
247, 272; Vivian girls manuscript, 135–37; and West
Madison Street, 34–35; and
the "wolf," 47; and word
play, 270; and Workingmen's
House, 128; and Yuki, 286
Darger, Henry, artworks of: 11. At
Norma Catherine. Are cap-
tured Again by Glandelinian
Calvary, 163; An Inhuman
Fiend Tormenting a Poor
Child, 161; At Cedernine,
Glandelinians Suspicious That
Little Vivian Girls Are Among
Child Slaves, 193; At Jennie
Richee again escape, 317; At
Jennie Richee. The blunder of
one of the Glandelinian rug
carriers causes the others to
fall with him, foiling the at-
tempt of the Little Girls none
too gently, 195; At Jennie
Ritchie. 2 of Story to Evans.
They attempt to get away by
rolling themselves in floor
rugs, 168; At Jullo Callo,
How They Were Rescued by
Four Christian Spies and
Three Secret Service Men and
Two Members of The Gemini,
193; At Norma Run, Later
During the Battle, Evans Succeeds in Rescuing Them, 193;
Battle of Calverhine, The,
214, 215, 304; Boys and

Man, Twice, 215; *Child with Glass of Milk*, 215; *How They Were Rescued by Four Christian Spies*, 193–95; *In Times Like These*, 269; *Nude Children in Meadow with Clouds*, 193; *Pictures of Fires Big or Small in Which Firemen or Persons Lose Their Lives*, 161; *Playhouse Dolls*, 271; *Reference Ledger*, 173; *Religious Collage with Madonna and Child*, 215; *They are almost murdered themselves though they fight for their lives, Typhoon save them*, 317; *Weather Report of Cold and Warm, Also Summer Heats and Cool Spells, Storms, and Fair or Cloudy Days, Contrary to What the Weatherman Says, and Also True Too*, 247
Darger, Henry, written works of: "Confirmed," 310; "Found on Sidewalk," 199, 234; "From a French Guiana to Little Princess Jennie," 310; "Jennie Ritchie Notations," 310. See also *Crazy House*, and *History of My Life, The*, and *Realms, The*
Darger, Rosa, 33, 36–37
Dear Friends: American Photographs of Men Together, 1840–1918 (Deitcher), 149
Deitcher, David, 149
DeLang, Quincy, 143
Dewey, Ella A., 68, 69, 127, 229
Dillon, Mary, 269, 271–72, 274, 276, 305
"dirt," 82

Dorothy, Sister, 204, 205, 207
Drinker, Frederick E., 292
Duff, Maud C., 102
Duncan Clark's Female Minstrels, 143
Dunning, 47, 51–53, 57, 118

Edlin, Andrew, 316
Ellis, Havelock, 170
Emmerich, Anne, 160
Epstein, Andrew J., 272–73
Evans, Jack, 172, 227, 280–81
Evening Journal, 64

Fabian, Brother, 249–50
Factory Inspector, The, 130
Fairyland, 142
Feldkamp, Edna, 211
Fernald, Walter E., Dr., 99
Feseri, Jacob, 262, 265
fire. *See* Darger, Henry, and fire
Fisher, Bud, 195
"Found on Sidewalk" (Darger), 199, 234
Fox, John, 100
"From a French Guiana to Little Princess Jennie" (Darger), 310
Fuchs, Betsy. *See* Berglund, Betsy
Further Adventures in Chicago: Crazy House (Darger). See *Crazy House*

Gannon, Mrs., 76–77, 87, 90, 156
Gay Deceiver, The, 144
Gay, Lesbian, Bisexual, and Transgender Myths from the Arapaho to the Zuñi: An Anthology (Elledge), 18
Gehr, Henry and Margy, 214–15
Gemini, 183–89, 191–95, 200, 227
George, Webber, as alter ego for Darger, 235–37, 285; as

enemy, 221; and Janet Theatre, 230; and Teacher's Infirmary, 228–29
Girls on the Run (Ashbery), 316
Giroux, Ben M., 104–5
Giroux, Frank, 104–5
Guernsey, Henry, 82

Hall, G. Stanley, *Adolescence,* 84–85
Hamilton, George, 101
Hamowy, Ronald, 106
Hardt, Harry G., 96, 104, 106, 108–11, 113, 155
Harry, Joseph, 261–62
Hartland, Claude, 169
Haymarket Theatre, 55, 222
Healy, Dr., 50
"Henry Darger" (Merchant), 316
Henry Darger Study Center, 19, 316
"Herman," 231
Hermaphrodite-Angel of Peladan, The (Czanara), 169
Hill, John W., 105
History of My Life, The (Darger), 40, 287–94, 298; and Angel Guardian Orphanage, 290; and Child Refuge Settlement, 290; and Mr. Cigarover, 292; and Gleason Orphanage, 290; and God, 292; and "great book of Records," 291; and the four soldiers, 290; and Illinois Asylum for Feeble-Minded Children, 290; manuscript of, 293–94; and Norma Pietri, 294; and Sacred Heart Convent, 290; and St. Joseph's Hospital, 290; themes of, 287–88; and whitewashing, 287; and *Wonderful Wizard of Oz, The,* 289. *See also* Sweetie Pie
hoarders, 306–10
homosexuality, early twentieth-century definition of, 81–84
Horrors of Tornado, Flood, and Fire (Drinker), 292
"hot dog sandwiches," 278
How They Were Rescued by Four Christian Spies (Darger), 193–95
Hughes, Robert, 22, 317
Hunter, Warren, Dr., 182
Hyde Park Art Center, 22, 314

Illinois Asylum for Feeble-Minded Children, 85; application to, 29–31; design of, 94; grounds of, 96–97; inmate makeup of, 92; staff of, 93
Ilmbergers, Alois and Annie, 100–01
In Times Like These (Darger), 269
International Association of Factory Inspectors, 130
Intuit: The Center for Intuitive and Outsider Art, 24, 319
invert, 82–83, 174, 229

Jack-Roller: A Delinquent Boy's Own Story, The ("Stanley"), 48
"Jennie Ritchie Notations" (Darger), 310
Jessop Virgene, 106
Johnson, John E., 163
Johnson, John, 101–2, 162–63
Jones, Daniel, 103, 122
Jones, Edgar, 111
Jordain, Lucille, 106
Juvenile Protective Association, 184

Kellogg, John Harvey, *Plain Facts About Sexual Life*, 80–81
"kid," 46, 52, 238
Kingston, E. A., 181
Krafft-Ebing, Richard von, 170
Kuback, Johanna, 207–8
Kutz, Eddie, 112

"lamb," 46, 52, 238
Lambden, Frank W., 104–5
Lannon, Charles E., 283–84
Larsen, E. Tage, 317
LeCount, E. R., 182
Leno, Sister, 126–27
"Leonard, Mr." *See* Lerner, Nathan
Lerner, Nathan: and Darger, care of, 277, 279, 298, 300, 302, 304; and Darger, discovery of, 21–22, 311–18; and Darger, landlord of, 256–57; and Darger, loan to, 295; and Darger, relating to, 271, 272, 274
Lincoln Park, 144, 208, 226
Lindquist, Theo, 118, 122
Little Sisters of the Poor, 29–30, 299, 304, 314
Logan, Richard, 202

Macferran, Charles S., 197
MacGregor, John, 22, 161–62, 195, 318
Mahoney, Dennis S. H., 57, 64–65, 69, 70–71, 76–78, 84, 214
Mahoney, John, 177
Mangela, Tony, 178
Manley, John, 71, 73–77, 90, 121, 156, 162, 221, 284
Marchi, Michael, Dr., 303, 313
Marcus, Jacob, 103
Marcus, Paul, 103

Masquerade: Queer Poetry in America to the End of World War II (Elledge) 18
Massachusetts School for Idiotic Children, 99
masturbation, 83; and devices for prevention of, 80–81; and self-castration, 107–8
McKenzie, John, 63
Meldorf, 32, 133
Merchant, Natalie, "Henry Darger," 316
Miller, T. H., 111
Mission of Our Lady of Mercy, 57, 62, 64–68
mômes, 239
Moon, Michael, 195
Morrison, C. F., 317
Morthland, John K., 106–7, 108
"Mr. D.," 231
"Mr. R.," 231
Murphy, Thomas J., 278–79
Museum of Contemporary Art, 314
Museum of Modern Art, 317
Mutt and Jeff, 195

Namath, Joe, 269
Nelson, Florence and Edward, 211
Nero, General, 162
New York's Willard Asylum for the Chronic Insane, 99
Newboys' Home. *See* Mission of Our Lady of Mercy
Newsome, Thomas A., 183, 185–86
Niles, Blair, *Condemned to Devil's Island*, 237–39
Nordstrom, Ernst, 119, 122
Nude Children in Meadow with Clouds (Darger), 193